P9-ARB-710

E
D
C
B
A

Easy Microsoft® Office PowerPoint® 2003

International Standard Book Number: 0-7897-2964-4

Library of Congress Catalog Card Number: 2003103666

Printed in the United States of America

First Printing: September 2003

06 05 04 03 4 3 2 1

Trademarks

All terms mentioned in this book that are known to be trademarks or service marks have been appropriately capitalized. Que Publishing cannot attest to the accuracy of this information. Use of a term in this book should not be regarded as affecting the validity of any trademark or service mark.

PowerPoint is a registered trademark of Microsoft Corporation.

Microsoft is a registered trademark of Microsoft Corporation.

Warning and Disclaimer

Every effort has been made to make this book as complete and as accurate as possible, but no warranty or fitness is implied. The information provided is on an "as is" basis. The author and the publisher shall have neither liability nor responsibility to any person or entity with respect to any loss or damages arising from the information contained in this book.

Bulk Sales

Que offers excellent discounts on this book when ordered in quantity for bulk purchases or special sales. For more information, please contact:

U.S. Corporate and Government Sales
1-800-382-3419
corpsales@pearsontechgroup.com

For sales outside of the U.S., please contact:

International Sales
+1-317-581-3793
international@pearsontechgroup.com

Associate Publisher
Greg Wiegand

Acquisitions Editor
Stephanie J. McComb

Development Editor
Kate Shoup Welsh

Managing Editor
Charlotte Clapp

Project Editor
Tonya Simpson

Copy Editor
Benjamin Berg

Indexers
Ken Johnson
Mandie Frank

Proofreader
Linda Seifert

Technical Editor
Mark Hall

Team Coordinator
Sharry Lee Gregory

Interior Designer
Anne Jones

Cover Designer
Anne Jones

Page Layout
Kelly Maish

Dedication

To my uncle, Gary Wyant, for his good cheer and loving spirit. He will be dearly missed.

Acknowledgments

I would like to say thanks to the team at Que Publishing for all their efforts in producing this book. Special thanks go to Stephanie McComb for her acquisitions work; to Kate Shoup Welsh for her fine development work; to Tonya Simpson for shepherding this book every step of the way until its final form; to Benjamin Berg for dotting the Is and crossing the Ts; and to Mark Hall for checking to make sure everything is technically accurate. Extra special thanks to the production group for assembling this visual masterpiece. Finally, much thanks to Jeremiah Hughes for loaning me his school project made especially on PowerPoint.

About the Author

Sherry Kinkoph has authored more than 50 computer books over the past 10 years on a variety of topics, including books for both adults and children. *How to Use Microsoft Office XP*, *The Complete Idiot's Guide to Excel 2000*, *Master Visually Dreamweaver MX and Flash MX*, and *Teach Yourself Adobe Premiere 6 VISUALLY* are only a few of Sherry's recent publications. A native of the Midwest, Sherry currently resides in the Indianapolis area and continues in her quest to help users of all levels and ages master ever-changing computer technologies.

Tell Us What You Think!

As the reader of this book, *you* are our most important critic and commentator. We value your opinion and want to know what we're doing right, what we could do better, what areas you'd like to see us publish in, and any other words of wisdom you're willing to pass our way.

As an associate publisher for Que, I welcome your comments. You can email or write me directly to let me know what you did or didn't like about this book—as well as what we can do to make our books better.

Please note that I cannot help you with technical problems related to the *topic* of this book. We do have a User Services group, however, where I will forward specific technical questions related to the book.

When you write, please be sure to include this book's title and author as well as your name, email address, and phone number. I will carefully review your comments and share them with the author and editors who worked on the book.

Email: `feedback@quepublishing.com`

Mail: Greg Wiegand
Que Publishing
800 East 96th Street
Indianapolis, IN 46240 USA

For more information about this book or another Que title, visit our Web site at `www.quepublishing.com`. Type the ISBN (excluding hyphens) or the title of a book in the Search field to find the page you're looking for.

Each step is fully illustrated to show you how it looks onscreen.

It's as Easy as 1-2-3

Each part of this book is made up of a series of short, instructional lessons, designed to help you understand basic information that you need to get the most out of your computer hardware and software.

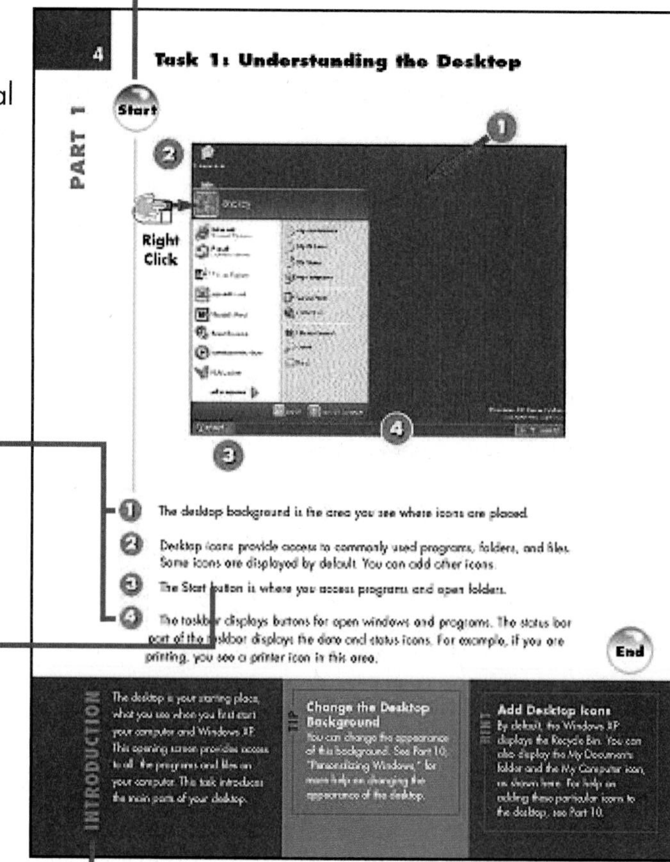

2. Each task includes a series of quick, easy steps designed to guide you through the procedure.

3. Items that you select or click in menus, dialog boxes, tabs, and windows are shown in **bold**.

Introductions explain what you will learn in each task, and **Tips and Hints** give you a heads-up for any extra information you may need while working through the task.

How to Drag:
Point to the starting place or object. Hold down the mouse button (right or left per instructions), move the mouse to the new location, then release the button.

See next page:
If you see this symbol, it means the task you're working on continues on the next page.

End Task:
Task is complete.

Selection:
Highlights the area onscreen discussed in the step or task.

Click:
Click the left mouse button once.

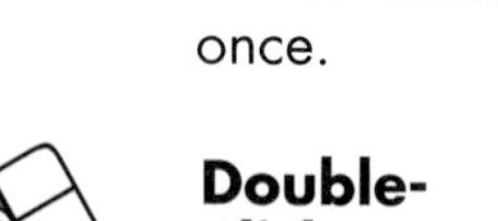

Right-Click:
Click the right mouse button once.

Type:
Click once where indicated and begin typing to enter your text or data.

Double-Click:
Click the left mouse button twice in rapid succession.

Pointer Arrow:
Highlights an item on the screen you need to point to or focus on in the step or task.

Introduction to *Easy Microsoft Office PowerPoint 2003*

Whether you're learning a program for the first time or getting acquainted with the latest upgrade, finding your way around new tools, dialog boxes, and program features can be daunting as well as time-consuming. *Easy Microsoft Office PowerPoint 2003* can help you get up and running fast.

Easy Microsoft Office PowerPoint 2003 gives you simple, step-by-step instructions that show you exactly what to expect on your own computer screen. Most people are visual learners, so seeing how to perform a task is a much faster way to learn about a program than wading through pages of text. With *Easy Microsoft Office PowerPoint 2003*, you'll learn all the basics for starting and working on your own slide-show presentations. You'll find out how to create a presentation, populate it with text and graphics, add slide transitions to make your show more interesting, and present your show when it's ready for an audience. Along the way, you'll pick up valuable skills and tips for making PowerPoint work the way you want.

You can start in Part 1 and read until the end of the book, or you can skip around and tackle just the tasks that interest you. You can also use the book as a reference for times when you need just a bit of extra help with the program. With the *Easy* visual format, you'll feel confident and up-to-date with PowerPoint in no time at all.

PART 1

Getting Started with PowerPoint

Before you begin creating slide shows and other presentations with PowerPoint, first acquaint yourself with the various program elements and how they work. The PowerPoint window is composed of a menu bar and several toolbars, along with several panes, such as the Task pane, which contains links to common PowerPoint tasks. The first step to mastering the program is knowing how to navigate its onscreen elements.

You can customize different aspects of the program window, including the appearance of the Task pane, toolbars, and your view of the slide area. For example, you can zoom in to see a closer look at a slide object or zoom out to see the entire slide. You can also switch between viewing single slides one at a time, or all the slides in a presentation.

If you run into a problem or question about a PowerPoint command or task, you can consult the PowerPoint Help files for assistance. The Help files offer quick instructions and explanations for using the program, along with links to online Help sources on the Web.

The PowerPoint Program Window

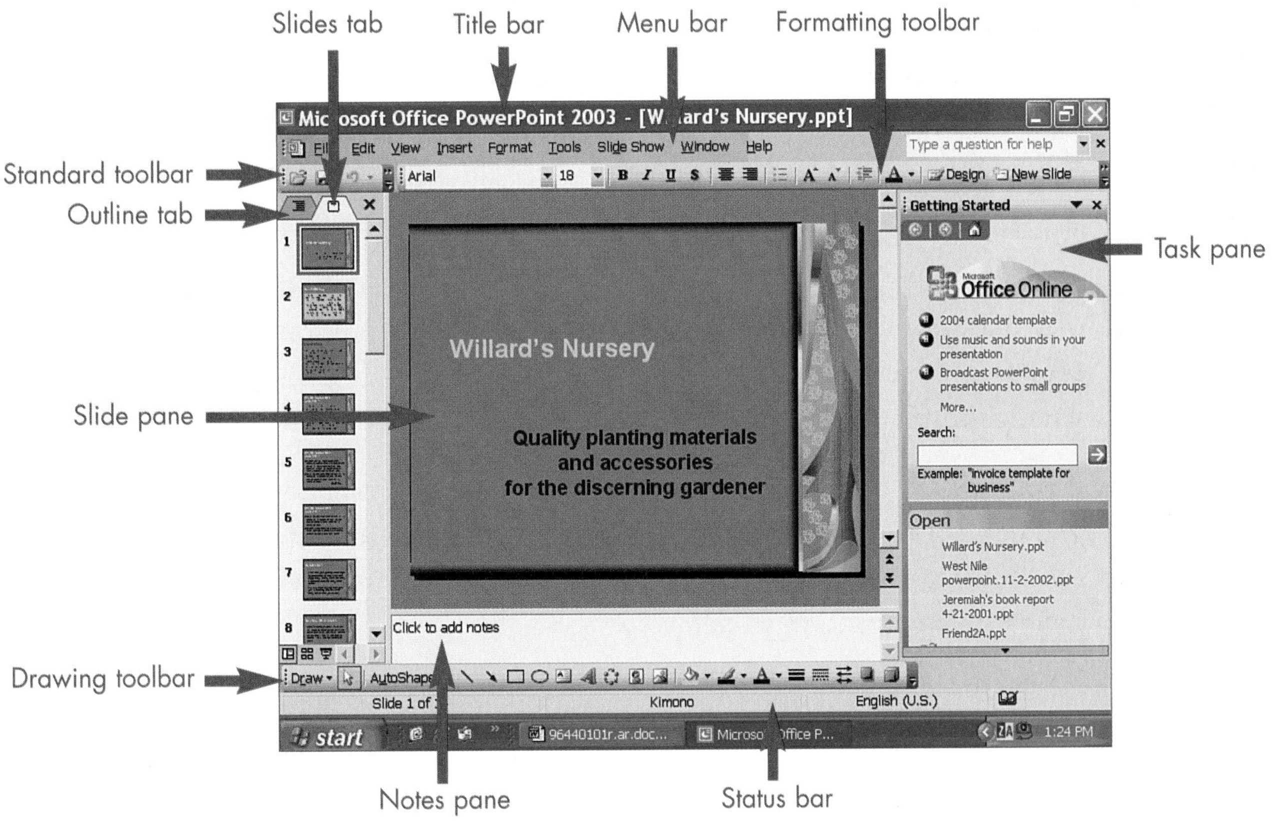

Starting PowerPoint

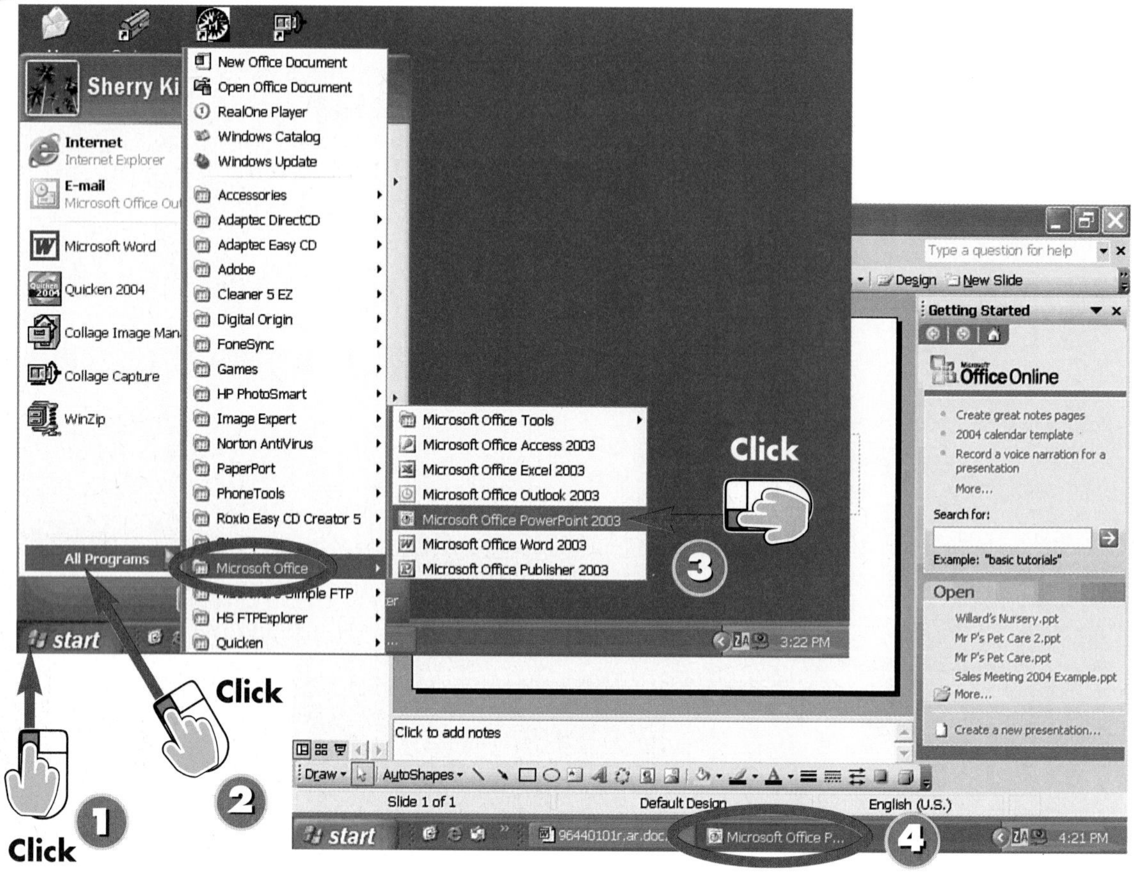

1. Click the **Start** button.
2. Click **All Programs**.
3. Click **Microsoft Office, Microsoft Office PowerPoint**.
4. The PowerPoint program window opens and a taskbar button for the program appears on the Windows taskbar.

INTRODUCTION

PowerPoint 2003 is a powerful presentation program you can use to create slide presentations and other visual documents. Whether you are giving a business presentation, a lecture, or book report, you can use PowerPoint to communicate important information visually. You can start PowerPoint using the Windows Start menu.

TIP

Another Way to Start PowerPoint

If your Windows desktop includes a PowerPoint shortcut icon, you can use it to start the program. Simply double-click the icon to open the program.

TIP

Start Menu Shortcut

Windows XP keeps track of recently used programs and lists them at the top of the Start menu. If you recently opened PowerPoint, you can click the program name from the Start menu to quickly access the program.

Exiting PowerPoint

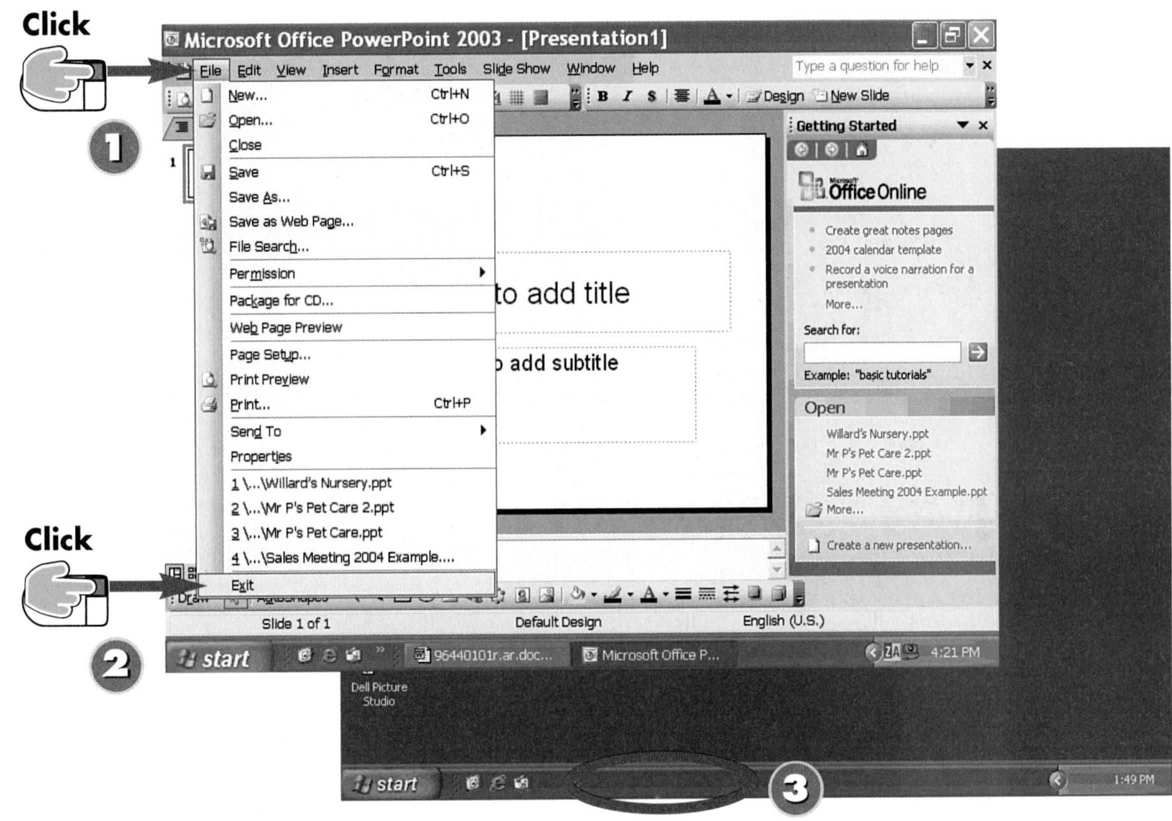

1. In the PowerPoint window, click the **File** menu.
2. Click **Exit**.
3. The PowerPoint window closes, and the taskbar button for the program no longer appears on the Windows taskbar.

INTRODUCTION

You can close PowerPoint when you finish working on a presentation. Closing the application frees up system memory. If you leave too many programs open at a time, your computer's processing power slows down.

HINT

Caution

If you have not saved your work, PowerPoint prompts you to do so before closing the program window. Click **Yes** to save the file or click **No** to exit the program without saving your work.

TIP

Using the Close Button

You can also click the **Close** button (×) located in the upper-right corner of the program window to quickly close PowerPoint.

Understanding the PowerPoint Window

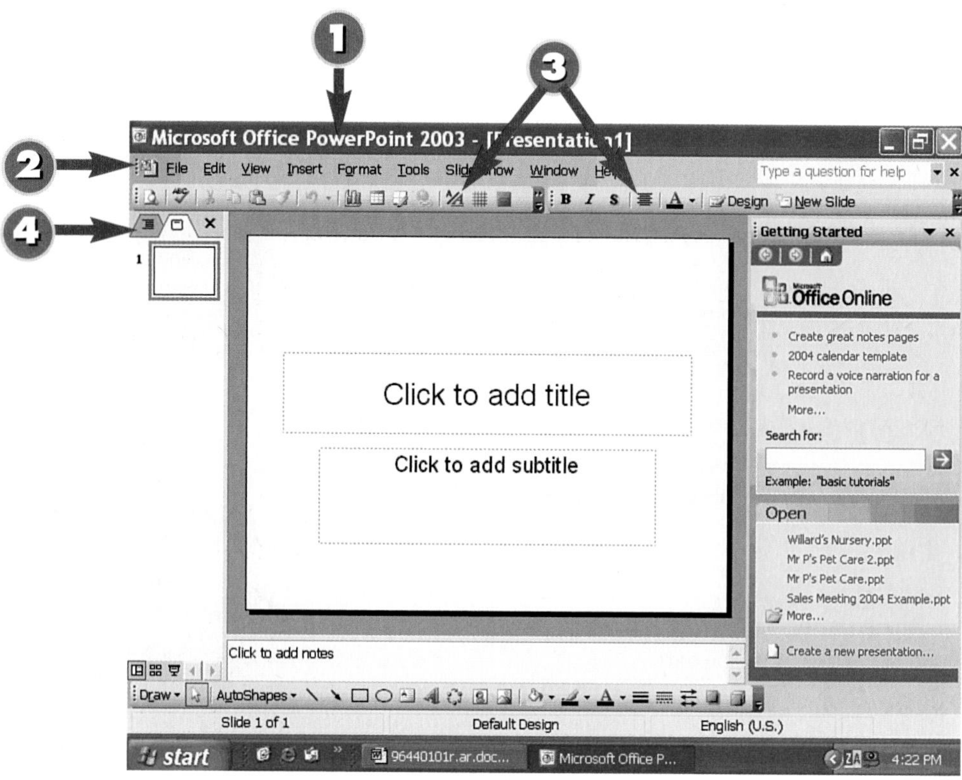

1. The title bar displays the name of the program and current file.
2. The menu bar displays menus and commands.
3. The Standard toolbar contains buttons for common tasks, and the Formatting toolbar contains buttons for formatting commands.
4. The Outline and Slides tabs allow you to switch between viewing your presentation as slides or in an outline format.

INTRODUCTION

The PowerPoint program window contains several elements, some of which are unique to PowerPoint, such as the Outline and Slides tabs. Other elements, such as the menu bar and toolbars, are common among most programs. The various onscreen elements enable you to quickly perform tasks and execute commands.

TIP

Viewing Toolbar Buttons

By default, the Standard and Formatting toolbars share the same area in the PowerPoint window. Depending on your screen-resolution setting, you may see more or fewer buttons on the toolbars. You can view other buttons by clicking the **Toolbar Options** button located at the far right-end of each toolbar, and then clicking the toolbar button you want to activate.

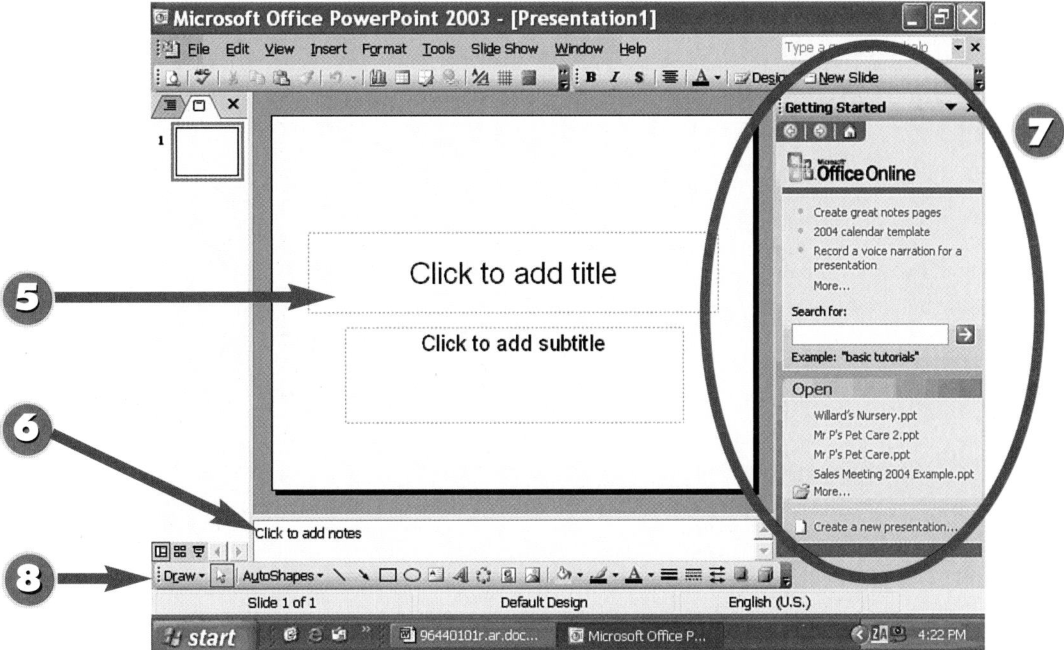

5 The Slide pane displays the current slide.

6 The Notes pane displays notes for the current slide.

7 The Task pane contains links to common tasks.

8 The Drawing toolbar contains buttons for working with slide objects, while the Status bar displays information about the current slide and presentation.

TIP

Freeing Up Workspace
To allow yourself more room to work on a slide, you can close panes to free up onscreen workspace. For example, you can close the Task pane or the Outline and Slides tabs. See the task "Using the Task Pane" later in this part to learn more.

TIP

Your Window Might Look Different
Depending on your monitor's screen-resolution setting, the arrangement of PowerPoint program elements on your computer can differ from those shown in this book. If you share your computer with other users, various features may have been turned on or off by someone else.

Working with Menus and Toolbars

Start

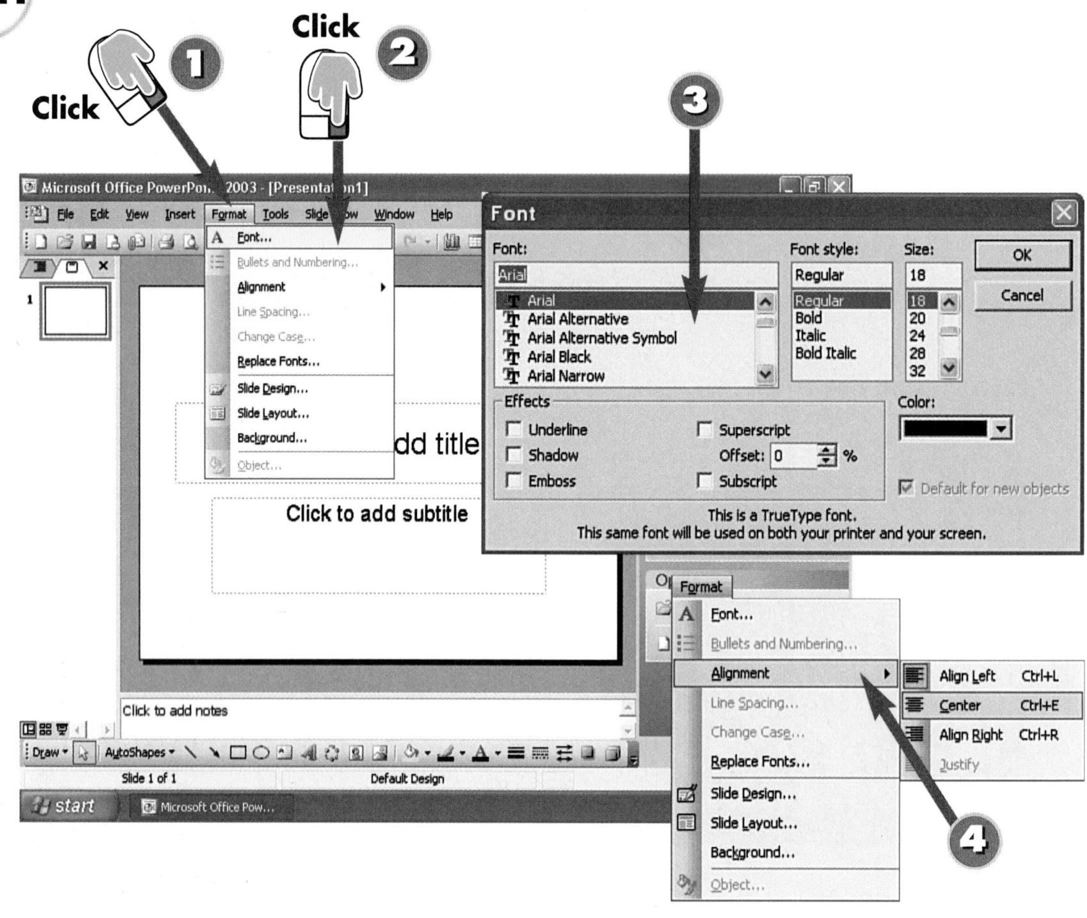

1. To view the contents of a menu, click the menu name. The menu drops down from the menu bar to reveal a list of commands.

2. To execute a command, click the command name.

3. PowerPoint carries out the command, which may sometimes involve you selecting additional options from a dialog box.

4. Some commands reveal an additional submenu of commands. Move the mouse pointer over the command to view a submenu.

INTRODUCTION

Use PowerPoint's menus and toolbars to execute commands and perform tasks. The menu bar groups related commands and tasks under menu names. For example, the File menu includes commands to help you work with PowerPoint files. Toolbars contain clickable shortcuts, in the form of buttons, to common commands.

NOTE

Opening Dialog Boxes
Menu commands followed by three dots open a dialog box of more options you can choose from.

TIP

Issuing Keyboard Commands
You can also use your keyboard to execute menu commands in PowerPoint. Pressing the **Alt** key along with the underlined letter in a menu name opens the menu onscreen.

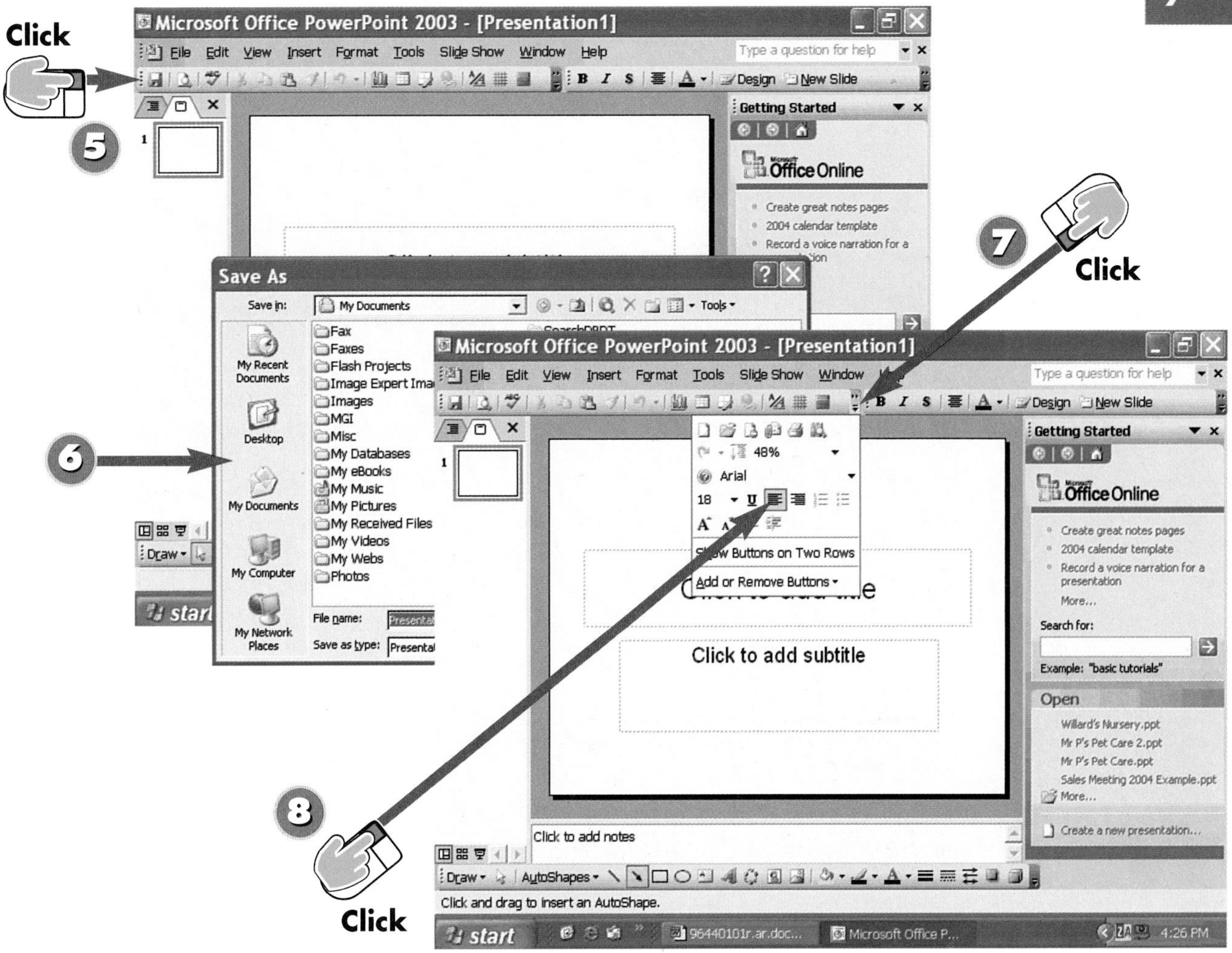

5. To execute a toolbar command, click the command's toolbar button.

6. PowerPoint carries out the command, which may involve you selecting additional options from a dialog box.

7. To view additional toolbar buttons, click the **Toolbar Options** button.

8. A pop-up menu of additional buttons appears. Click a button to execute the command.

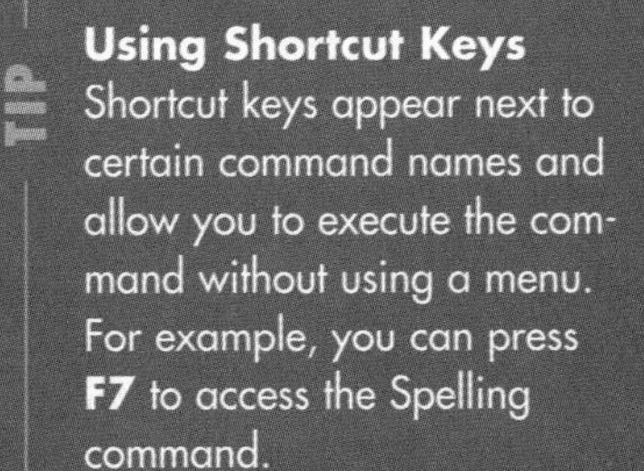

TIP

Using Shortcut Keys
Shortcut keys appear next to certain command names and allow you to execute the command without using a menu. For example, you can press **F7** to access the Spelling command.

TIP

Which Button Is Which?
To find out the name of any toolbar button, simply move your mouse over the button and pause. A ScreenTip appears with the button name.

TIP

Hiding and Displaying Toolbars
To hide a toolbar so that it no longer appears on the screen, select **View**, **Toolbars**, and then select the toolbar you want to hide. To display the toolbar again, repeat this procedure.

Customizing Toolbars

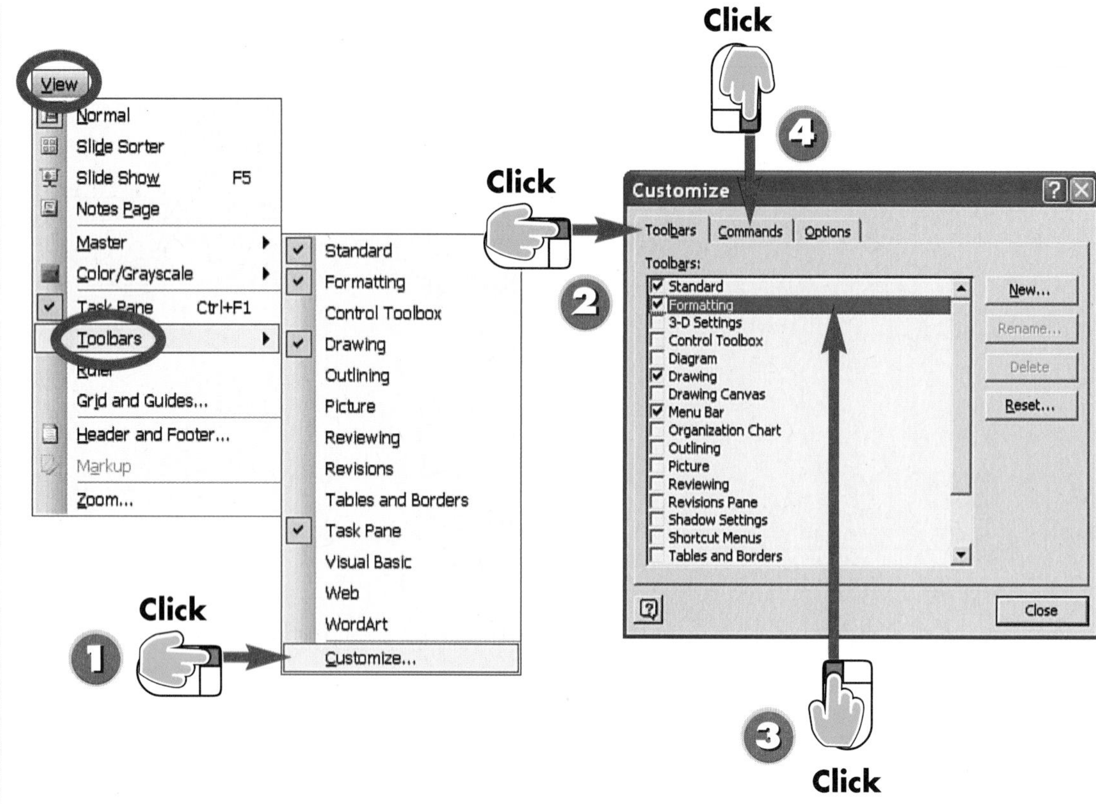

1. Click **View**, **Toolbars**, **Customize**.
2. The Customize dialog box opens. Click the **Toolbars** tab.
3. Click the toolbar you want to customize.
4. Click the **Commands** tab.

INTRODUCTION

Each toolbar in PowerPoint displays a default set of buttons. You can customize which buttons appear on each toolbar, or add new buttons for other tasks you perform frequently.

TIP

Seeing the Full Toolbars
Click **View**, **Toolbars**, **Customize**, and then click the **Options** tab and select **Show Standard and Formatting Toolbars on Two Rows**. Click **Close** to apply the change.

TIP

Displaying Larger Buttons
You can enlarge toolbar buttons onscreen to see them better. To do so, click **View**, **Toolbars**, **Customize**, click the **Options** tab, and select **Large icons**. Click **Close** to apply the change.

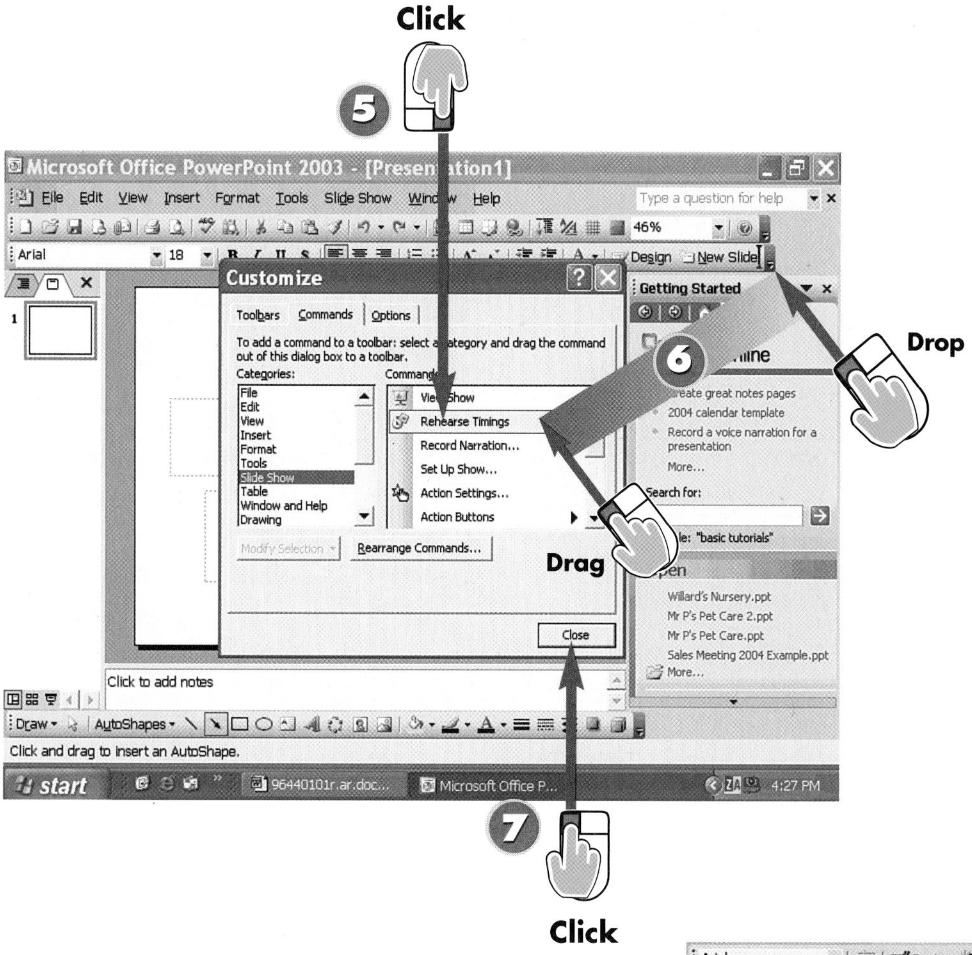

5 Select the category and button you want to add to the toolbar. (Categories group similar commands together, often by menu name.)

6 Drag the selected button from the list, and drop it onto the toolbar where you want it to appear.

7 Click **Close**.

8 The button appears on the toolbar.

End

TIP
Removing a Button
To remove a button from a toolbar, first select **View**, **Toolbars**, **Customize** to open the Customize dialog box. (This dialog box must be open to edit any toolbar.) Next, drag the button from the toolbar and drop it anywhere in the work area. The button is immediately removed, and all the other buttons in the toolbar shift to fill the space. Close the dialog box to complete the customization process.

TIP
Hiding ScreenTips
Select **View**, **Toolbars**, **Customize** to open the Customize dialog box. Click the Options tab and deselect **Show ScreenTips on Toolbars**. Click **Close**.

Using the Task Pane

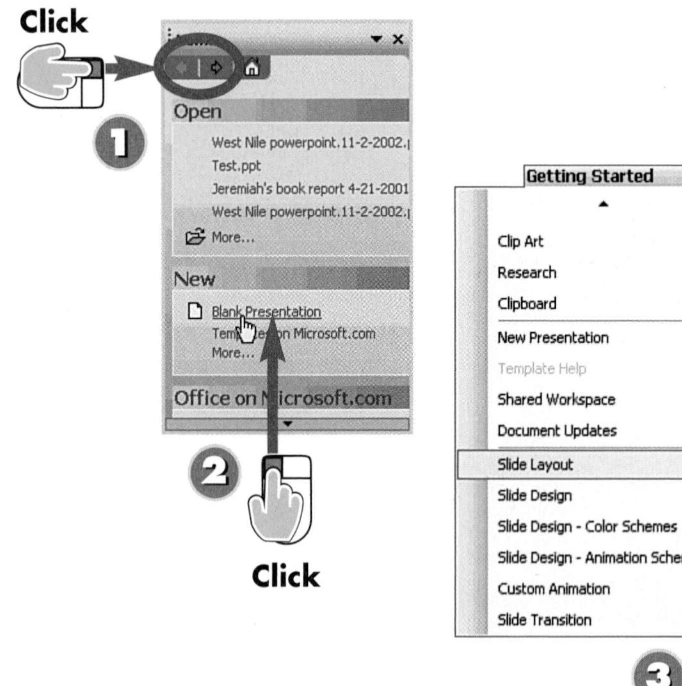

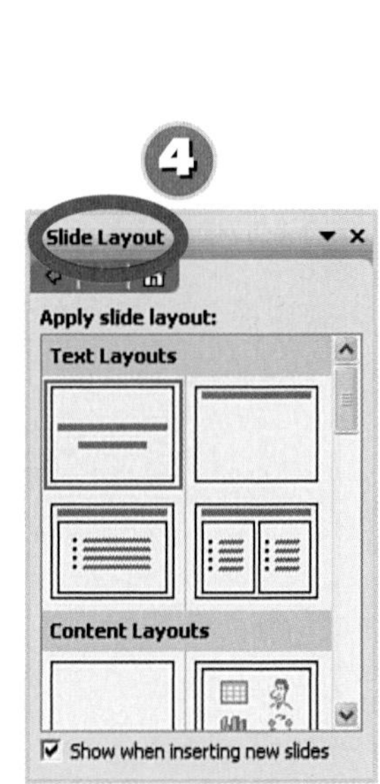

1. If two or more panes are open at the same time, you can click the navigation buttons to move between them.
2. You can click a link to activate a feature, or you can select from available options.
3. To open a particular pane, click the **Other Task Panes** button (the **down arrow** button in the upper-right corner of the Task pane), and then click the pane you want to view.
4. The new pane's contents appear in the Task pane.

INTRODUCTION

The Task pane is a handy way to access common commands and controls. By default, the Task pane is displayed on the right side of the PowerPoint window. You can view several different panes within the Task pane area. For example, you can view slide layouts in the Slide Layout pane, or clip art in the Clip Art pane.

TIP

Clicking Home

Click the **Home** button at the top of the Task pane to return to the default Getting Started pane that appears whenever you open PowerPoint.

TIP

Seeing It All

Depending on your screen resolution, you might not be able to see all the information in the Task pane. Click the scroll up or down arrows at the top or bottom of the pane to view more options inside the pane.

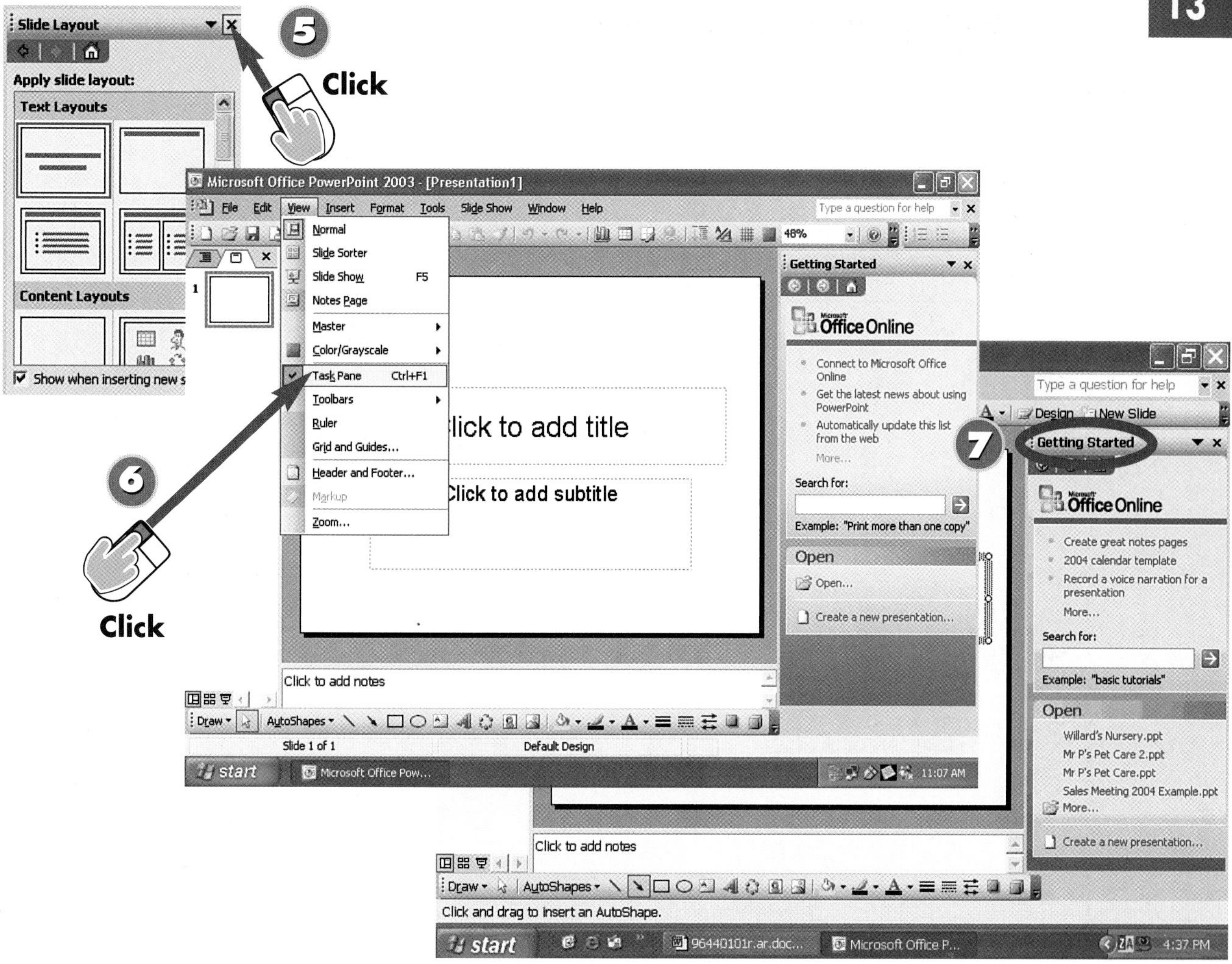

5 To close the pane, click the **Close** button.

6 PowerPoint closes the pane area. To display the Task pane again, select **View**, **Task Pane**.

7 The Task pane opens again, displaying the Getting Started pane.

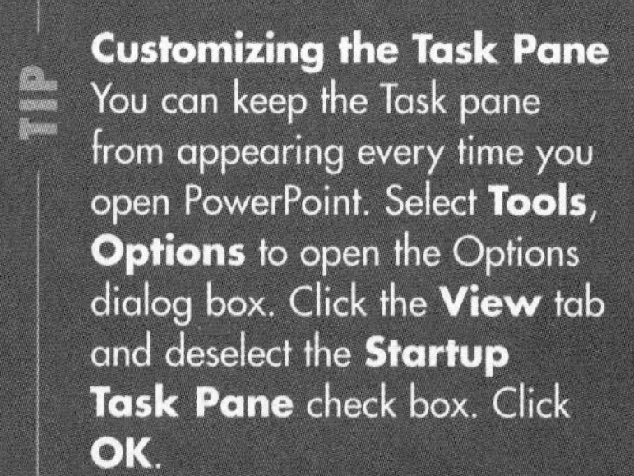

TIP

Customizing the Task Pane
You can keep the Task pane from appearing every time you open PowerPoint. Select **Tools**, **Options** to open the Options dialog box. Click the **View** tab and deselect the **Startup Task Pane** check box. Click **OK**.

TIP

Hiding It Quickly
You can right-click over the Task pane to reveal a shortcut menu of related commands. Click **Task Pane** to quickly hide the pane from view. To display it again, select **View**, **Task Pane**.

TIP

Your Screen May Differ
The figures in the remaining parts of this book show the Task pane closed, unless it is related to the task at hand. Your own screen will look different if your Task pane remains open.

Changing PowerPoint Views

Click

Click

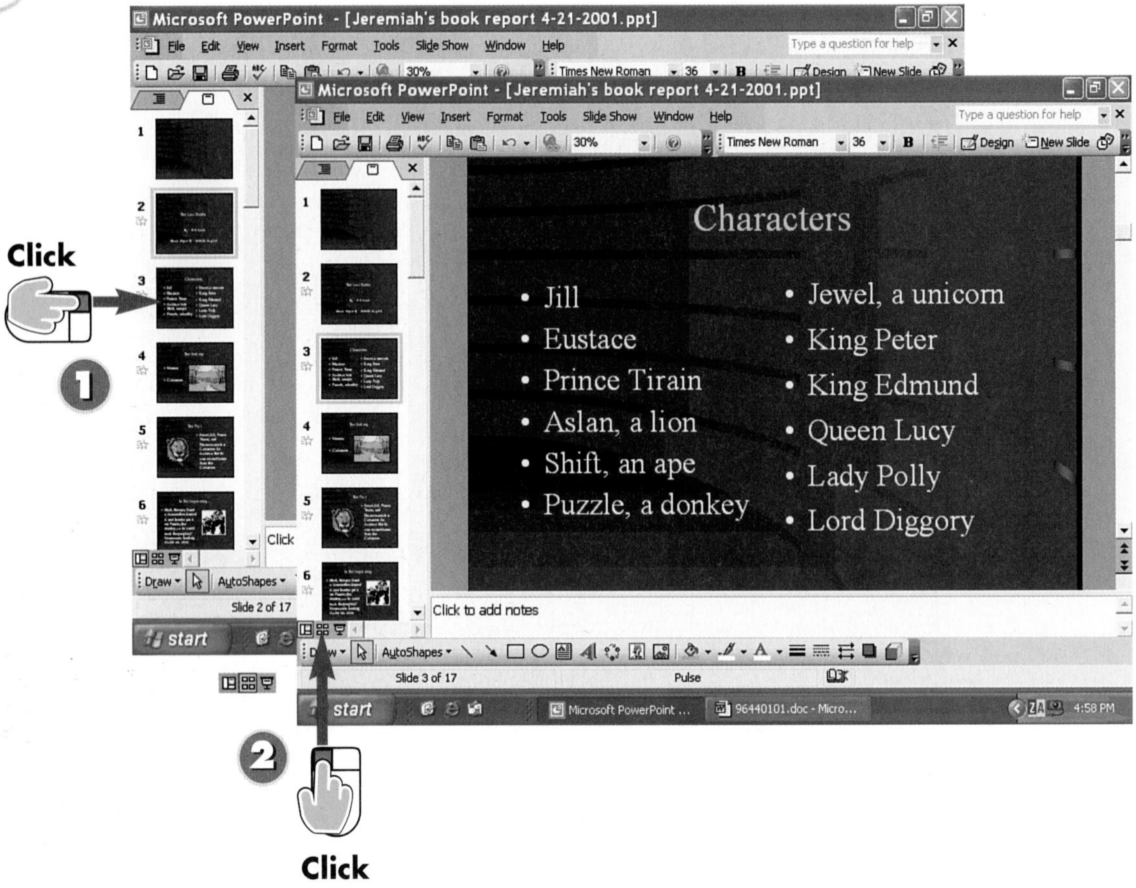

1. Normal view displays by default. To view another slide in your presentation, click the slide in the Slides tab.

2. PowerPoint displays the slide. To view all the slides, click the **Slide Sorter View** button.

INTRODUCTION

You can use PowerPoint's View buttons to change how you view slides in a presentation. By default, PowerPoint displays a single slide in the work area, called Normal view. You can switch views to see all the slides in a presentation or to view the actual presentation.

TIP

Closing the Outline and Slides tabs

To free up more workspace onscreen, you can close the Outline and Slides tabs. Click the **Close** button at the top of the pane. To view the panes again, select **View**, **Normal (Restore Panes)**.

TIP

Rearranging Slides

You can use Slide Sorter view to rearrange and reorder the slides in your presentation. See Part 10, "Fine-Tuning a Presentation," to learn more.

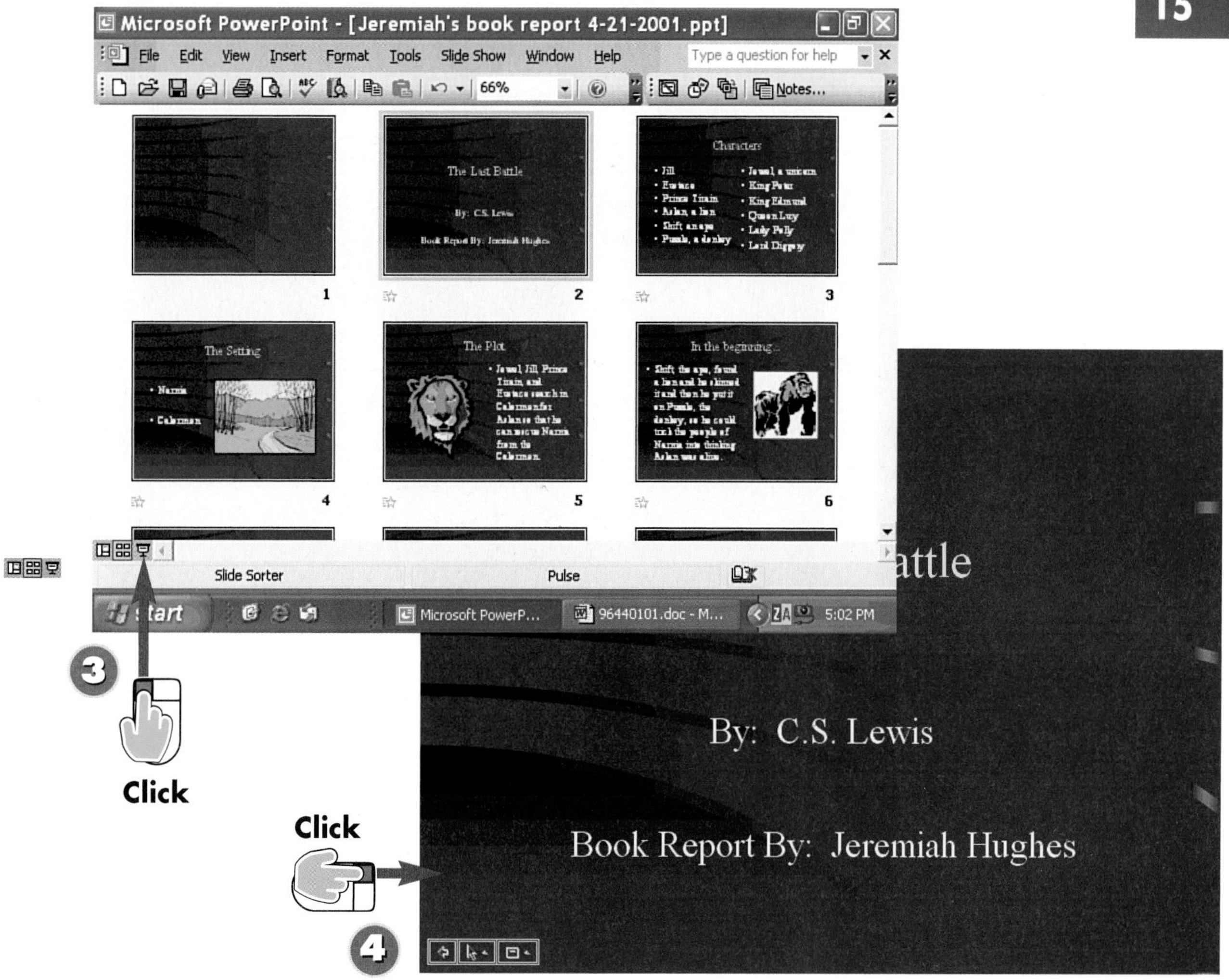

Click

Click

3. PowerPoint displays all the slides in your presentation. Click the **Slide Show View** button.

4. PowerPoint displays your presentation in full-screen mode. Click anywhere onscreen or press **Enter** to advance each slide, or press **Esc** to exit at any time.

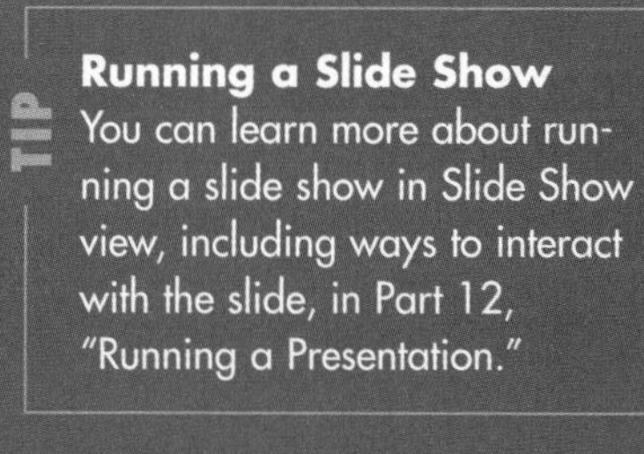

TIP

Running a Slide Show
You can learn more about running a slide show in Slide Show view, including ways to interact with the slide, in Part 12, "Running a Presentation."

TIP

Using the View Menu
You can also use the View menu to switch between PowerPoint view modes. Select **View**, and then click the view mode you want to apply.

Zooming In and Out

Start

Click

Click 3

1. To zoom in, click the **Zoom** drop-down arrow and select a zoom percentage.
2. PowerPoint zooms your view of the slide.
3. To return a slide to its regular size, click the **Zoom** drop-down arrow and select **Fit**.
4. PowerPoint displays the entire slide in the Slide pane.

INTRODUCTION

You can use the Zoom command to change your view of slide elements. You can zoom in for a closer view, or zoom out to see more of the slide. The Zoom feature is based on percentages; the higher the percentage, the closer the view.

TIP

Using the Zoom Dialog Box

Another way to set a zoom percentage is to use the Zoom dialog box. Select **View**, **Zoom** to display the dialog box, and then select a view percentage to use. Click **OK** to apply the zoom.

TIP

Zooming into a Specific Area

To zoom into a specific part of your slide, first click over that area, and then execute the **Zoom** command.

Finding Help

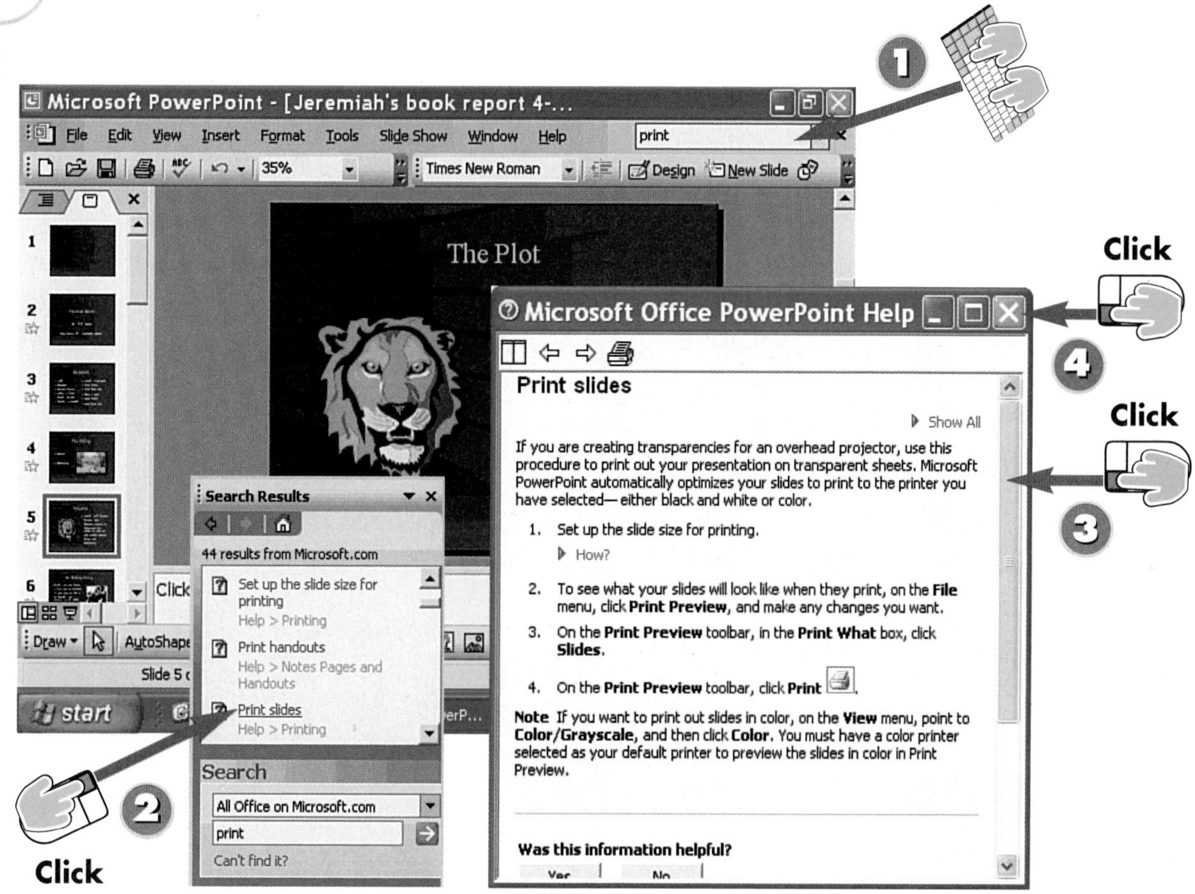

1. Click inside the **Ask A Question** box; type a question, word, or phrase you want to find help with; and press **Enter**.

2. The Search Results pane appears with a list of possible matches. Click a topic.

3. A Help window opens with information about the chosen topic. You can read the information and use the scrollbars to view more.

4. Click the window's **Close** button to exit the Help file.

INTRODUCTION

From time to time, you might find yourself needing some additional help with the PowerPoint program. PowerPoint offers several ways you can look up information about a particular task or feature. The Help menu lists a variety of features, or you can type in a topic or question directly into the Ask a Question box.

TIP

Finding Help on the Web

You can also log on to the Microsoft Web site to find more help resources for PowerPoint 2003. To log on to the Web site, you must have an Internet connection. When you do, select **Help**, **Office on Microsoft.com**. Your Web browser opens to the Microsoft Web site, where you can peruse other information and search for more help with PowerPoint.

PART 2

Creating Presentations

PowerPoint 2003 offers you a variety of ways to create your slide show presentations. You can build a presentation from scratch by adding text and other slide elements to blank slides. Or you can use the AutoContent wizard to assist you with creating a presentation step-by-step. By utilizing preformatted templates, you simply add your own text to create a quick slide show tailored for your specific audience. You can also select from numerous design templates and then add slides that share the same look and feel.

Once you have started a presentation, you can fill in placeholder text, add clip art, and add more slides. You can also modify the layout of a slide to change the way in which information and graphics are presented.

As you build your presentation, you can save it to work on it a little at a time, assign a password to protect your work, and open multiple slide shows.

The Slide Design Task Pane

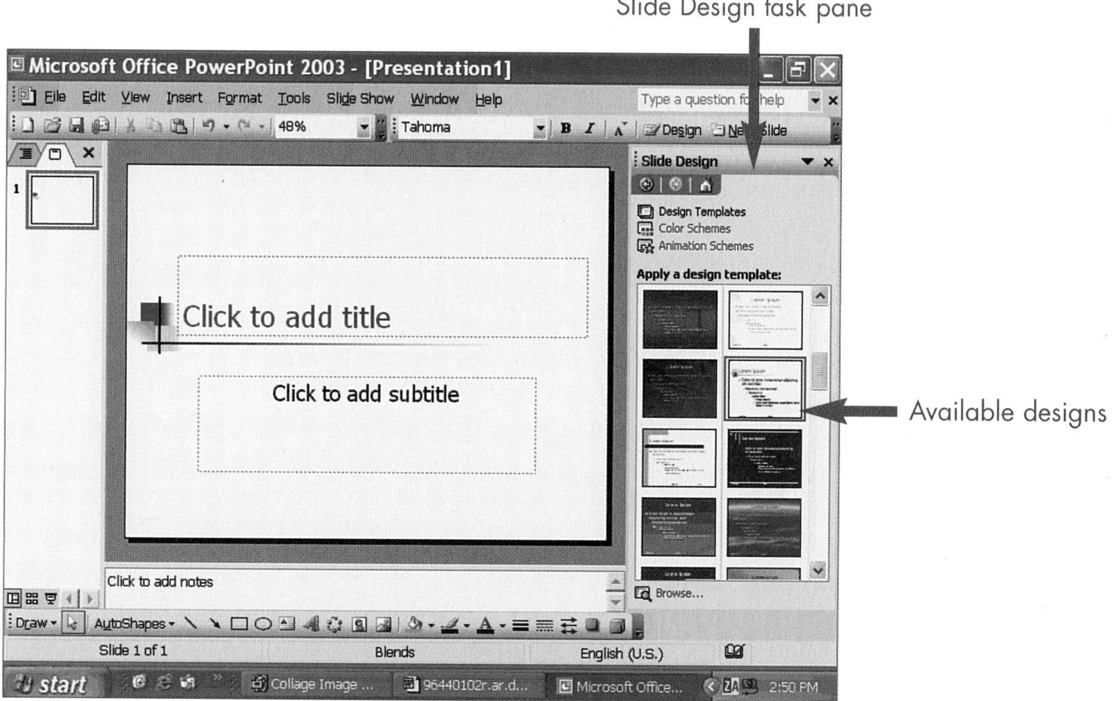

Creating a Blank Presentation

Start

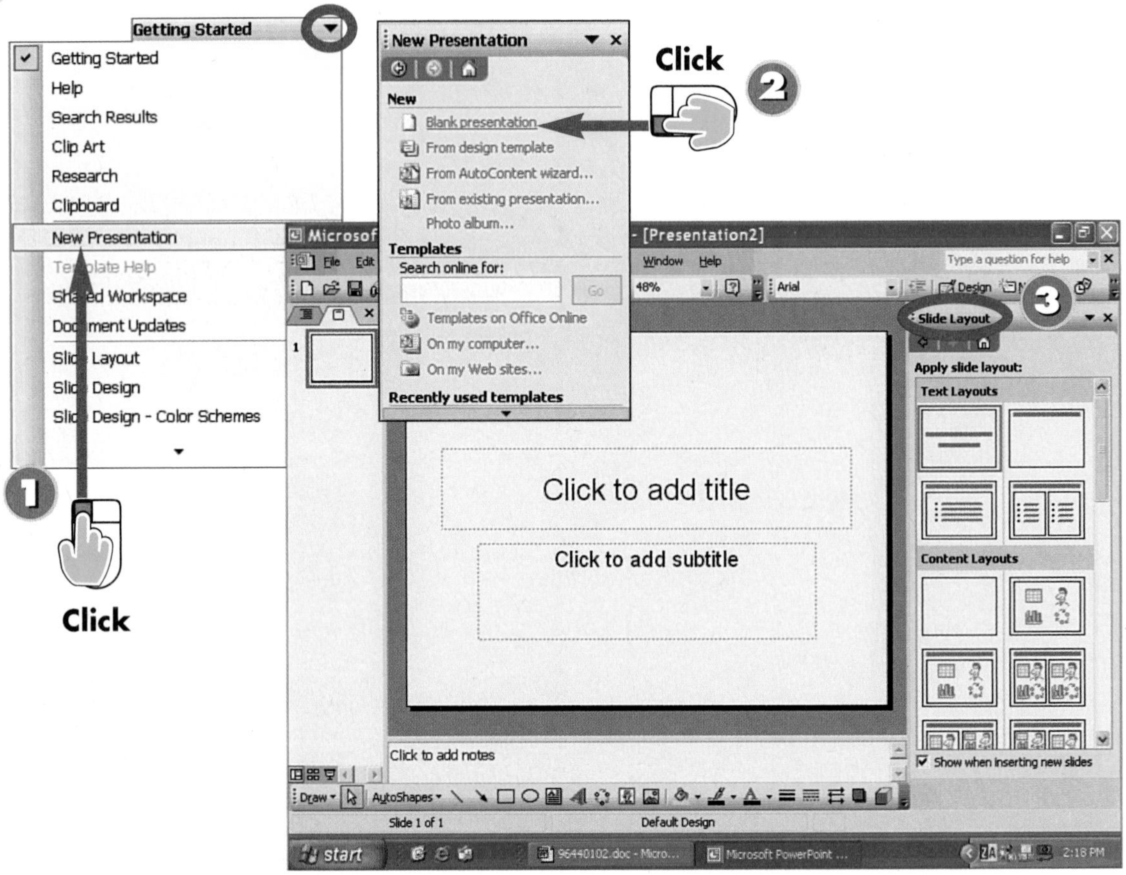

1. Click the **Other Task Panes** button and click **New Presentation**.

2. Click the **Blank Presentation** link in the New Presentation pane.

3. PowerPoint immediately starts a new presentation with a single slide and a default layout. The Slide Layout pane also opens.

INTRODUCTION

When you create a blank presentation, PowerPoint starts with a single slide and a plain white background. You can add a background, graphics, and other objects to the slide later. You can use the Slide Layout pane to assign a layout for the slide. A *layout* is simply the arrangement of slide objects.

TIP

Other Ways to Start a Blank Presentation

You can also click the **New** button on the Standard toolbar, or select **File**, **New** to create a blank presentation. Alternatively, you can click the **Blank Presentation** link on the New Presentation pane.

TIP

Where Is My Task Pane?

If you closed your Task pane, you must open it again to click the Blank Presentation option. See Part 1, "Getting Started with PowerPoint," to learn how to display and hide the Task pane and how to view different panes in the Task pane.

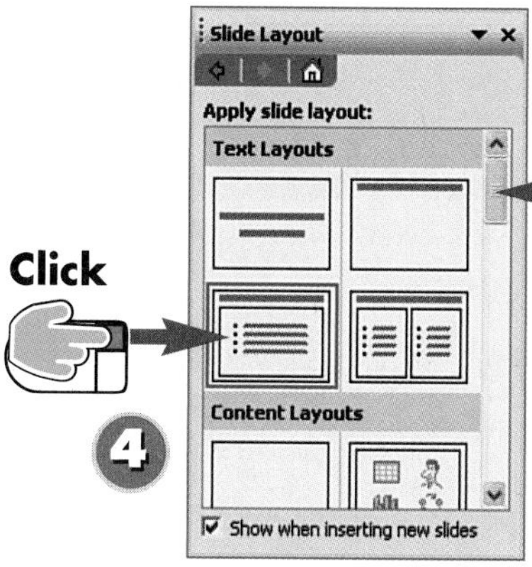

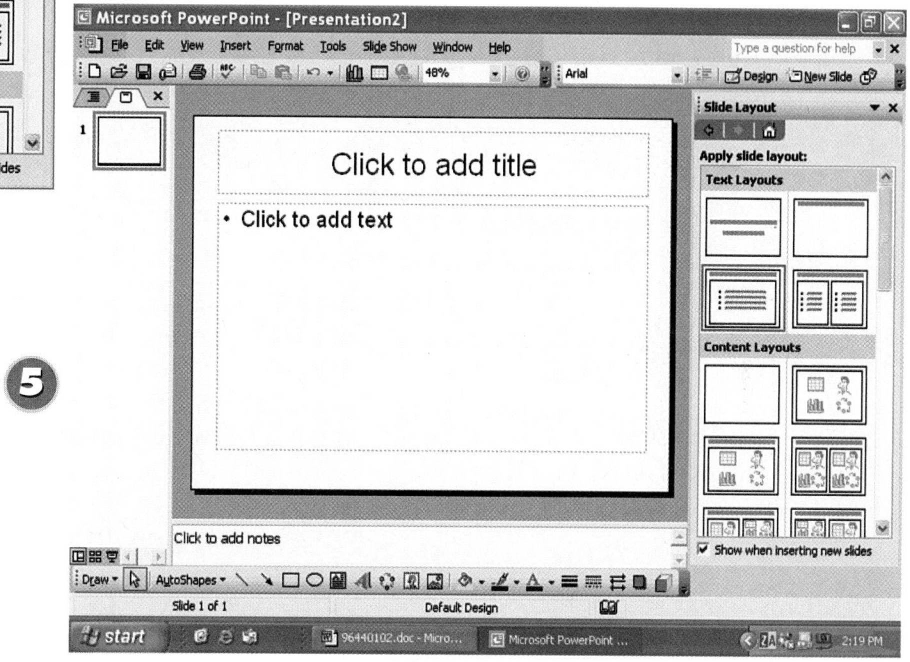

Click

4

5

4 Use the scroll arrows on the right side of the pane to scroll through the Slide Layout pane to view layouts. When you find a layout you like, click it.

5 PowerPoint changes the blank slide's layout.

TIP

Adding Text
You can click placeholder text and start typing your own text for the slide. To learn more about adding text, see the task "Replacing Placeholder Text" later in this part.

TIP

Do I Have to Choose a Layout?
If you prefer to design your own layout from scratch, you can select the Blank layout, located in the Content Layout section of the Slide Layout pane, and add your own text boxes and other slide objects later.

Creating a Presentation Using the AutoContent Wizard

Start

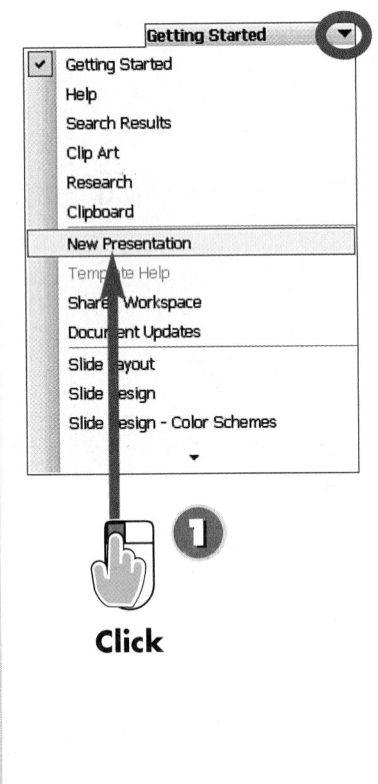

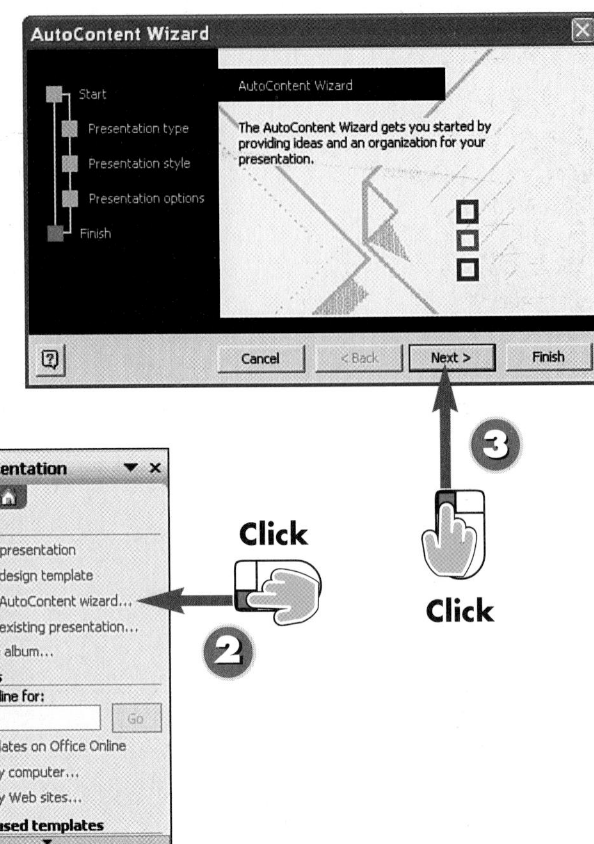

1. In the Task pane, click the **Other Task Panes** button (the down arrow in the pane's upper-right corner), and then click **New Presentation**.
2. The New Presentation pane appears. Click **From AutoContent Wizard**.
3. The AutoContent wizard opens. Click **Next** to continue.

INTRODUCTION

To create a quick and easy slide show, use the AutoContent wizard. This wizard walks you through each step in designing a presentation. You select the type of presentation, and PowerPoint creates an outline. When you finish building the presentation with the wizard, you can add your own text to each slide.

TIP

Opening the Task Pane
Is your Task pane closed? To open it quickly, press **Ctrl+F1** on the keyboard, or select **View, Task Pane** on the menu bar.

TIP

Another Way to the AutoContent Wizard
You can also select **File, New** to open the New Presentation pane and access the AutoContent Wizard.

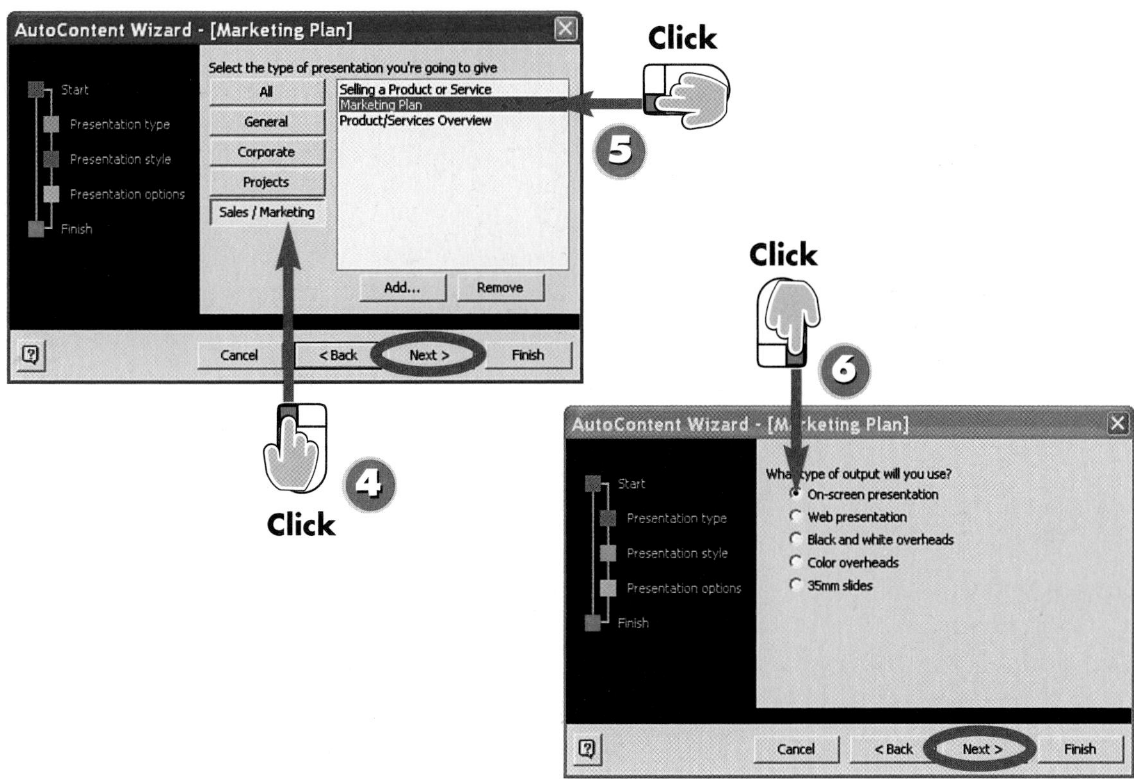

4 Click a category to select it.

5 PowerPoint lists presentations associated with the category you clicked. Select a presentation type, and then click **Next** to continue.

6 Click the type of method that best describes how you want to give your presentation, and then click **Next** to continue.

See next page

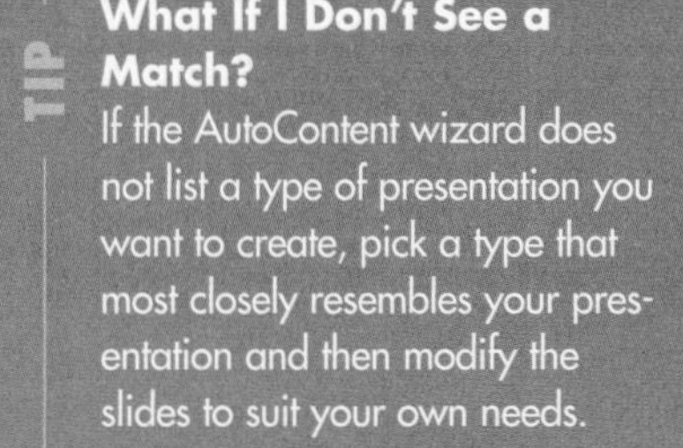

TIP

What If I Don't See a Match?
If the AutoContent wizard does not list a type of presentation you want to create, pick a type that most closely resembles your presentation and then modify the slides to suit your own needs.

TIP

Displaying All Categories
Click the **All** button in the AutoContent wizard in step 4 to view all the different types of preformatted presentations that PowerPoint offers.

Creating a Presentation Using the AutoContent Wizard Continued

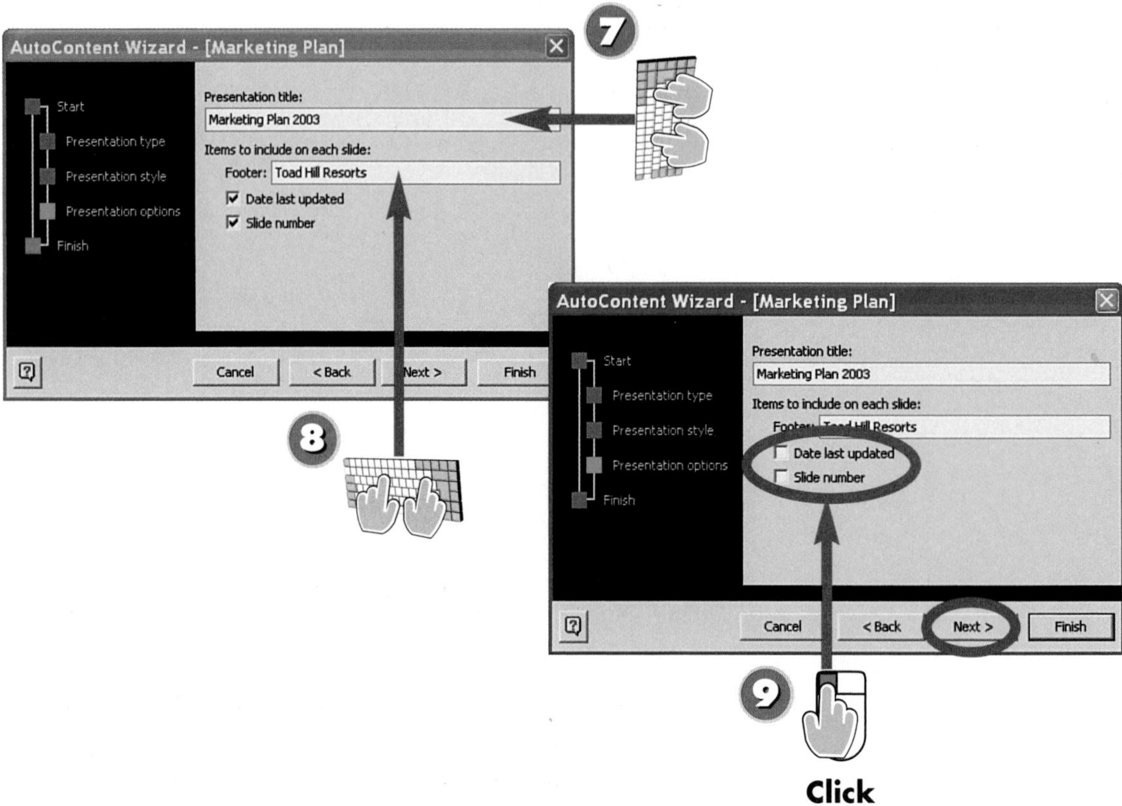

7. Type a title for the presentation, if desired. The title appears on the first slide in the presentation.
8. Optionally, type in any footer text you'd like to appear at the bottom of each slide.
9. By default, the AutoContent wizard includes the date and slide number at the bottom of each slide. To turn off these features, deselect the check boxes. Click **Next** to continue.

INTRODUCTION

The AutoContent wizard offers 18 different types of presentations you can choose from. Each one employs a different design background. The placeholder text on each slide is preformatted, so all you have to do is add your own text.

TIP

Going Back or Jumping Forward
You can click the **Back** button in the AutoContent Wizard dialog box to return to the previous screen and make any changes. You can also skip steps by clicking the **Finish** button, when applicable.

TIP

Stopping the Wizard
You can stop the AutoContent wizard at any stage during the process by clicking the **Cancel** button.

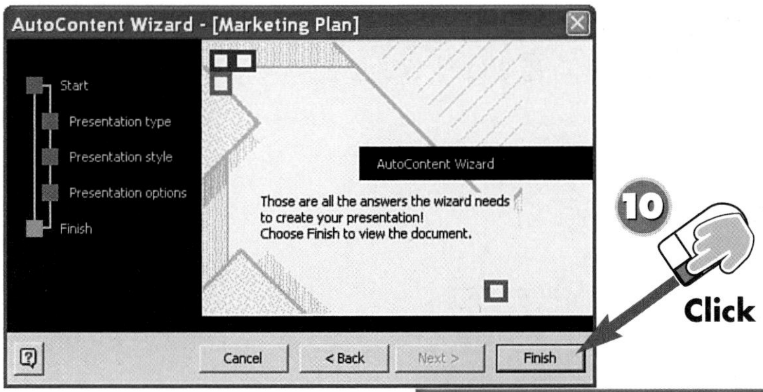

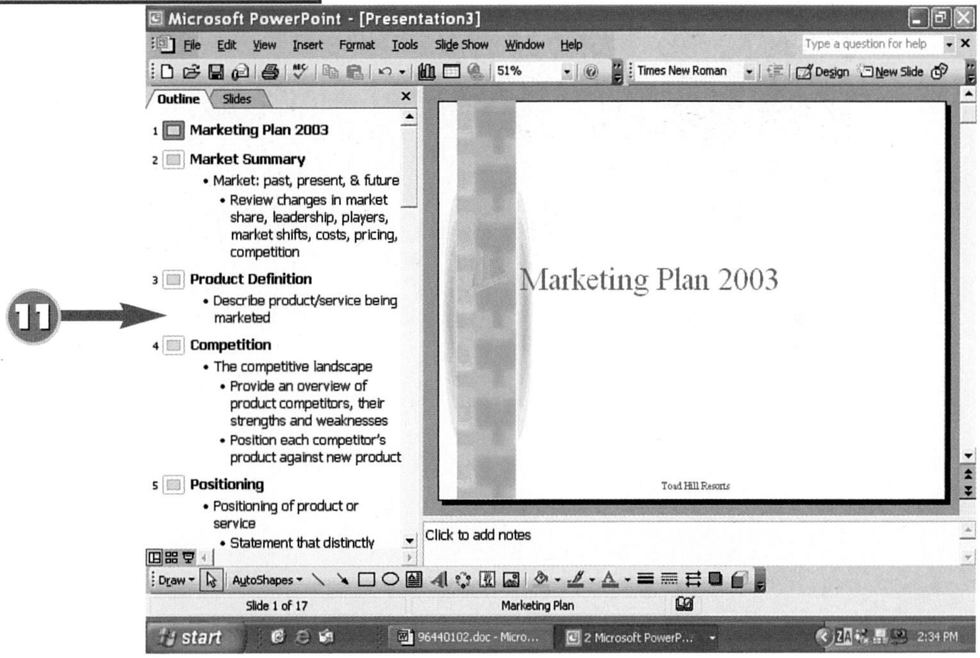

10 Click **Finish**.

11 PowerPoint creates the presentation and lists each slide in Outline view. You can now add your own text to each slide.

TIP

Adding Text
Each slide created with the AutoContent wizard includes placeholder text. You can replace the placeholder text with your own text. See the task "Replacing Placeholder Text" later in this part to learn more.

TIP

What If I Don't Like the Design?
If you don't like the design that the AutoContent wizard assigns to a presentation, you can change the presentation's design template. See the next task, "Creating a Presentation Using a Design Template," to learn how.

Creating a Presentation Using a Design Template

Start

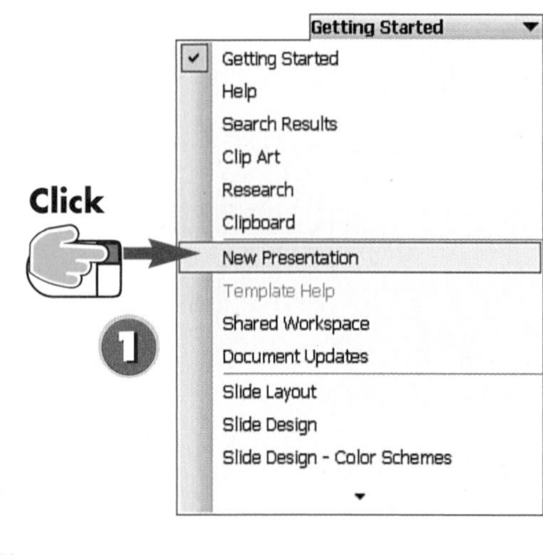

1. From the Task pane, click the **Other Task Panes** button (the down arrow in the pane's upper-right corner), and then click **New Presentation**.

2. The New Presentation pane appears. Click **From Design Template**.

INTRODUCTION

PowerPoint 2003 installs with 24 presentation design templates you can use for your slide shows. Plus, you can install additional designs, or download more from the Microsoft Web site. A *design template* is simply a preformatted color scheme, font style, and background for a presentation.

TIP

Finding More Designs
To find more designs, scroll to the bottom of the Slide Design pane and click the **Additional Design Templates** option. PowerPoint prompts you to insert the CD-ROM you used to install the program, and then installs the additional design templates.

TIP

Getting Task Pane Help
To learn more about working with the Task pane, see Part 1.

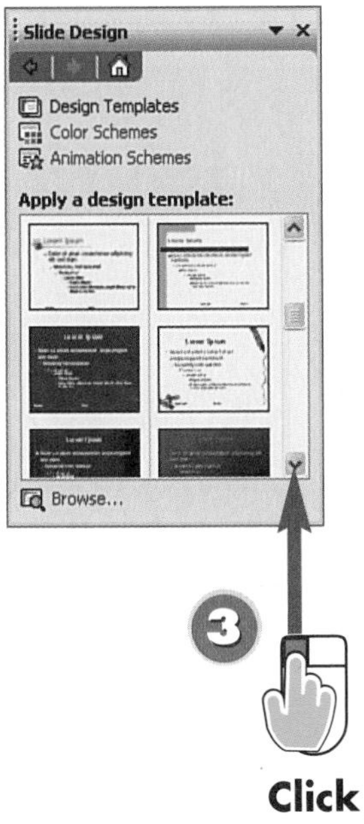

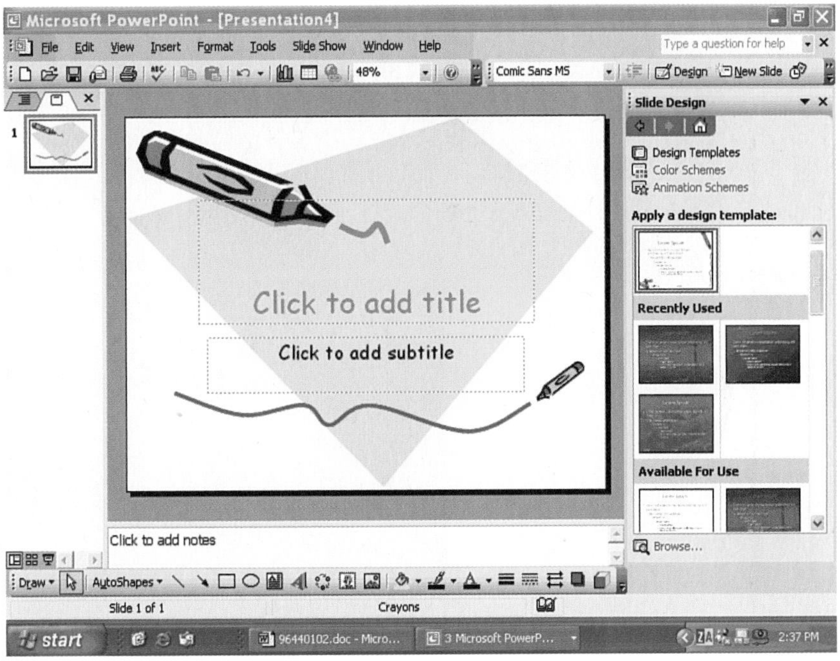

Click

3. The Slide Design pane opens. Scroll through the list of designs and click the one you want to apply.

4. PowerPoint immediately applies the design. Each new slide you add to the presentation will share the design you selected.

TIP

Finding Design Templates on the Web
If you scroll to the bottom of the Slide Design pane and click the **Design Templates on Microsoft.com** option, your Web browser opens to the Microsoft Web page, where you can explore other templates available for downloading.

TIP

Undoing a Selection
If you don't like the design you selected, you can select another, or click the **Undo** button located on the Standard toolbar to return to the previous design.

Understanding Slide Elements

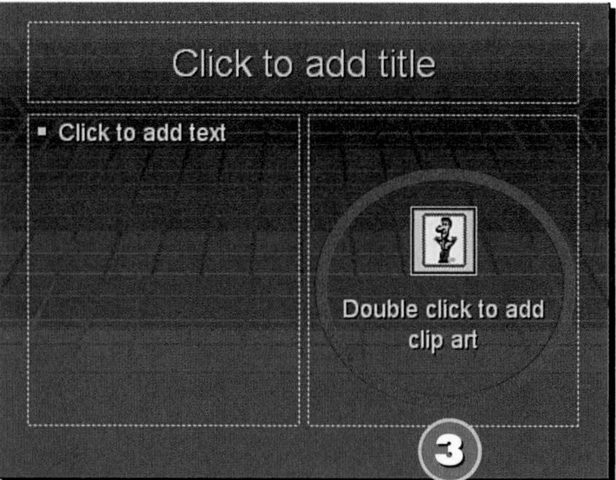

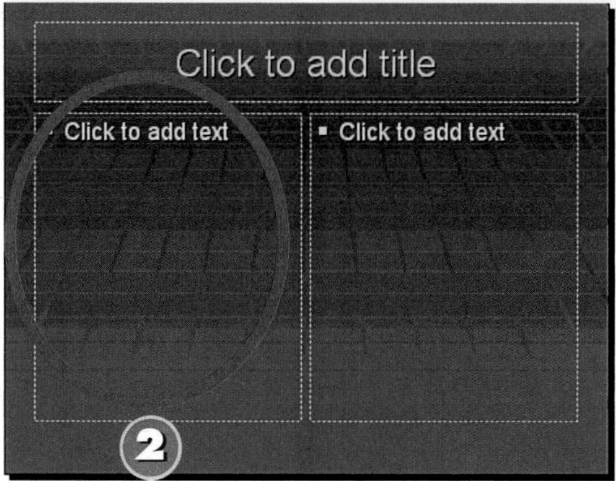

1. Just about every slide in a presentation includes text. Text boxes allow you to enter words and paragraphs into your slide.
2. You can use bulleted lists to present data succinctly and focus the audience on specific points you want to make.
3. You can use clip art to illustrate your slides.

INTRODUCTION

A *slide* can include a variety of elements, such as text, clip art, charts, and more. Each slide element is treated as an *object* on the slide, which means you can move or resize it as needed. The layout you select indicates what kind of object you can use; some offer a variety of object types. You can also add and delete slide objects. When selecting layouts from the Slide Layout pane, you can choose from several distinct slide elements as well as a combination of how those elements are arranged in a layout.

TIP

Defining Layouts

A *layout* is simply a design that tells PowerPoint where slide objects should appear on a slide. You can use the preset layouts in the Slide Layout pane, or you can build your own layouts from scratch starting with a blank slide.

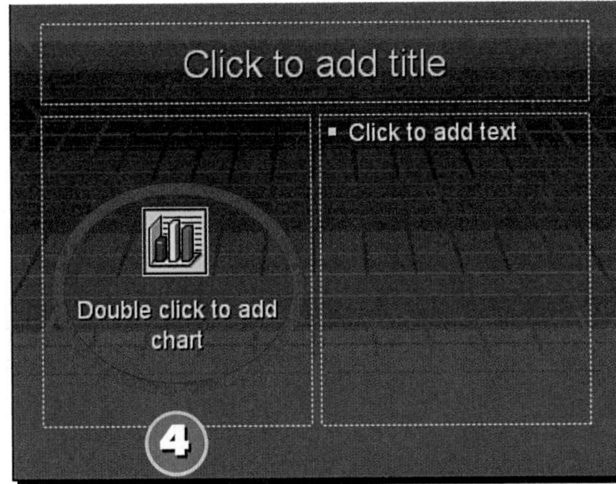

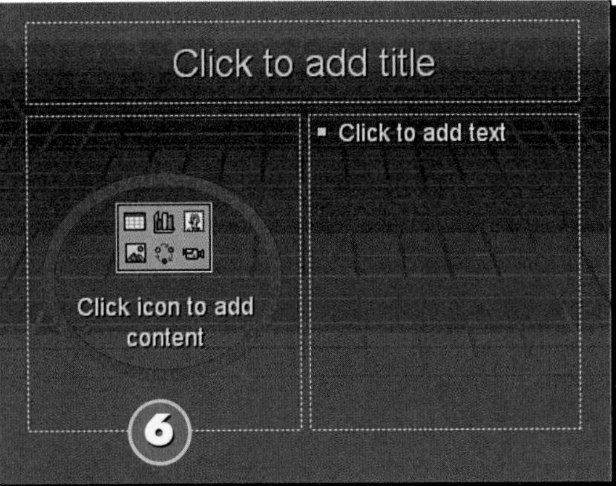

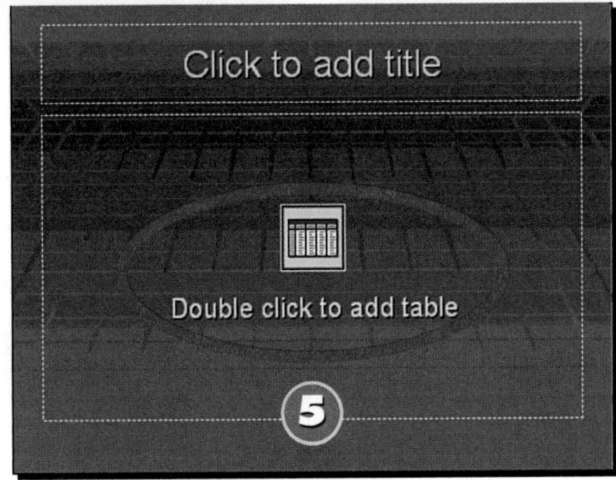

4 You can use charts to present data in a visual manner.

5 You can add tables to your slides to organize and present data in an easy-to-read format.

6 Content boxes allow you to choose the type of object you want to add, such as a media clip, a diagram, or a picture file from another source.

TIP

Selecting Objects

When you select a slide element, the object is surrounded by *selection handles*. You can drag the handles to resize the object. You'll learn more about resizing in Part 5, "Illustrating Your Slides."

TIP

What Is a Media Clip?

Media clips are sound and video clips that, when activated, run on a slide. For example, you might include a brief audio interview in a slide show.

TIP

Defining Clip Art and Graphics

Clip art is predrawn artwork you can insert onto a slide; graphics or picture files are drawings from other sources, such as a photo from Adobe Photoshop or an illustration from Macromedia FreeHand.

Replacing Placeholder Text

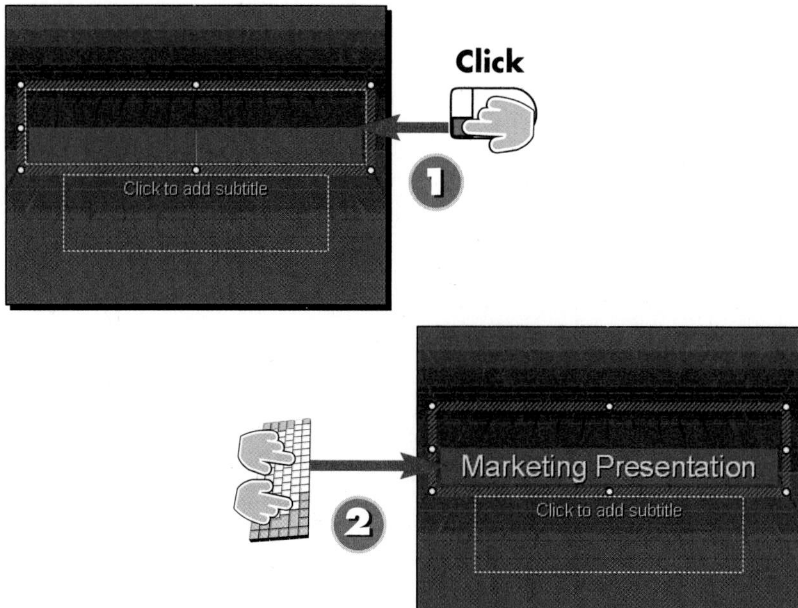

1. Click the text box to which you want to add text. The slide element is immediately surrounded by selection handles (tiny square boxes at each corner of the text box).

2. Type the text you want.

INTRODUCTION

Many of PowerPoint's slide layouts include text boxes with place-holder text. This placeholder text gives you an idea of what type of text to add to the slide, such as a title or subtitle. You replace the placeholder text with your own text.

TIP

Making Mistakes
If you make a mistake while typing slide text, press the **Delete** key to erase characters to the right or press the **Backspace** key to delete characters to the left of the insertion point.

TIP

Using Outline View
You can also use Outline view to replace placeholder text. See Part 3, "Building Presentations Using Outline View," to learn more.

Adding New Slides

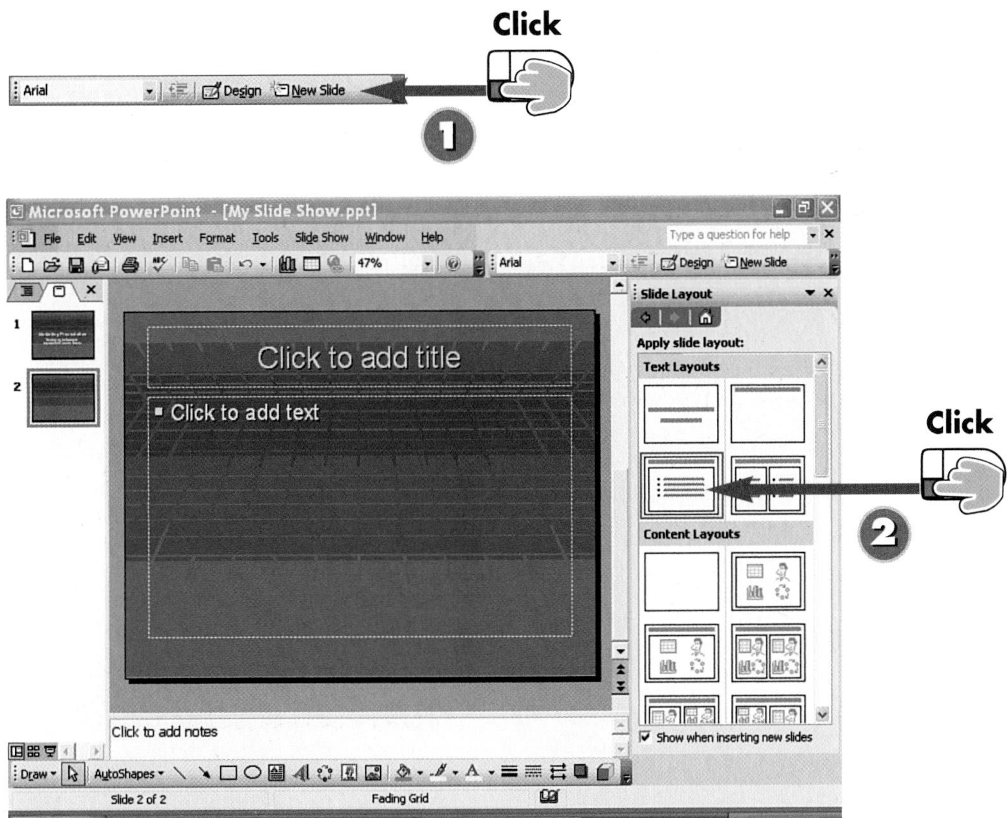

1. Click the **New Slide** button on the Formatting toolbar.

2. PowerPoint immediately opens the Slide Layout pane. Click a layout, and the new slide is ready to go.

INTRODUCTION

If you create a presentation using a blank slide or a design template, PowerPoint starts you out with a single slide. You can add more slides as you go. You can also add slides wherever you like in an existing presentation, such as one you create using the AutoContent wizard.

TIP

Using the Menu
You can also select **Insert**, **New Slide** to quickly add a slide to your presentation.

TIP

Using Slide Sorter View
To insert a slide amid existing slides, display the presentation in Slide Sorter view. Click the slide that precedes where you want a new slide inserted, then click the **New Slide** button on the Standard toolbar.

Changing the Slide Layout

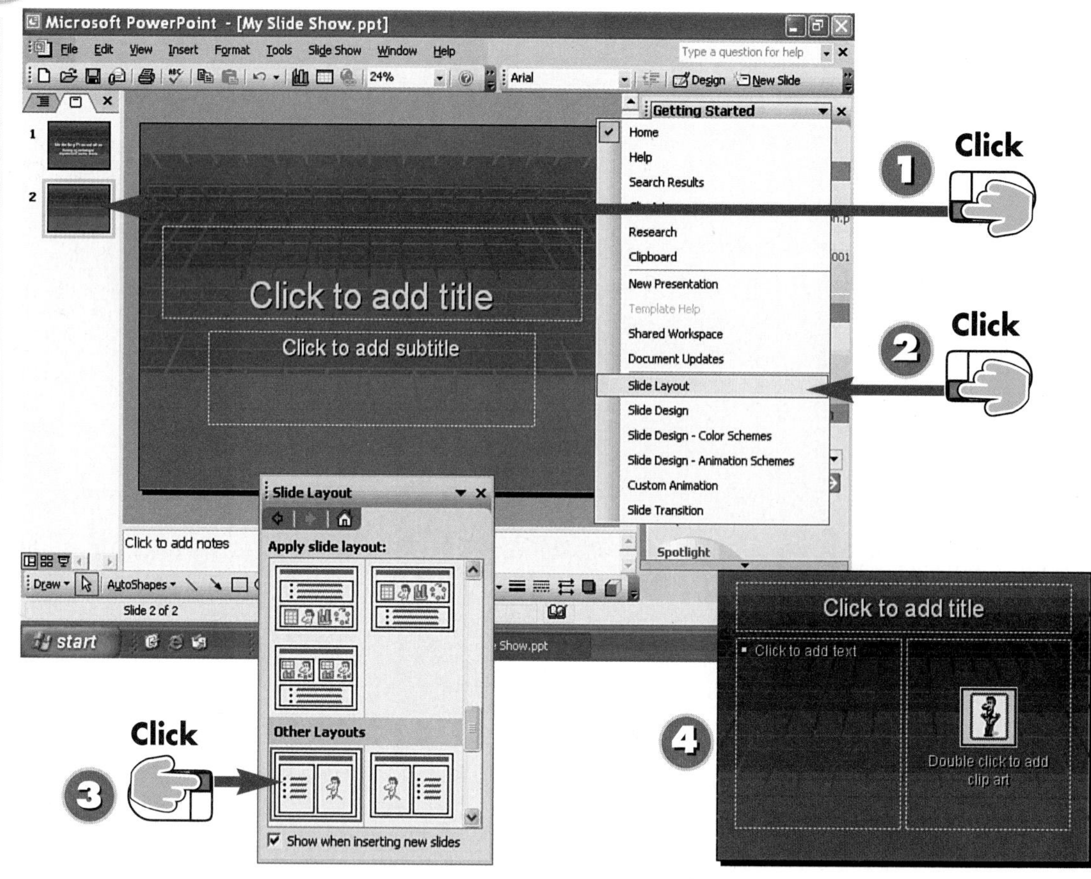

1. Click the slide you want to change.
2. From the Task pane, click the **Other Task Panes** button (the down arrow in the pane's upper-right corner), and then click **Slide Layout**.
3. The Slide Layout pane appears. Scroll through the available layouts and click the one you want to assign.
4. PowerPoint assigns the layout to the current slide.

INTRODUCTION

PowerPoint offers a variety of slide layouts you can use. If you don't like the current slide's layout, you can use the Slide Layout pane to select a new layout.

TIP

Undoing the Layout
If you assign a new layout to a slide that has existing text and artwork, the new layout may make the slide elements appear worse. To undo any new layout after you apply it, click the **Undo** button on the Standard toolbar.

TIP

Changing Designs
You can also change the slide's design, which includes the fonts, color scheme, and background of the slide. See Part 6, "Changing the Appearance of Slides," to learn more.

Saving a Presentation

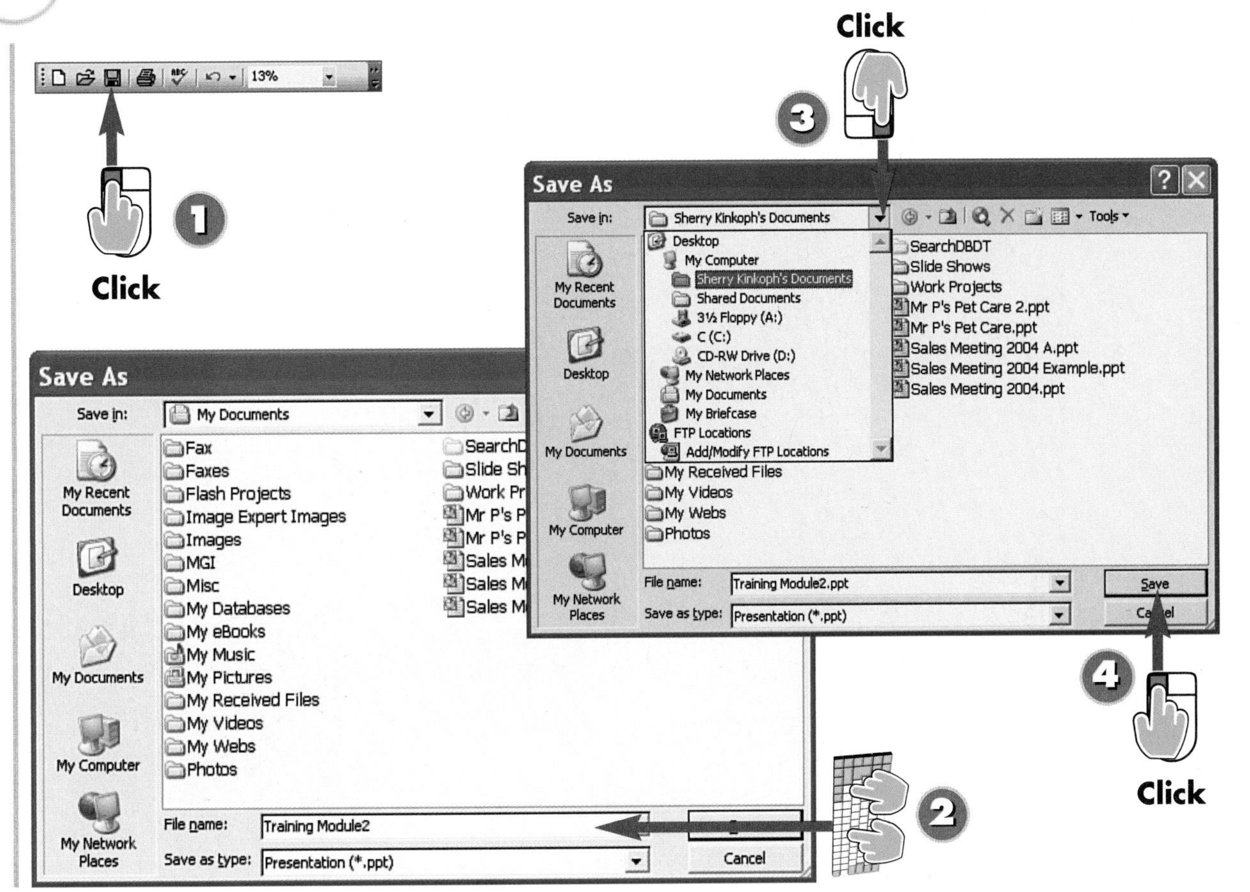

1. Click the **Save** button on the Standard toolbar.
2. The Save As dialog box opens. Type a name for the presentation.
3. To save the file in another folder, click the **Save In** drop-down arrow and select another folder or drive.
4. Click **Save**. PowerPoint saves the presentation.

INTRODUCTION

You must save your presentations to reuse them or to continue working on the slides later. When you save a PowerPoint file, you assign the presentation a unique name. You can also save the file to a specific folder or disk. After you've saved a file, subsequent saves do not require assigning a filename or location unless you want to create a duplicate of the presentation under a different filename.

TIP

The Default Folder
By default, PowerPoint saves your presentations in the **My Documents** folder. If you prefer to save your work in another folder or on a CD or floppy disk drive, you must use the Save in drop-down list to choose the folder or drive.

Opening and Closing an Existing Presentation

Start

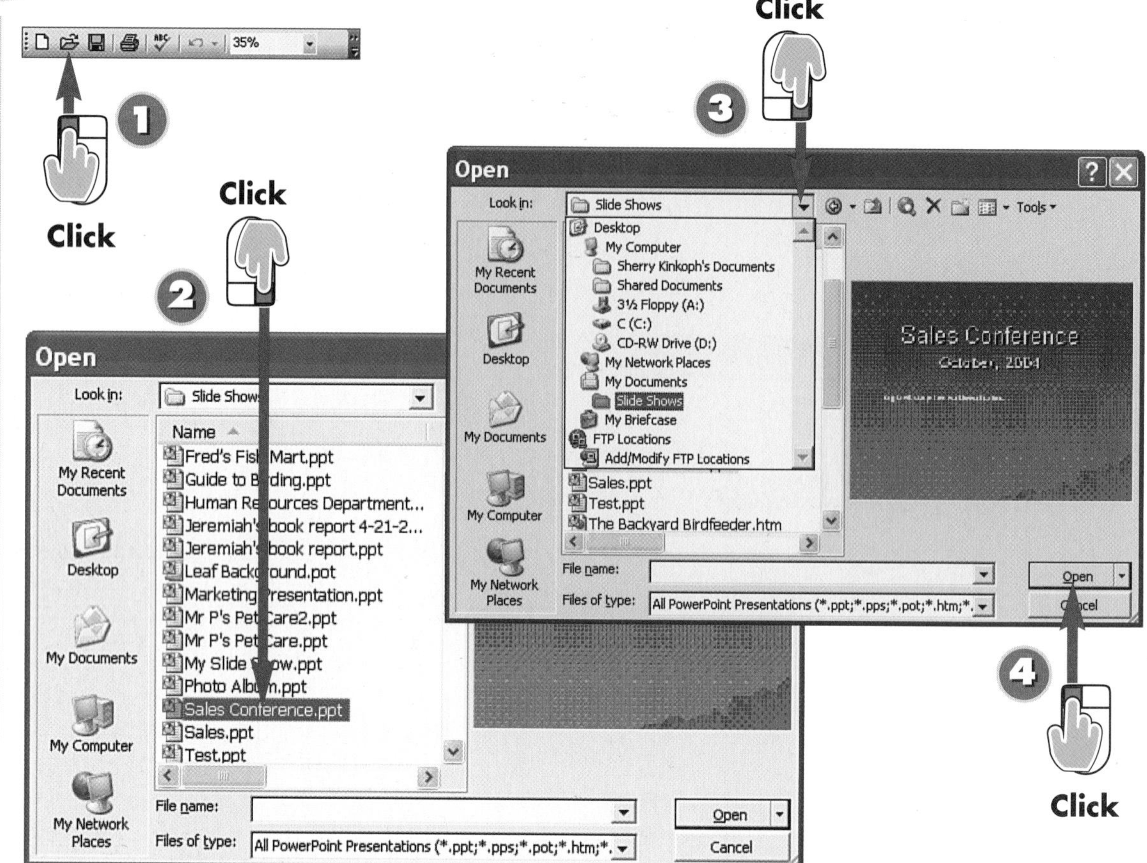

1. Click the **Open** button on the Standard toolbar.

2. The Open dialog box opens. Click the file you want to open to select it.

3. To locate the file in another folder or drive, click the **Look In** drop-down list, navigate to the folder or drive, and then select the file.

4. Click **Open**. PowerPoint opens the presentation.

INTRODUCTION

You can open a presentation you have previously saved in order to work on the slides some more. In addition, you can close a file you no longer want to work on, yet keep the PowerPoint window open to start new files.

TIP

Using the Menu Method

You can also display the Open dialog box using the **File** menu. Select **File**, **Open**.

TIP

Double-clicking

A quick method of opening a file from the Open dialog box is to simply double-click the filename.

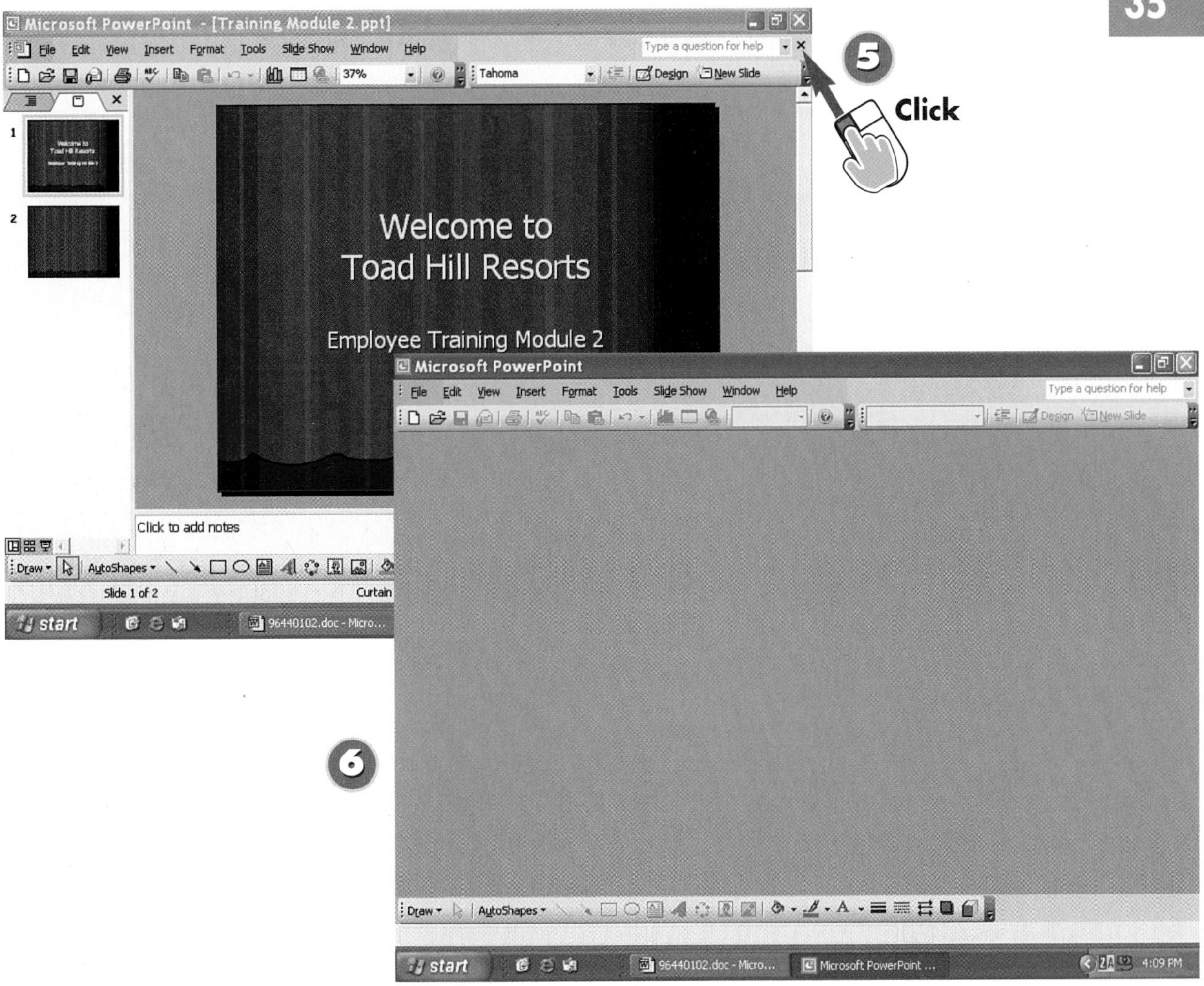

5 To close a presentation, click the file's **Close** button.

6 PowerPoint immediately closes the presentation.

TIP

Switching Between Multiple Files

You can open multiple files in PowerPoint and switch between them; use the Task bar or the Window menu to select which presentation to view.

TIP

Saving First

If you have made changes to your presentation, PowerPoint prompts you to save your work before closing the file. Click **Yes** to save.

HINT

Caution

Be careful not to click the program window's Close button, or you will end up closing PowerPoint entirely. The program window's Close button is located in the upper-right corner, directly above the file's Close button.

Navigating Between Slides

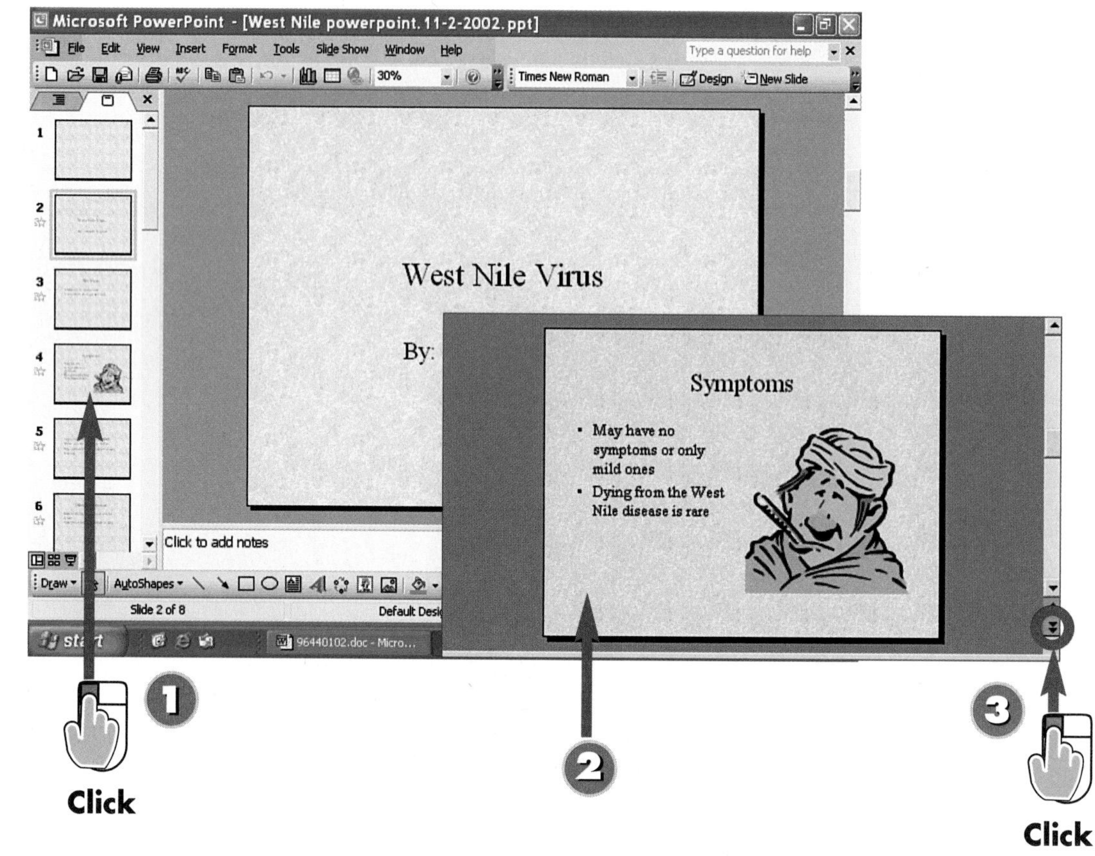

1. In the Slides tab, click the slide you want to view.
2. The slide immediately appears in the work area, also called the Slide pane.
3. Click the **Next Slide** button to display the next slide in the presentation.

INTRODUCTION

As you begin building your presentation, you will need to navigate back and forth between slides. In Normal view, you can view different slides using the navigation buttons located in the bottom-right corner of the Slide pane, or you can use the pane's scrollbar.

TIP

Using Keyboard Shortcuts

You can press the Page Up and Page Down buttons on your keyboard to move through a presentation in Normal view. See Part 1 to learn more about view modes.

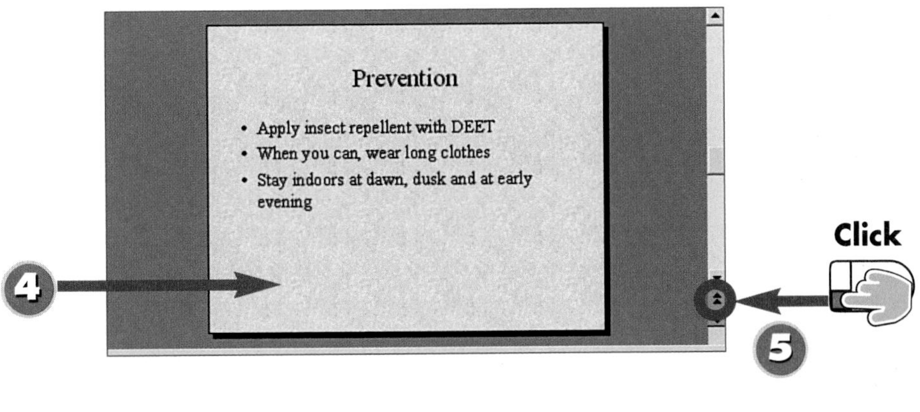

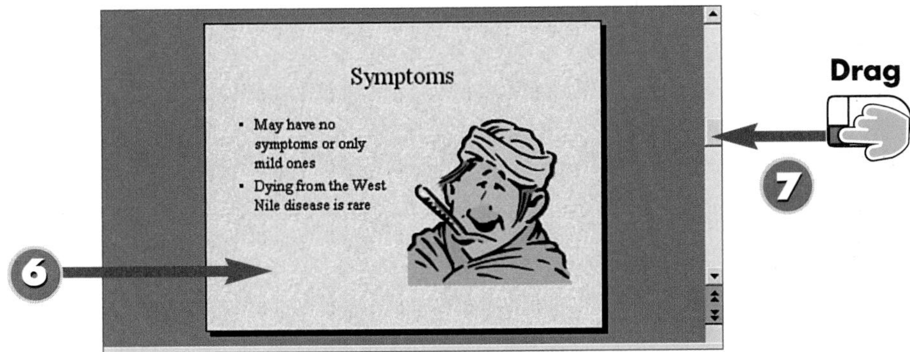

4. The next slide is displayed.
5. Click the **Previous Slide** button to move back a slide.
6. The previous slide is displayed.
7. You can also drag the scrollbar to navigate forward and backward in your presentation.

TIP

Using ScreenTips

When you drag the scrollbar in the Slide pane, a ScreenTip box appears, detailing the name and number of each slide as you drag.

TIP

Using Slide Sorter View

To view all the slides in a presentation, switch to Slide Sorter view. See Part 1 to learn more about using PowerPoint view modes.

Assigning a Password to a Presentation

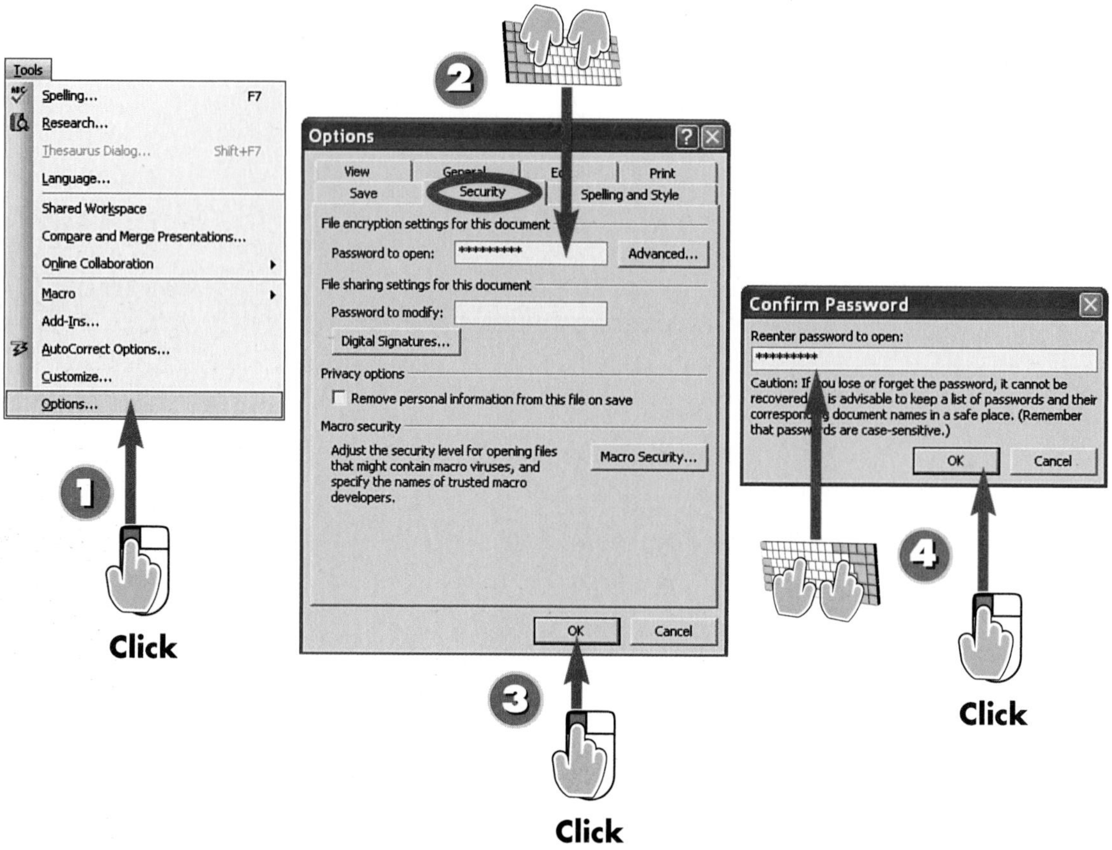

1. Open the **Tools** menu and click **Options**.

2. The Options dialog box opens. Click the **Security** tab, click inside the **Password to Open** box, and type a password.

3. Click **OK**.

4. The Confirm Password dialog box opens. Type the password again and click **OK**.

INTRODUCTION

PowerPoint 2003 includes a security feature that you can use to assign a password to your presentation file. This prevents other users from opening your presentation. Passwords can contain up to 15 characters, including any combination of letters, numbers, and special characters.

CAUTION

PowerPoint passwords are case sensitive, which means you must retype the password exactly as you entered it when you set up the password. Be sure to write down your password and keep it somewhere safe.

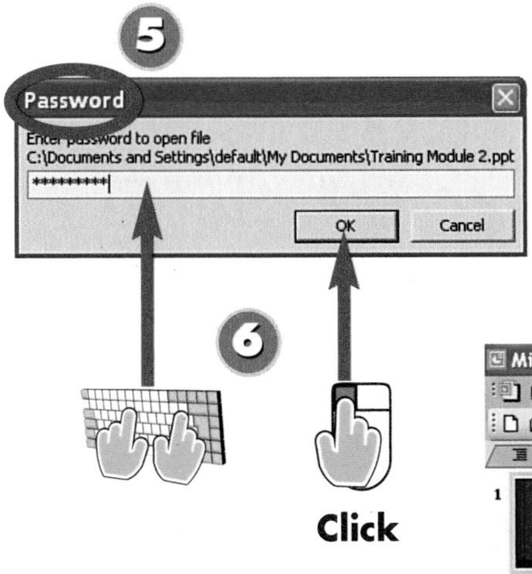

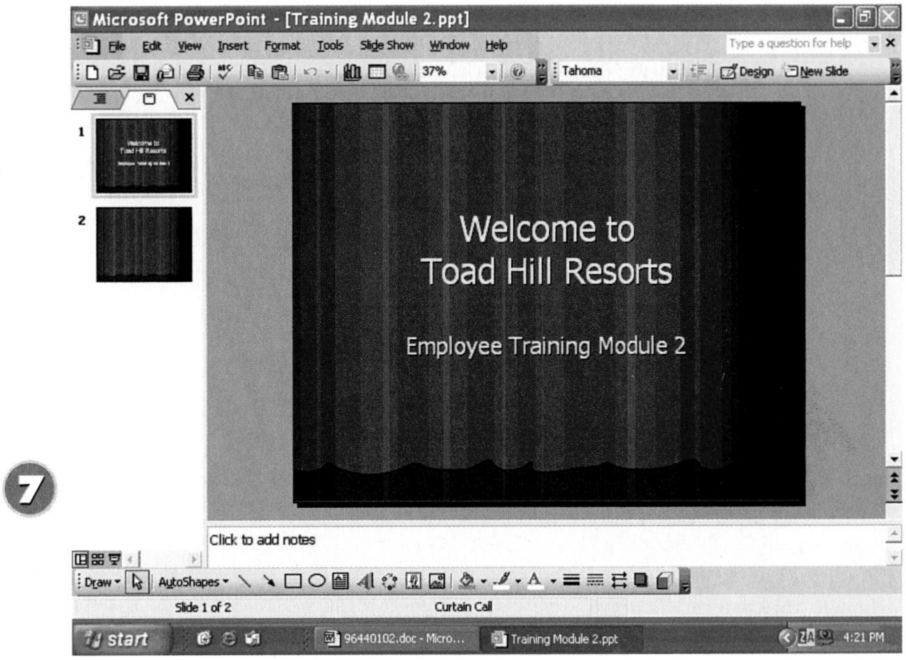

5 To test the password, save and close your presentation, and then open it again. The Password dialog box appears.

6 Type the password and click **OK**.

7 PowerPoint opens the presentation.

Password to Modify

TIP: You can use the **Password to Modify** option in the **Options** dialog box to allow other users to access the file, but not make any changes to the presentation. When they open the file, a Password dialog box appears. They can click a **Read Only** button that lets them view the presentation without making changes.

Removing a Password

TIP: To remove a password you have previously assigned to a presentation, reopen the **Options** dialog box and the **Security** tab, select the current password, and press the **Delete** key. Click **OK** and save the presentation.

PART 3

Building Presentations Using Outline View

While Slide view allows you to focus on the slide's visual appeal, Outline view lets you focus on the structure of your presentation's message. You can use Outline view to concentrate on your presentation's text, such as the main points and subpoints you want to convey. The Outline feature is simply another way in which you can view your presentation in PowerPoint.

In Outline view, you can see your presentation in an outline format. Each slide in your show is numbered in Outline view. Slide text appears in levels, which can be demoted or promoted in the outline. For example, titles are listed prominently as headings in the outline, while subtitles and bulleted text are listed as subheadings. You can use the Outlining toolbar to quickly edit your presentation structure in Outline view.

Outline View

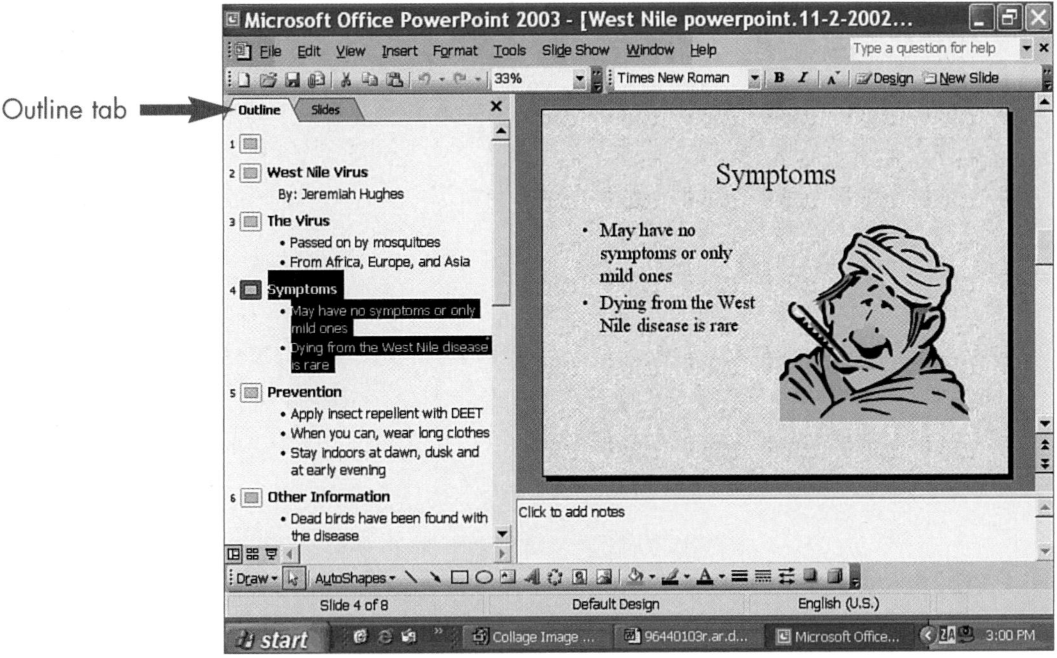

Working with the Outline Pane

Click

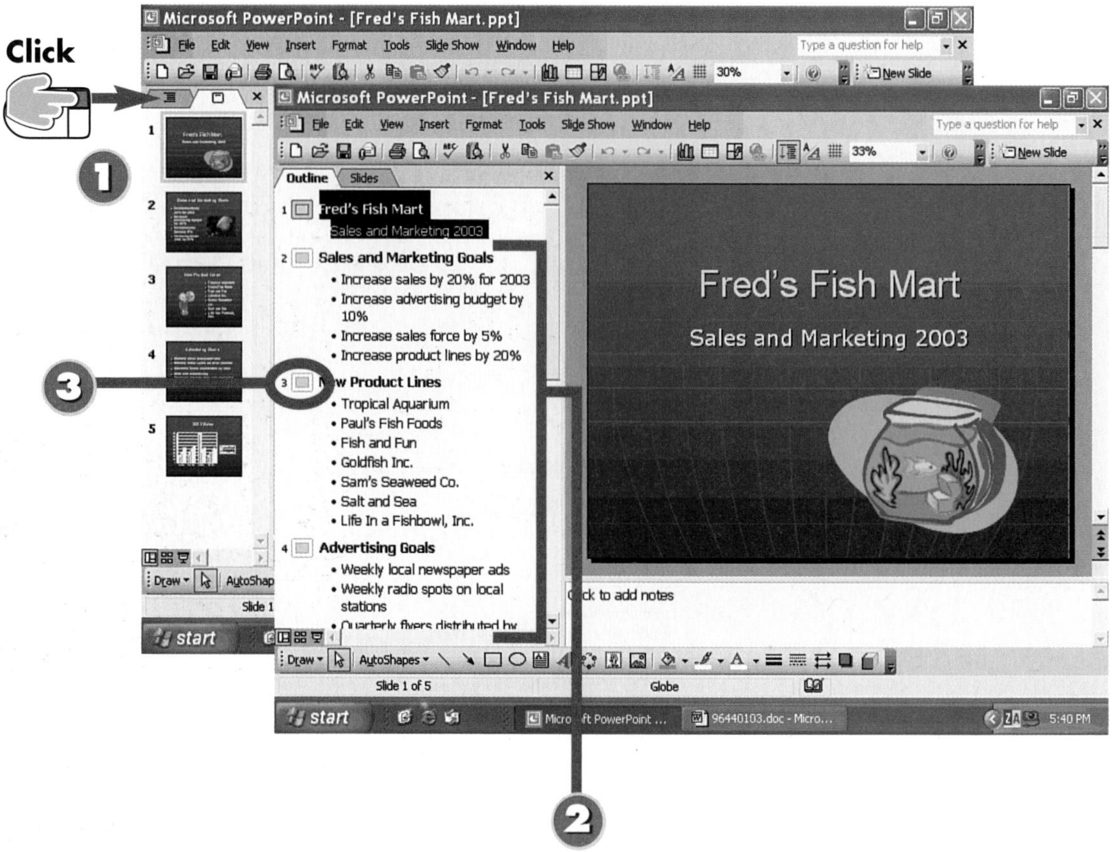

1. Click the **Outline** tab.
2. PowerPoint displays your presentation in outline format.
3. To view a specific slide in the Slide pane, click the slide number.

INTRODUCTION

The Outline view shares space with the Slides tab. When you select the Outline tab, however, the pane expands to show all your presentation headings and subheadings. You can use the Outlining toolbar to quickly access commands for rearranging and editing the outline.

TIP

Bigger Pane

You can resize panes in PowerPoint to view more information, or in the case of Outline view, more of your presentation outline. Move the mouse pointer over a pane border, and then drag the border to resize the pane.

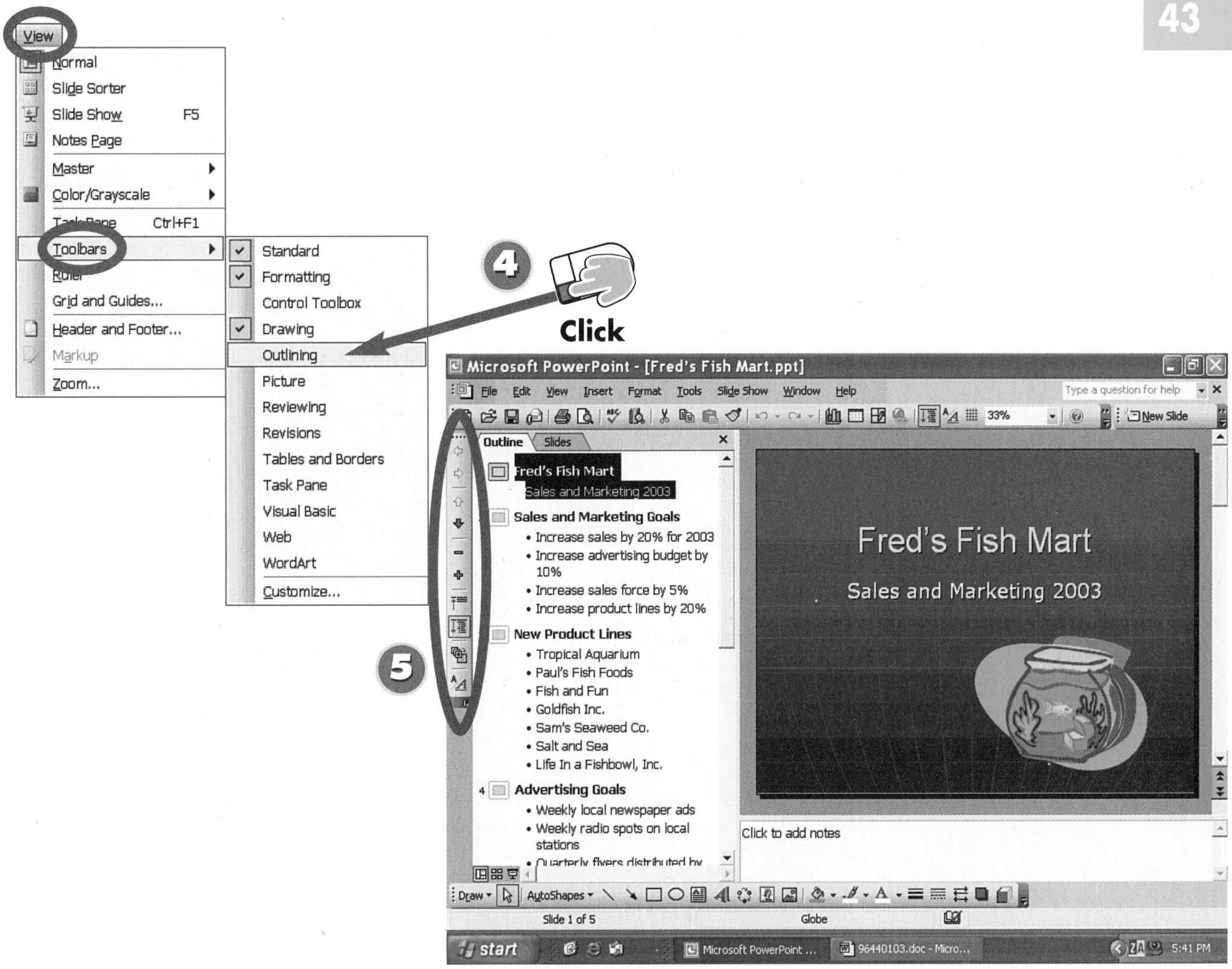

4. To display the Outlining toolbar, open the **View** menu and select **Toolbars**, **Outlining**.

5. The Outlining toolbar appears.

TIP

Closing the Pane
You can close the Outline and Slides tab pane to free up onscreen workspace. However, you will gain more space by closing the Task pane. See Part 1 to learn how. To close the Outline view pane, click the pane's **Close** button. To open it again, open the **View** menu and choose **Normal (Restore Panes)**.

TIP

Hiding Formatting
Another way to focus on your presentation's content is to hide the formatting shown in Outline view. Click the **Show Formatting** button on the Outlining toolbar or on the Formatting toolbar to toggle the formatting on or off.

Adding and Editing Outline Text

Start

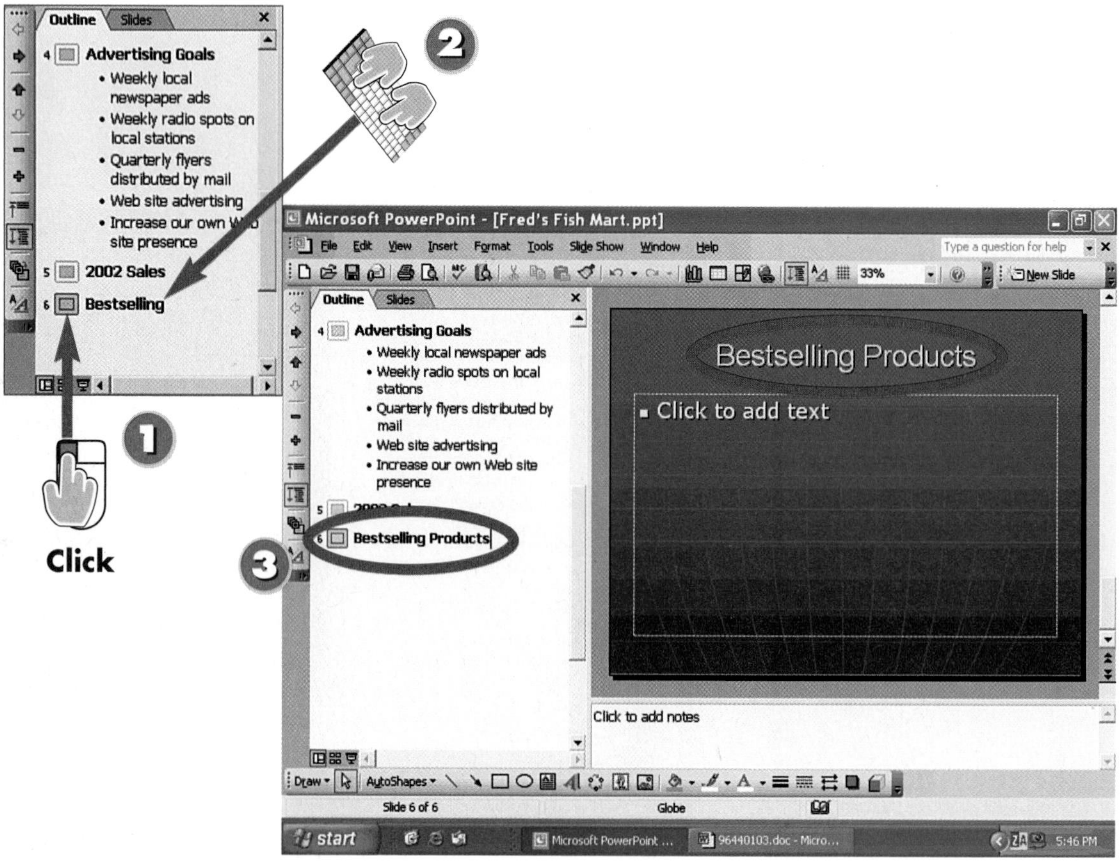

Click

1. In Outline view, click the slide you want to edit.
2. Type the text you want to add.
3. PowerPoint adds the text to the outline as well as to the slide in the Slide pane.

INTRODUCTION

You can easily add new text in Outline view, as well as edit existing slide text. When adding text to a new slide, you can simply type the text in Outline view.

TIP

Adding Subordinate Text
You can click the **Demote** button on the Outlining toolbar to turn any slide text into subordinate text for the previous slide or heading. See the task "Promoting and Demoting Outline Text" to learn more.

TIP

Adding New Slides
To add a new slide to the outline, press **Enter** or click the **New Slide** button on the Formatting toolbar.

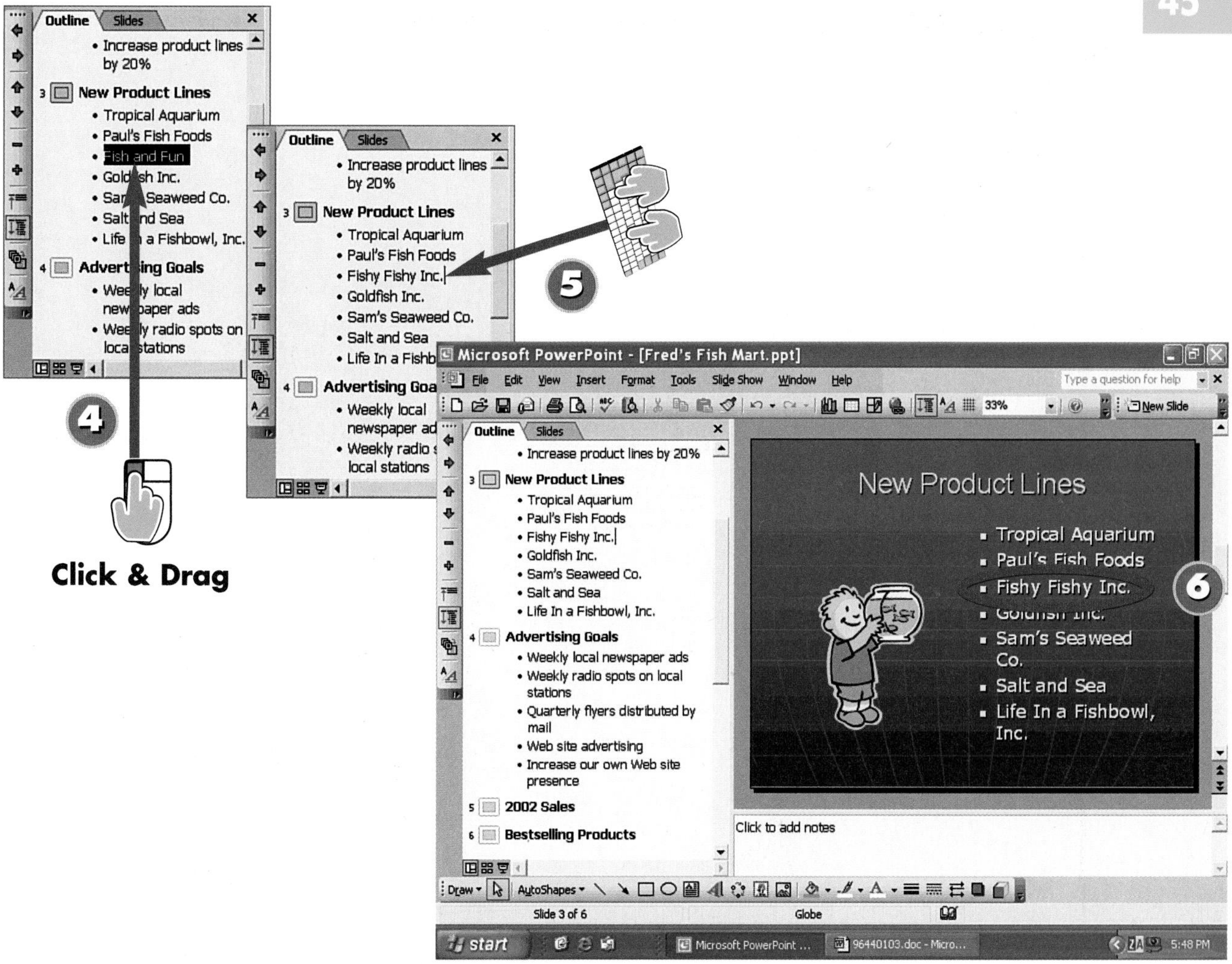

Click & Drag

4. To edit existing slide text, click and drag over the text.

5. Type the replacement text.

6. Your edits immediately appear on the slide in the Slide pane.

End

TIP

Scrolling Along
For longer presentations, you can use the Outline view's scrollbar to move up and down a presentation outline.

TIP

Selection Techniques
To select a single word in Outline view, double-click the word. To select all the text found on a slide, triple-click a word on that slide or click the slide number to the left of the outline text.

Promoting and Demoting Outline Text

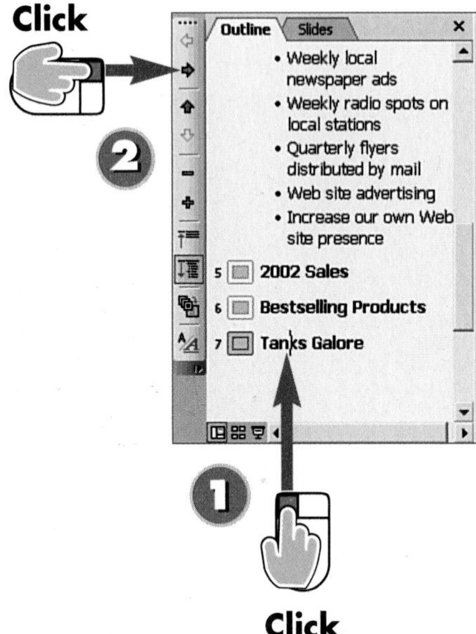

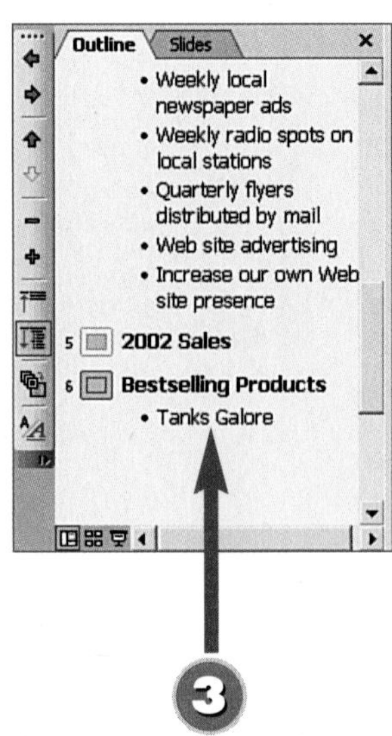

1. To demote a line of text, click anywhere in the text. In this example, a new slide is being demoted to subordinate text.
2. Click the **Demote** button on the Outlining toolbar.
3. PowerPoint demotes the text to subordinate text.

INTRODUCTION

You can quickly make changes to the structure of your outline by demoting and promoting text. Using the Demote and Promote buttons on the Outlining toolbar, you can quickly create headings, subheadings, and subordinate text.

TIP

Handling New Paragraphs
When you press **Enter** in Outline view, PowerPoint starts a new slide for you. To turn the new paragraph into subordinate text, click the **Demote** button. PowerPoint immediately deletes the new slide and adds the text to the previous slide.

TIP

Where's My Toolbar?
Open the **View** menu and select **Toolbars**, **Outlining** to display the Outlining toolbar. Follow the same procedure to turn the toolbar off again.

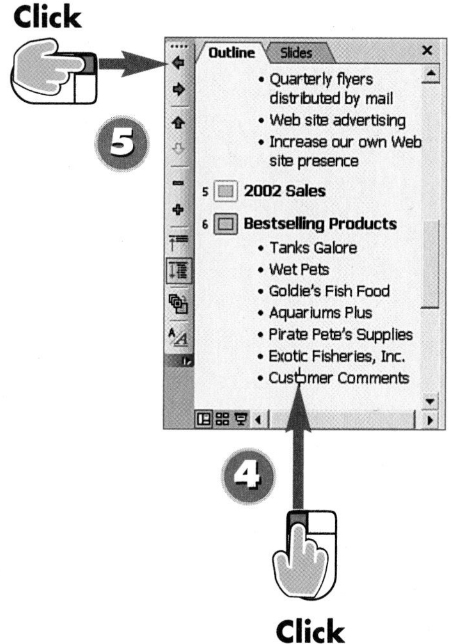

4. To promote a line of text, click anywhere in the text.
5. Click the **Promote** button.
6. PowerPoint promotes the text.

TIP

Using the Indent Buttons
You can also use the **Increase Indent** and **Decrease Indent** buttons on the Formatting toolbar to change the level of text in Outline view.

TIP

Keyboard Shortcuts
You can press **Alt+Shift+Left Arrow** on the keyboard to promote a line of text in your presentation outline. To demote a paragraph, press **Alt+Shift+Right Arrow**.

Moving Outline Text

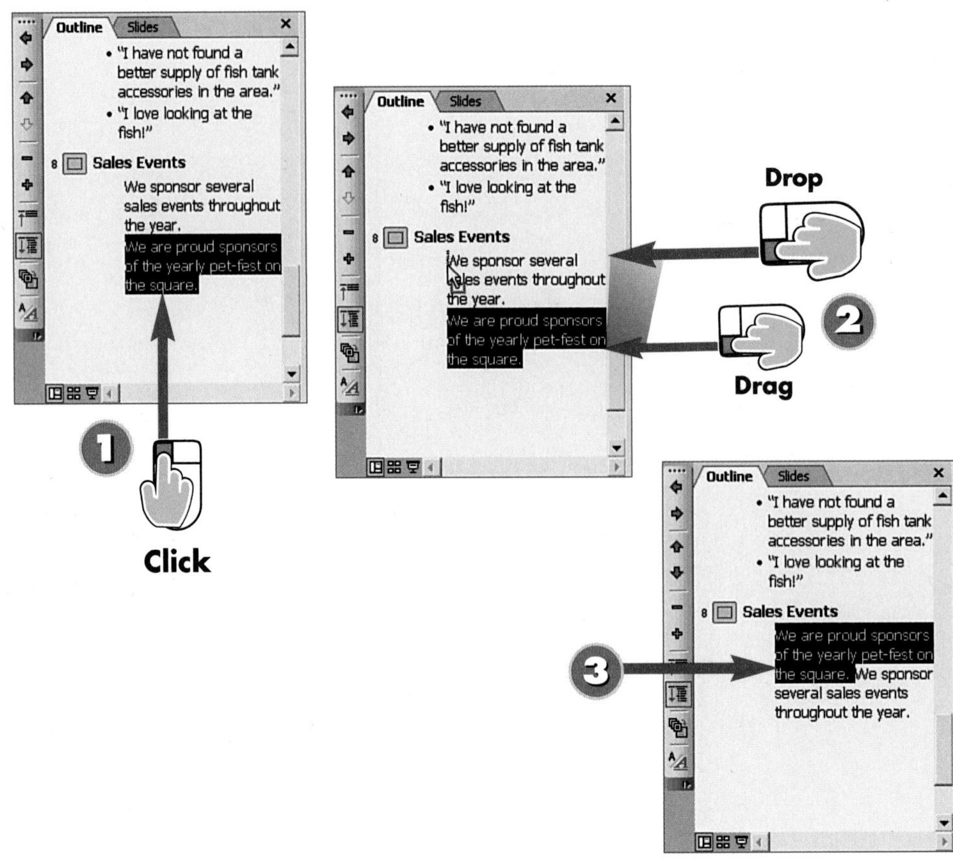

1. To move portions of text, first select the text you want to move.
2. Click and drag the text, dropping it where you want it to appear in the outline.
3. PowerPoint moves the text.

INTRODUCTION

You can rearrange slide text in Outline view by dragging the text around the Outline pane. By doing so, you can rearrange bullet points, headings, single words, and more.

TIP

Undoing a Move
If you make a mistake while moving your slide text around the outline, you can undo your changes. Click the **Undo** button on the Standard toolbar, or press **Ctrl+Z** to undo your last edit.

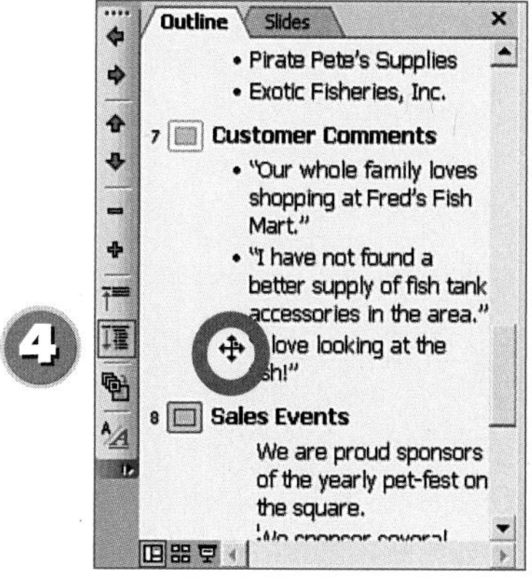

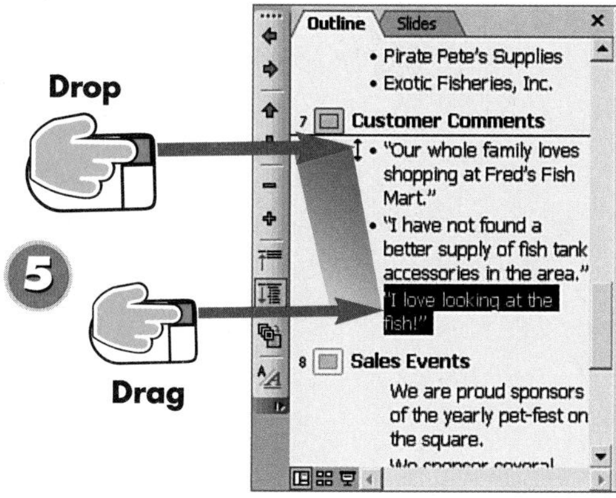

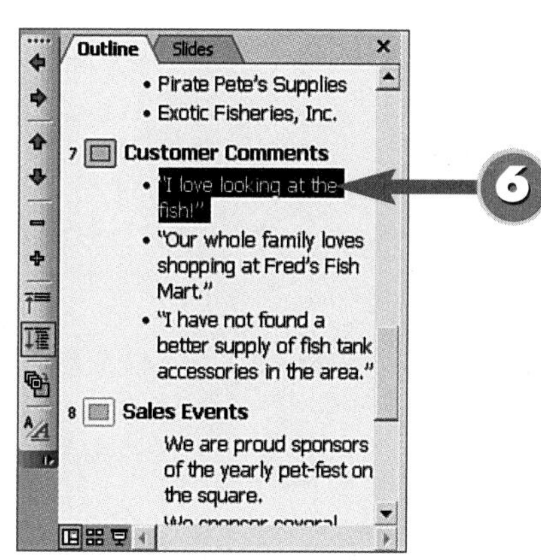

4. To move a bullet point, point to the bullet you want to move. The mouse pointer changes to a four-cornered arrow icon.
5. Click and drag the bullet to a new location in the outline, dropping it where you want it to appear.
6. PowerPoint moves the text.

TIP

Using the Up and Down Buttons

Another way to move a line of text in the outline is to click the **Move Up** or **Move Down** buttons on the Outlining toolbar. To learn how to display the Outlining toolbar, see the task "Working with the Outline Pane" earlier in this part.

Expanding and Collapsing the Outline

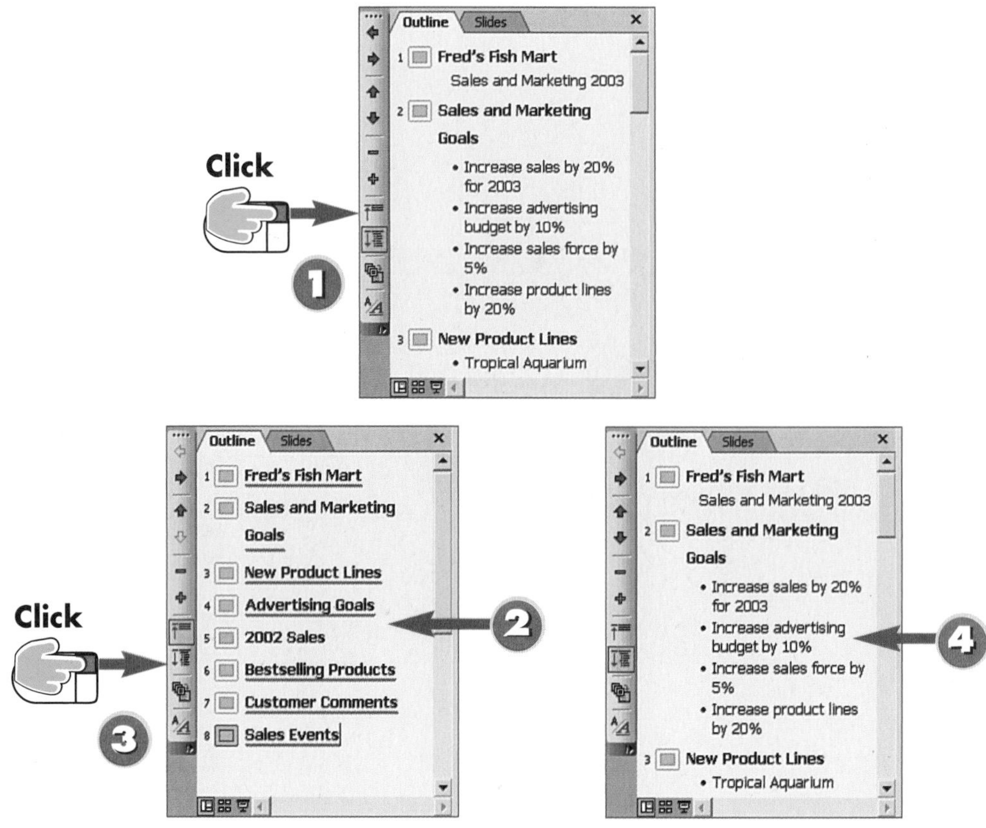

1. To collapse the outline, click the **Collapse All** button in the Outlining toolbar.
2. PowerPoint collapses the outline.
3. To expand the outline again, click the **Expand All** button.
4. The full outline is again displayed.

INTRODUCTION

To help you concentrate on slide titles without viewing the subordinate text associated with each slide, you can collapse the outline. This allows you to view titles only. You can expand the outline again to view body text.

TIP

Collapsing a Single Slide
To collapse just a single slide in the outline, select the slide and click the **Collapse** button on the Outlining toolbar. To expand it again, click the **Expand** button.

Creating a Summary Slide

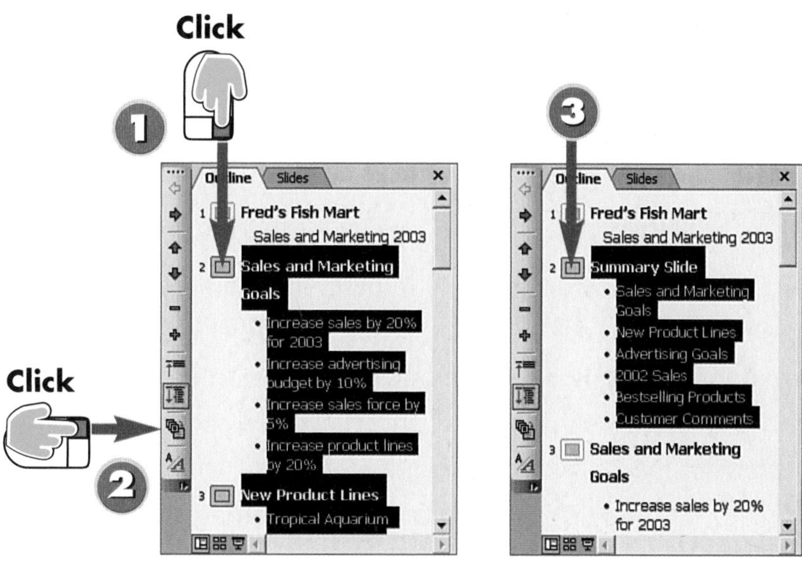

1. Select the slides you want to include on the summary slide. You can click to select individual slides in the outline, or press **Ctrl+A** to select all the slides.
2. Click the **Summary Slide** button on the Outlining toolbar.
3. PowerPoint creates a summary slide and places it before the first selected slide. You can type a new title for the summary slide or use the default title.

INTRODUCTION

A *summary slide* shows the titles of slides included in your presentation. You can use a summary slide at the beginning of your slide show to let your audience know what you plan to talk about or present.

PART 4

Working with PowerPoint Text

The most common type of slide object you work with in PowerPoint is the text object. Text objects, which are simply boxes for holding text, contain the information you want to convey to your audience. Slide text includes titles, subtitles, and body text. Body text typically takes the form of bulleted lists, but can also be paragraphs of text.

You can work with PowerPoint text in much the same way you work with text in other programs, such as Microsoft Word. You select text to perform edits on it, such as changing the text font and size, or making the text bold. You can also change the alignment of slide text, insert special characters and symbols, and even customize the bullets used in a bulleted list. This section of the book introduces you to a variety of ways to modify the appearance of text in your presentation.

PowerPoint Text Objects

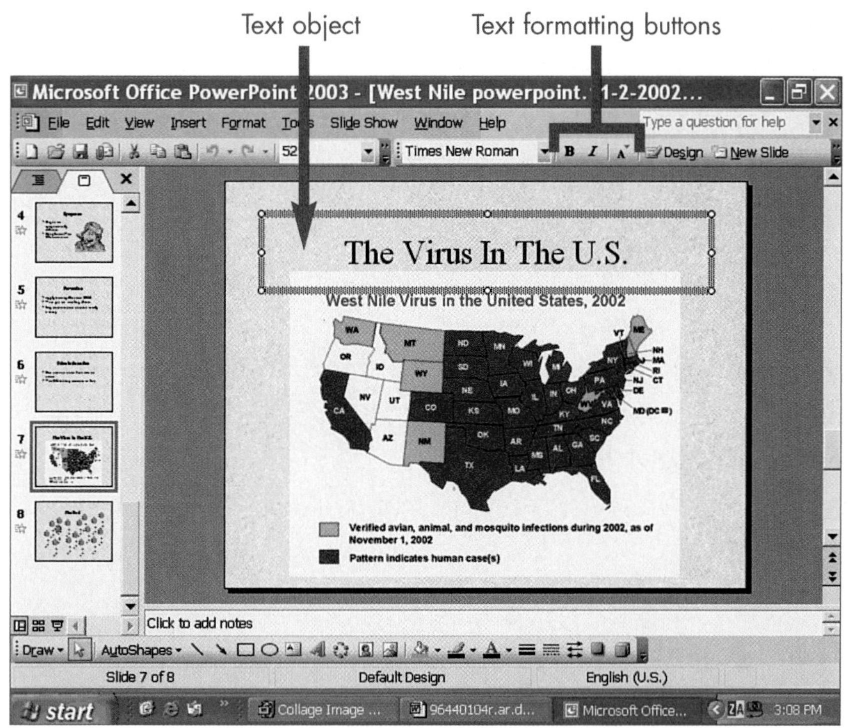

Selecting Text

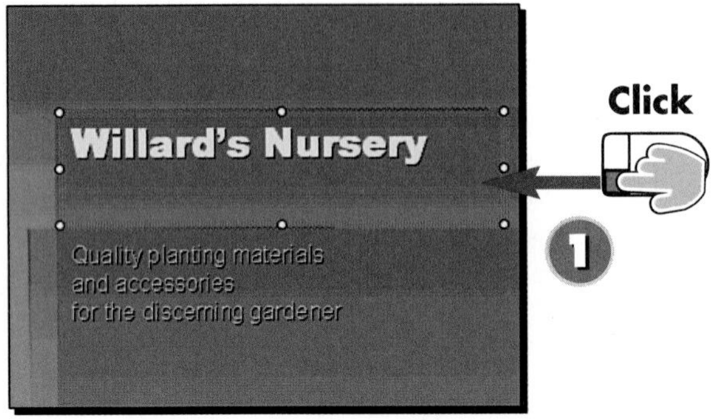

1. Click the text block you want to edit.
2. Click and drag across the text you want to select.
3. PowerPoint immediately highlights the selected text onscreen.

INTRODUCTION

To make changes to your text, you must first select the text to which you want to apply modifications. Selecting text in PowerPoint 2003 works the same as selecting text in other programs—you highlight the text onscreen before applying any commands or changes.

TIP

Other Selection Methods
To quickly select an entire word, double-click on the word. To select an entire sentence, triple-click on a word in the sentence.

TIP

Deselecting Text
If you change your mind about selecting text, click anywhere outside the selected text to deselect it.

Deleting Text

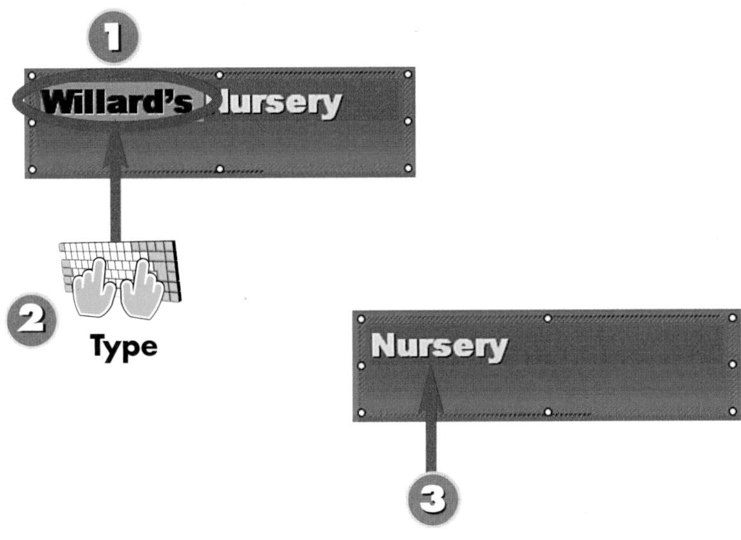

1. Select the text you want to delete.
2. Press the **Delete** key on your keyboard.
3. PowerPoint removes the text.

INTRODUCTION

You can delete text you no longer want to include on a slide, or delete text and replace it with new text.

TIP

Deleting an Entire Text Box

To delete an entire text box, first click on the border of the text box to select it, then press the **Delete** key. PowerPoint removes the entire text block from the slide. See the task "Adding New Text Boxes" later in this part to learn how to add new text blocks to your slides.

Moving and Copying Slide Text

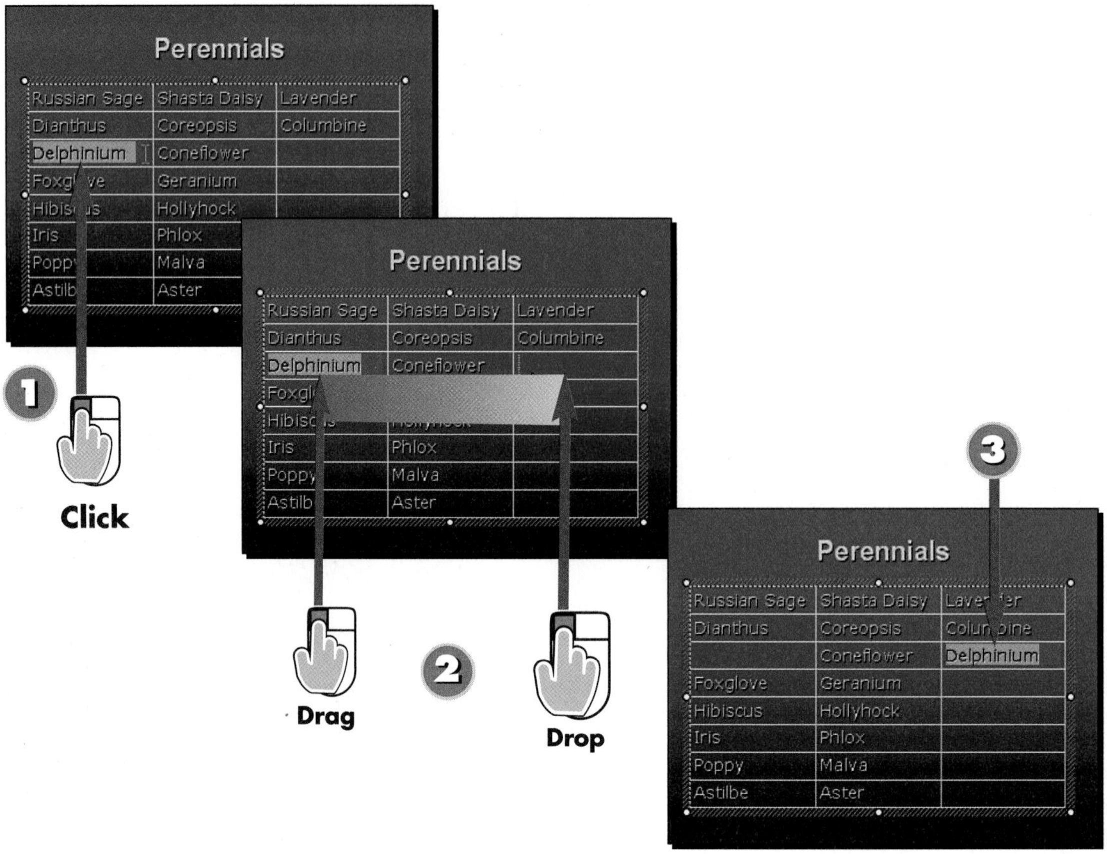

1. Select the text you want to move or copy.
2. To move the text, click the text and drag it to a new location. To copy the text, press the **Ctrl** key while clicking and dragging.
3. Drop the text where you want it to go. PowerPoint moves or copies the text.

INTRODUCTION

You can use PowerPoint's Cut, Copy, and Paste commands to move and copy slide text. You can also drag and drop text to quickly move it around on a slide.

TIP

Selecting Text
See the task "Selecting Text" earlier in this part to learn how to select slide text.

TIP

Using the Clipboard Pane
If you copy or cut two or more text items, PowerPoint opens the Clipboard pane in the Task pane area. To paste an item from the Clipboard, click where you want it to go, and then click the item in the Clipboard pane.

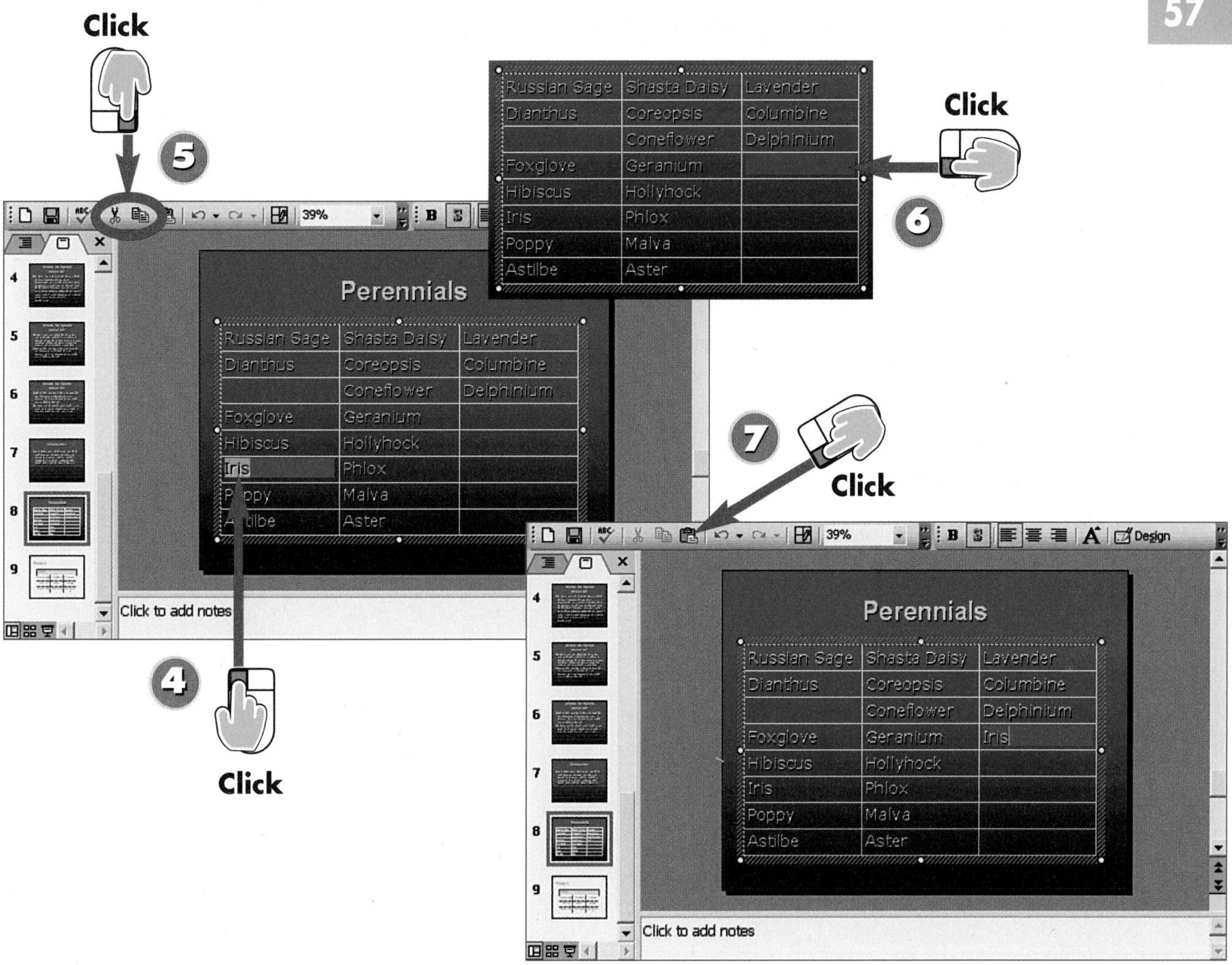

4. To move or copy the text using the Cut, Copy, and Paste commands, first select the text you want to move or copy.

5. Click the **Cut** button to move the text or click the **Copy** button to copy the text.

6. Click the spot on the slide where you want to place the text.

7. Click the **Paste** button. PowerPoint moves or copies the text.

TIP

Using the Edit Menu
You can also use the **Edit** menu to cut, copy, and paste text. Select the text, and then select **Edit**, **Cut** or **Edit**, **Copy**. Then, click where you want to insert the text, and select **Edit**, **Paste**.

TIP

Using Keyboard Shortcuts
Press **Ctrl+X** on the keyboard to cut text, or press **Ctrl+C** to copy text. Click where you want to insert the text, and press **Ctrl+V** to paste the text.

Inserting Symbols

Click
Click
Click

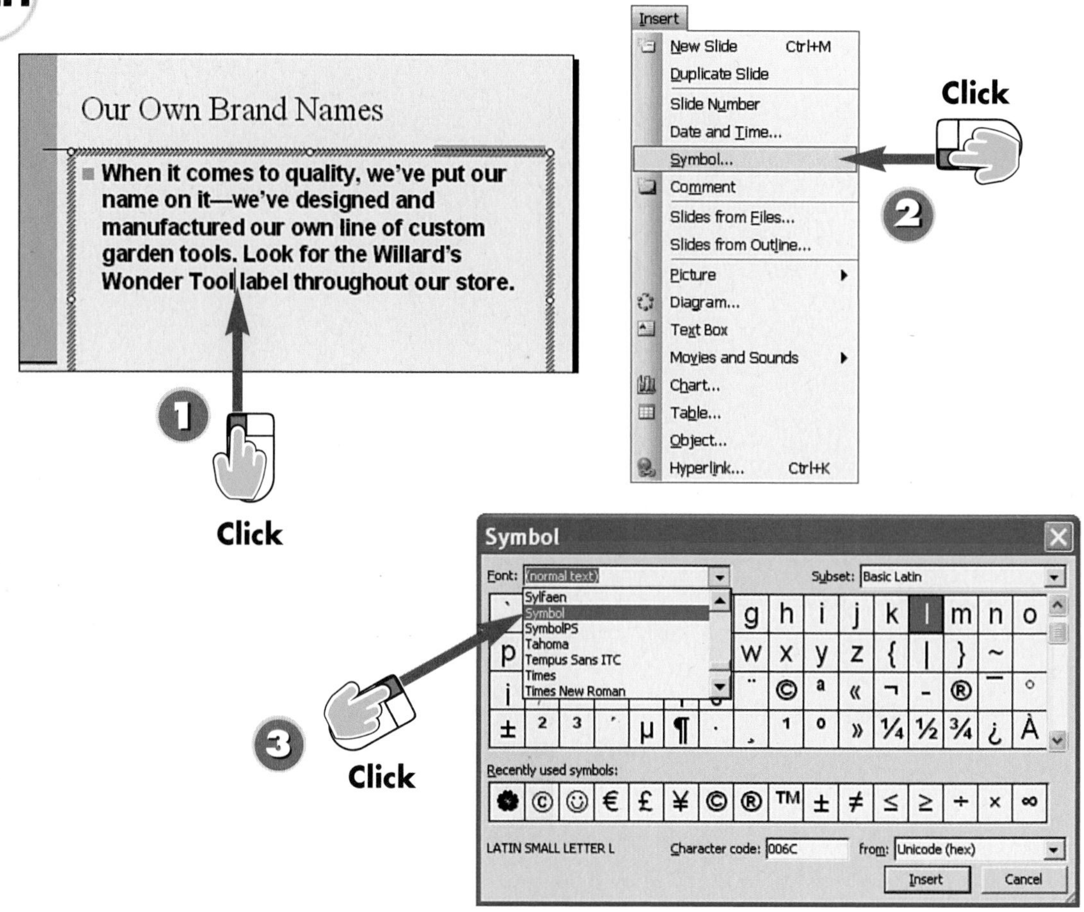

1. Click in the slide text where you want to insert a symbol.

2. Open the **Insert** menu and choose **Symbol**.

3. The Symbol dialog box opens. Click the **Font** drop-down arrow and click the font you want to display.

INTRODUCTION

If your slide text requires special characters or symbols not found on the keyboard, you can use the Symbol dialog box to add them to your slides. Simply choose a particular font library, such as Wingdings or Symbol, peruse the available symbols, and then insert the one you want to use.

TIP

Which Fonts Have Which Symbols?
Use the Symbols font if you are looking for mathematical equation symbols. Use the Wingdings fonts if you are looking for a variety of icons, bullet, and arrow symbols.

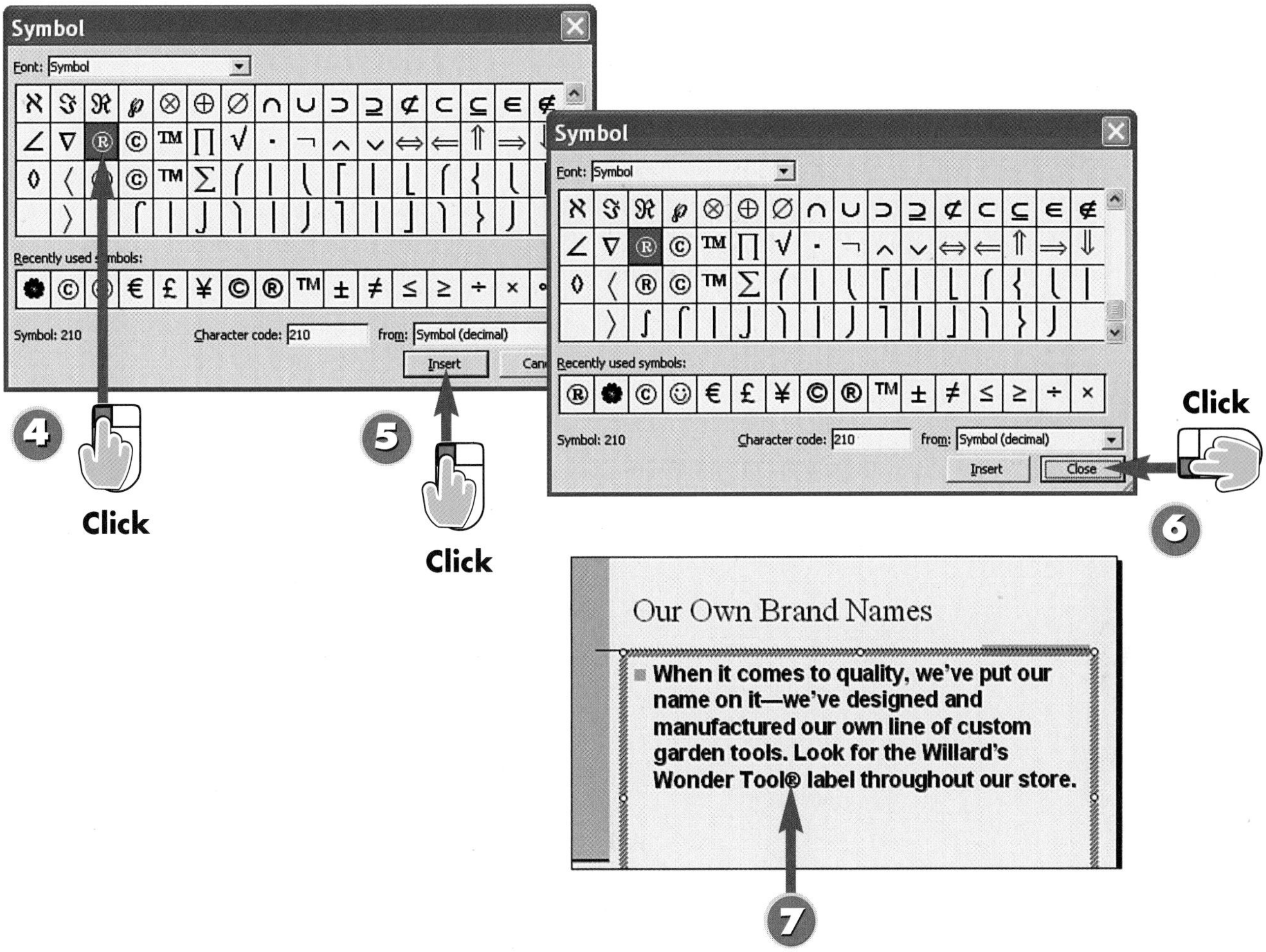

4 Click the symbol you want to use.

5 Click **Insert**. PowerPoint adds the symbol to your slide.

6 Click **Close** to exit the dialog box.

7 The symbol appears in the text.

TIP

Removing Unwanted Symbols
By default, PowerPoint attempts to insert certain common symbols based on what you type. For example, if you type **(c)**, PowerPoint inserts a copyright symbol automatically. If you do not want the symbol, open the **Edit** menu and choose **Undo** immediately after PowerPoint converts the text; the characters you typed are immediately restored to their original status.

TIP

Reusing Symbols
The Symbol dialog box keeps track of the symbols most recently used. If you want to reuse a symbol, open the Symbol dialog box and click the symbol in the **Recently Used Symbols** list at the bottom of the dialog box.

Adding New Text Boxes

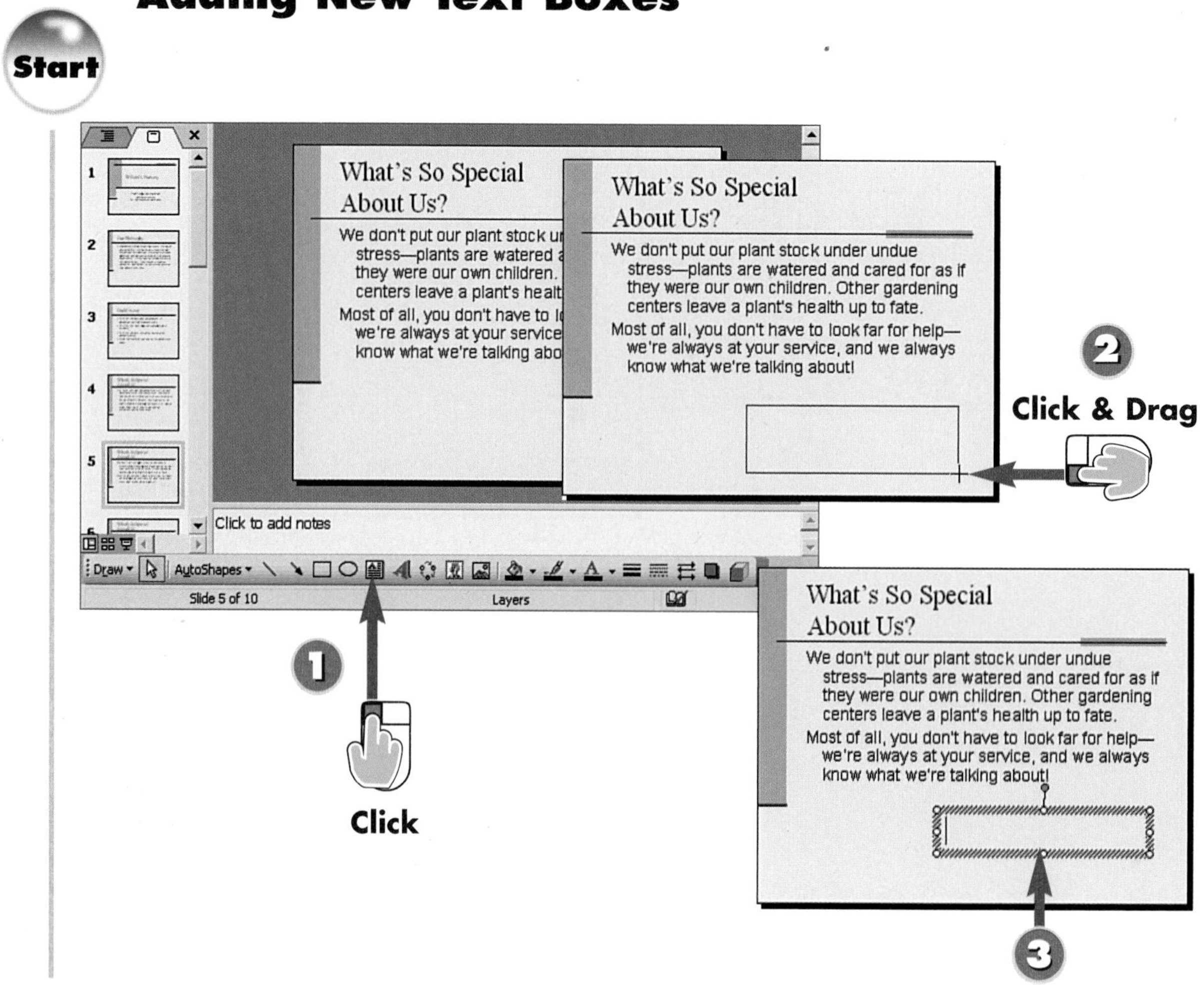

1. Click the **Text Box** button on the Drawing toolbar.
2. Click and drag the mouse on the slide where you want the text box to appear until the text box is the size you want.
3. Release the mouse button; the text box is created.

INTRODUCTION

If your slide layout does not supply the number of text boxes you need to present your slide text, you can add text objects. A text object is simply a box that contains text. Like other slide objects, a text object can be moved and resized.

TIP

Selecting a Text Box

To select an existing text box on a slide, click any border around the box. When selected, the box displays handles around the corners of the box. If you move the mouse over a handle of a selected box, a double-sided arrow appears, indicating you can drag the handle to resize the box. If you move the mouse over a border, a four-sided arrow appears, indicating you can move the box to reposition it on the slide.

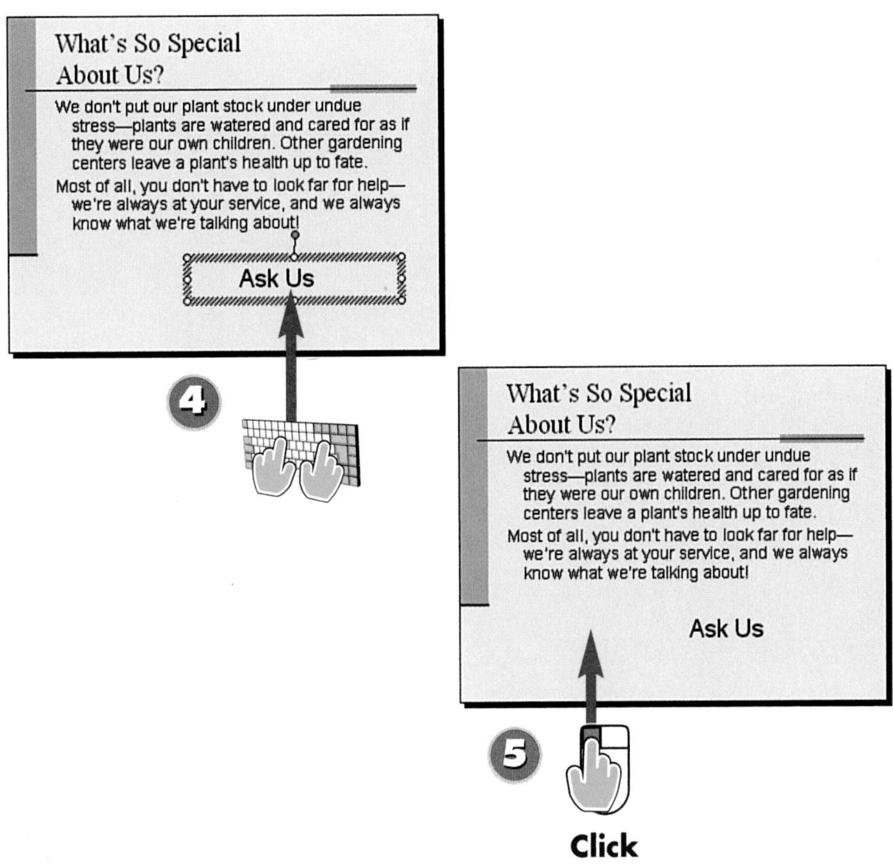

4. Type the text you want to include in the text box.

5. Click anywhere outside the text box to deselect the text object.

TIP

Formatting Text
You can apply formatting to a text box before or after you draw the box. Simply select from the tools available on the Formatting toolbar. See the remaining tasks in this section to learn more about formatting techniques.

TIP

Moving a Text Box
You can move a text box to reposition it in the slide layout. First select the text box, then move the mouse pointer over any border or edge and drag the box to a new location on the slide.

TIP

Deleting Text Boxes
You can delete text boxes you do not need in your slide layout, including text objects that came with the layout. Simply click any text box border to select the box, and then press the **Delete** key. PowerPoint immediately removes the box.

Creating a Bulleted or Numbered List

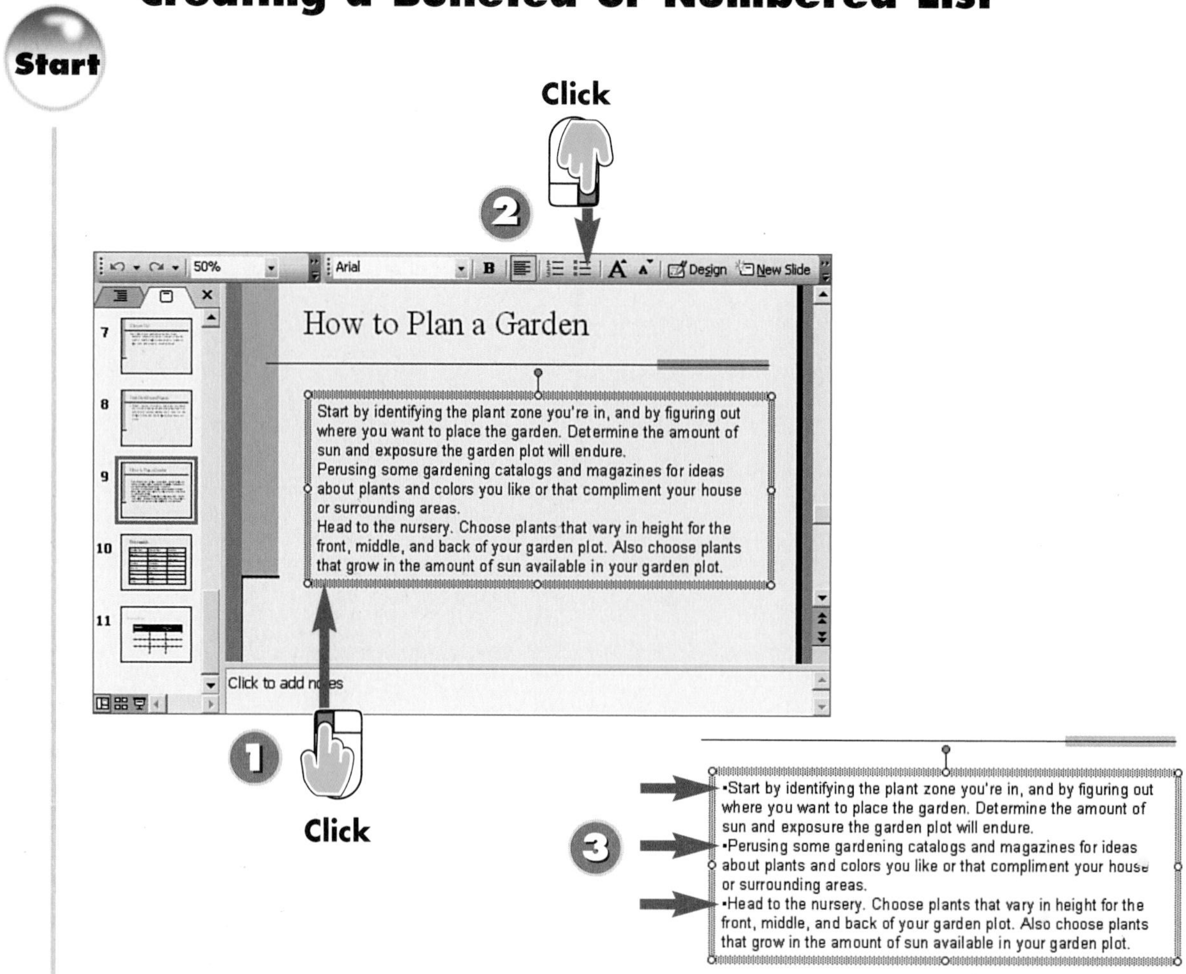

Start

Click

Click

1. To add bullets, click the text box you want to change.
2. Click the **Bullets** button on the Formatting toolbar.
3. PowerPoint inserts bullets in front of each line of text.

INTRODUCTION

Although many of PowerPoint's preformatted layouts include bulleted lists, you might need to create a new list for a new text box you add, or turn an existing bulleted list into a numbered list.

TIP

Changing the Bullets

You can customize the bullets and numbers used in bulleted lists. See the next task, "Customizing Bullets," to learn more.

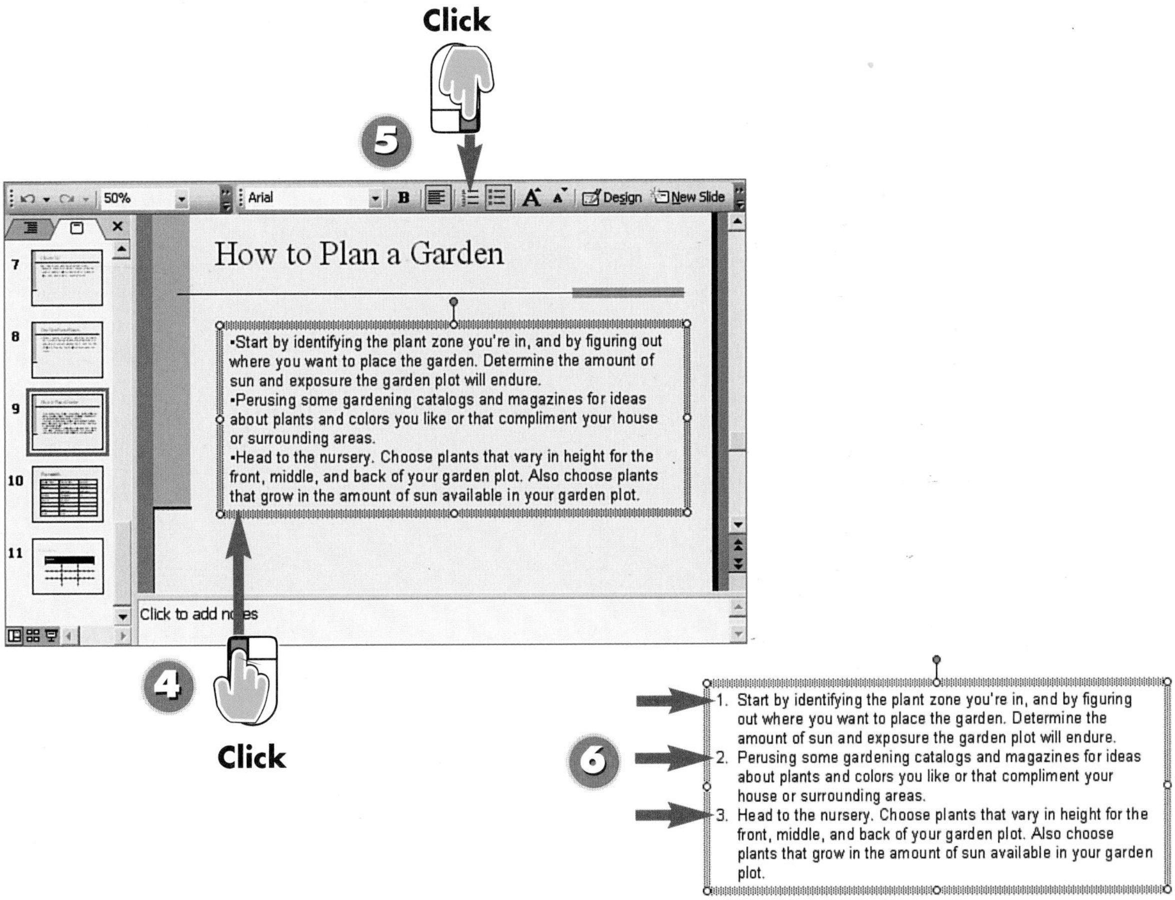

4. To add numbers, click the text box you want to change.

5. Click the **Numbers** button on the Formatting toolbar.

6. PowerPoint inserts numbers in front of each line of text.

Removing Bullets

TIP

To turn a bulleted or numbered list back into regular text, first select the text box, and then click on the **Bullets** or **Numbers** button on the Formatting toolbar.

Removing a Single Bullet

TIP

To remove a single bullet, click in the line of text containing the bullet you want to remove, and then click the **Bullets** button on the Formatting toolbar. PowerPoint turns off the bullets feature for that particular line of text.

Customizing Bullets

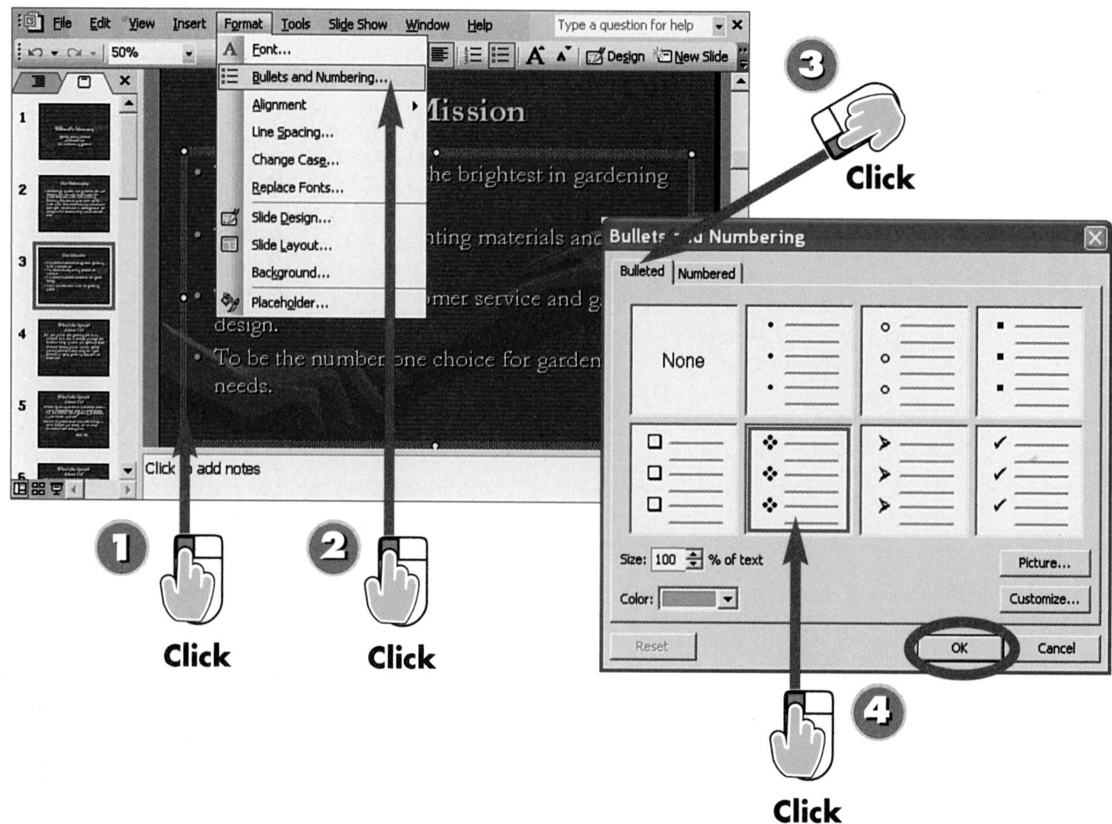

1. Click the text box you want to change.
2. Open the **Format** menu and choose **Bullets and Numbering**.
3. PowerPoint opens the Bullets and Numbering dialog box. Click the **Bulleted** tab.
4. Click the bullet style you want to apply and click **OK** to apply it to the text box.

INTRODUCTION

PowerPoint inserts a default bullet in front of bulleted lists, but you can customize the bullet and change its shape or picture. For example, you might use your company logo as a bullet point, or use arrows or check marks instead.

TIP

Changing the Bullet Color

You can use the **Color** drop-down list in the Bullets and Numbering dialog box to change the color of your bullets. Click the drop-down arrow, and then click the color you want to apply. Be sure to choose a color that complements your slide design.

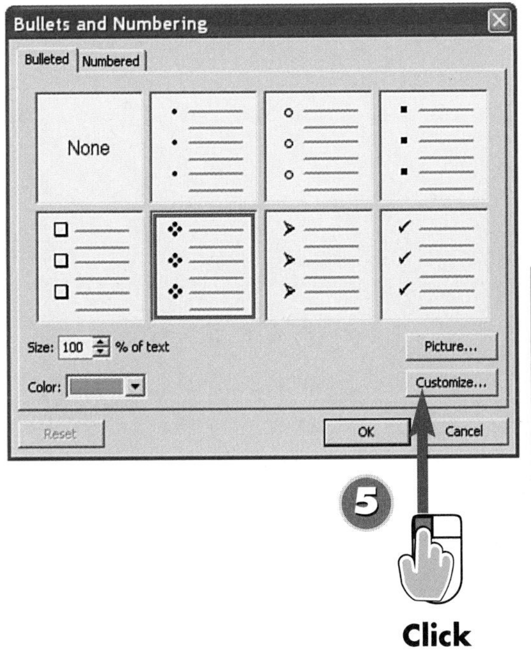

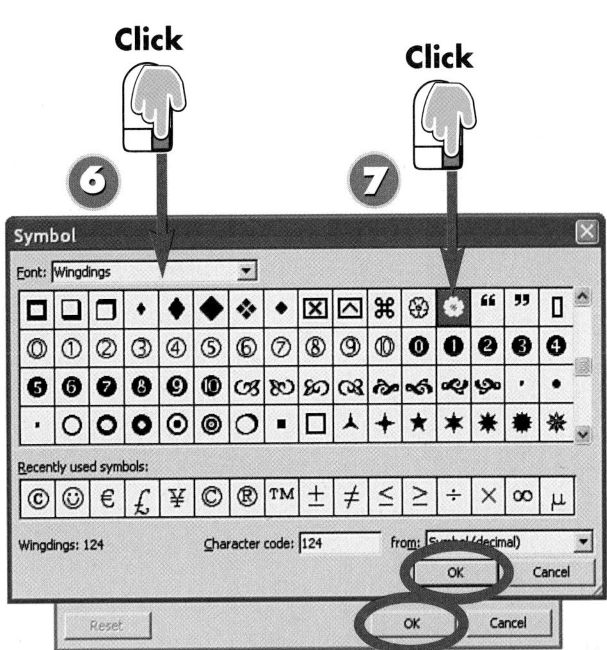

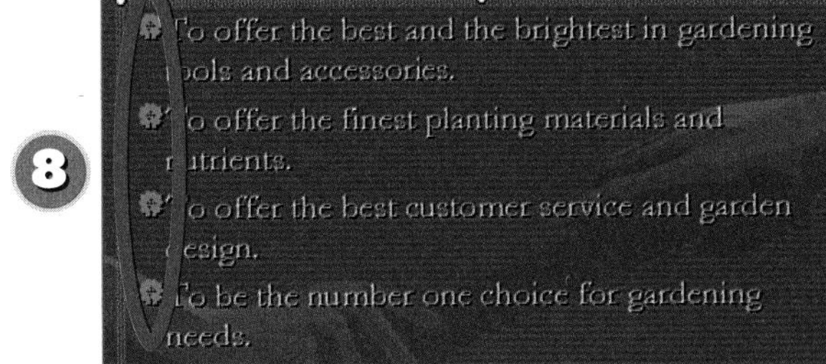

5 To further customize the bullet style, click the **Customize** button.

6 The Symbol dialog box opens. Select a font from the **Font** drop-down list.

7 Click a bullet type and click **OK** to close the Symbol dialog box, and then click **OK** again to close the Bullets and Numbering dialog box.

8 PowerPoint applies the customized bullet to the list.

TIP

Customizing Numbers

You can also customize the style of numbers displayed in a numbered list. Click the **Numbered** tab and choose a number style to apply. Click **OK**, and PowerPoint applies the style.

TIP

Using Picture Bullets

You can use the Picture button in the Bullets and Numbering dialog box to add picture bullets. Click **Picture** to open the Picture Bullet dialog box. Click the picture bullet you want to use, and click **OK** to return to the Bullets and Numbering dialog box. To use an imported picture, click the **Import** button, locate and select the image you want to use, and click **Add** to return to the Picture Bullet dialog box. Select the image and click **OK**.

Changing Text Alignment

Start

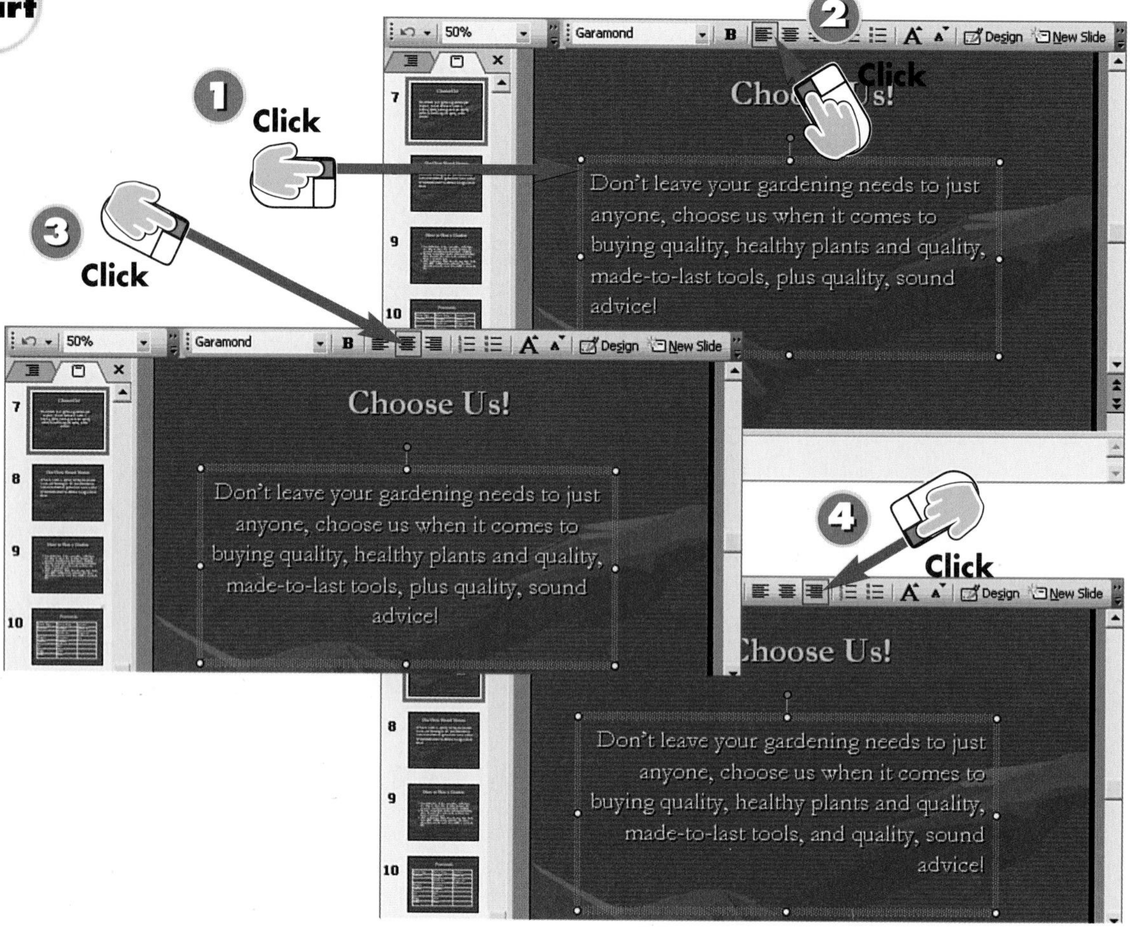

1. Click the text box whose alignment you want to change.
2. Click the **Align Left** button in the Formatting toolbar to align text to the left.
3. Click the **Center** button to center text in the text box.
4. Click the **Align Right** button to align text to the right.

INTRODUCTION

You can control the alignment of text within a text box. By default, text aligns to the left of any new text boxes you add. Other text objects, like titles, automatically center the text. You can use the alignment buttons on the toolbar to quickly change text alignment in a slide.

TIP

Using the Format Menu
You can also find the alignment commands listed on the Format menu. Open the **Format** menu, choose **Alignment**, and then click the alignment you want to apply.

Indenting Text

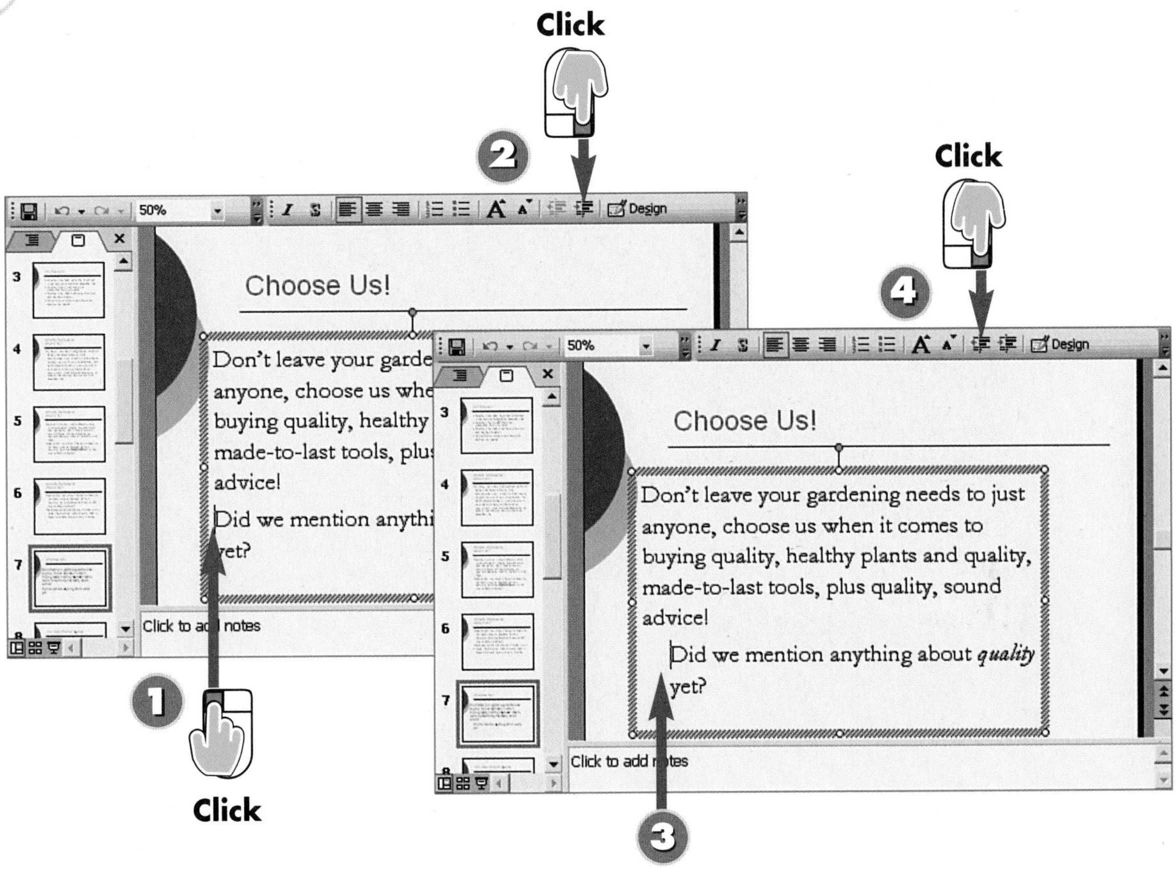

1. Click in front of the line of text to be indented.

2. Click the **Increase Indent** button in the Formatting toolbar to indent the text.

3. PowerPoint indents the text.

4. Click the **Decrease Indent** button to decrease the indent.

INTRODUCTION

You can use the Increase Indent and Decrease Indent buttons to quickly indent paragraph text in a slide.

TIP

Using the Ruler
If you prefer using a ruler to control indents, you can display the ruler at the top of the slide and use the ruler's indent markers to change indents. Open the **View** menu and choose **Ruler** to open the ruler. Click and drag the indent markers to adjust indents. To turn the ruler off, select **View**, **Ruler** again.

Changing Line Spacing

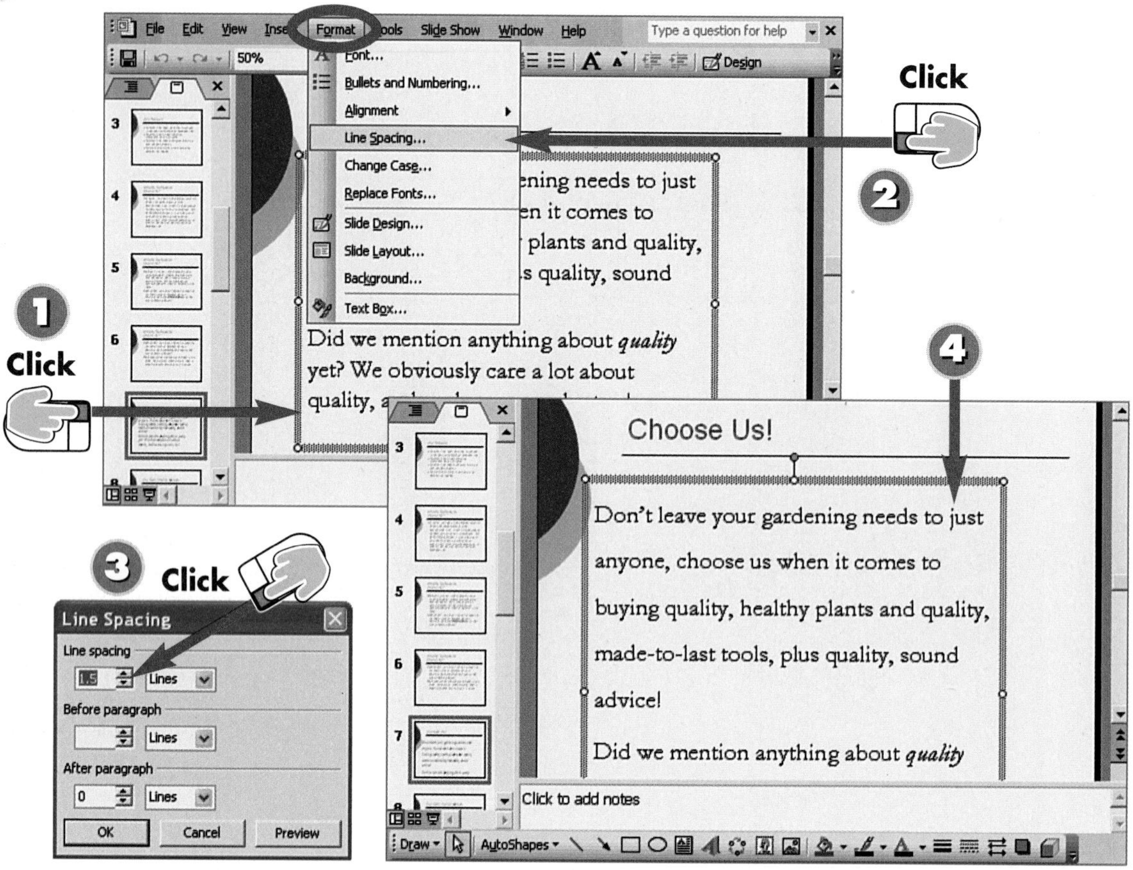

1. Select the text or text box you want to edit.

2. Open the **Format** menu and choose **Line Spacing**.

3. The Line Spacing dialog box opens. Click the **up** or **down arrow** to change the amount of spacing between lines of text, and then click **OK**.

4. PowerPoint adjusts the line spacing.

INTRODUCTION

Line spacing refers to the amount of space between lines of text in a paragraph. You can control line spacing in PowerPoint using the Line Spacing dialog box.

TIP

Other Line-Spacing Options

The Line Spacing dialog box also offers controls for setting the amount of spacing before and after paragraphs. Generally, however, if you use too many paragraphs on a slide, it's more difficult for the audience to read the material.

Changing the Text Style

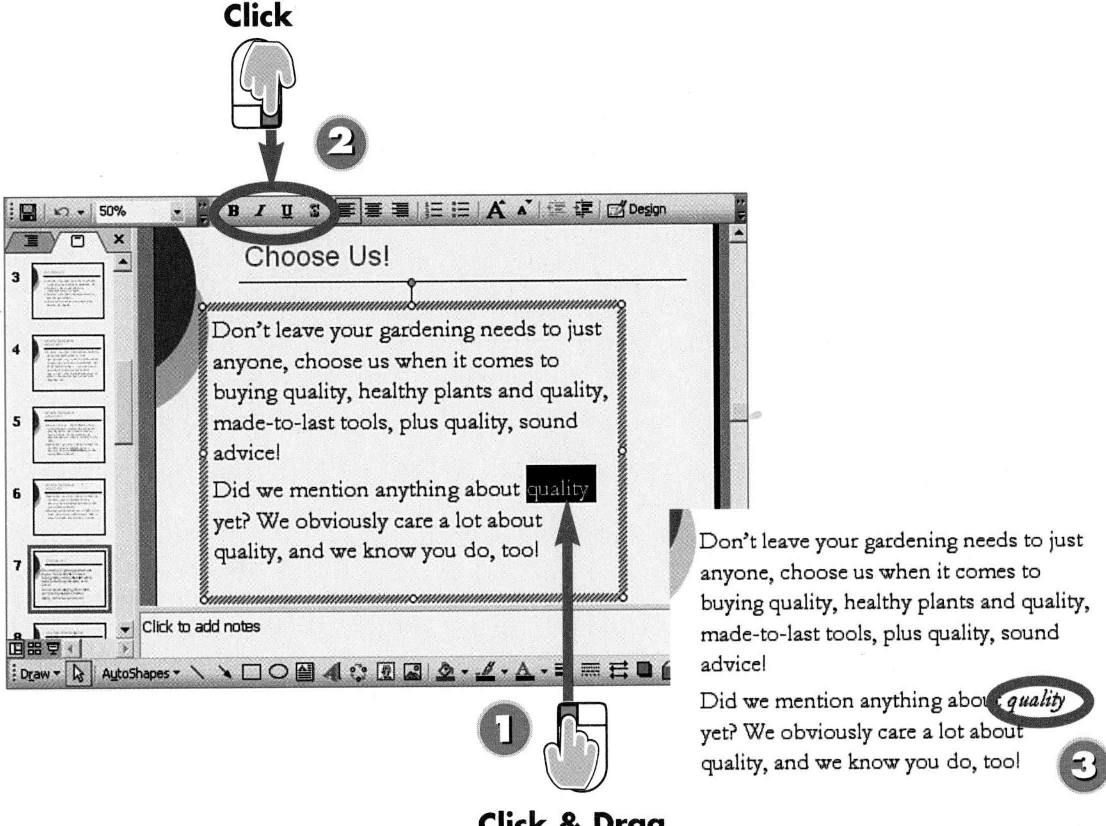

1. Select the text you want to format.
2. Click the appropriate style button (**Bold** to make text bold, **Italic** to italicize the text, **Underline** to add underlining to the text, or **Shadow** to add a shadow to the text).
3. PowerPoint applies the selected style to the text. In this example, the text is italicized.

INTRODUCTION

A quick way to change the appearance of text on a slide is to make the text bold, italic, or underlined, or to add a shadow to the text characters. You can find shortcut buttons for each embellishment on the Formatting toolbar. The buttons toggle the style effect on or off.

TIP

Copying Formatting

You can easily copy any formatting you assign to slide text to another text object in the slide or on another slide. First select the text that uses the formatting you want to copy, and then click the **Format Painter** button on the Standard toolbar. Drag the mouse over the text you want to copy the formatting to; PowerPoint immediately applies the same formatting to the new text.

Changing the Font and Size

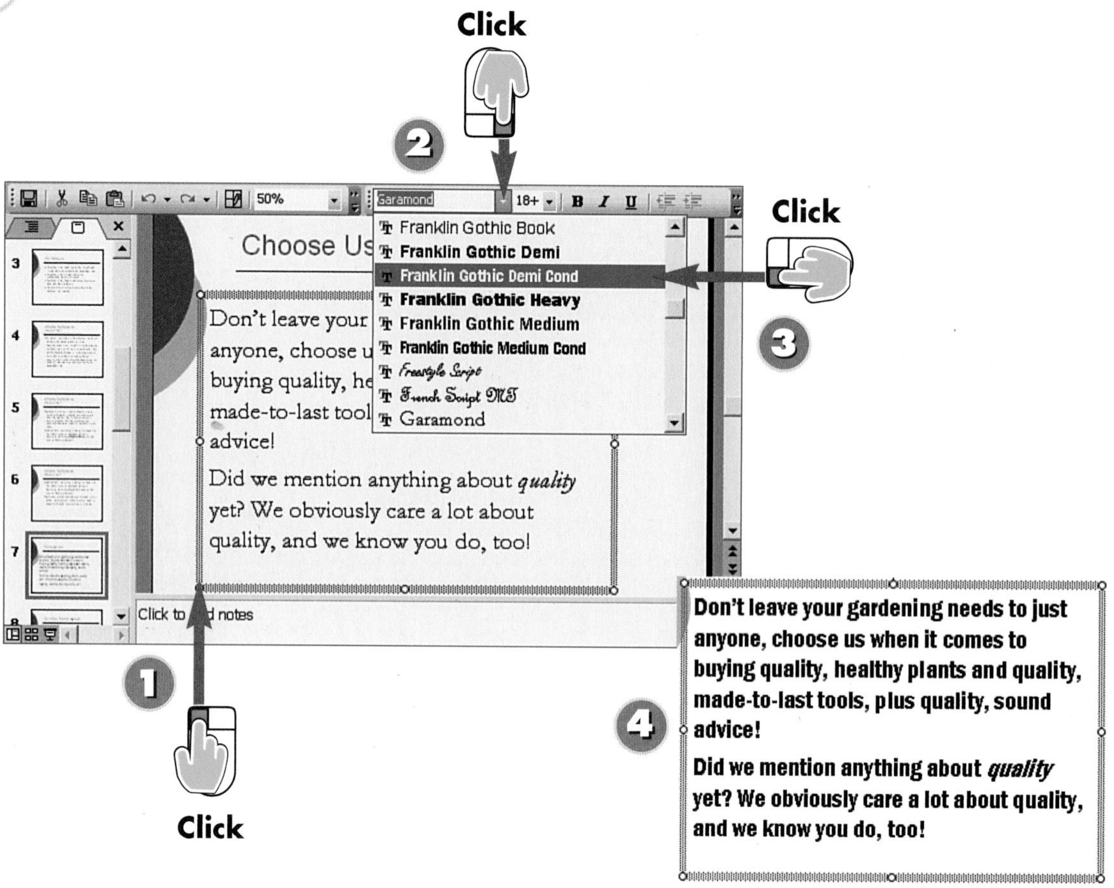

1. Select the text or text box you want to edit.
2. Click the **Font** drop-down list on the Formatting toolbar.
3. Click a new font.
4. PowerPoint applies the new font to the text.

INTRODUCTION

When you assign a slide layout to a slide, the layout includes a default font and size for the various text objects it includes. You can change the font and size of text as needed. For example, you can increase the size of your title text to make it more prominent.

TIP

Using the Font Dialog Box

Another way to change the font is to open the Font dialog box (open the **Format** menu and choose **Font**). From the Font dialog box, you can change the font style and size, and set any special effects, such as superscript text or embossing. Click **OK** to apply any changes.

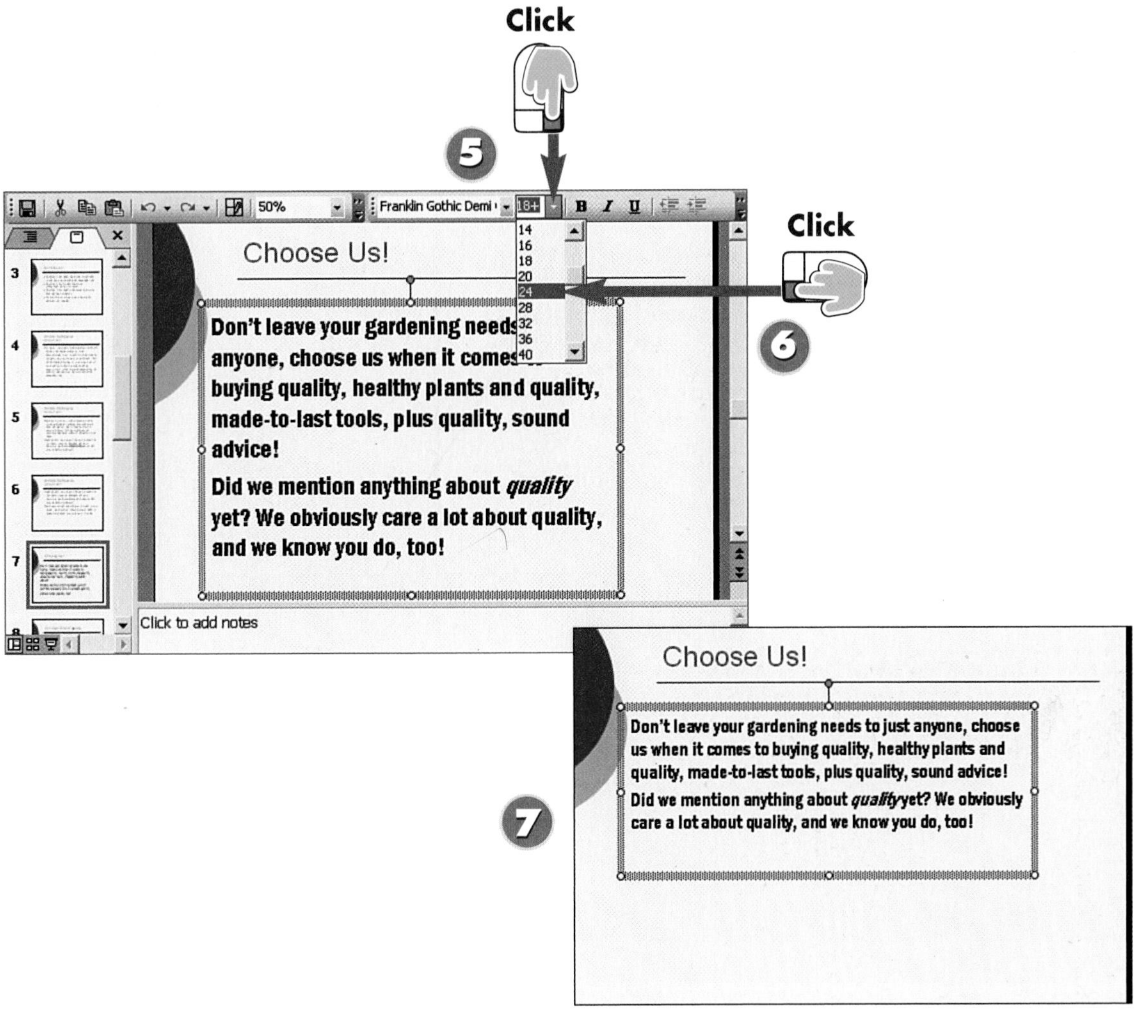

5. To change the font size, click the **Size** drop-down list on the Formatting toolbar.

6. Click a new size.

7. PowerPoint applies the new size to the text.

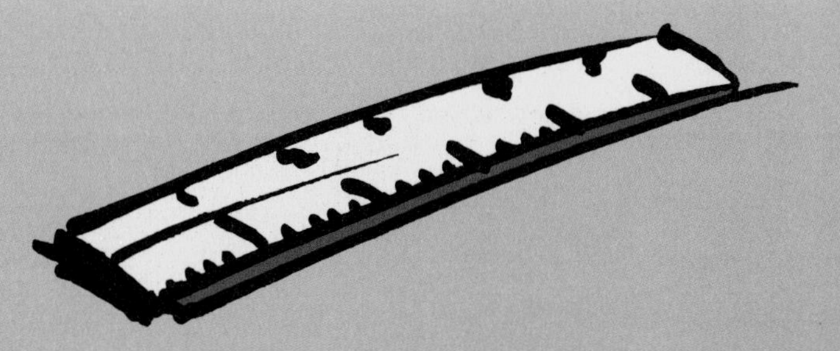

TIP

Using the Toolbar Buttons
Another way to increase or decrease font sizes is to click the **Increase Font Size** or **Decrease Font Size** buttons on the Formatting toolbar. This allows you to change the size incrementally without knowing an exact size measurement.

Changing the Text Color

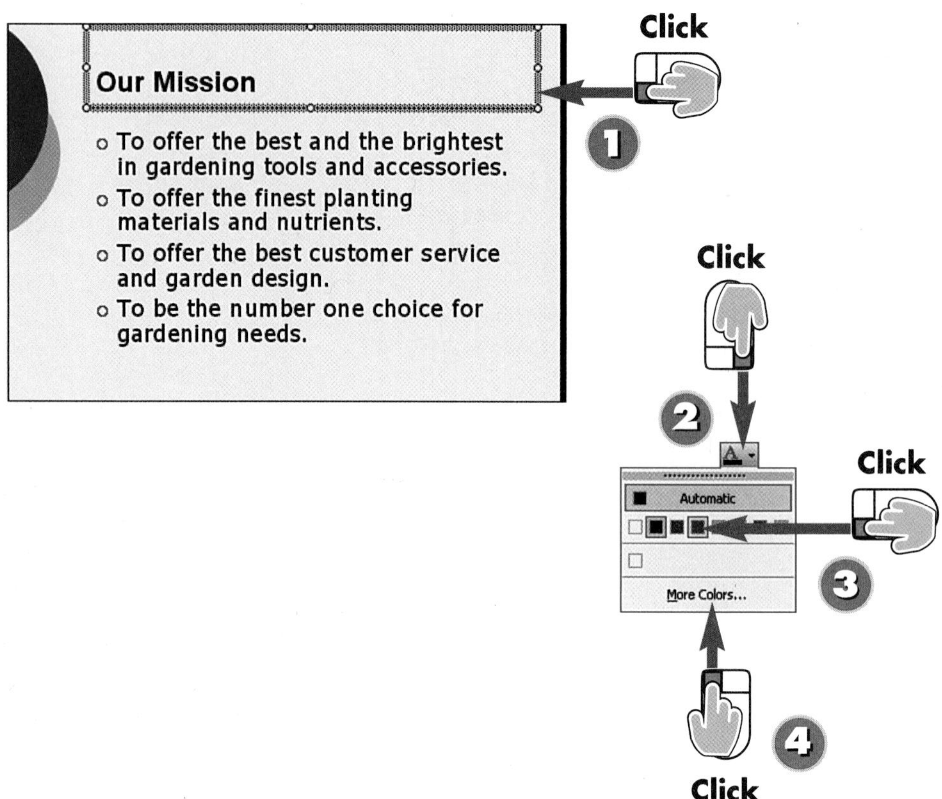

1. Select the text or text box you want to format.
2. Click the **Font Color** button on the Formatting toolbar.
3. PowerPoint displays a menu of color options that coordinate with your current slide design. Click the color you want to apply.
4. If you do not see a color you like, click **More Colors**.

INTRODUCTION

As you work with different slide designs, you might need to change the color of slide text to make it more legible against the background, or you might want to use color to emphasize a word or line of text. You can change text color quickly using the Font Color button on the Formatting toolbar.

TIP

Understanding Color Schemes
The colors that appear on the Font Color menu are coordinated with the slide design's color scheme. You'll learn more about changing slide designs and color schemes in Part 6, "Changing the Appearance of Slides."

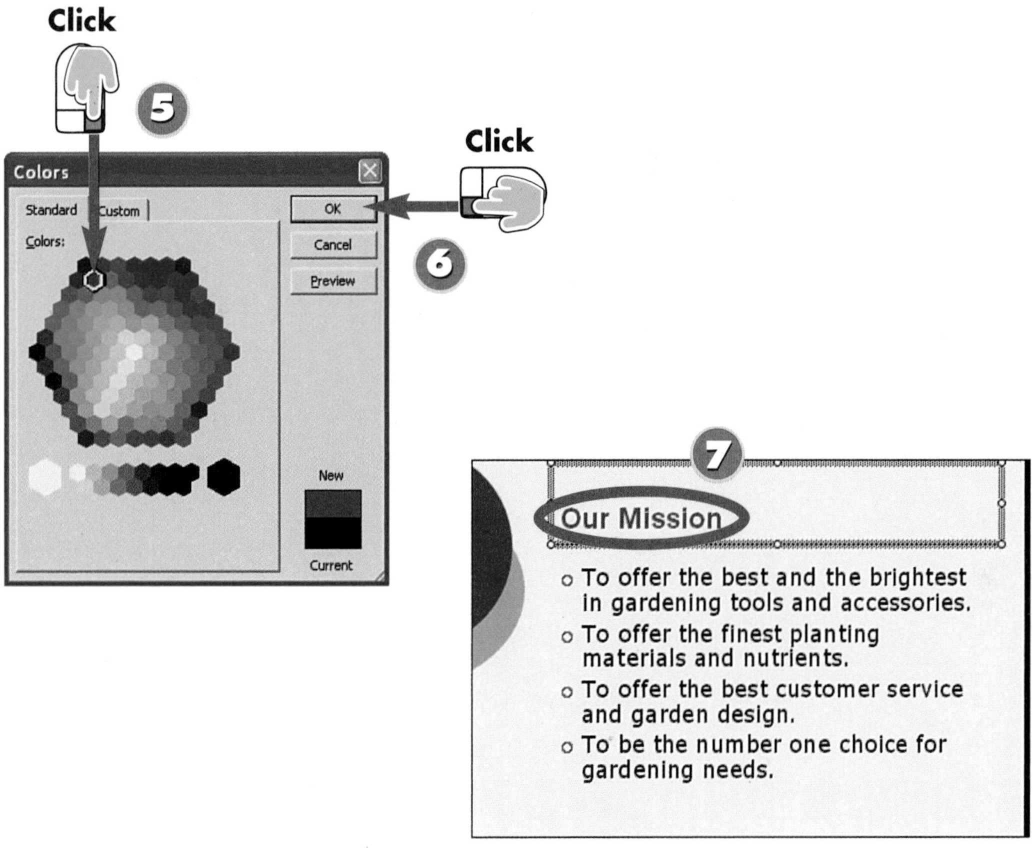

5. The Colors dialog box opens. Click a color.
6. Click **OK**.
7. PowerPoint applies the color.

TIP

Previewing First

The Colors dialog box enables you to preview how the color actually looks on the slide text before applying it. (This works only if you have selected the entire text box.) Click a color in the Colors dialog box, and then click the **Preview** button to see what it looks like on the slide. You can drag the dialog box out of the way to better see your slide text.

TIP

Undoing a Color Choice

If your color choice turns out to be less than what you envisioned, you can quickly undo the edit. Click the **Undo** button on the Standard toolbar, or open the **Edit** menu and choose **Undo**.

Changing the Text Box Background Color

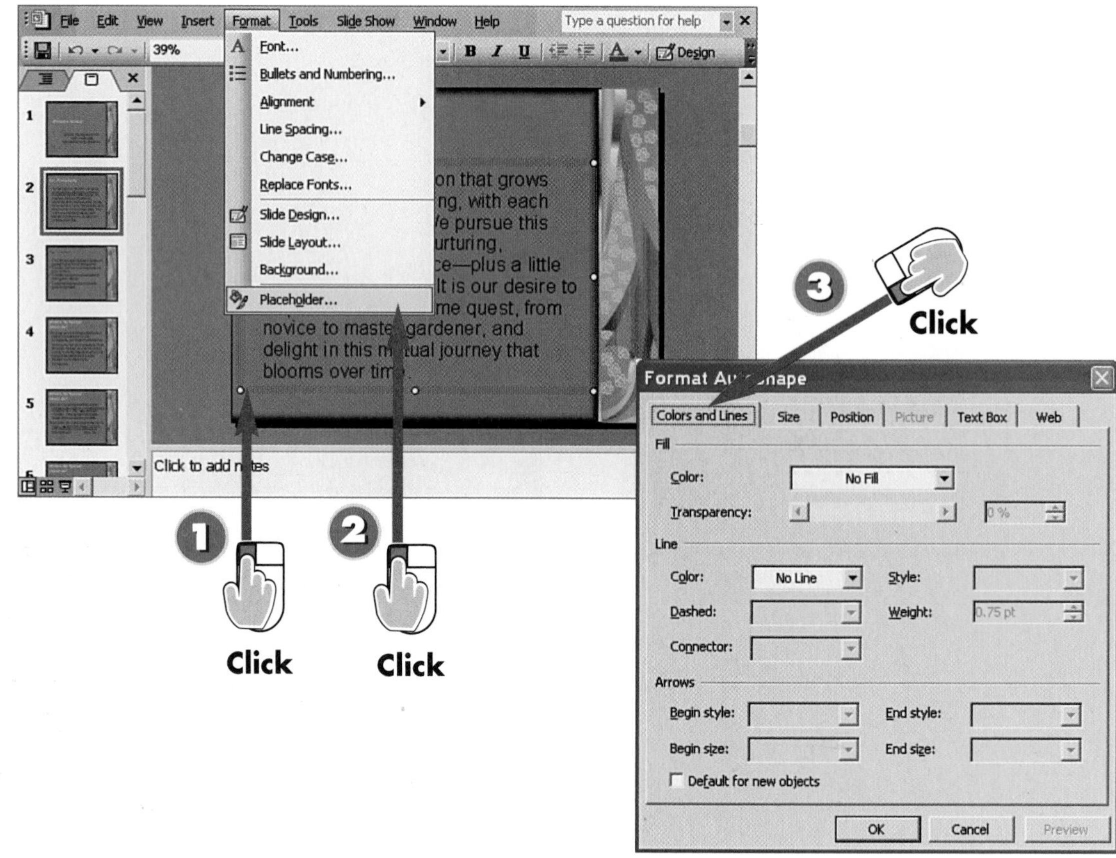

1. Select the text box you want to edit.
2. Open the **Format** menu and choose either **Text Box** or **Placeholder**.
3. The Format dialog box opens. (The dialog box will be labeled Format AutoShape or Format Text box, depending on the type of box you selected.) Click the **Colors and Lines** tab.

INTRODUCTION

Text object backgrounds appear separately from overall slide backgrounds. Using the Format dialog box, you can edit the fill color to change the text box background. The dialog box uses a different name depending on the type of text box you edit. For example, if you edit a placeholder text box, a text box that is part of the original slide layout, the Format AutoShape dialog box appears. If you edit a text box you added to the slide layout, the Format Text Box dialog box appears. Both dialog boxes offer the same options for setting the text object's background color.

HINT

Caution

Use caution when applying colors behind your text. Slide text must be easy to read, so don't choose a text box background color that conflicts with the text color. Instead, choose a color that complements the text color.

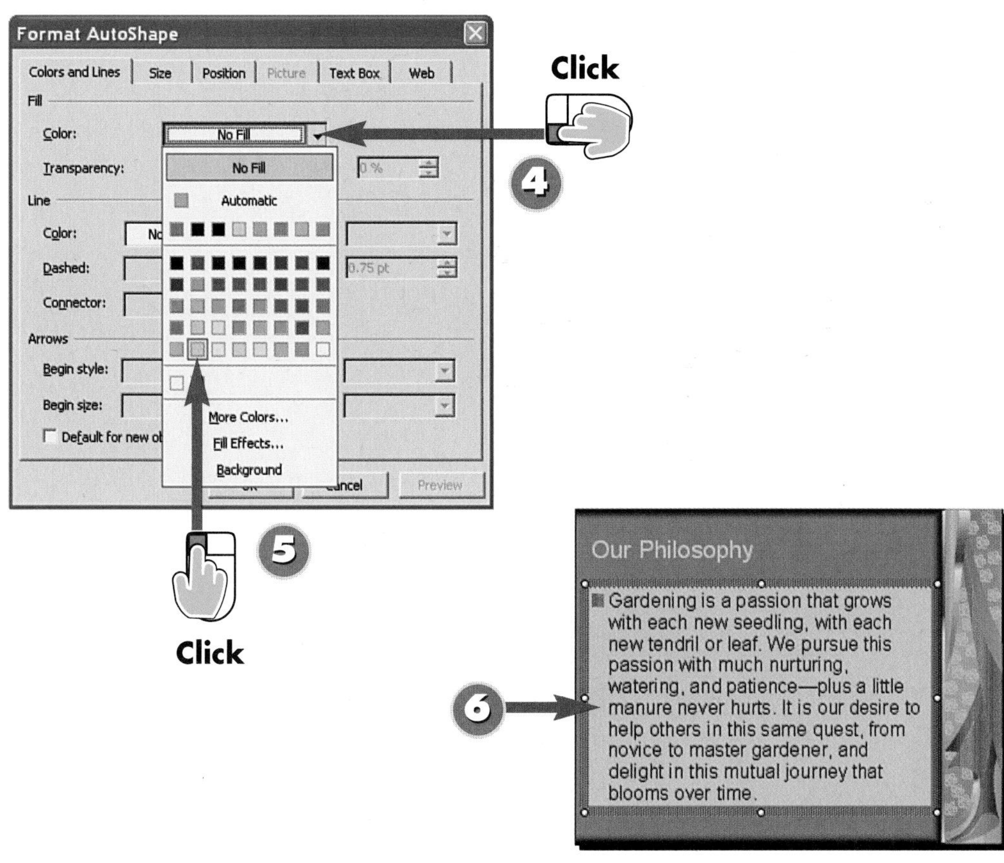

4. Click the **Color** drop-down arrow.

5. Click a color, and click **OK**.

6. The background color is applied behind the text box.

TIP

Finding More Colors
To choose from a full palette of color options, click the **More Colors** option in the Color drop-down list in the Format dialog box. This opens the Colors dialog box; you can pick another color from the palette.

TIP

Setting the Slide Background Color
To change the entire slide's background, use the Background dialog box. See Part 6 to learn more about the various options for setting slide backgrounds.

Spell Checking Slide Text

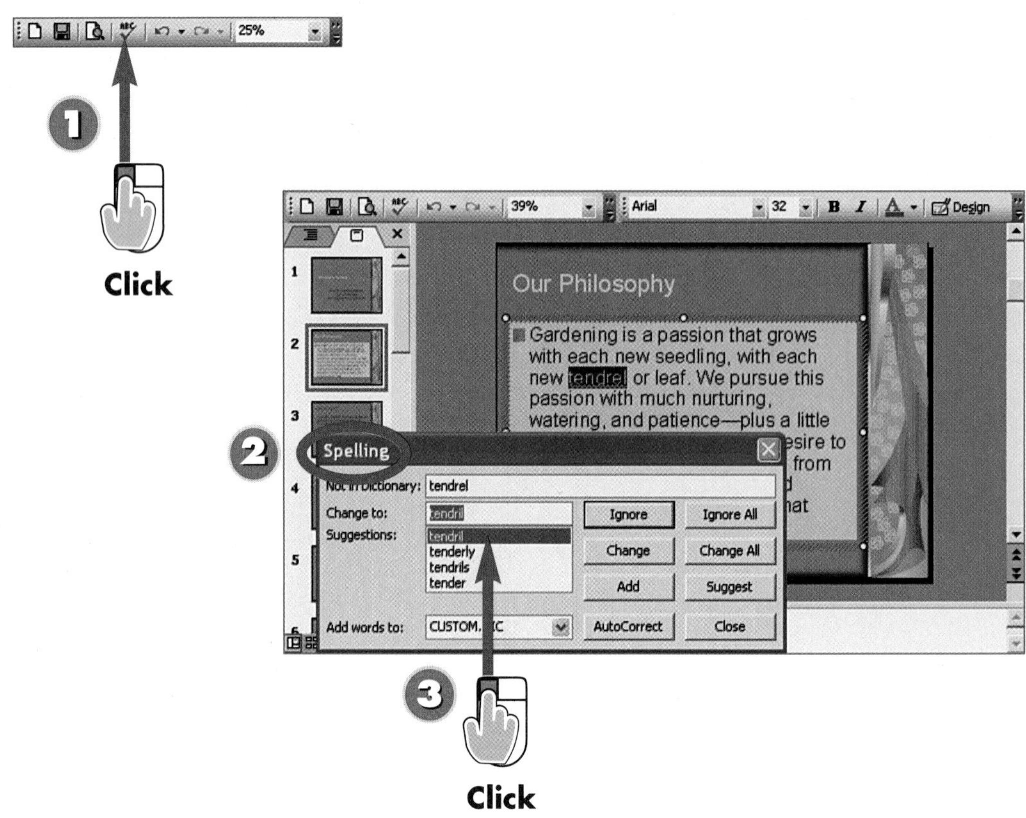

1. Click the **Spell Check** button on the Standard toolbar.
2. PowerPoint launches the spell check. If it finds an error, it highlights the misspelled word and opens the Spelling dialog box.
3. Click a correct spelling from the list of suggestions.

INTRODUCTION

As you build your presentation, do not neglect the important task of proofreading your text for errors. PowerPoint includes a spell check tool you can use to check your slides for spelling mistakes.

TIP

Using AutoCorrect

By default, PowerPoint's AutoCorrect feature is turned on. This feature automatically underlines misspelled words with a red wavy line as you type. To correct a word, right-click it to reveal a list of suggestions, and then click a suggestion in the list.

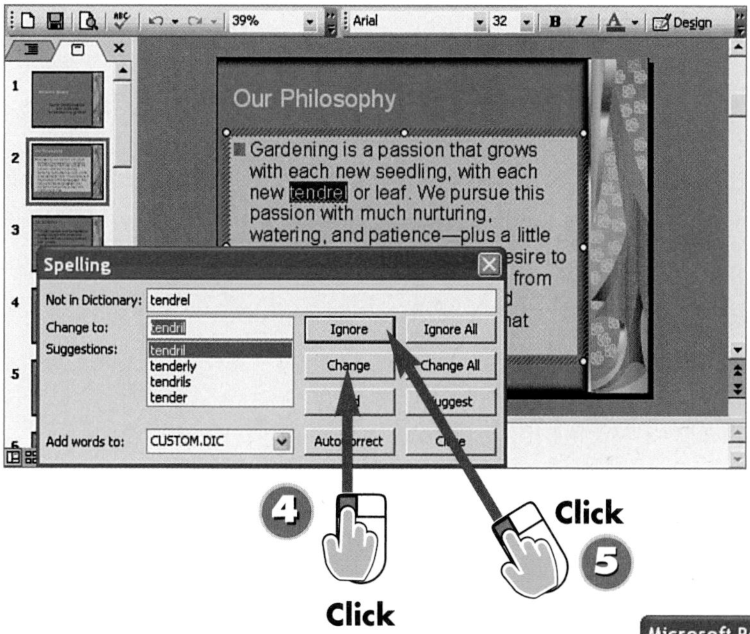

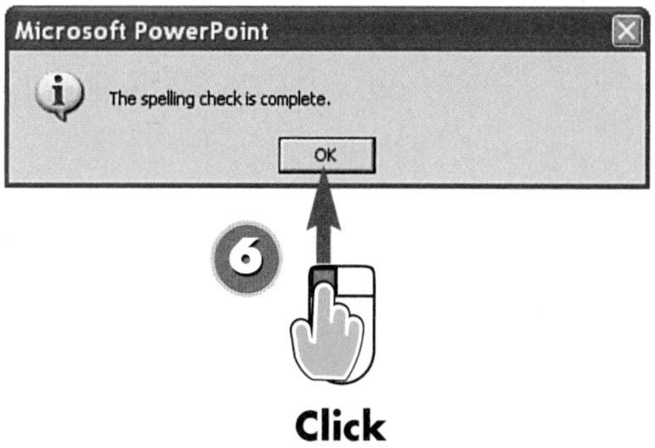

4. Click **Change** to replace the highlighted word with the new word you selected.
5. If the word is not actually misspelled (for example, if it's a proper name or a product name), click **Ignore** to skip the word.
6. When the spell check is complete, click **OK**.

CAUTION

Although the spell check feature is helpful for catching misspellings of words, it is always good practice to read through your presentation's text carefully. The spell checker cannot find mistakes in grammar or words used out of context.

TIP

Adding Words to the Dictionary

If you plan to frequently use a word that PowerPoint's spell check feature thinks is a mistake, consider adding the word to the program's dictionary. Click the **Add** button in the Spelling dialog box to add the word to the dictionary.

PART 5

Illustrating Your Slides

PowerPoint presentations are very visual by nature, and you can enhance your message by including different types of illustrations on your slides. For example, you can add one of thousands of clip-art images to a slide. PowerPoint and Microsoft Office ship with a clip-art collection that includes a variety of illustration categories and styles.

You can also add illustrations created in other programs. For example, if you have a company logo created in Illustrator, you can import the file and place it on a PowerPoint slide.

In addition to adding images to presentations, you can use PowerPoint's drawing tools to draw your own shapes and turn text into graphics. The Drawing toolbar offers tools for tweaking illustrations by adding lines, fill colors, shadows, borders, and more.

All illustrations are considered slide objects in PowerPoint. Slide objects can be moved and resized to enhance your presentation message.

The Clip Art Task Pane

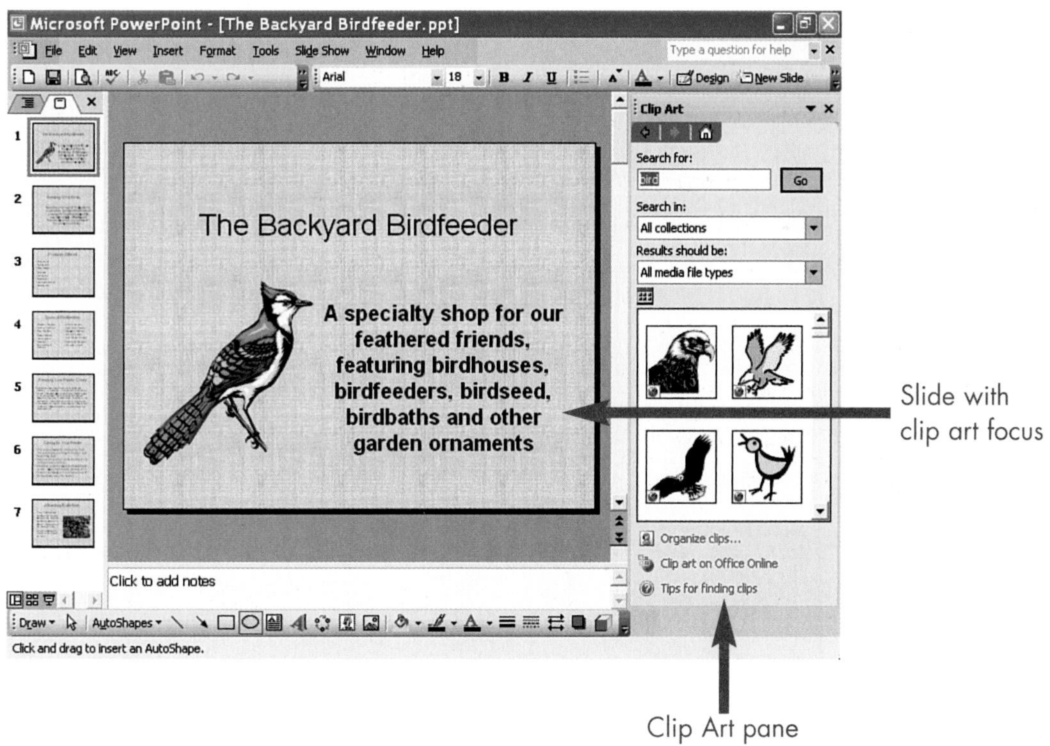

Adding Clip Art

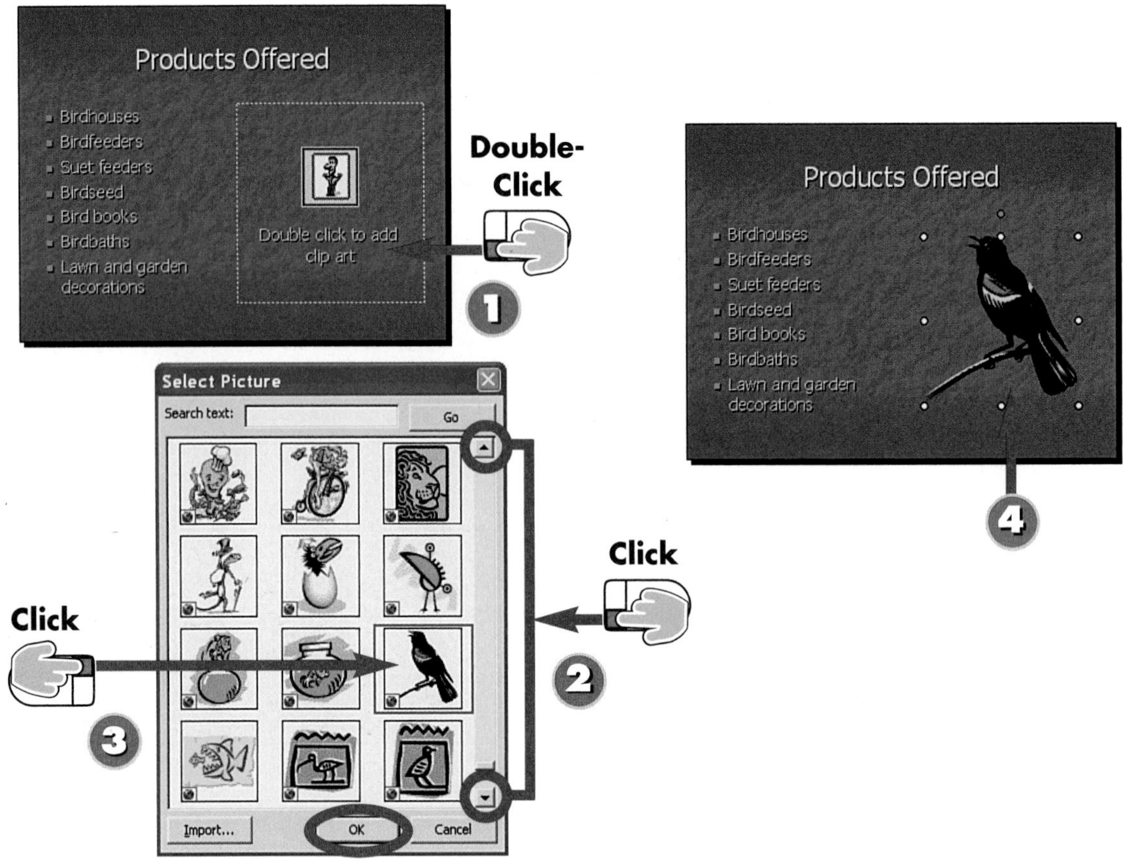

1. Double-click the clip-art slide object.
2. The Select Picture dialog box opens. Click the **scroll arrows** to scroll through the clip-art collection.
3. Click the image you want to add to your presentation and click **OK**.
4. PowerPoint adds the clip art to the slide.

INTRODUCTION

If you choose a layout that includes a placeholder slide object for clip art, you can use the Select Picture dialog box to browse the available clip art that installs with PowerPoint 2003. *Clip art* is simply a collection of pre-drawn images. Clip art can also include photos, sound, and motion clips.

TIP

Searching for an Image
If you are looking for a specific type of drawing, you can type a keyword in the **Search Text** field in the Select Picture dialog box, then click the **Go** button. PowerPoint locates any matching clip art and displays it in the list box.

TIP

Swapping Images
To exchange one clip-art image for another, first select the clip-art object and press the **Delete** key on your keyboard. Click or double-click the clip-art object box again to reopen the Select Picture dialog box, and choose another clip-art image.

Adding a New Clip-Art Slide Object

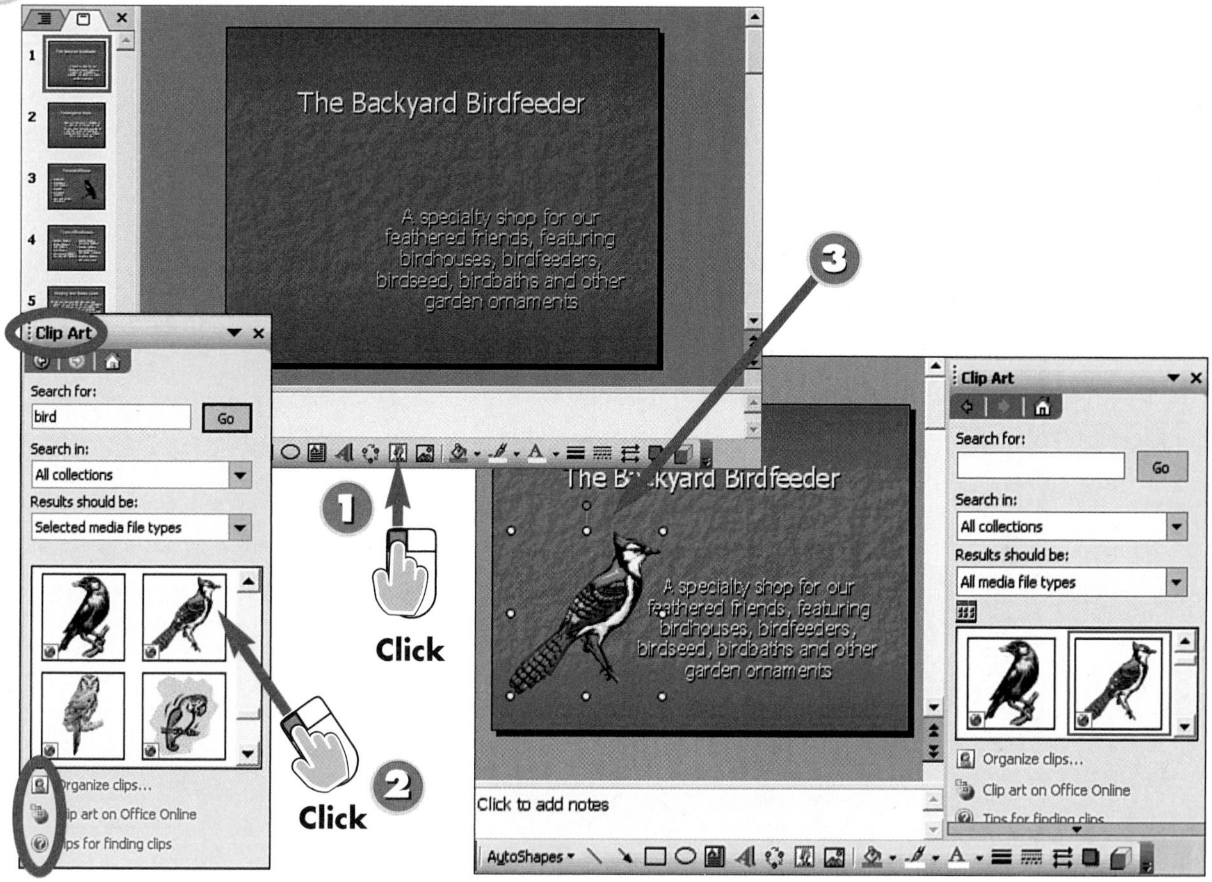

1. Click the **Insert Clip Art** button on the Drawing toolbar.

2. The Clip Art Task pane opens. Click the image you want to add.

3. PowerPoint adds the clip art to the slide.

INTRODUCTION

If your layout does not include a clip-art slide object, you can add one to illustrate your slide.

TIP

Editing the Clip-art Object
If you double-click a clip-art object, the Format Picture dialog box appears, enabling you to make changes to the image's cropping or brightness.

TIP

Searching in the Clip Art Task Pane
To search for a specific image in the Clip Art Task pane, click inside the **Search For** box and type a keyword. Click **Go**, and PowerPoint locates any matching clip art and displays it in the pane.

Adding a Picture

Start

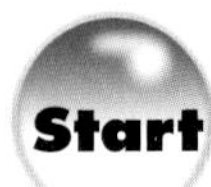

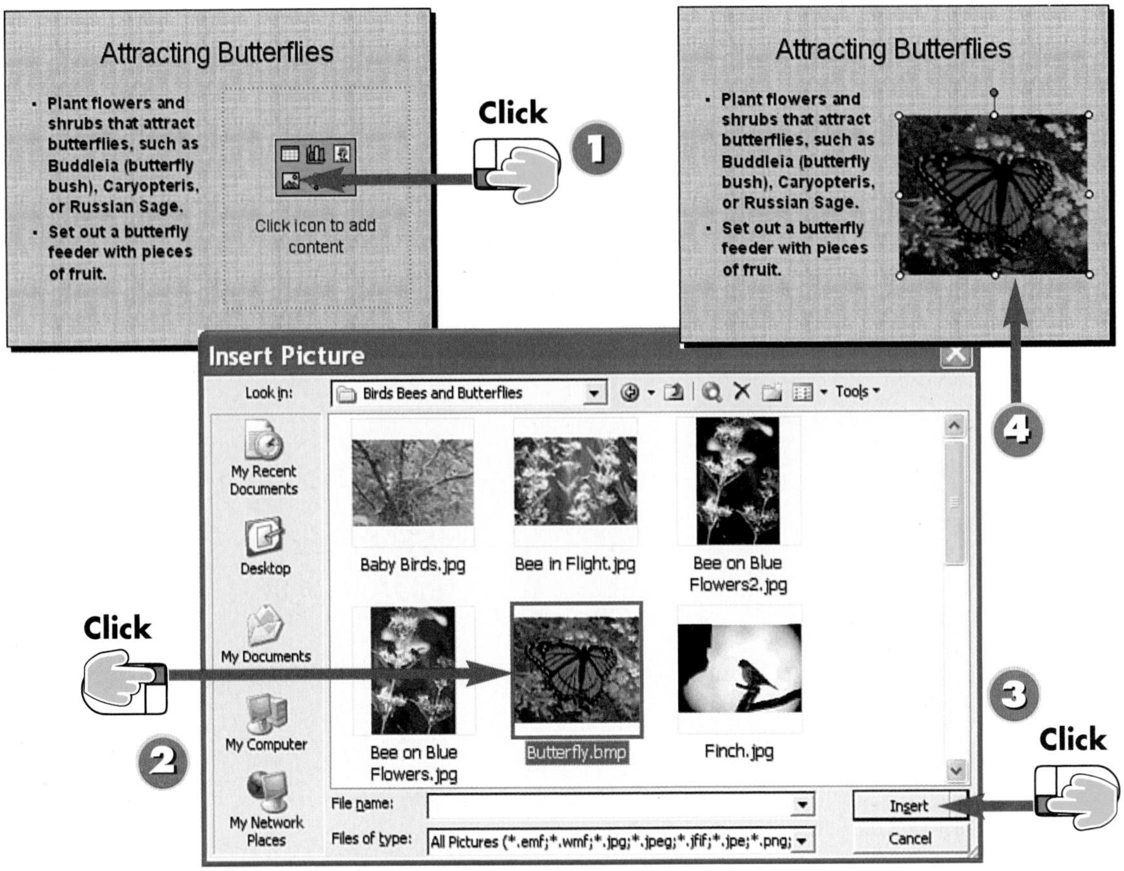
Attracting Butterflies
Plant flowers and shrubs that attract butterflies, such as Buddleia (butterfly bush), Caryopteris, or Russian Sage.
Set out a butterfly feeder with pieces of fruit.
Click icon to add content
Click
1
Insert Picture
Look in: Birds Bees and Butterflies
Tools
My Recent Documents
Desktop
My Documents
My Computer
My Network Places
Baby Birds.jpg
Bee in Flight.jpg
Bee on Blue Flowers2.jpg
Bee on Blue Flowers.jpg
Butterfly.bmp
Finch.jpg
File name:
Files of type: All Pictures (*.emf;*.wmf;*.jpg;*.jpeg;*.jfif;*.jpe;*.png;
Insert
Cancel
Click
2
3
Click
4
Attracting Butterflies
Plant flowers and shrubs that attract butterflies, such as Buddleia (butterfly bush), Caryopteris, or Russian Sage.
Set out a butterfly feeder with pieces of fruit.

1. Click the **Insert Picture** icon on the slide object box.
2. The Insert Picture dialog box opens. Locate and select the image file you want to use.
3. Click **Insert**.
4. PowerPoint adds the picture to the slide.

End

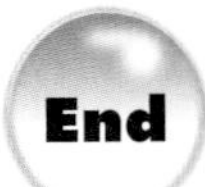

INTRODUCTION

In addition to adding clip art to your presentation, you can add picture files created in other programs. For example, you might have a company logo saved as a graphic file, or a photo you want to insert onto a slide.

TIP

Adding a New Picture Slide Object
If your layout does not include a slide object box, you can add a picture by clicking the **Insert Picture** button on the Drawing toolbar. This opens the Insert Picture dialog box; follow steps 2–4 in this task to complete the operation.

TIP

Editing the Picture Object
If you double-click a picture, the Format Picture dialog box appears, enabling you to make changes to the picture's cropping or brightness.

Deleting a Slide Object

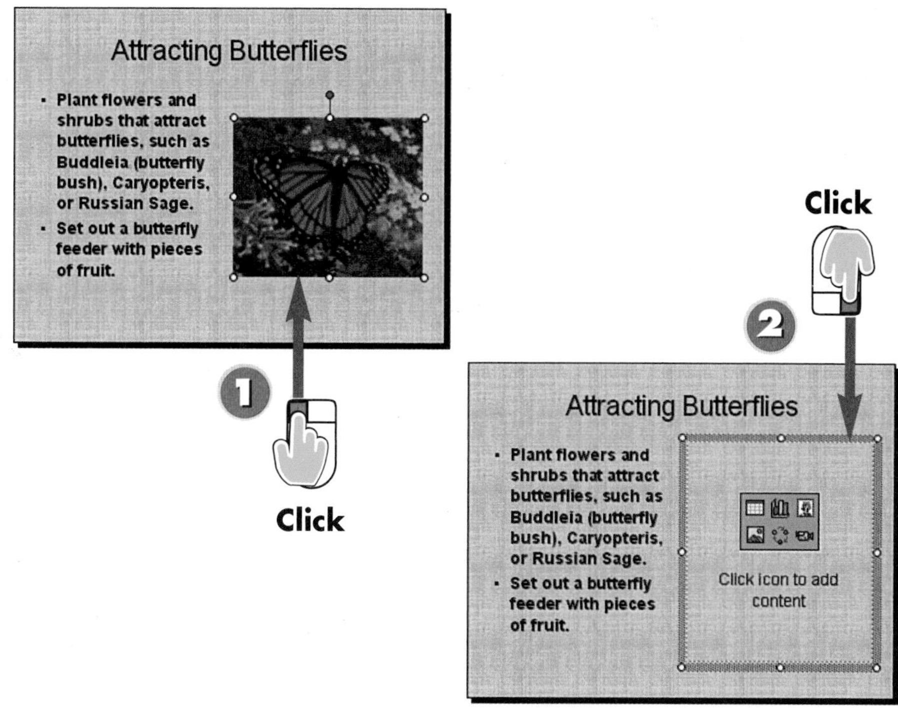

1. Click the slide object to select the object, and press the **Delete** key on your keyboard.
2. PowerPoint removes the illustration from your slide. In this example, the placeholder box reappears.

INTRODUCTION

You can remove a slide object you no longer need. For example, you can delete clip art or a picture file from your slide. If you delete a slide object that was part of the original layout, PowerPoint displays the original placeholder box for the object on the slide. If you delete a slide object that was later added to the layout, no placeholder box appears.

TIP

Permanently Removing Placeholders

To completely remove a placeholder object from your slide layout, select the empty placeholder, and then press the **Delete** key on your keyboard.

Adding WordArt Objects

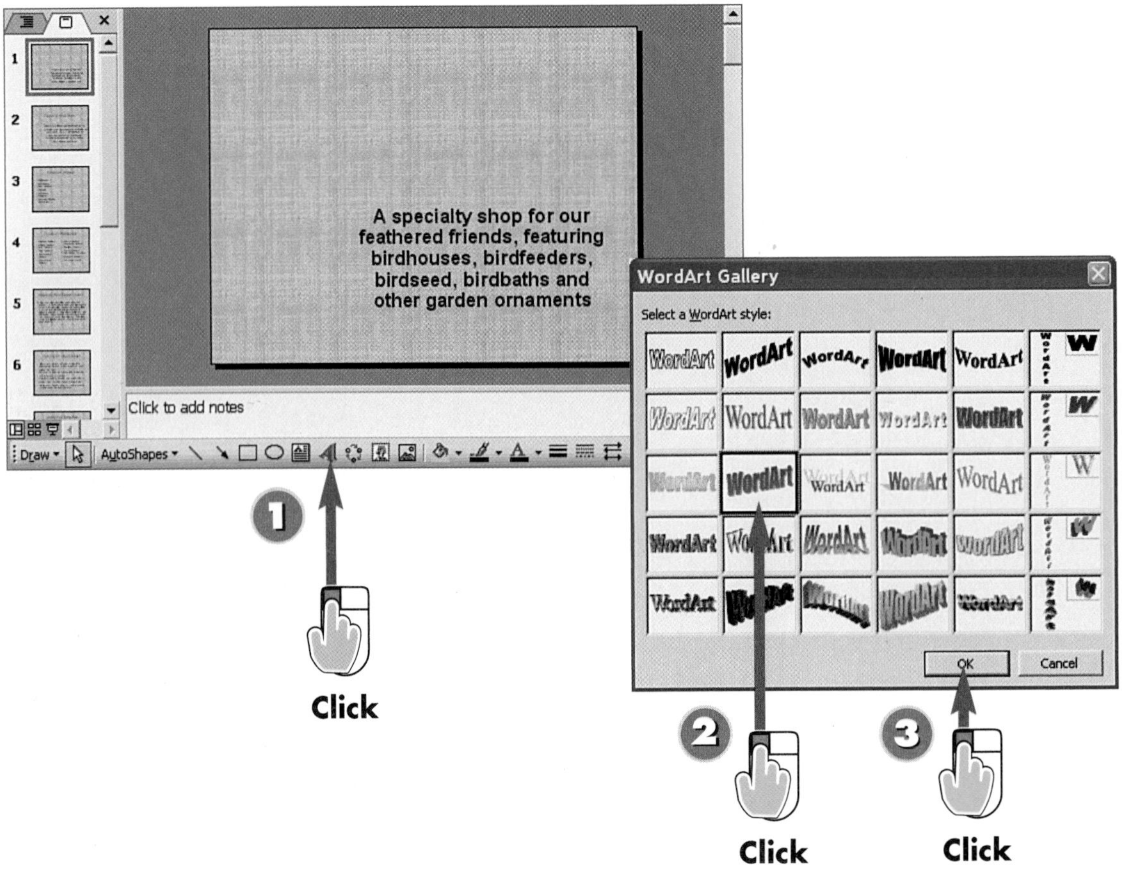

1. Click the **Insert WordArt** button on the Drawing toolbar.
2. The WordArt Gallery dialog box opens. Click the WordArt style you want to apply.
3. Click **OK**.

INTRODUCTION

You can turn text into a graphic using the WordArt feature. With WordArt, you can apply a variety of designs—such as curved text or text that uses a gradient fill—to ordinary text. You can also create vertical text.

TIP

Changing the WordArt Design
To swap the current WordArt design for another, click the **WordArt Gallery** button on the WordArt toolbar. This reopens the WordArt Gallery dialog box, where you can select another text design.

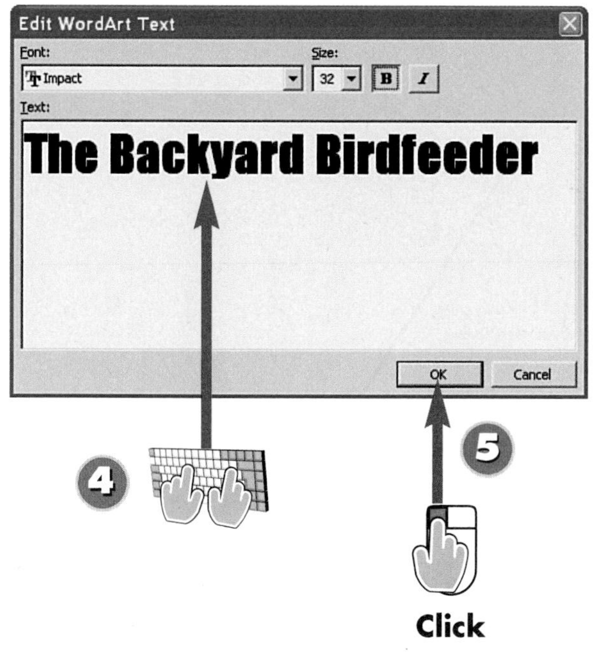

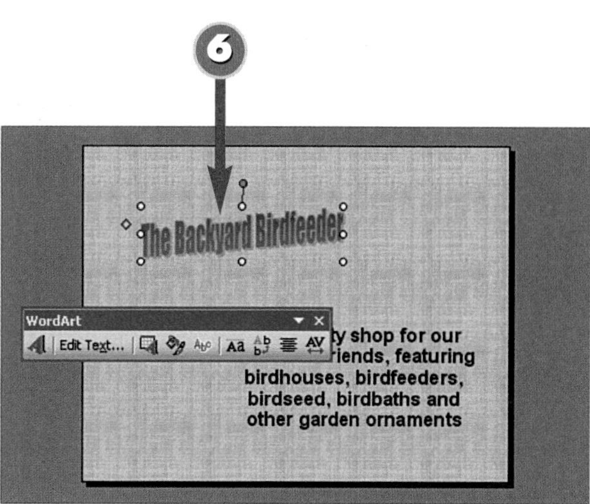

4 The Edit WordArt Text dialog box opens. Type the text you want to use as your WordArt object.

5 Click **OK**.

6 PowerPoint adds the WordArt object to the slide and the WordArt toolbar appears. You can use the toolbar tools to edit the WordArt object, such as change text alignment or character spacing.

TIP

Correcting Spelling Mistakes

You can return to the Edit WordArt Text dialog box to make changes to your text, such as correcting a misspelling. Simply double-click on the WordArt object, make the corrections, and click **OK**.

TIP

Viewing the WordArt Toolbar

If you accidentally close the WordArt toolbar and need it again later, select **View**, **Toolbars**, **WordArt** to bring it back.

TIP

Formatting the Text

In the Edit WordArt Text dialog box, you can choose another font, size, or style using the formatting controls at the top of the dialog box.

Drawing Shapes on a Slide

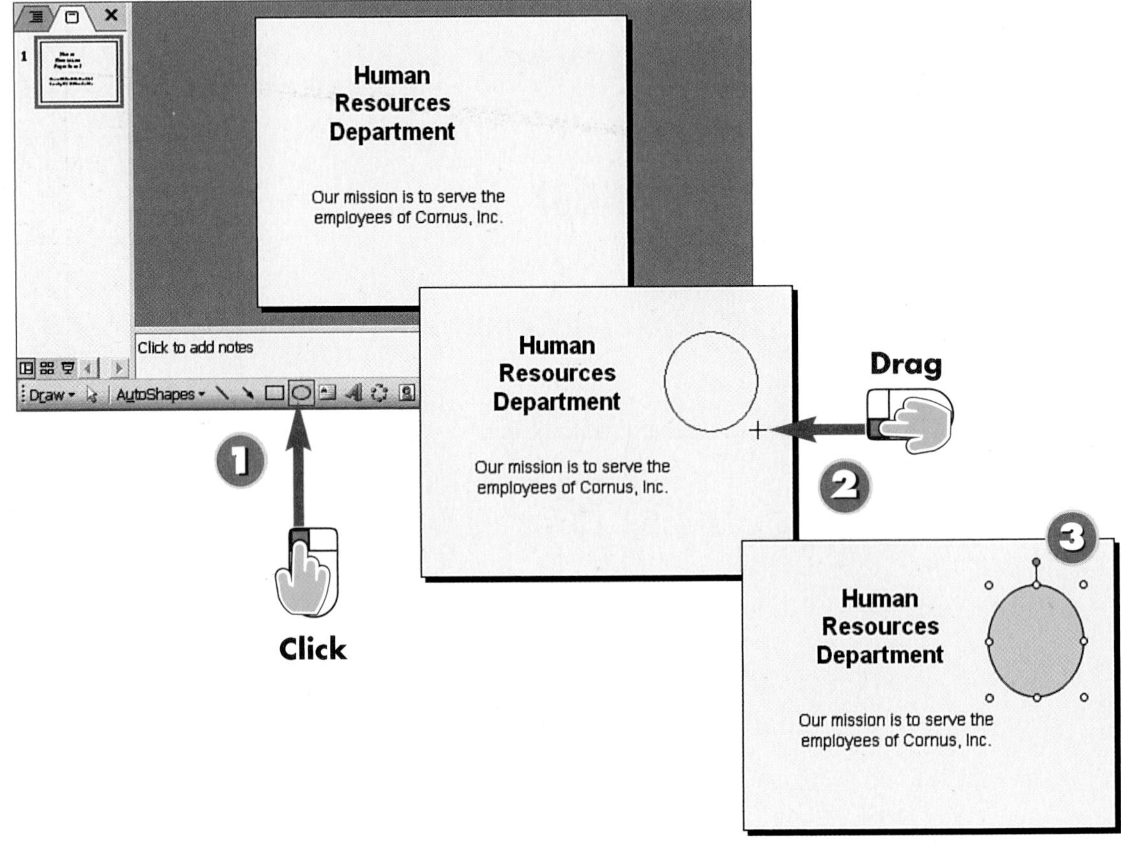

1. Click a drawing tool on the Drawing toolbar. In this example, the **Oval** tool is selected.
2. Click and drag on the slide to draw the shape.
3. Release the mouse button; the shape is created.

INTRODUCTION

You can draw your own illustrations on your slides using the tools available on the Drawing toolbar. The toolbar contains buttons for drawing simple shapes, such as ovals and rectangles, as well as lines and lines with arrows. You can control the shape's line color and thickness as well as apply a fill color to your shapes.

TIP

Drawing a Perfect Shape
To draw a perfect circle or square, press and hold the **Shift** key while drawing with the Oval or Rectangle tools.

TIP

Drawing Lines
To draw just a single line or a line with an arrow, simply click the **Line** or **Arrow** button on the Drawing toolbar and drag on the slide to create the line.

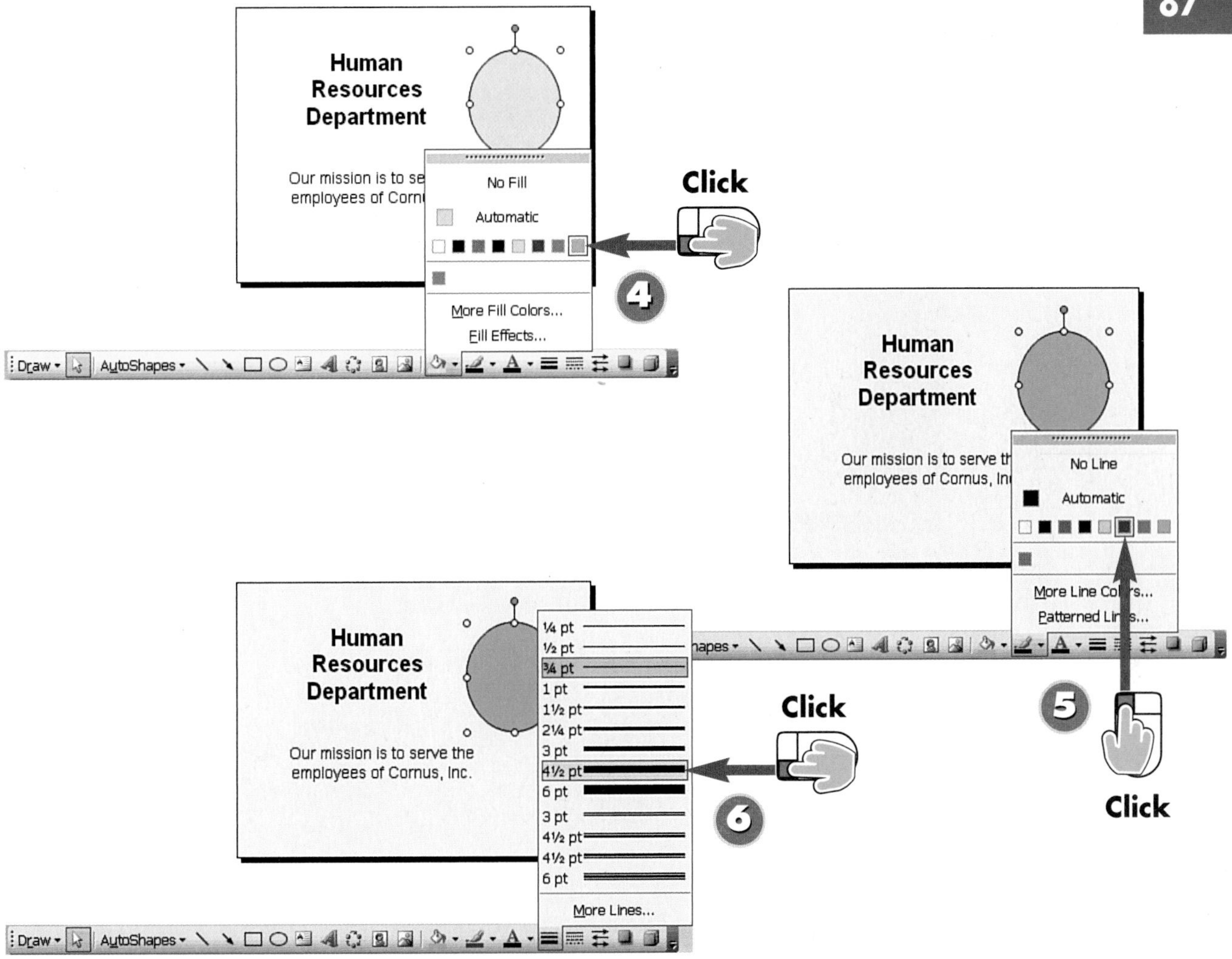

Click

Click

Click

4 Click the **down arrow** next to the **Fill Color** button in the Drawing toolbar and click a color to fill the inside of the shape.

5 Click the **down arrow** next to the **Line Color** button in the Drawing toolbar and click a color for the line.

6 Click the **Line Style** button and click a thickness or style for the line.

TIP

Editing Shapes

You can edit the shape or line you draw by double-clicking the object to open the Format AutoShape dialog box. Here, you can reset the fill color, line thickness, and more.

TIP

Quickly Inserting a Circle or Square

Click the **Oval** or **Rectangle** button on the Drawing toolbar, and then click on the slide where you want to insert a circle or square. PowerPoint inserts the shape for you using the default drawing settings.

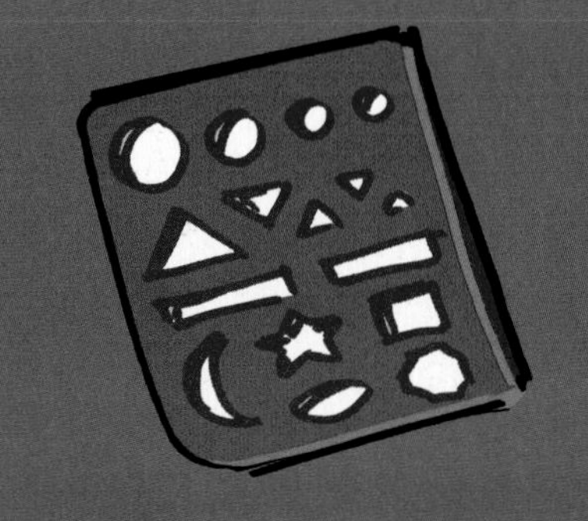

Adding AutoShapes

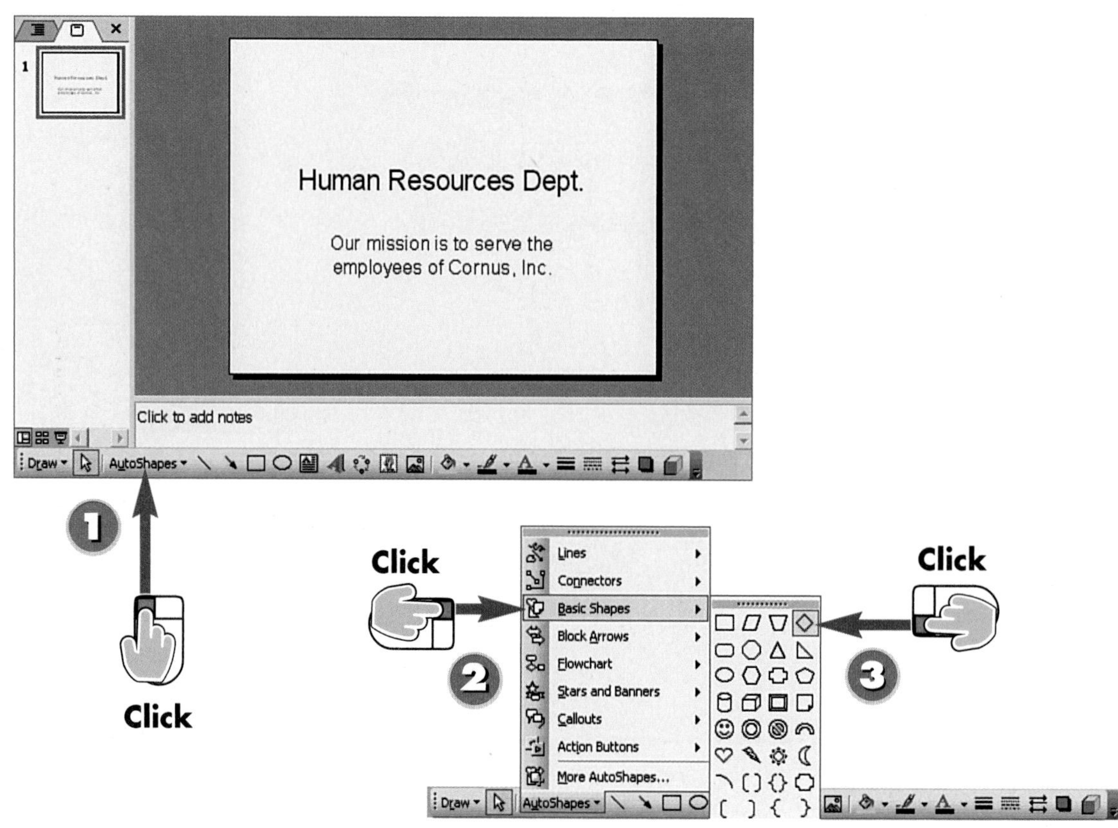

1. Click the **AutoShapes** button on the Drawing toolbar.
2. Click an AutoShape category (in this example, **Basic Shapes**).
3. Click an AutoShape.

INTRODUCTION

Rather than drawing your own shapes on your slides, you can choose from dozens of predrawn shapes, called *AutoShapes*. Among the AutoShapes catalog, you can find callout shapes, block arrows, and basic shapes, such as triangles.

TIP

Setting a Fill Color

You can set the fill color or line style for the AutoShape before drawing it on the slide. To do so, click the **Fill Color** button on the Drawing toolbar to change the fill color, or click the **Line Color** and **Line Style** buttons to change line color or style (for help, see the preceding task). You can now draw an AutoShape using your selections. You can also apply formatting options to a shape you have already created.

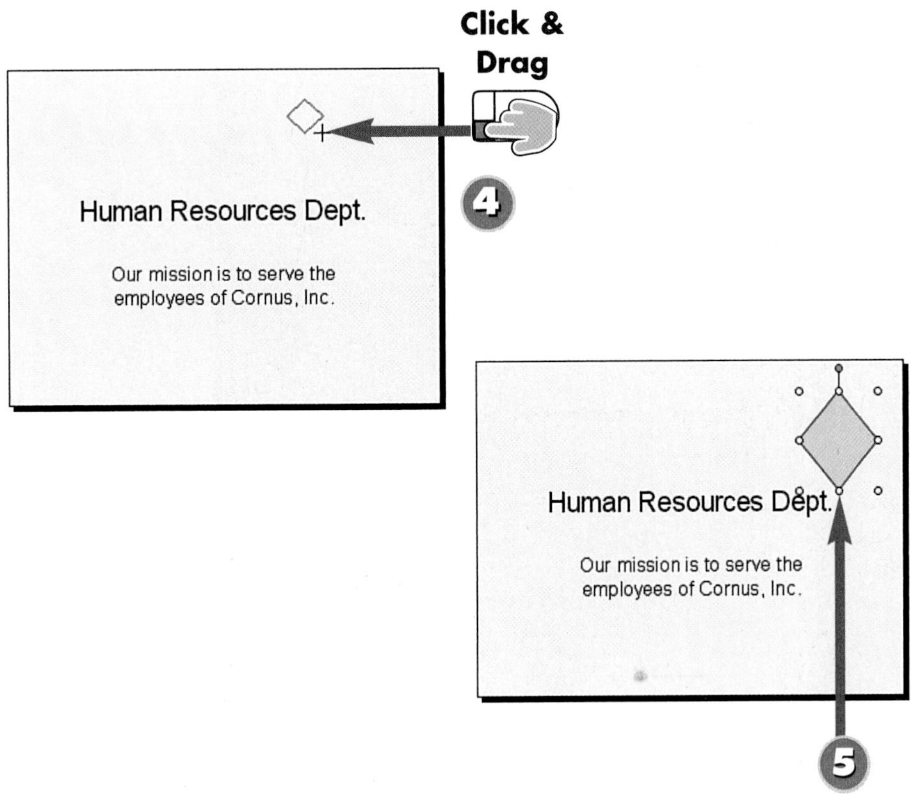

4. Click and drag on the slide to draw the shape.

5. Release the mouse button; the shape is created.

TIP

Adding Text to an AutoShape
Most AutoShapes allow you to add text within the shape. To do so, choose an AutoShape as you did in steps 1–3, click on the slide where you want to insert the shape, then start typing the text you want to appear.

TIP

Deleting an AutoShape
To remove an AutoShape object from a slide, click to select the object, and then press the **Delete** key on your keyboard.

TIP

Editing an AutoShape
If you double-click an AutoShape, the Format AutoShape dialog box opens, enabling you to make changes to the shape's fill color or line style.

Moving a Slide Object

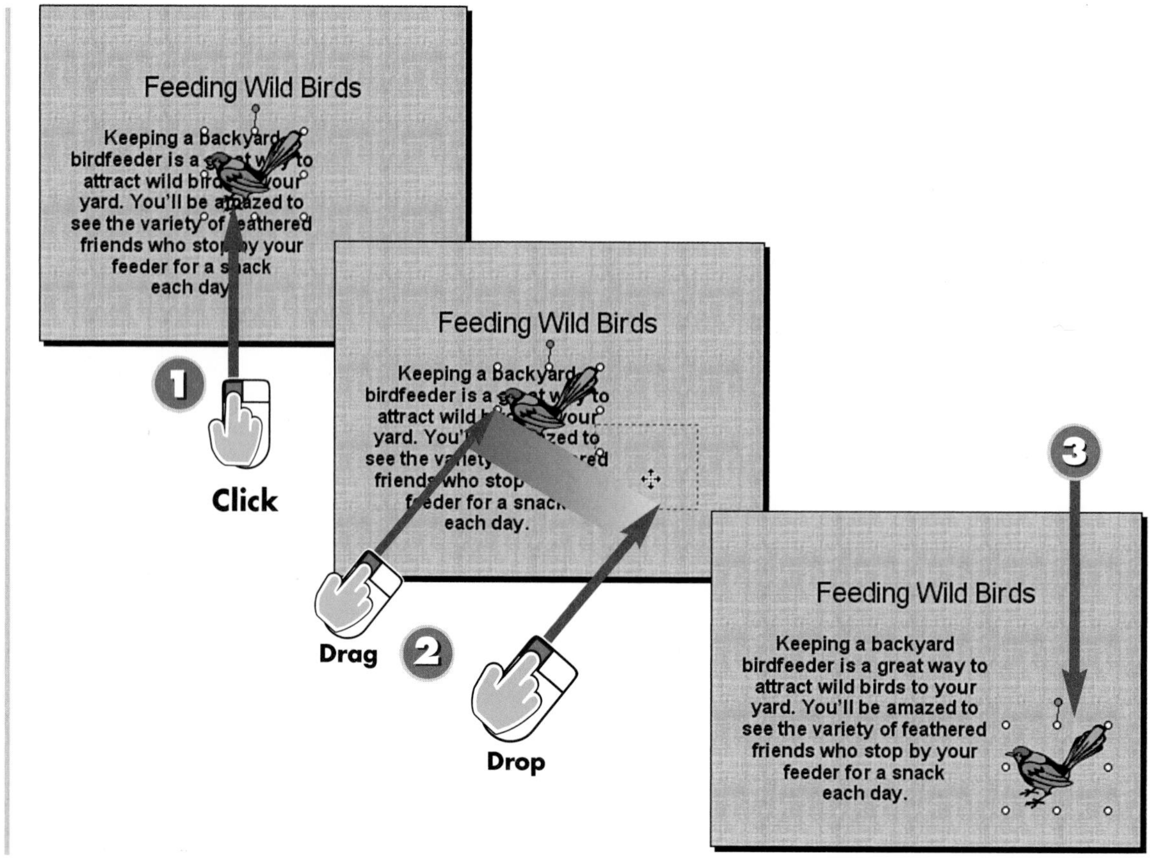

1. To move an object, click on the object to select it.
2. Drag the slide object to a new location.
3. Release the mouse button; the slide object is moved.

INTRODUCTION

You can move any slide object, including clip art, pictures, shapes, and even text boxes. You might move an object to change the slide layout, or to better position the object on the slide.

TIP

Restricting Movement
If you press and hold the **Shift** key while dragging the slide object you want to move, the object can be moved only vertically or horizontally.

TIP

Nudging a Slide Object
To move a slide object ever so slightly on the slide, use the Nudge command. Select the object, click the **Draw** button on the Drawing toolbar, select **Nudge**, and then select a direction to nudge the object.

Resizing a Slide Object

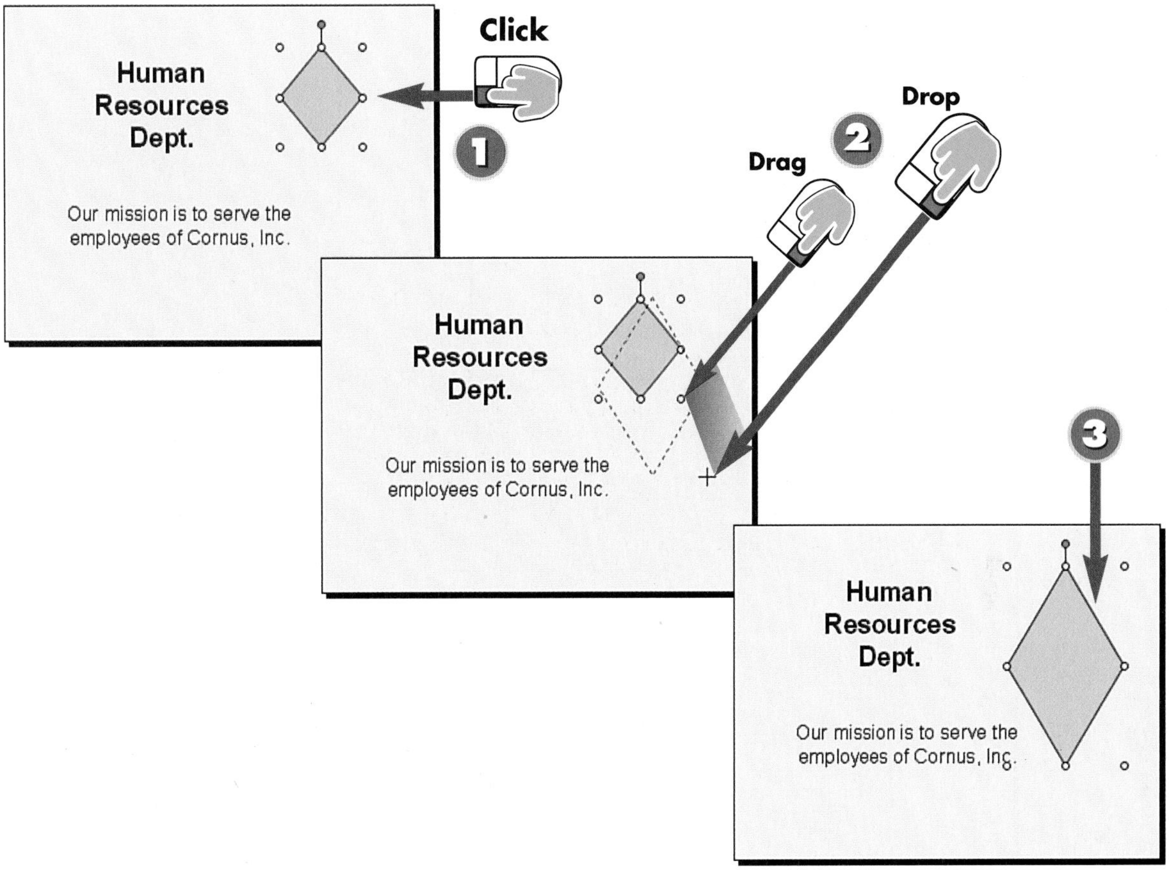

1. To resize an object, click on the object to select it.
2. Drag a handle.
3. Release the mouse button; the object is resized.

INTRODUCTION

You can resize any type of slide object—including clip art, pictures, shapes, and text boxes—to make it appear larger or smaller on the slide. When an object is selected, it is surrounded by handles; you use these handles to resize different sides of the object.

TIP

Keeping It Proportional
Press and hold the **Ctrl** key while dragging an object handle to keep the slide object size proportional to its original size. This prevents you from making one side of the object appear distorted. All sides stay the same relative size as you drag.

TIP

Changing the Object's Shape
To change an AutoShape, select the object, then click the **Draw** button on the Drawing toolbar. Select **Change AutoShape**, and choose another shape from the AutoShape categories.

Adding Borders to Slide Objects

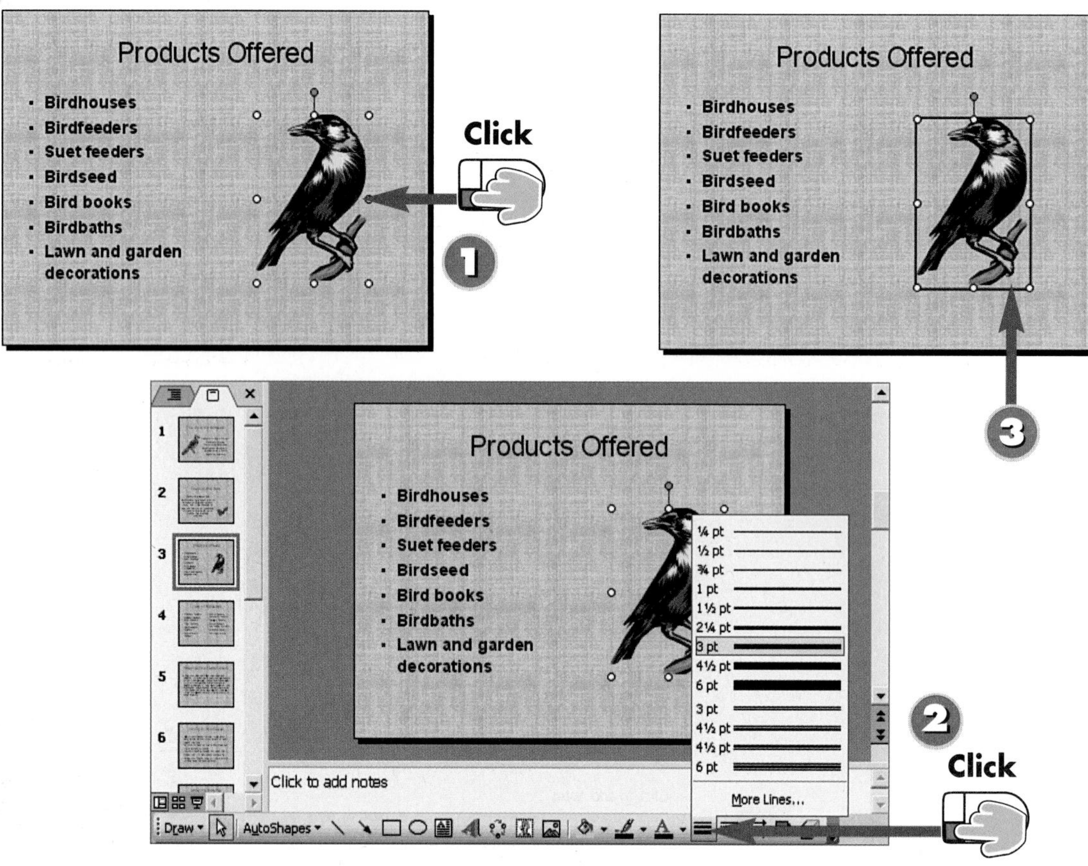

1. To add a border to an object, click on the object to select it.
2. Click the **Line Style** button on the Drawing toolbar and select a line thickness for the border.
3. PowerPoint adds a line around the entire slide object as a border.

INTRODUCTION

To make a slide object stand out on a slide, or to separate it from other slide objects, you can apply a border around the object. *Borders* are simply lines surrounding the outside of the slide object. You cannot add borders to a shape or WordArt object, but you can add borders to objects such as clip art, pictures, and text boxes.

TIP

Changing the Border Color

To change the color of a border, select the object and click the **Line Color** button on the Drawing toolbar. Select another color, and PowerPoint immediately applies it to the border.

Adding Shadows to Slide Objects

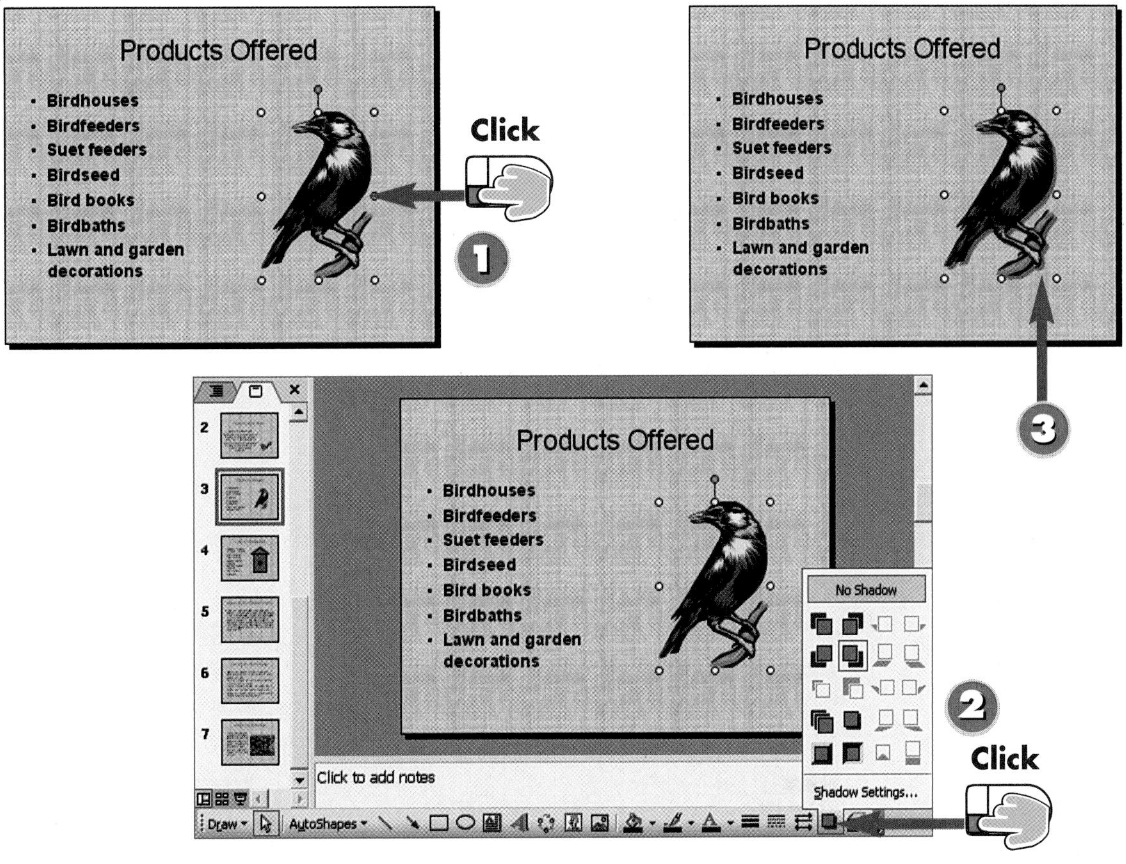

1. To add a shadow to an object, click on the object to select it.
2. Click the **Shadow** button on the Drawing toolbar and click a shadow style.
3. PowerPoint applies the shadow.

INTRODUCTION

To make your illustration pop off the slide, you can add shadow effects. Shadows create the illusion of depth by making it appear as though light is shining on the object. You can add shadows to any slide object.

TIP

Shadow Control
For added control, you can click the **Shadow Settings** option in the **Shadow** drop-down list to display the Shadow Settings toolbar. This toolbar has buttons for changing the placement of the shadow as well as the shadow color.

TIP

Undoing Mistakes
If you do not like the effect of a formatting setting you apply to a selected object, simply click the **Undo** button on the Standard toolbar to undo your work.

Adding 3D Effects to Shapes

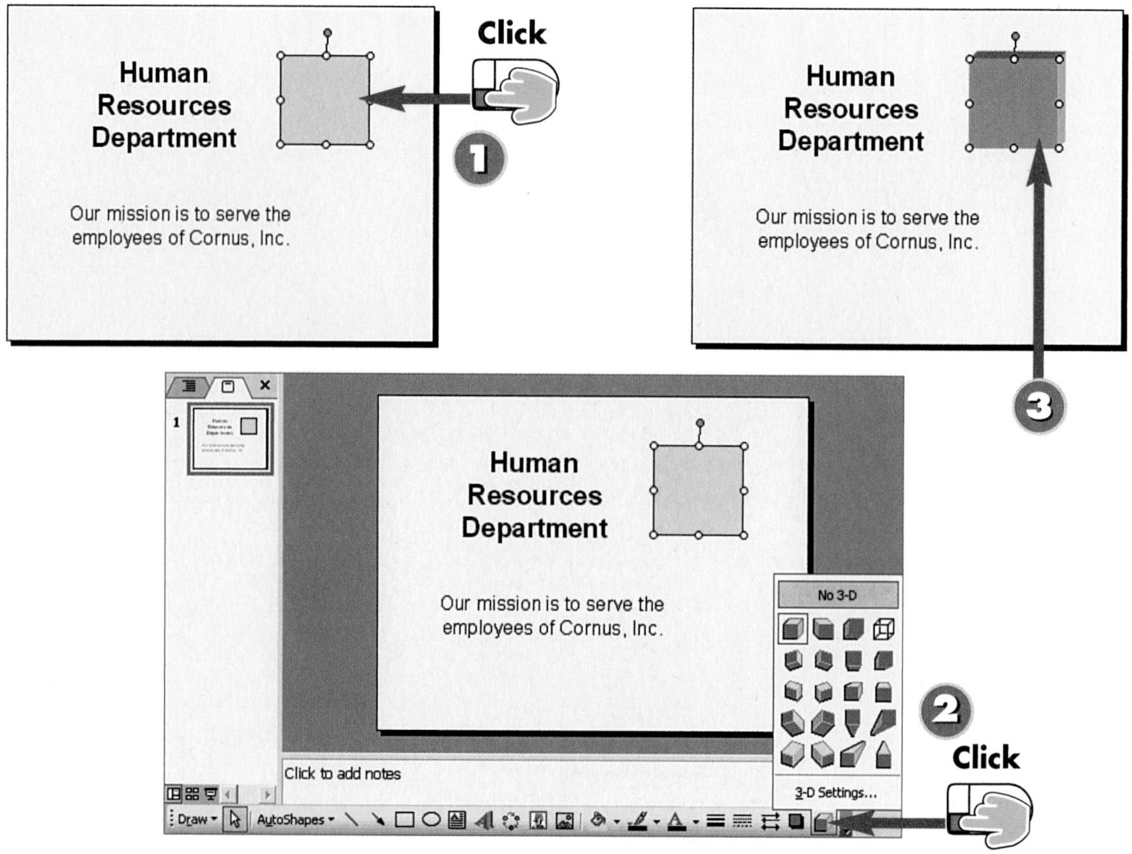

1. To apply a 3D effect to an object, click on the object to select it.
2. Click the **3D** button on the Drawing toolbar and select an effect.
3. PowerPoint applies the 3D effect to the object.

INTRODUCTION

You can apply a 3D effect to any shape or AutoShape on your slide to make it appear more lifelike. PowerPoint creates the effect by adding shadows and shading to the shape.

CAUTION

You cannot apply the 3D feature to clip art, pictures, WordArt, or text box objects.

Aligning Slide Objects

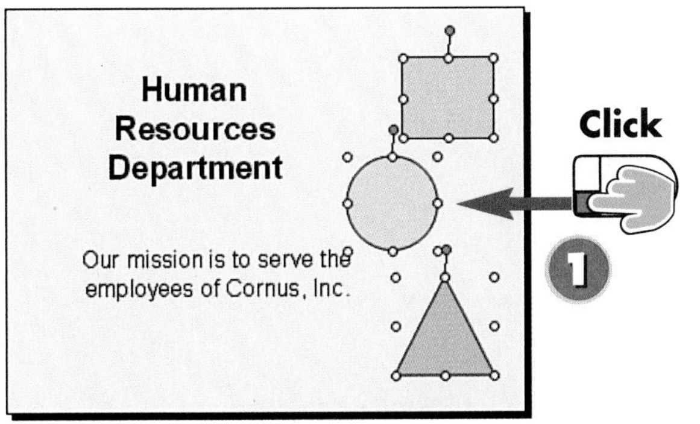

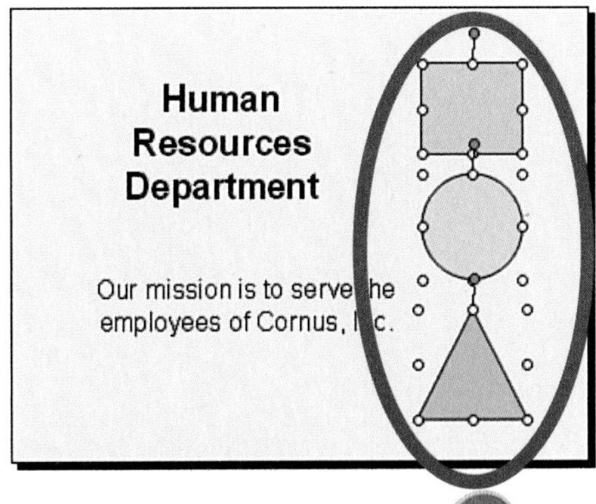

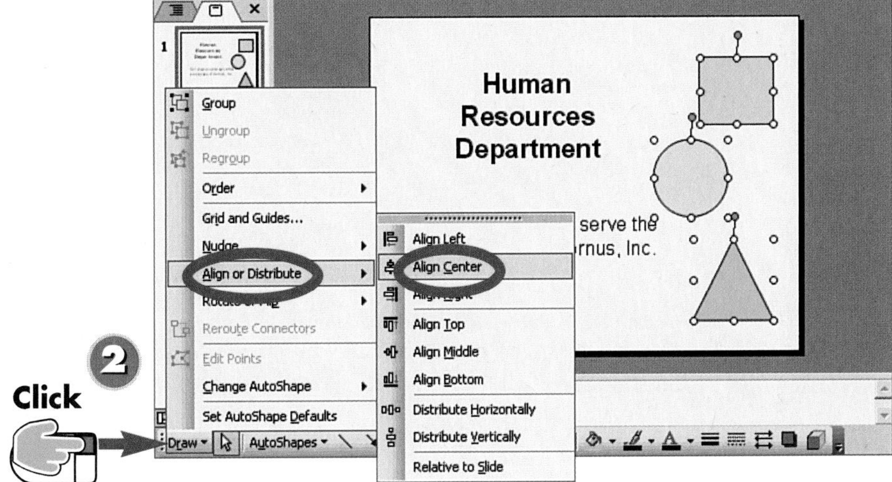

1. Select the slide objects you want to align. (To select multiple objects, press and hold down the **Ctrl** key on your keyboard as you click each object.)
2. Click the **Draw** button on the Drawing toolbar, select **Align or Distribute**, and then click an alignment.
3. PowerPoint aligns the objects.

INTRODUCTION

If your slide contains two or more illustrations, you might need to align them to improve your slide's appearance. To do so, use the alignment commands on the Draw menu to align selected objects on a slide; you can choose to align objects horizontally or vertically on the slide.

TIP

Distributing Objects

Use the Distribute options on the **Draw** menu to space your objects evenly on the slide in a vertical or horizontal manner.

Flipping and Rotating Slide Objects

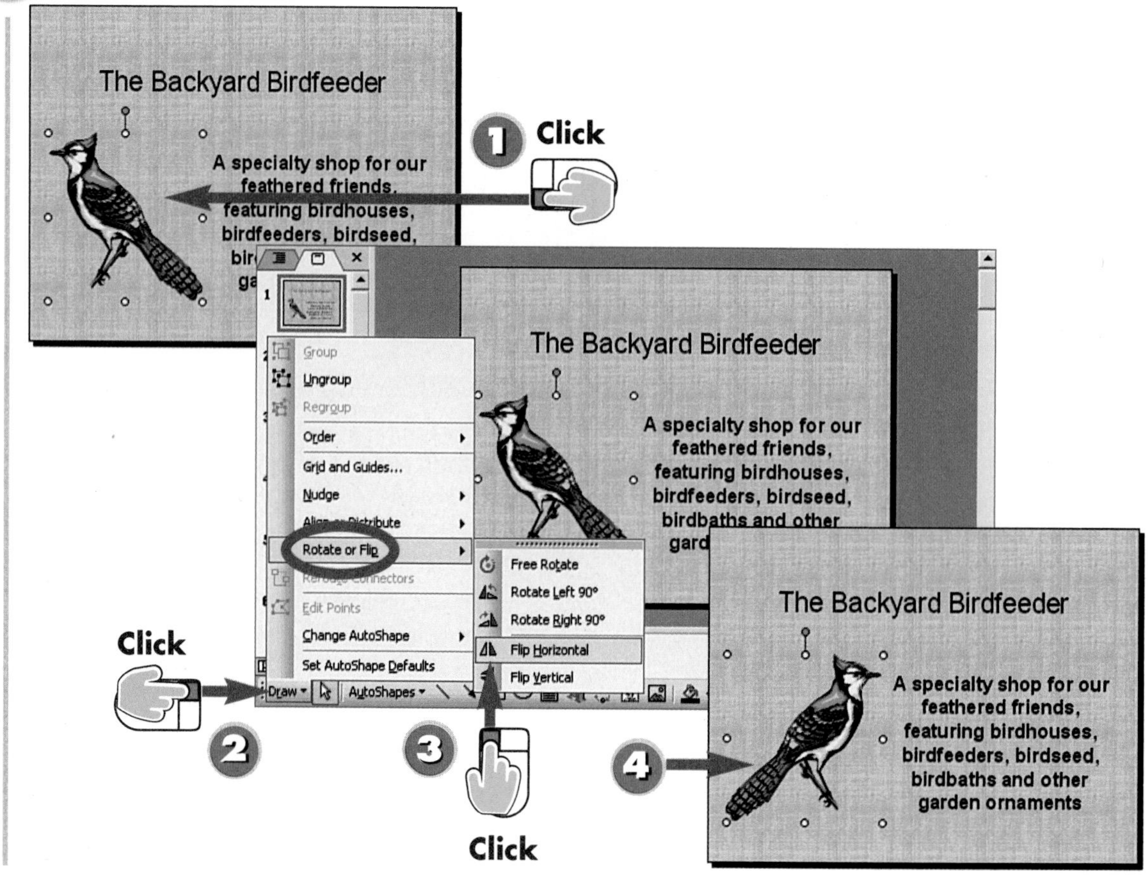

1. To flip an object, click the object to select it.
2. Click the **Draw** button on the Drawing toolbar and click **Rotate or Flip**.
3. Click **Flip Horizontal** or **Flip Vertical**.
4. PowerPoint flips the object.

INTRODUCTION

Another way to modify your slide illustrations is to change their position by flipping or rotating. *Flipping* an object simply turns it over, making it a mirror-image of the original. You can flip objects horizontally or vertically. *Rotating*, on the other hand, moves an object on an invisible axis, changing the direction of the object in a clockwise or counterclockwise fashion.

CAUTION

Use caution when flipping an image that includes text. Flipping will cause the text to read backward, as if held to a mirror.

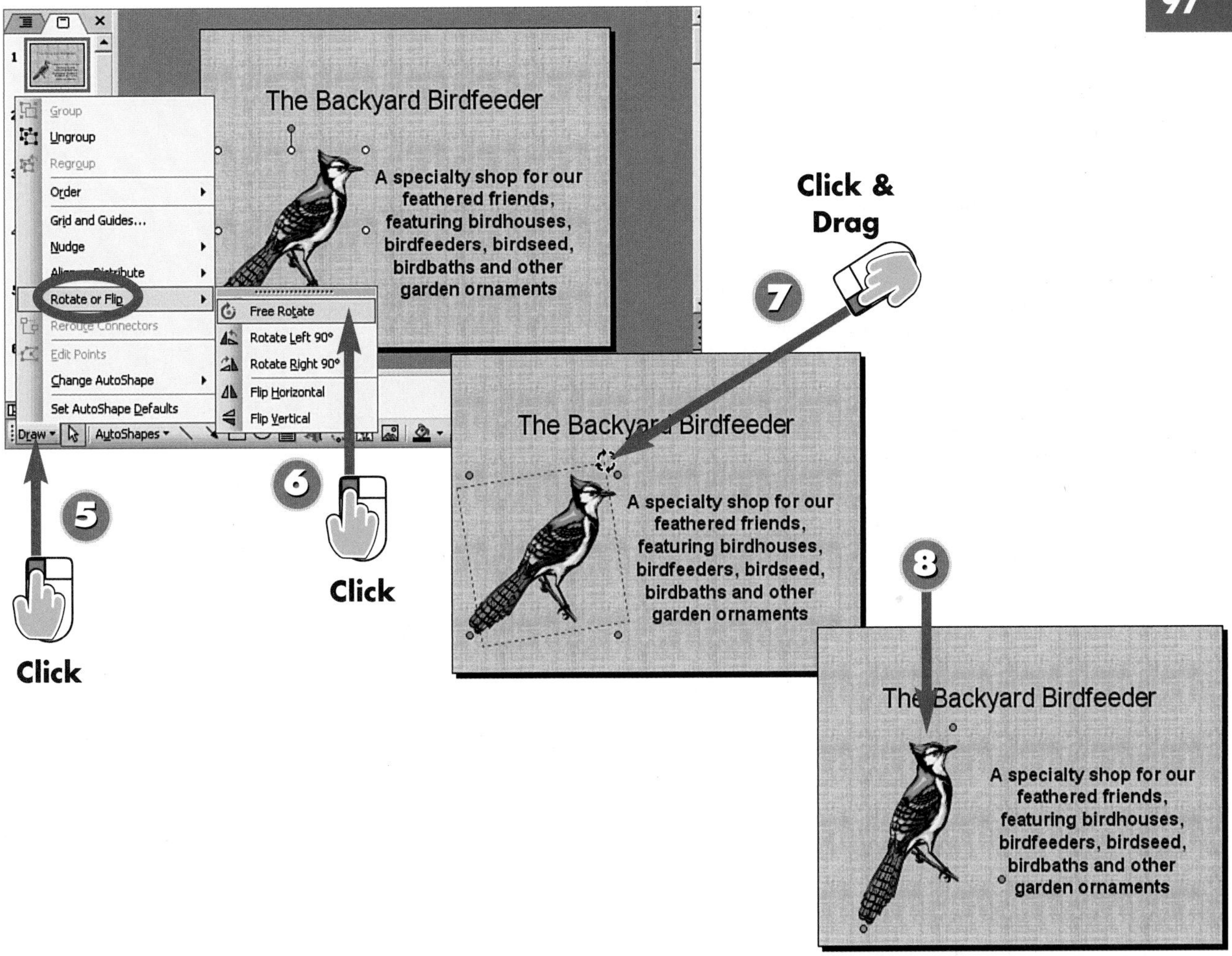

Click & Drag

Click

Click

1. To rotate a selected object, click the **Draw** button on the Drawing toolbar and click **Rotate or Flip**.
2. Click **Free Rotate**.
3. Rotation handles surround the object. Click and drag a handle to rotate the object.
4. Release the mouse button; the object is rotated.

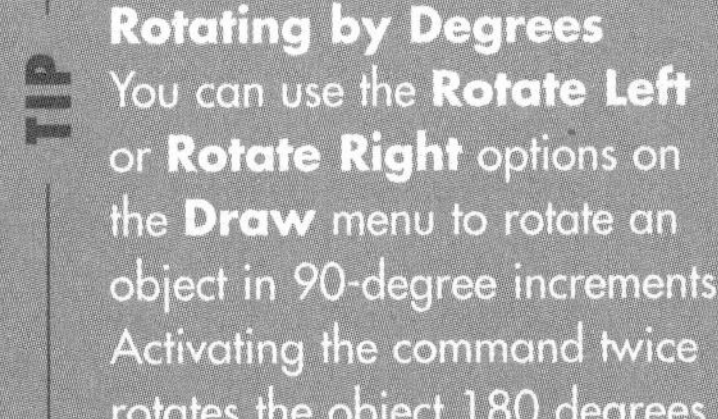

TIP

Rotating by Degrees
You can use the **Rotate Left** or **Rotate Right** options on the **Draw** menu to rotate an object in 90-degree increments. Activating the command twice rotates the object 180 degrees.

TIP

Restricting Rotation
If you press and hold the **Shift** key while dragging an object's rotation handle, PowerPoint restricts the rotation to 15-degree increments.

Recoloring Clip Art

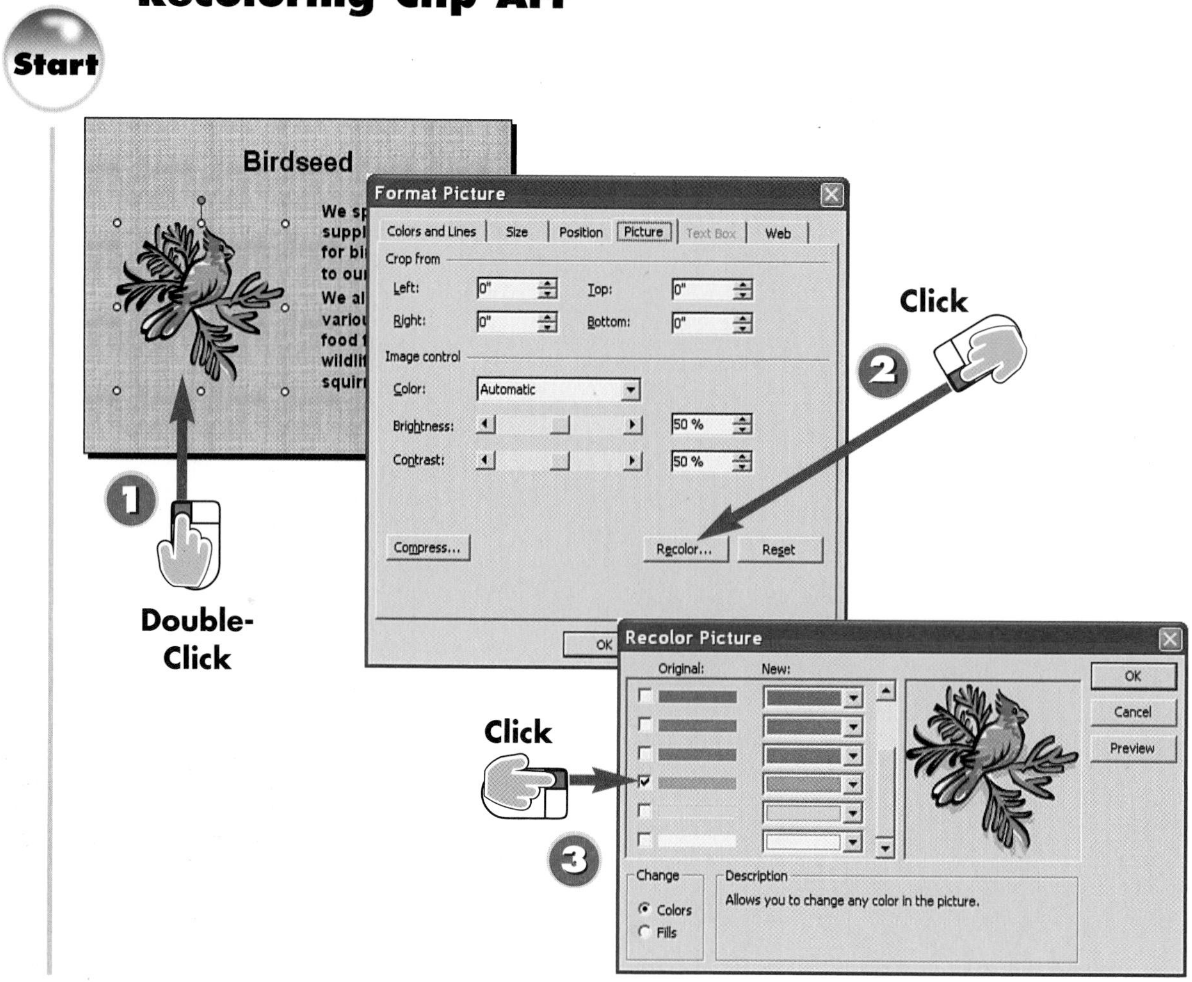

1. Double-click the clip-art object.
2. The Format Picture dialog box opens and displays the Picture tab. Click the **Recolor** button.
3. The Recolor Picture dialog box opens. Click the check box next to the color you want to edit to place a check mark in it.

INTRODUCTION

If the colors in the clip-art image you insert onto your slide do not match your slide's color scheme, you can change them. Recoloring clip art allows you to change the various colors associated with the image and choose colors that more closely coordinate with your slide's color scheme.

TIP

Clicking the Recolor Picture Button
Another way to access the Recolor Picture dialog box is to click the **Recolor Picture** button on the Picture toolbar. To view the toolbar, select **View**, **Toolbars**, **Picture**.

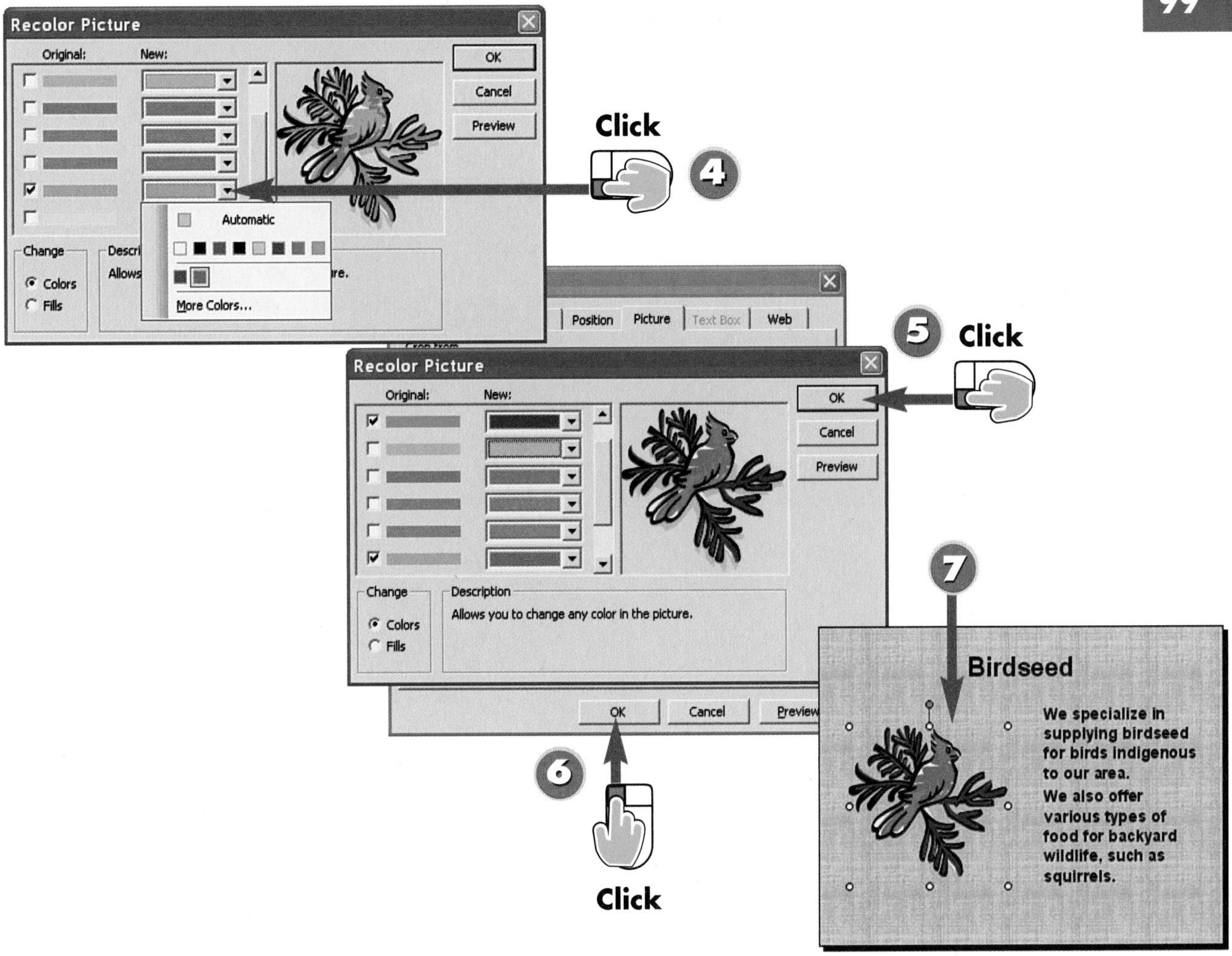

4. Click the **New** drop-down arrow and select a new color to apply.
5. Repeat steps 3 and 4 to modify other colors in the clip art, and then click **OK**.
6. Click **OK** in the Format Picture dialog box to apply your changes.
7. PowerPoint applies the new colors.

TIP

Leaving the Outline, Changing the Fill

To leave the outline color of the clip-art image unchanged, click the **Fills** option in the Recolor Picture dialog box before making changes to the clip-art colors. This tells PowerPoint to change the image's fill colors only.

Creating a Photo Album

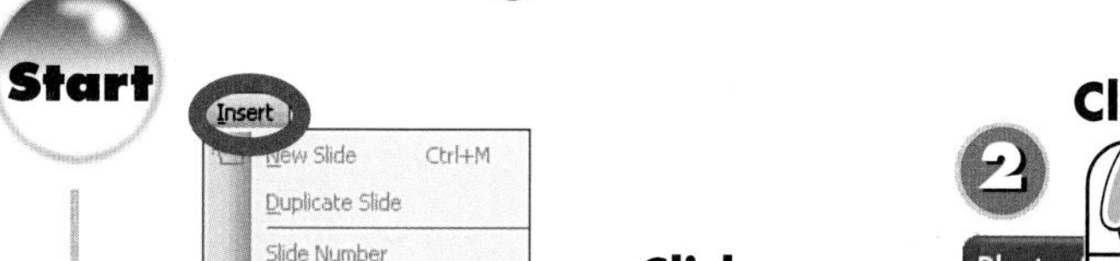

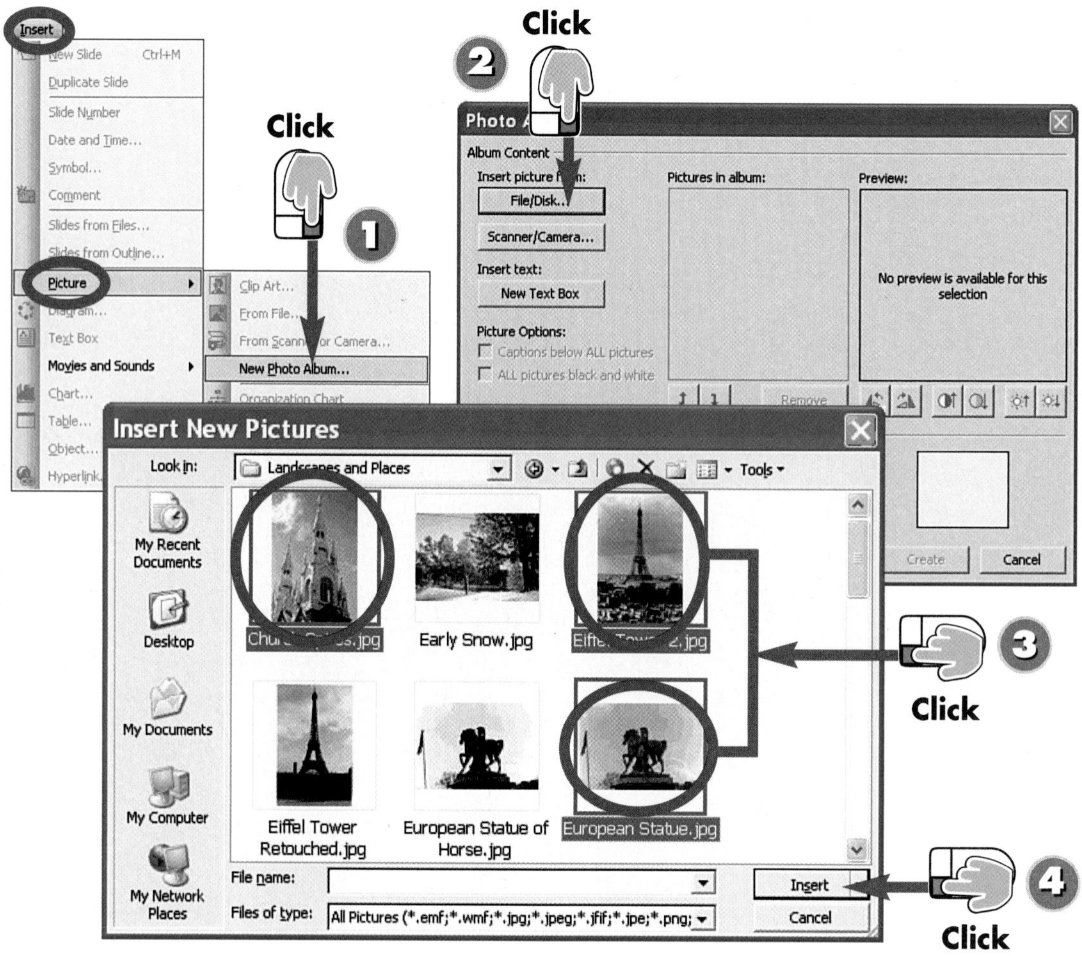

1. Click **Insert**, **Picture**, **New Photo Album**.

2. The Photo Album dialog box opens. Click the **File/Disk** button.

3. The Insert New Pictures dialog box opens. Locate and select all the photos you want to include. (Press and hold the **Ctrl** key while clicking photos to select multiple files.)

4. Click **Insert**.

INTRODUCTION

PowerPoint offers you a unique way to display photographs in a presentation: You can turn them into a photo album. The Photo Album feature takes the selected photograph files and turns them into slides.

TIP

Locating Photos
You can click the **Look In** drop-down arrow in the Insert New Pictures dialog box to look for photos in another folder or drive.

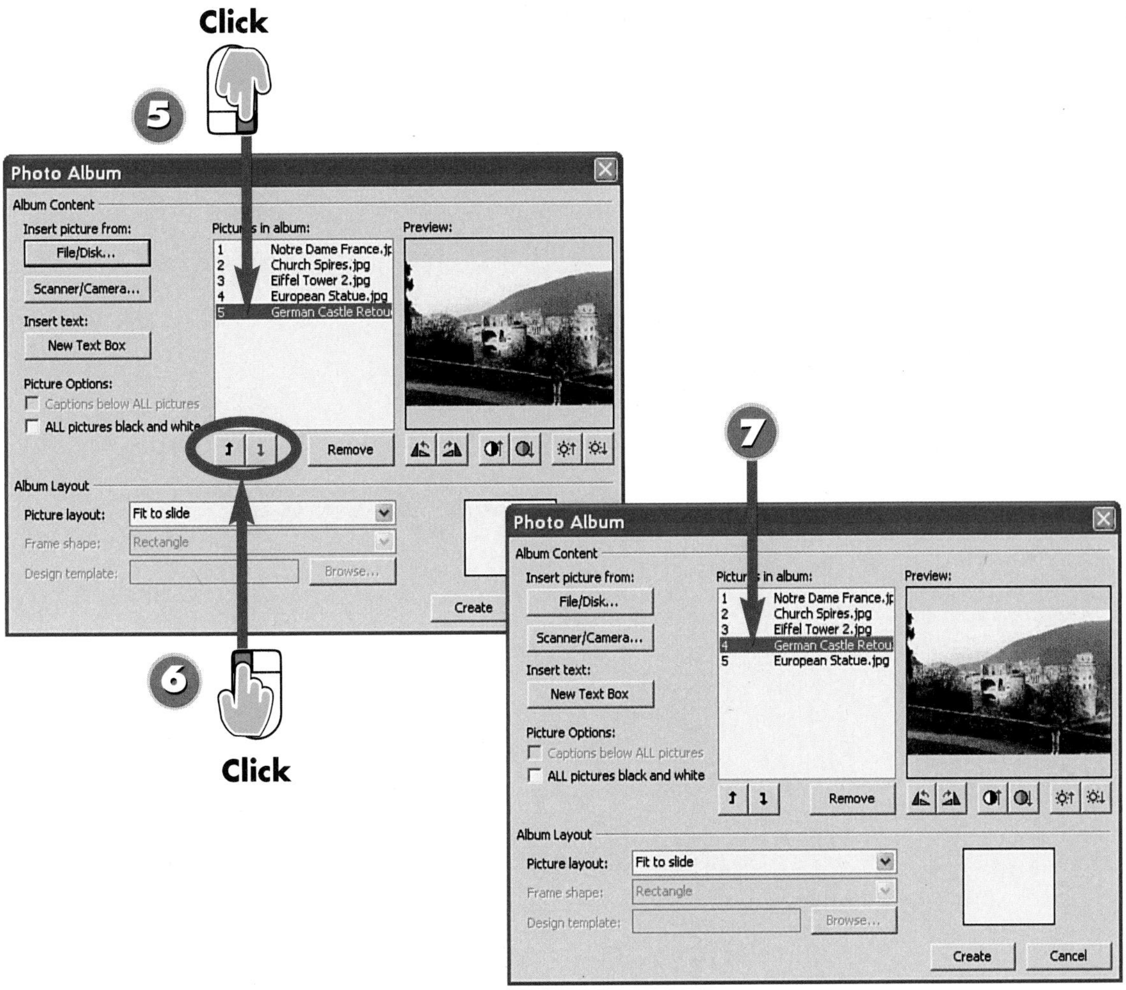

Click

Click

5 PowerPoint lists the names of the selected pictures. To move a picture in the list, first click the name to select the picture.

6 Click the **Up** or **Down** arrow to rearrange the selected picture in the list order.

7 The picture changes location in the list. Repeat steps 5 and 6 as needed until your photos appear in the desired order.

TIP

Removing a Photo from the List

If you accidentally selected pictures in the Insert New Picture dialog box that you do not need, you can easily remove them using the Photo Album dialog box. Click the name of the picture in the **Pictures in Album** list, and then click the **Remove** button to remove the picture.

TIP

Adjusting the Picture

In the Photo Album dialog box, you can adjust crooked pictures using the **Rotate Counterclockwise** or **Rotate Clockwise** buttons. Select the crooked image in the **Pictures in Album** list, and then click the button.

Creating a Photo Album (Continued)

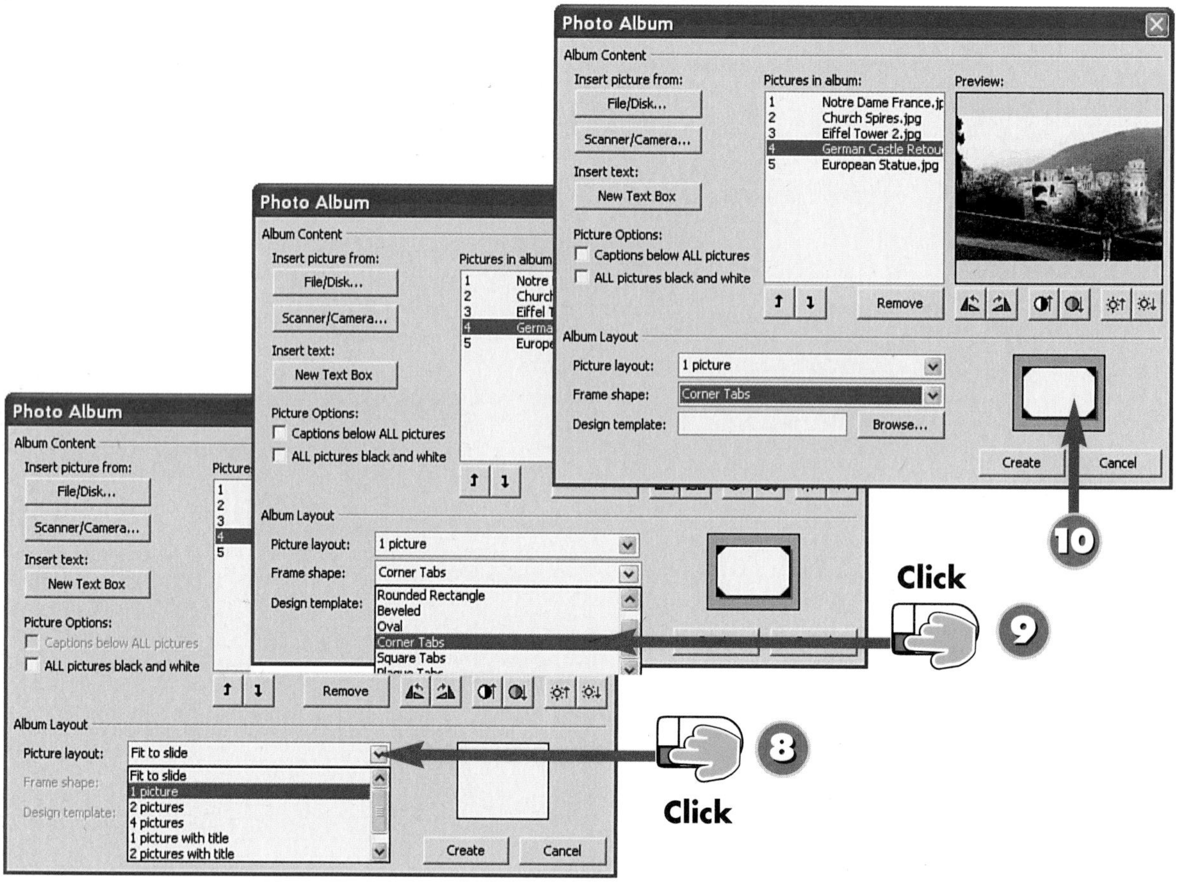

Click

Click

8 To specify how many pictures appear on each slide, click the **down arrow** next to the **Picture Layout** field and select the desired option (here, **1 Picture**).

9 To add a frame to the pictures in your photo album, click the **down arrow** next to the **Frame Shape** field and select a frame style (in this case, **Corner Tabs**).

10 The preview area displays how the pictures will appear on each slide, along with any special frames you select.

TIP

No Preview?
If you selected the **Fit to Slide** option for the picture layout, you will not see a preview of your layout or frame selection in the preview area.

HINT

Frame Styles
You can only apply one frame style for the entire album.

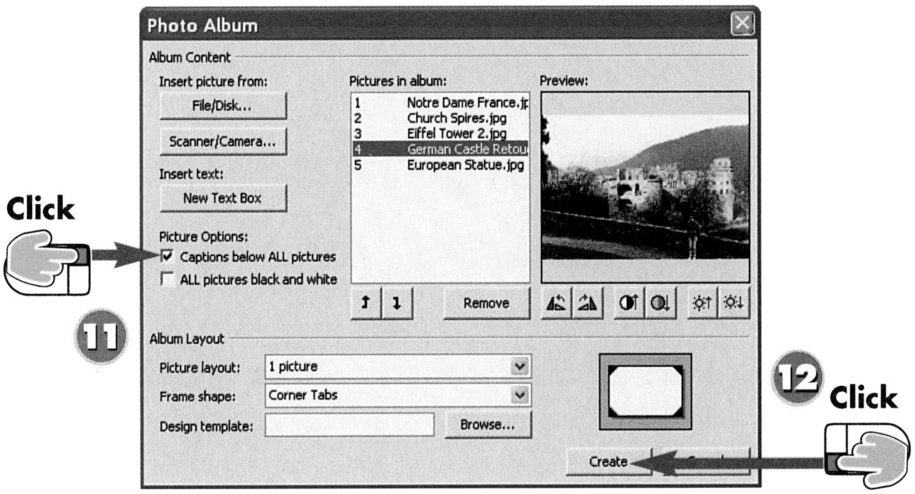

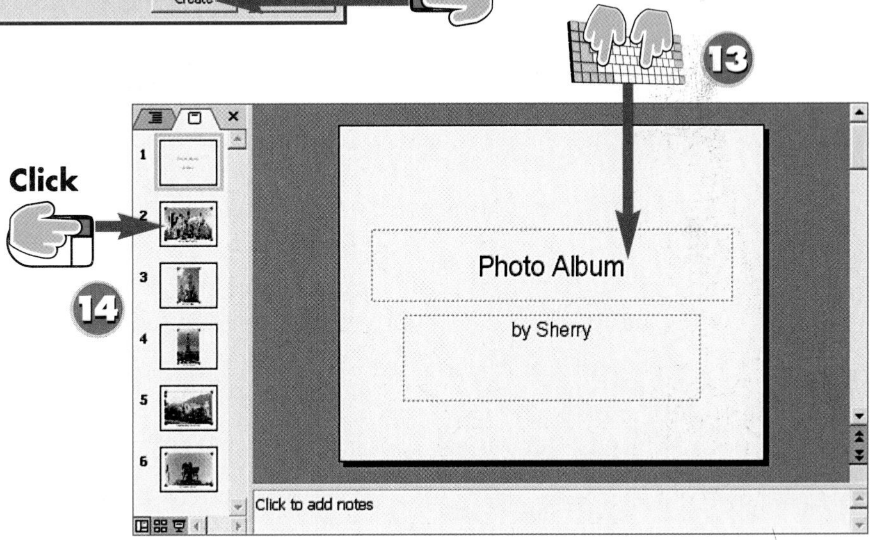

11 To include a caption for each image, click the **Captions Below ALL Pictures** check box.

12 Click **Create**.

13 PowerPoint creates the album, along with a title slide. To fill in the title slide placeholder, click the Photo Album text box and type another title, if desired.

14 The Slides tab lists all the photo slides. To view a photo, click a slide in the Slides tab area.

TIP

Adding Captions

If you chose to add captions below your photos, click the slide you want to add a caption to in the Slides tab, then click the caption area and type a new caption for the photo.

TIP

Saving the Album

You can save a photo album just like you save other presentations you create in PowerPoint. See Part 2 to learn more about saving PowerPoint files.

TIP

Editing the Album

To make changes to the pictures in your album, select **Format**, **Photo Album** to open the Format Photo Album dialog box. Here, you can change the picture order, frames, layout, and more.

Changing the Appearance of Slides

As you build your presentation, you might need to make changes to the appearance of your slides, such as changing backgrounds or adding header and footer text. PowerPoint offers a variety of ways to customize your slide's overall appearance. You can alter the slide's color scheme, for example, and even choose from an array of pre-coordinated schemes specially prepared by color professionals.

You can also customize slide backgrounds by assigning solid colors, patterns, and textures. You can even turn a picture into a slide background.

When making changes to the appearance of your slides, make sure your backgrounds do not conflict with the message text. You may need to make adjustments to text fonts, sizes, and styles to make sure slide text remains legible and easy to read.

Color Scheme Options

Color scheme options

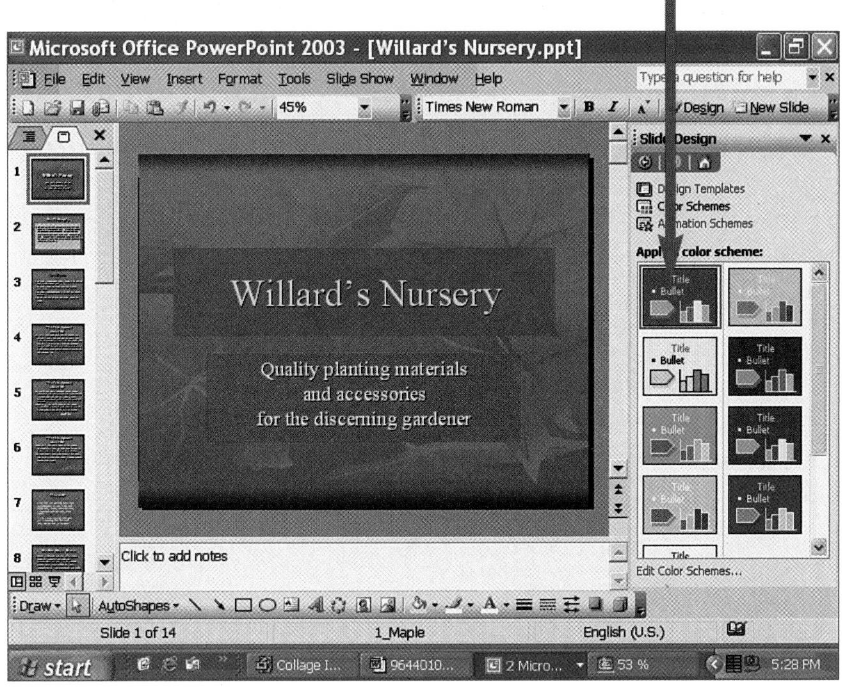

Changing the Design Template

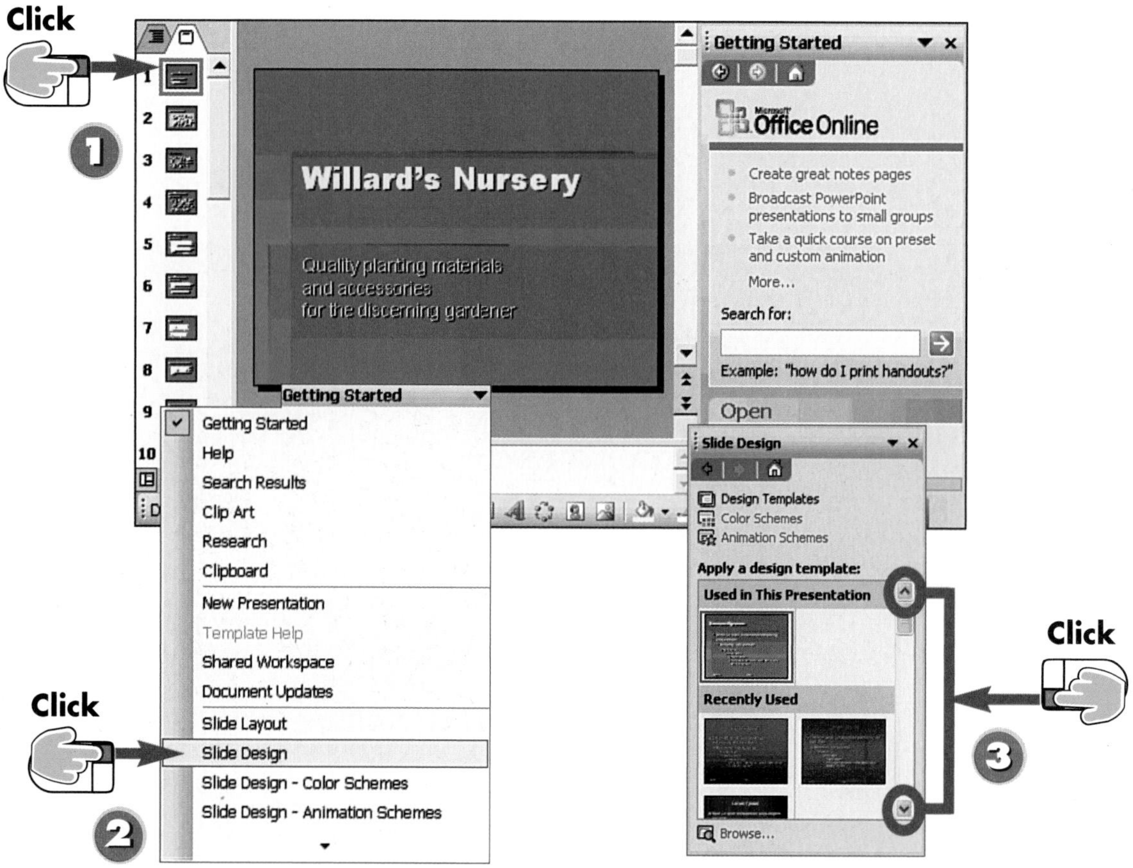

1. Click the slide to which you want to apply a new design.

2. From the Task pane, select **Other Task Panes**, and then click **Slide Design**.

3. The Slide Design Task pane appears. Click the scroll arrows to scroll through the list of available designs.

INTRODUCTION

As you learned in Part 2, you can use design templates to add color and backgrounds to your presentation. A *design template* is simply a preformatted color scheme, font style, and background for a presentation. You can use the Slide Design pane to try out other design templates.

TIP

Selecting Multiple Slides
To select multiple slides in the Slides tab, press and hold the **Ctrl** key while clicking on each slide you want to select.

TIP

Task Pane Help
To learn more about working with the Task pane, see Part 1.

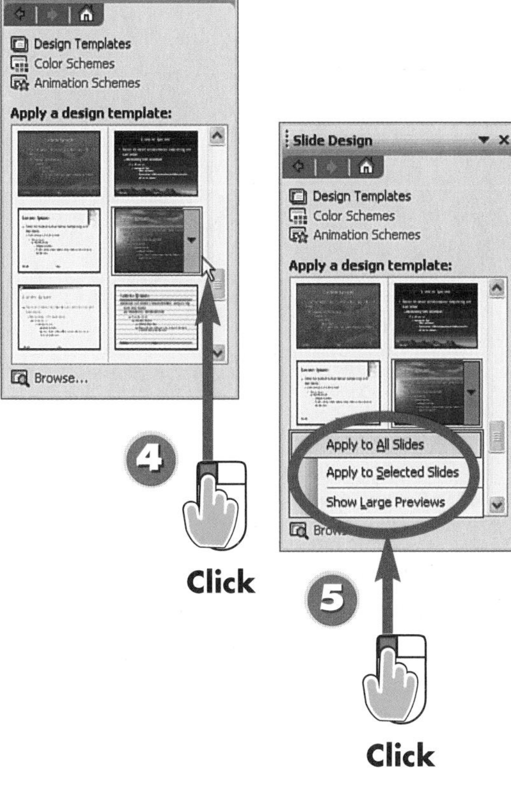

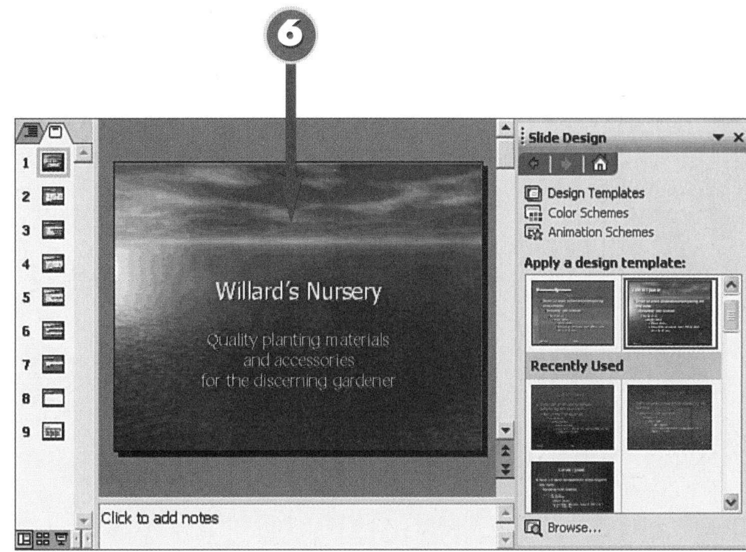

4. To control how a design is applied, move the mouse pointer over the design to display a drop-down arrow, then click the arrow.
5. Click **Apply to Selected Slides** to apply the design to the current slide, or click **Apply to All Slides** to apply the design to all the slides.
6. PowerPoint applies the new design. In this example, the design is applied only to the selected slide.

TIP

Showing Large Previews
You can zoom your view of the slide designs listed in the Slide Design pane. Move the mouse pointer over the design and click the drop-down arrow. Click **Show Large Previews** from the menu.

CAUTION

It's not a good idea to mix too many designs in a presentation. Viewing different slide backgrounds may be jarring to the presentation audience. The rule of thumb is to stick with a single design template throughout the presentation.

TIP

Finding More Designs
Scroll to the bottom of the Slide Design pane and click the **Additional Design Templates** option. PowerPoint prompts you to insert the CD-ROM you used to install the program, and then installs additional design templates.

Changing the Slide Color Scheme

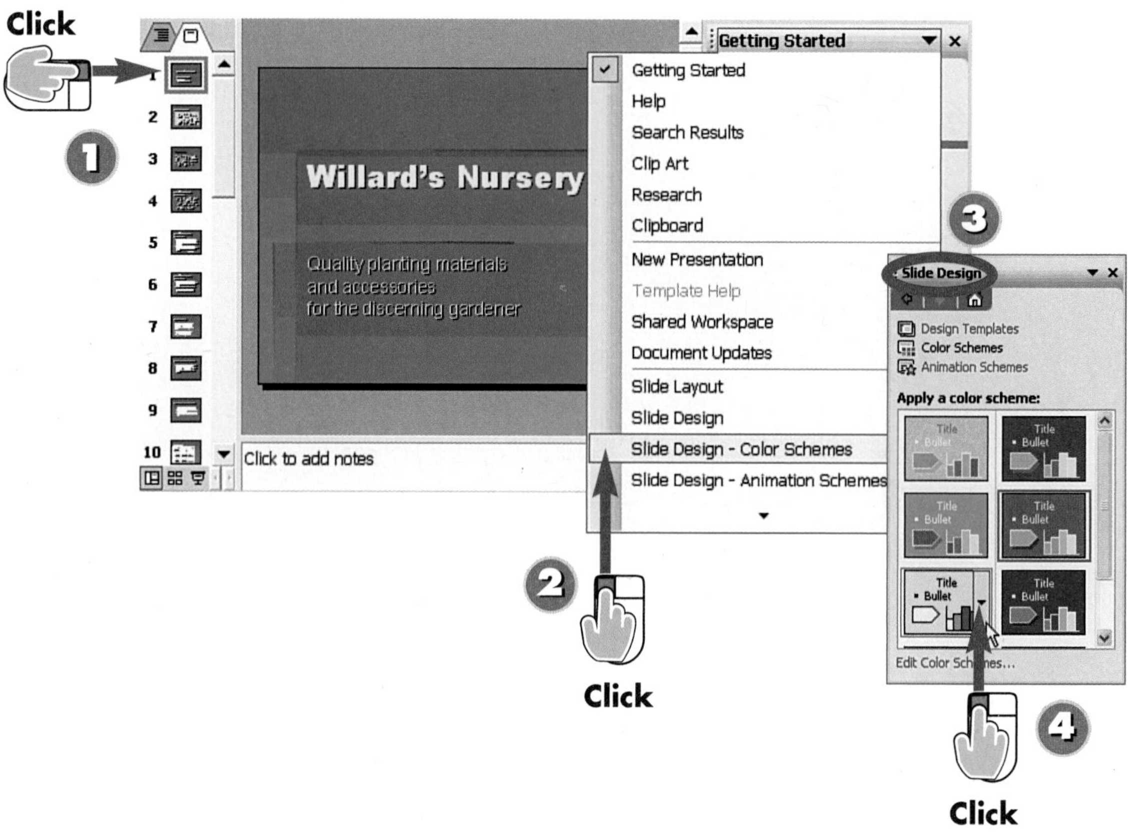

1. Select the slide to which you want to apply a new color scheme.

2. From the Task pane, select **Other Task Panes**, then click **Slide Design - Color Schemes**.

3. The Slide Design pane appears with a list of available color schemes.

4. Move the mouse pointer over the color scheme you want to apply and click the arrow that appears to the right of the color scheme.

INTRODUCTION

If you prefer to keep your slide designs simple, you can spruce up your slide backgrounds by changing the slide color scheme. Unlike design templates, which may use illustrations and textures, color schemes are professionally designed coordinated sets of colors. Each color scheme includes a background color, text and line colors, shadow colors, fill colors, and accent colors.

TIP

Selecting Multiple Slides
To select multiple slides in the Slides tab, press and hold the **Ctrl** key while clicking on each slide you want to select.

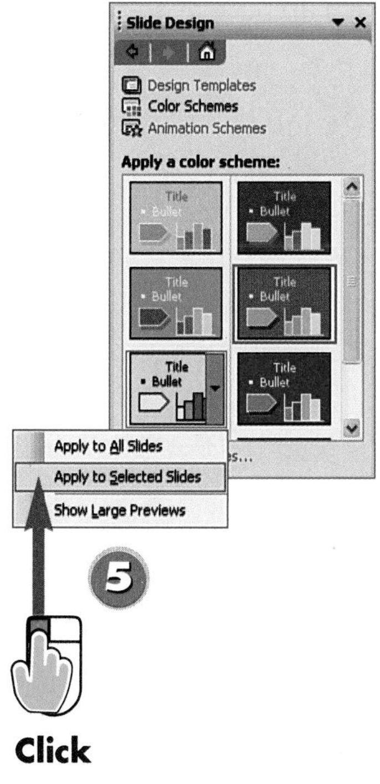

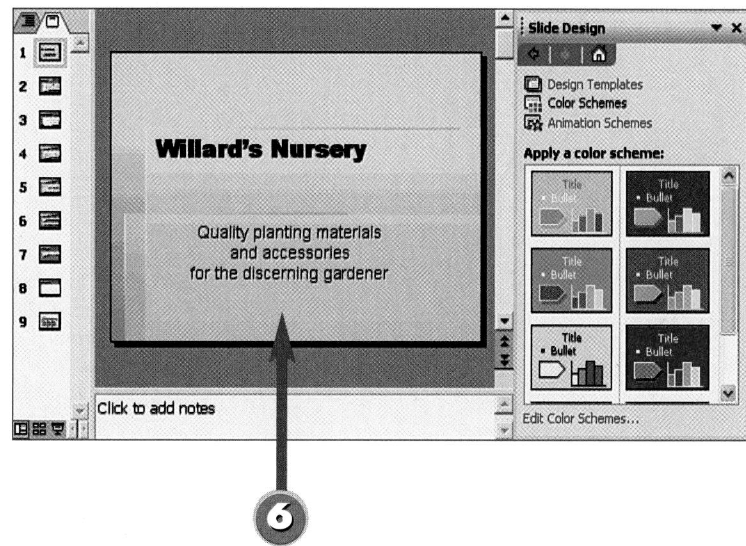

5. Click **Apply to All Slides** to assign the new color scheme to all the slides in the presentation, or **Apply to Selected Slides** to assign the scheme to selected slide.
6. The color scheme is applied.

TIP

Larger Previews

You can zoom your view of the slide color schemes listed in the Slide Design pane. To do so, move the mouse pointer over the color scheme and click the drop-down arrow that appears. Click **Show Large Previews** from the menu. PowerPoint displays larger versions of the color schemes in the pane.

TIP

What Are Animation Schemes?

Another link located below the Color Schemes link at the top of the Slide Design pane is **Animation Schemes**. You can use animation schemes to animate slide elements during a presentation.

Changing the Slide Background Color

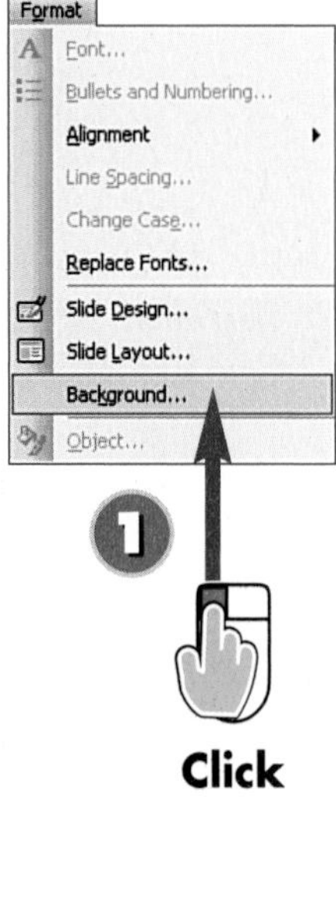

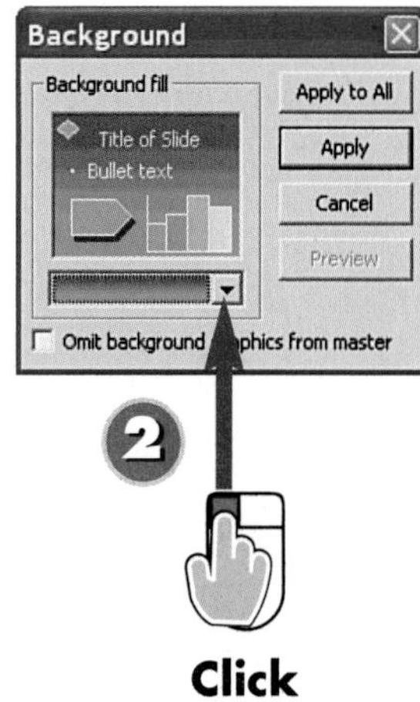

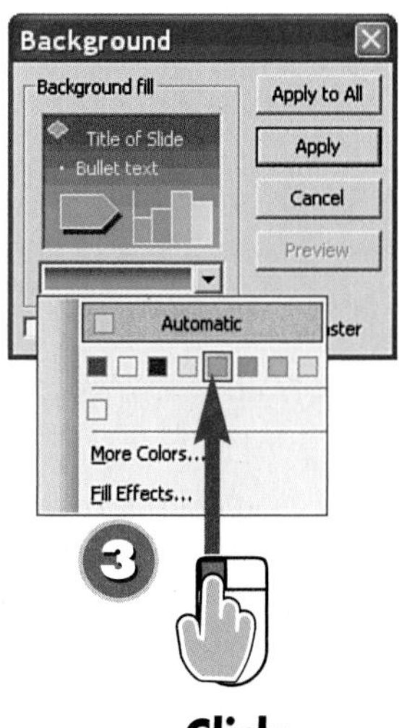

1. Open the **Format** menu and choose **Background**.
2. The Background dialog box opens. Click the **color** drop-down arrow.
3. Click a color.

INTRODUCTION

In addition to design templates and color schemes, you can also control the appearance of your slides by setting your own slide backgrounds. For example, you can choose a specific color for the background.

TIP

What If My Slide Already Has a Design?
If your slide already has a design template applied, changing the background color can change the overall design appearance. You can experiment with different color choices to change the design. To remove any background graphics associated with the design, click the **Omit Background Graphics from Master** check box in the Background dialog box.

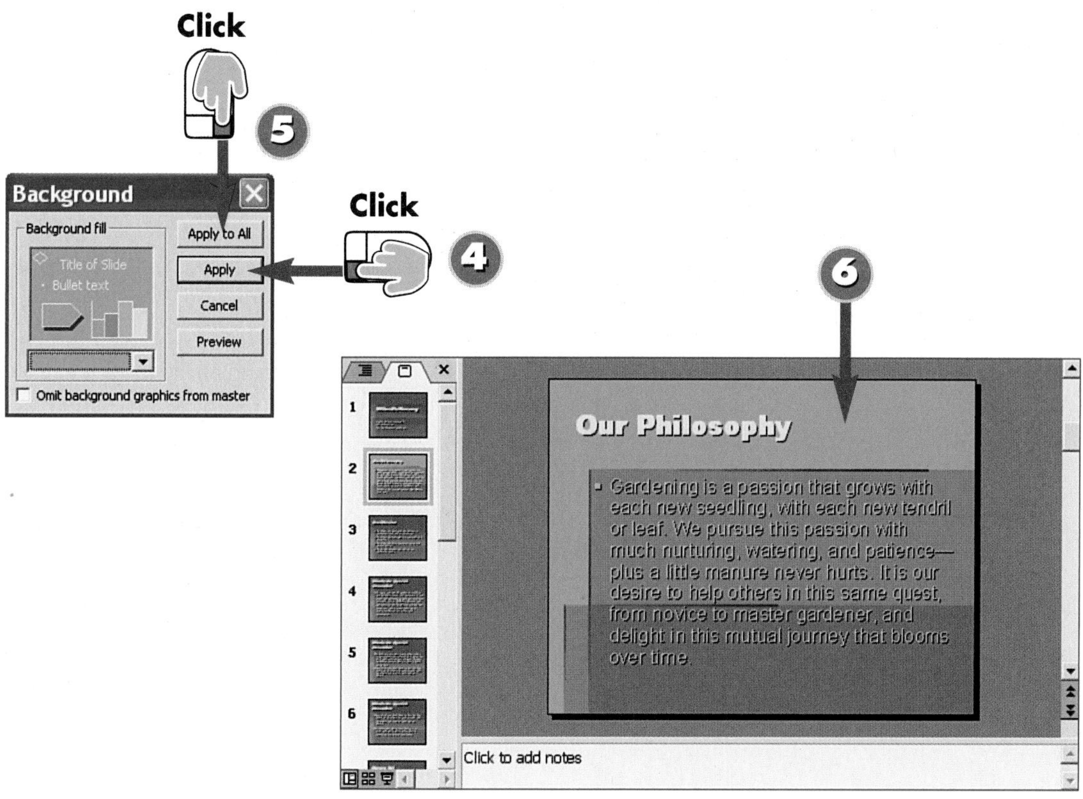

4. To apply the background to the current slide only, click **Apply**.
5. To apply the background to every slide in the presentation, click **Apply to All**.
6. The background color is applied.

TIP

Choosing from Additional Colors

The Background dialog displays colors based on the chosen color scheme. To choose from a full palette of colors, click the **More Colors** option in the color drop-down list in the Background dialog box. This opens the Colors dialog box, where you can pick another color from the palette.

TIP

Do Background Colors Affect a Text Boxes?

If you have previously assigned a background color to a text object, assigning a slide background color does not affect the text background. See Part 4 to learn more about assigning backgrounds to text boxes.

Changing the Slide Background Pattern or Texture

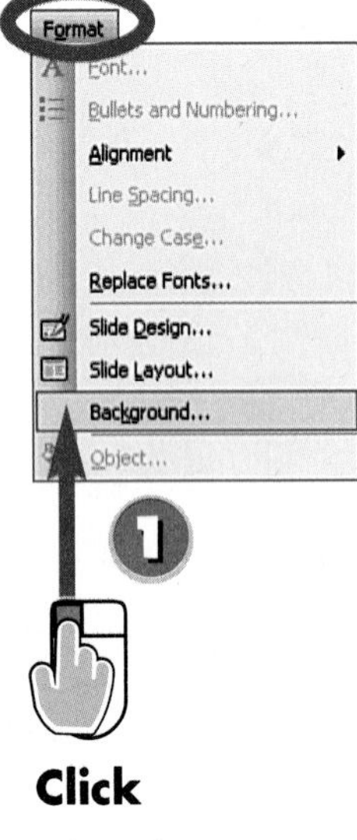

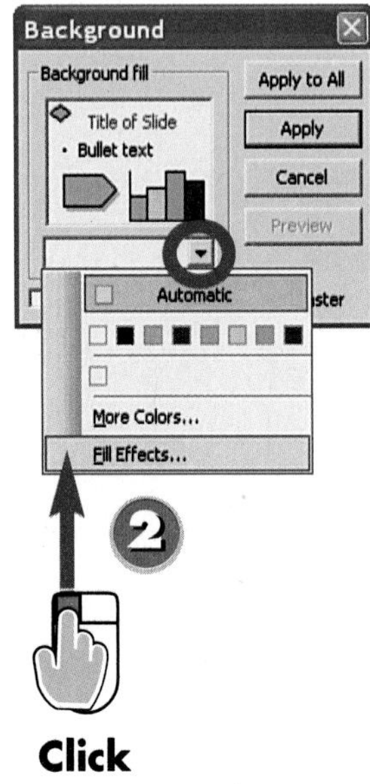

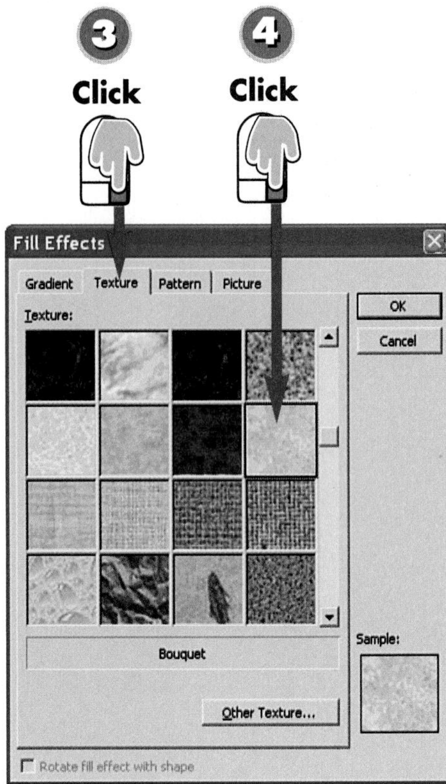

1. Open the **Format** menu and choose **Background**.
2. The Background dialog box opens. Click the **color** drop-down arrow and click **Fill Effects**.
3. The Fill Effects dialog box opens. Click the **Texture** tab.
4. Click the texture you want to use and click **OK**.

INTRODUCTION

You can apply a color pattern or texture to the slide background to create yet another choice of slide backgrounds. The Fill Effects dialog box offers a variety of textures and patterns you can apply.

HINT

Caution

Use caution when applying textures to your slides. Choosing a busy background texture can make your slide text difficult to read. You might need to adjust the boldness, color, or font size to remedy the situation, or try another texture. See Part 4 to learn more about working with slide text.

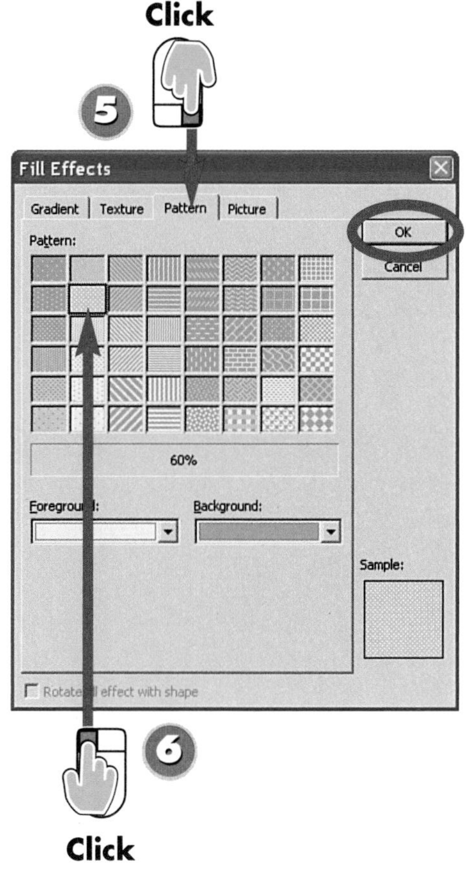

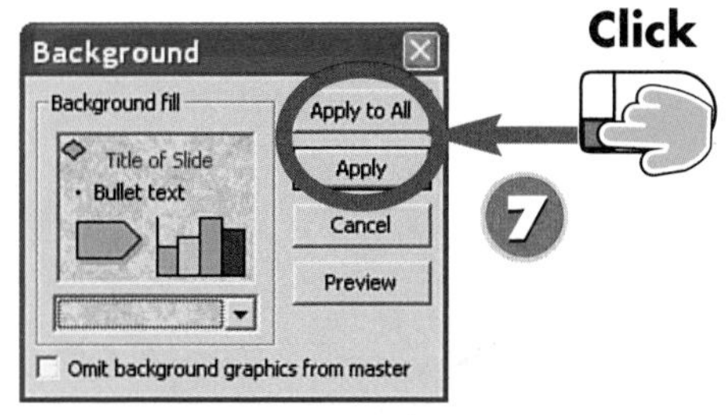

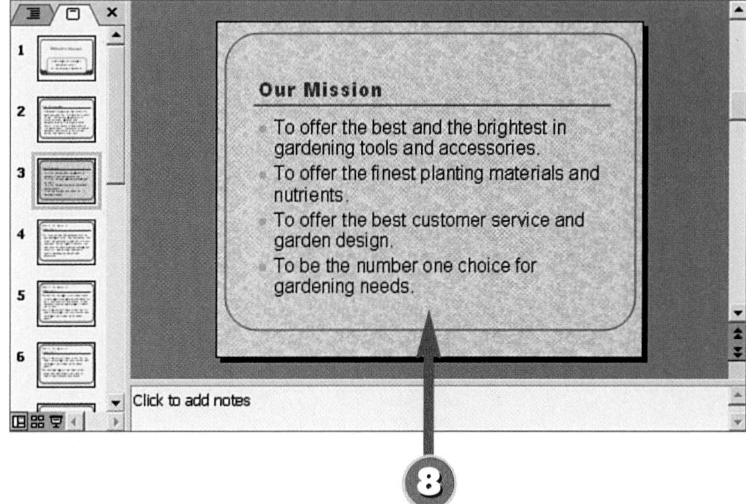

5. To apply a pattern instead of a texture, click the **Pattern** tab of the Fill Effects dialog box.

6. Click the pattern you want to use and click **OK**.

7. Click **Apply** to apply the texture or pattern to the current slide, or click **Apply to All** to apply it to all the slides in the presentation.

8. PowerPoint applies the new texture or pattern. In this example, a texture is applied to the current slide.

TIP

Choosing a Pattern Color
To choose a specific color for your background pattern, click the Foreground or Background drop-down arrow on the Pattern tab and specify a color.

TIP

Changing the Text Color
If you choose a texture or pattern that makes your slide text illegible, you can try changing the text color to alleviate the problem. See Part 4 to learn how to change the color of text in a text object.

Changing the Slide Background to a Gradient Effect

Start

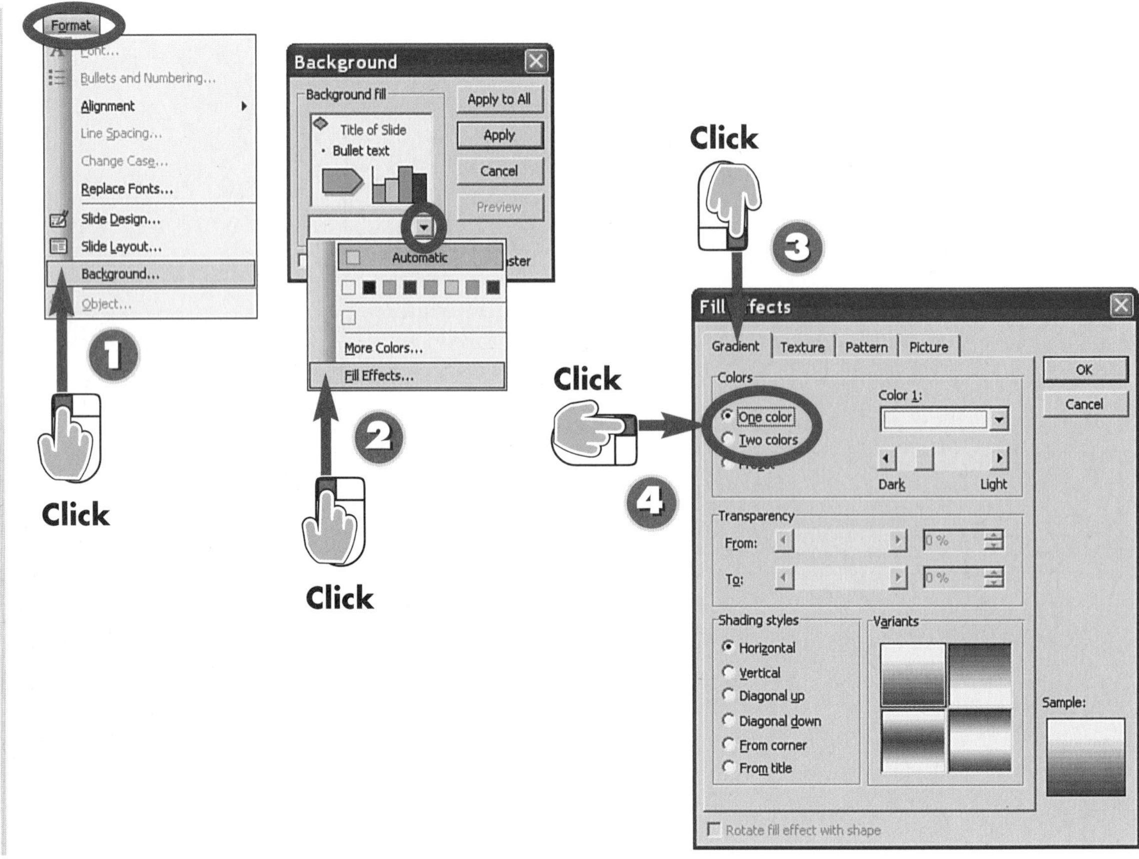

1. Open the **Format** menu and choose **Background**.
2. The Background dialog box opens. Click the **color** drop-down arrow and click **Fill Effects**.
3. The Fill Effects dialog box opens. Click the **Gradient** tab if it is not already displayed.
4. Click the **One Color** or **Two Colors** option. Use one color if you want to blend a color with white, or two colors to blend two different colors.

INTRODUCTION

You can use a gradient effect as a type of background for your slides. A *gradient effect* is simply the blending of two colors. You can blend a color with white, or you can blend two different colors. You can apply a gradient background to your slide presentation by mixing colors using options available in the Fill Effects dialog box. You can also control the direction of the blending effect.

TIP

Opening the Background Dialog Box

Another way to open the Background dialog box is to use a shortcut menu. Right-click on an empty area of the slide to reveal the shortcut menu, then select **Background**.

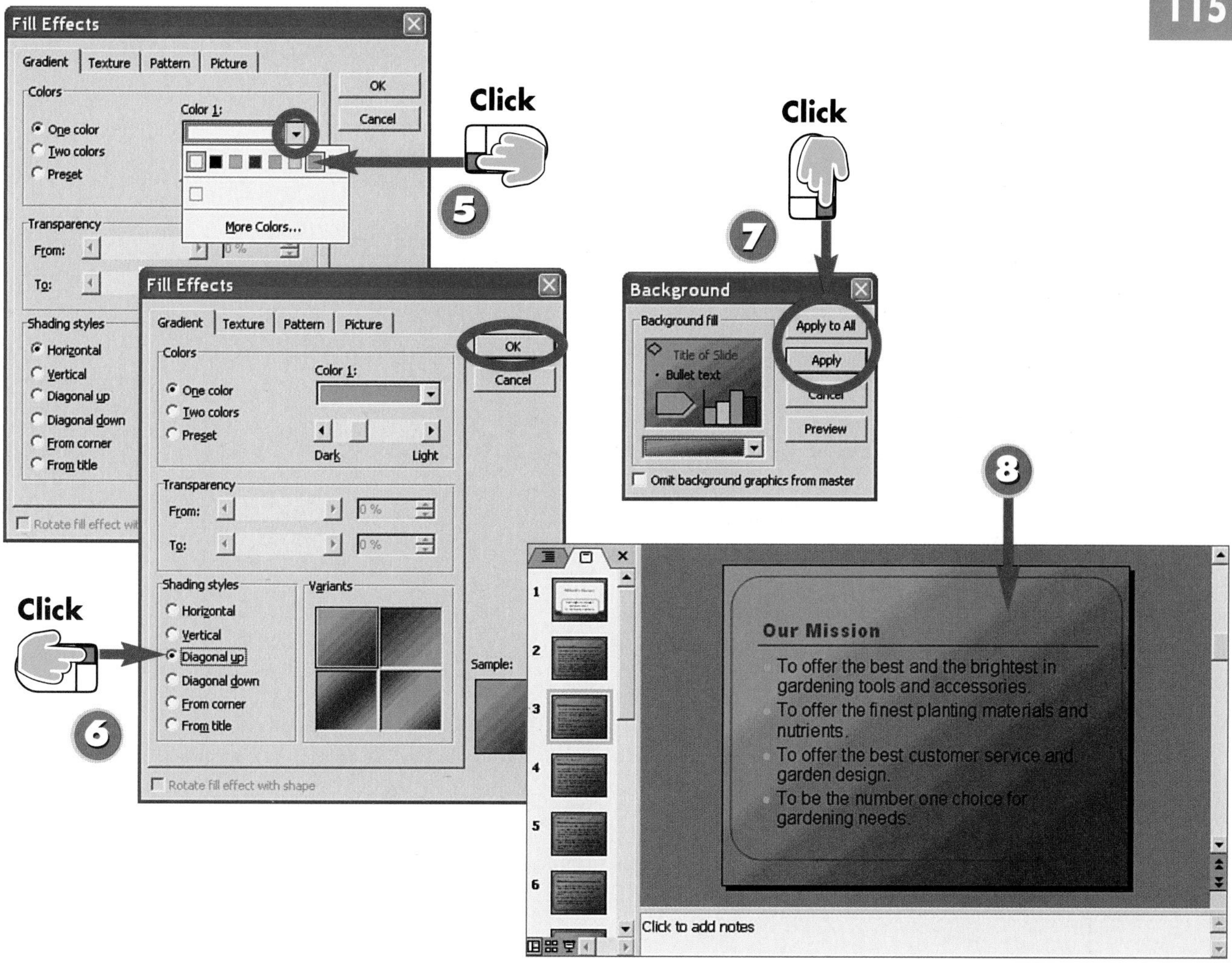

5 Select the **color** drop-down arrows and choose the gradient colors.

6 Select a shading style to control the direction of the gradient effect and click **OK**.

7 Click **Apply** or **Apply to All**.

8 PowerPoint applies the gradient effect. In this example, the effect is applied to all the slides.

TIP

Using Preset Gradients
PowerPoint offers several preset gradient effects you can apply. In the Fill Effects dialog box, click the **Gradient** tab and click the **Preset** option instead of choosing a color. This displays the **Preset Colors** option. Click the option to view a list of available gradients and select the one you want to apply. Click **OK** to apply the effect.

TIP

Controlling Color Intensity
If you choose the **One Color** option for your gradient effect, you can control the darkness and lightness levels of the effect by clicking the **Dark** and **Light** arrow buttons.

Start

Saving a Custom Background as a Design Template

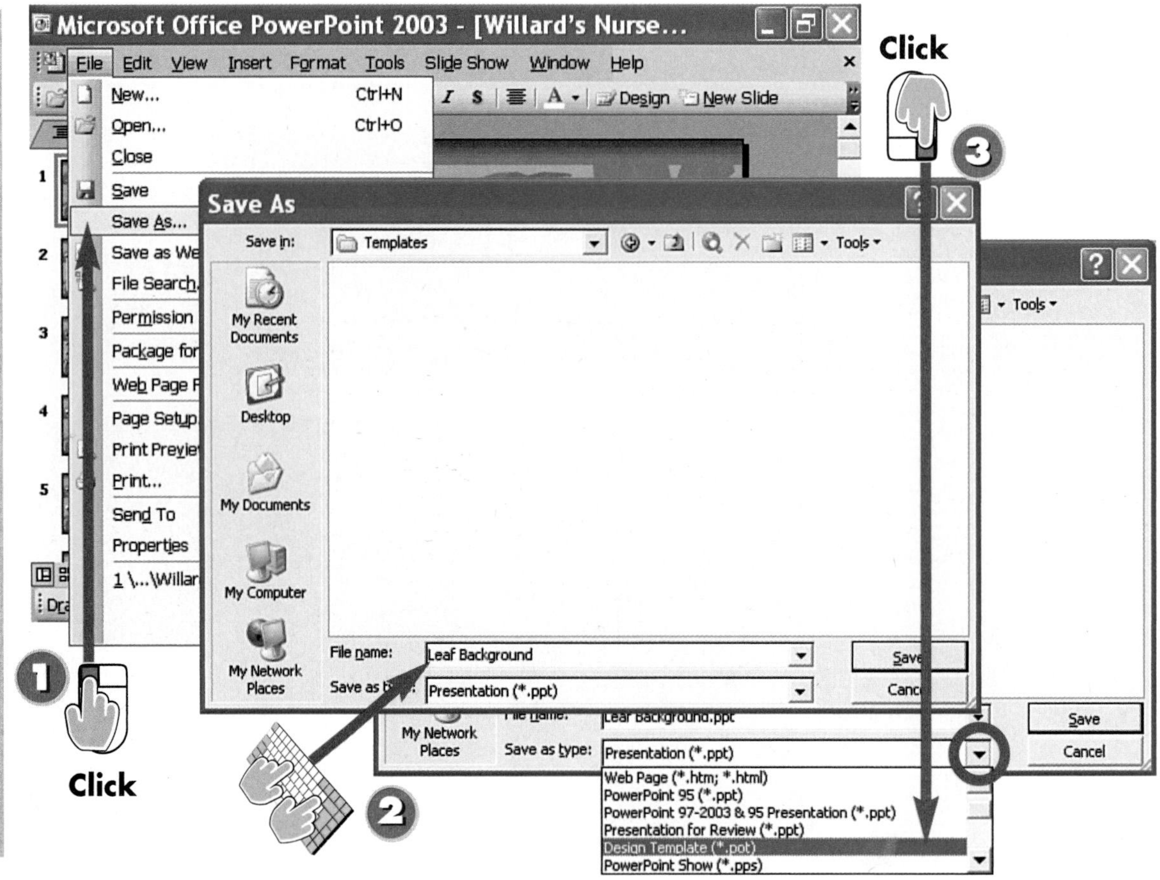

1. Open the **File** menu and choose **Save As**.
2. The Save As dialog box appears. Type a name for the slide design in the **File Name** field.
3. Click the down arrow next to the **Save As Type** field and choose **Design Template** from the list that appears.

INTRODUCTION

If you customize your slide background and get it just the way you want it, you can save your work and reuse the same settings again. To do so, save the customized background as a slide design template and then apply the design to other presentations as needed. Customized designs are saved by default to the Template folder.

TIP

Storing the Template in My Documents

You can save your template in any folder, but you will need to use the Browse feature to locate the template and apply it to your slides. It's faster to keep templates stored in the Templates folder.

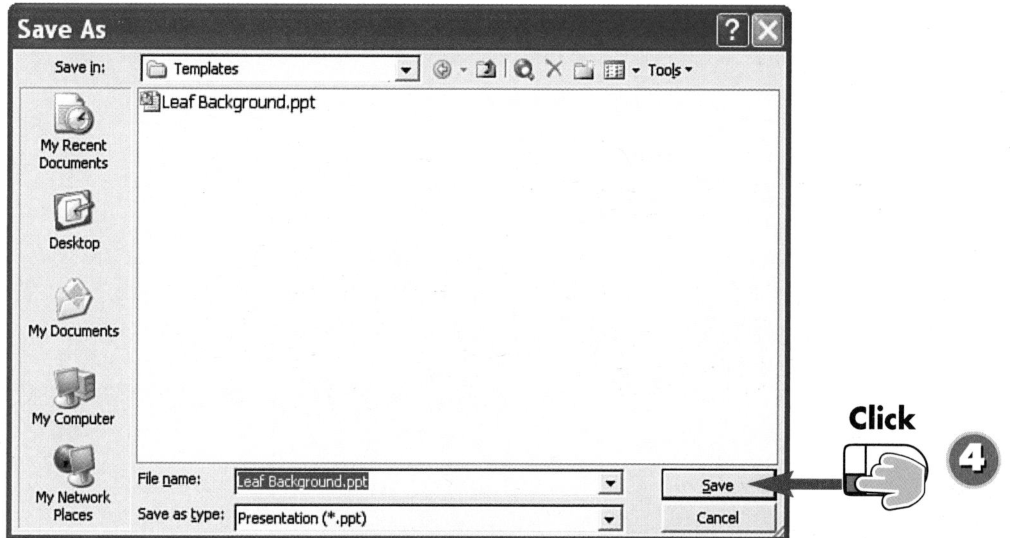

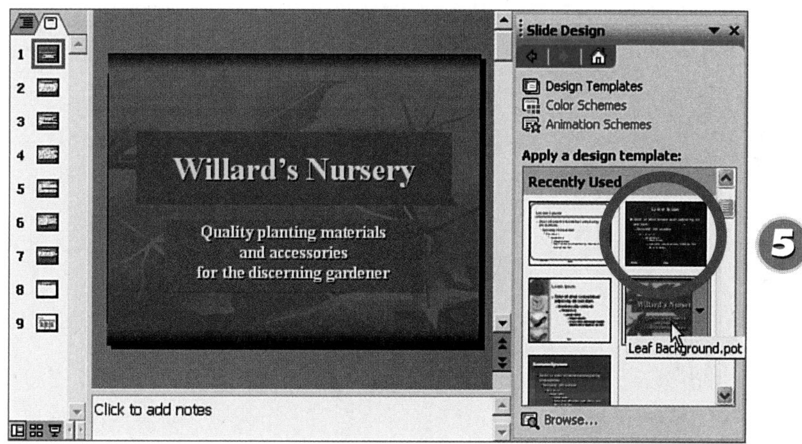

4. Click **Save**.

5. PowerPoint saves the design as a template file and lists it in the Slide Design pane.

TIP

Assigning the Design

When you create a new template, PowerPoint adds the template to the scrollable list of designs in the Slide Design pane. You can click the design to apply it to your presentation slides.

TIP

My Template Is Not Listed!

If you cannot find your design template listed, click the **Browse** link at the very bottom of the pane to open the Apply Design Template dialog box. Locate and select the template design and click **Apply**.

TIP

Removing a Template

To remove a custom template from the list, open the Slide Design pane and click the **Browse** link to open the Apply Design Template dialog box. Locate and select the template design and click **Delete**.

Setting Header and Footer Text

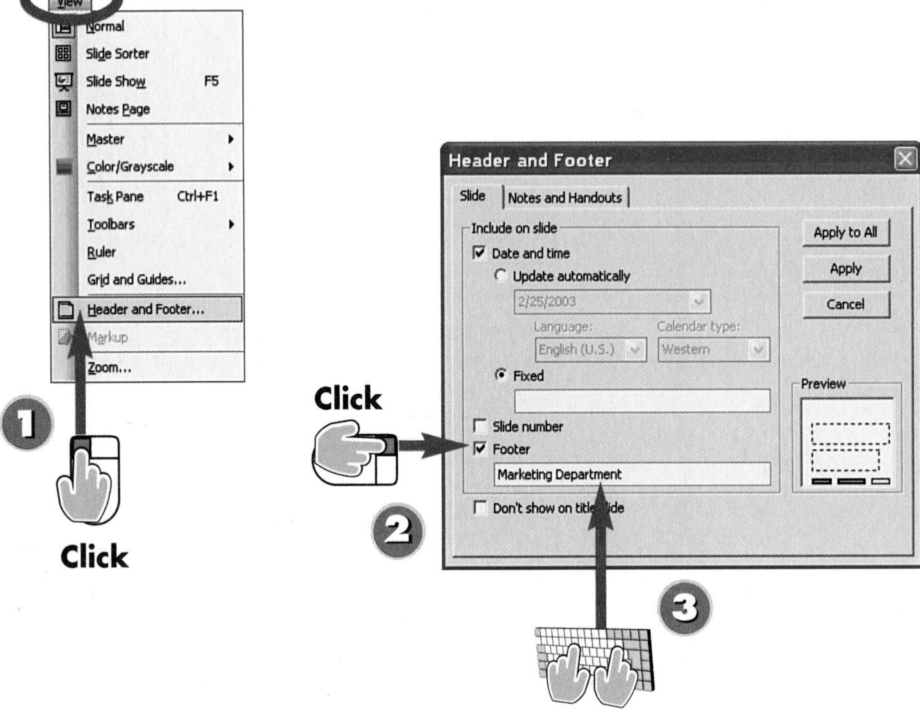

1. Open the **View** menu and choose **Header and Footer**.
2. The Header and Footer dialog box opens, displaying the Slide tab. To add a footer, click the **Footer** check box.
3. Type the text you want to appear at the bottom of each slide.

INTRODUCTION

Another way to alter the appearance of your slides is to add header and footer text. You can use header and footer text to display the same information on every slide in your presentation, such as the company name, your name, or the date. Header text appears at the top of the slide, while footer text appears at the bottom of the slide. Header text is limited to the date and time, while footer text can be any text you want to include on the slide.

TIP

AutoContent Wizard Slides

If you used the AutoContent wizard to create a presentation, header and footer text may appear automatically based on the presentation type you selected. Edit the text using the Header and Footer dialog box.

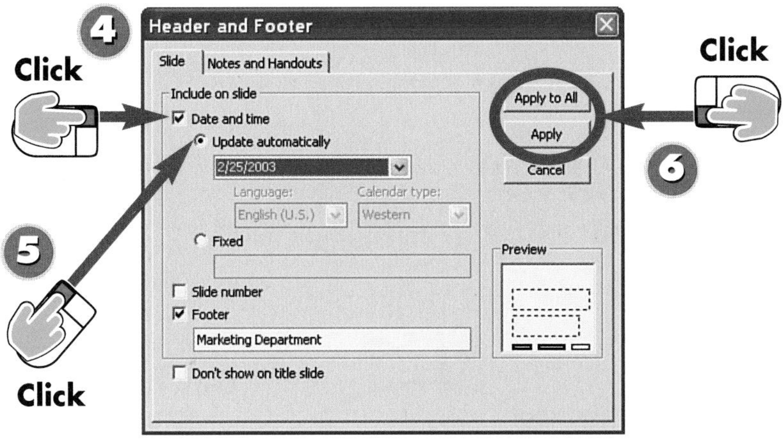

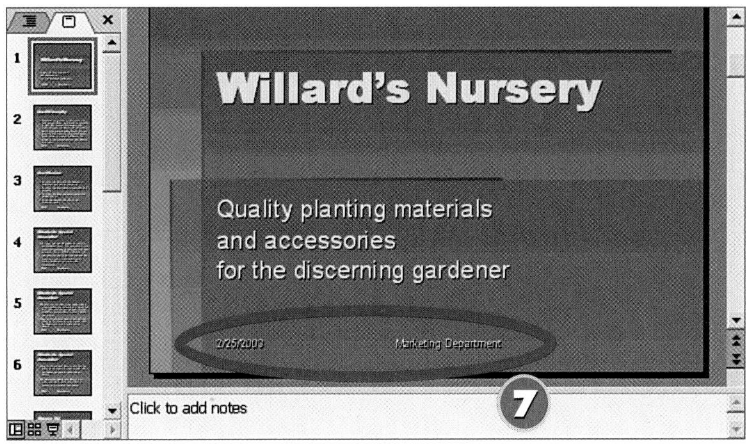

4. To include the date and time as header text, be sure the **Date and Time** check box is selected.

5. Click **Update Automatically** to let PowerPoint keep track of the current date, or click **Fixed** and enter a specific date.

6. Click **Apply to All** to add the header and footer text to every slide, or click **Apply** to add the text to the current slide only.

7. The header and/or footer text appears on the slide.

TIP

Editing the Placement of Headers and Footers

To change how header and footer text appears on a slide, or to change their font, you must edit the text objects in the Slide master. Select **View**, **Master**, **Slide Master** to open the Slide Master. You can now make changes to the various text boxes for headers and footers. For example, you can change alignment, remove boxes, or change the font and style. See the next task to learn more about editing the Slide master.

TIP

Setting Headers and Footers for Notes Pages

To set header and footer text for any notes or handout pages you plan to use, click the **Notes and Handouts** tab in the Header and Footer dialog box. Here you'll find additional options.

Changing Slides with the Slide Master

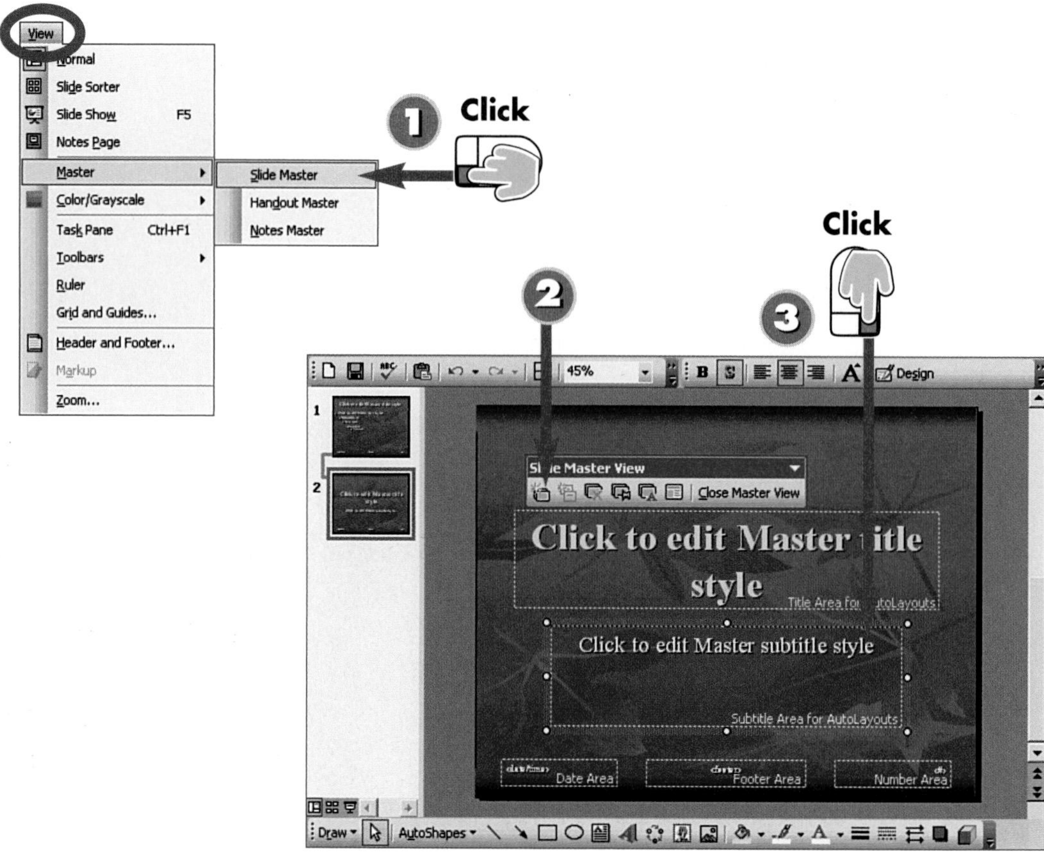

1. Open the **View** menu, choose **Master**, and choose **Slide Master**.
2. Slide Master view opens onscreen along with the Slide Master View toolbar.
3. Click the text object you want to edit and use the Formatting toolbar to make changes to the font, size, style, or alignment of the text.

INTRODUCTION

Slide masters control the overall appearance of a slide design, including the placement of slide objects, text fonts, and more. Every slide design in PowerPoint is based on a Slide Master that controls the slide appearance, even a presentation based on a blank slide. You can make changes to a design's Slide Master to customize all the slides in your presentation at once. Adjusting the Slide Master does not alter existing slide content, only the appearance of the slide.

TIP

Formatting Slide Text?
To learn more about using the various text-formatting commands available in PowerPoint, see Part 4.

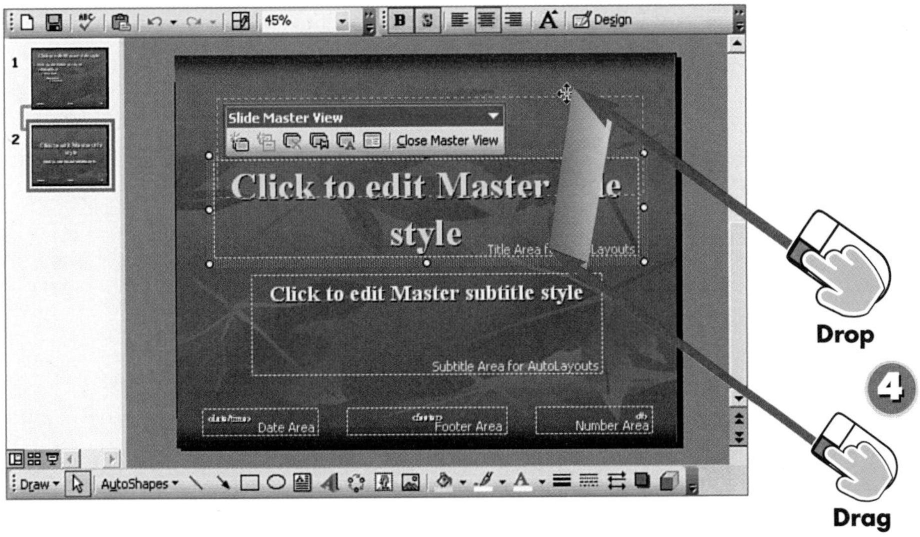

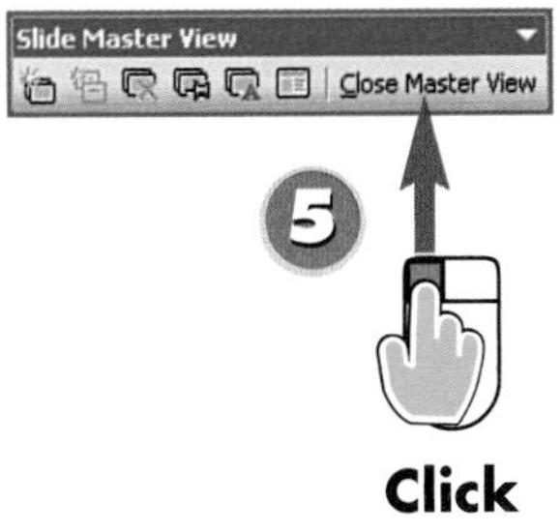

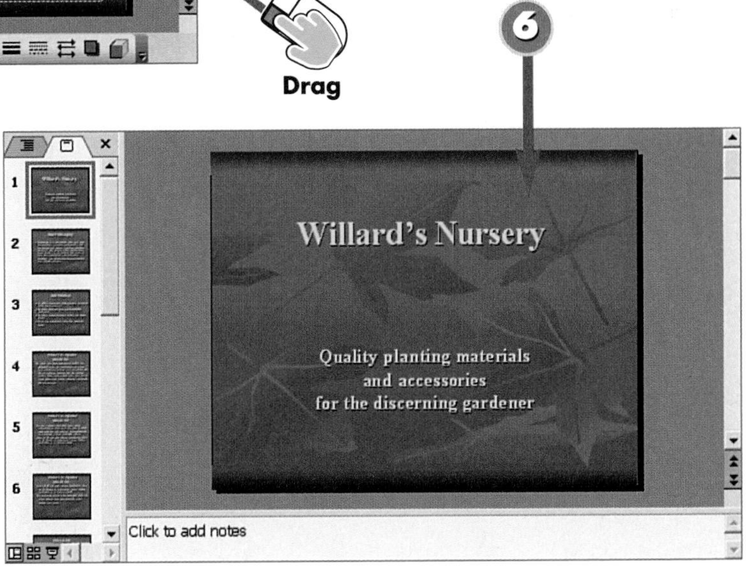

Drop

4

Drag

6

5

Click

4. To edit the placement of a text object, click and drag the object to a new location on the Slide Master.

5. When finished editing the Slide Master, click **Close Master View**.

6. PowerPoint returns you to the current slide and any changes you made are reflected in all the slides based on that particular Slide Master.

TIP

Using Other Masters

PowerPoint also includes masters for title slides, notes, and handouts. You can modify each type of master to customize the slide, notes, or handouts pages. See Part 10 to learn more about slide notes and handouts.

TIP

Adding Slide Elements to a Master

You can add text boxes and other slide objects, such as clip art or charts, so that each slide that uses that Slide Master includes the same elements. This saves you time from having to add each element to each slide yourself.

Adding Charts and Diagrams

Charts and diagrams are a great way to present data to your audience. PowerPoint includes a charting feature that allows you to enter your own data to create a chart. You can choose from a variety of chart types, such as pie charts and bar graphs, and select chart colors that coordinate with your slide's color scheme.

You can also create quick and easy diagrams such as organization charts, cycle diagrams, radial diagrams, pyramid diagrams, and more. Like the charting feature, the diagram feature lets you customize the appearance of the diagram as well as the information it displays.

PowerPoint's Charting Feature

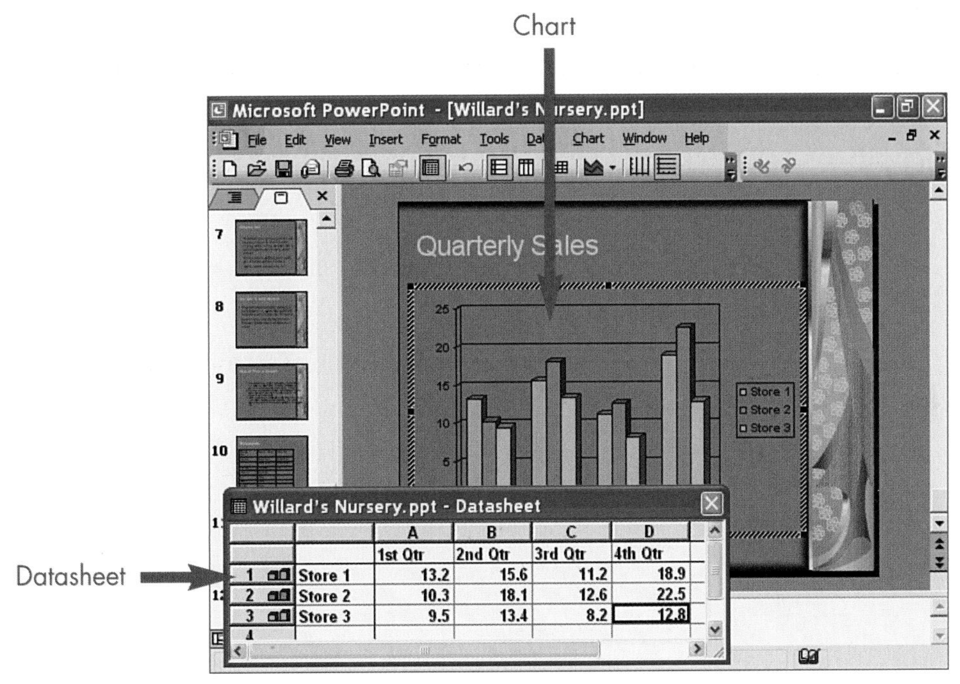

Adding a Chart

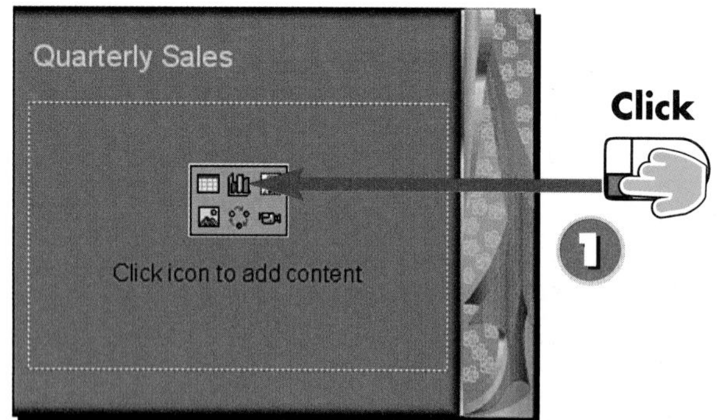

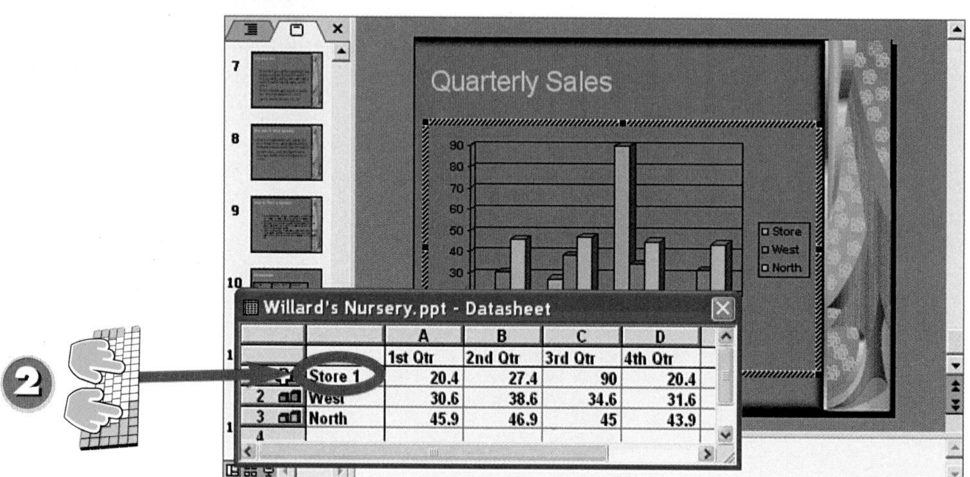

1. Click the **Insert Chart** icon in the placeholder slide object.

2. A datasheet appears, along with a default chart. To enter chart data, click in the first datasheet cell and type the data, and press **Enter**. PowerPoint moves the cursor to the next cell in the chart.

INTRODUCTION

You can create your own charts in PowerPoint using the charting feature. Several slide layouts include placeholder slide objects for creating charts. When activated, the chart feature opens a default column chart along with a datasheet. The datasheet resembles worksheets found in spreadsheet programs such as Microsoft Excel. You can enter your own chart information into the datasheet using rows and columns.

TIP

Adding a Chart Without a Chart Placeholder

You need not use a layout that already contains a chart placeholder; you can add a new chart to any slide. To do so, click the **Insert Chart** button on the Standard toolbar.

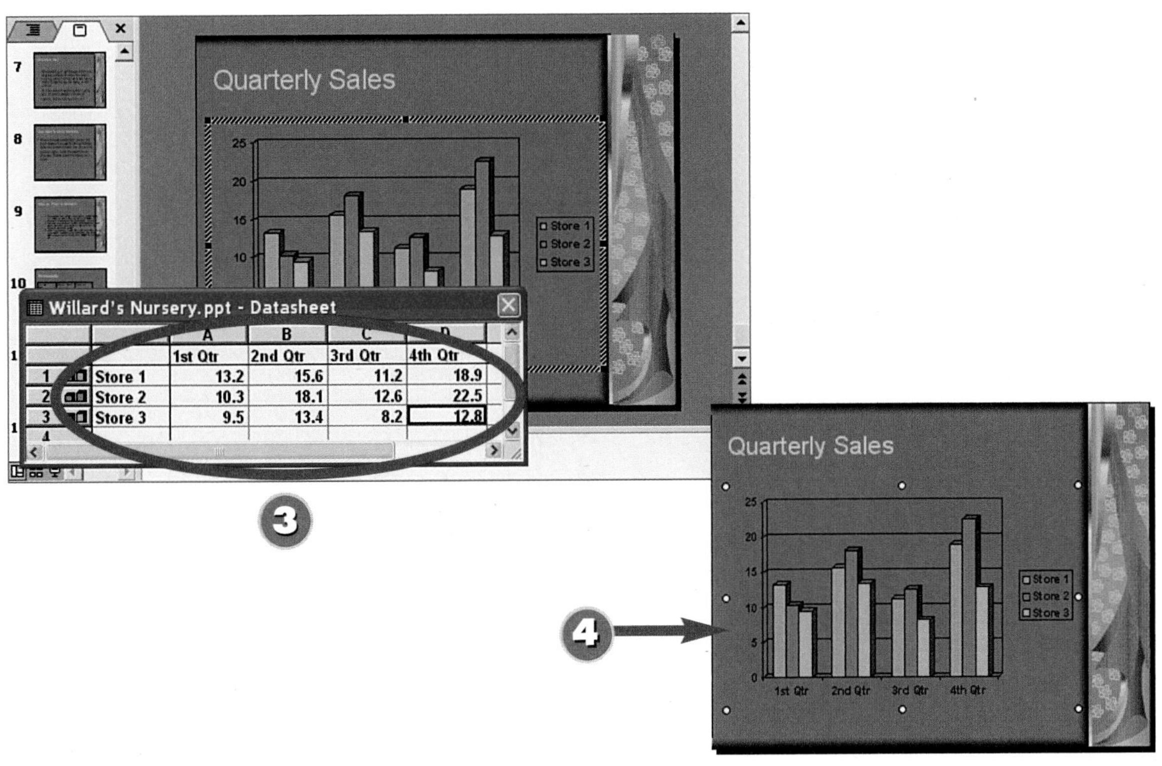

3 Continue adding your data to the cells. (Press **Tab** to move from cell to cell, or the arrow keys to move around the cells.) When you finish, click anywhere outside the datasheet.

4 PowerPoint returns you to Normal view, and the chart appears on the slide.

TIP

Enlarging the Datasheet
If you require more room in the datasheet for values, you can click and drag any corner of the datasheet to increase its size.

TIP

Resizing the Chart on the Slide
Click the chart to select it, and PowerPoint surrounds it with selection handles. You can then click and drag a handle to resize the chart. Charts act like any other slide object, which means you can resize them.

TIP

Deleting a Chart
To remove a chart object, first select the chart, and then press the **Delete** key on your keyboard.

Changing the Chart Type

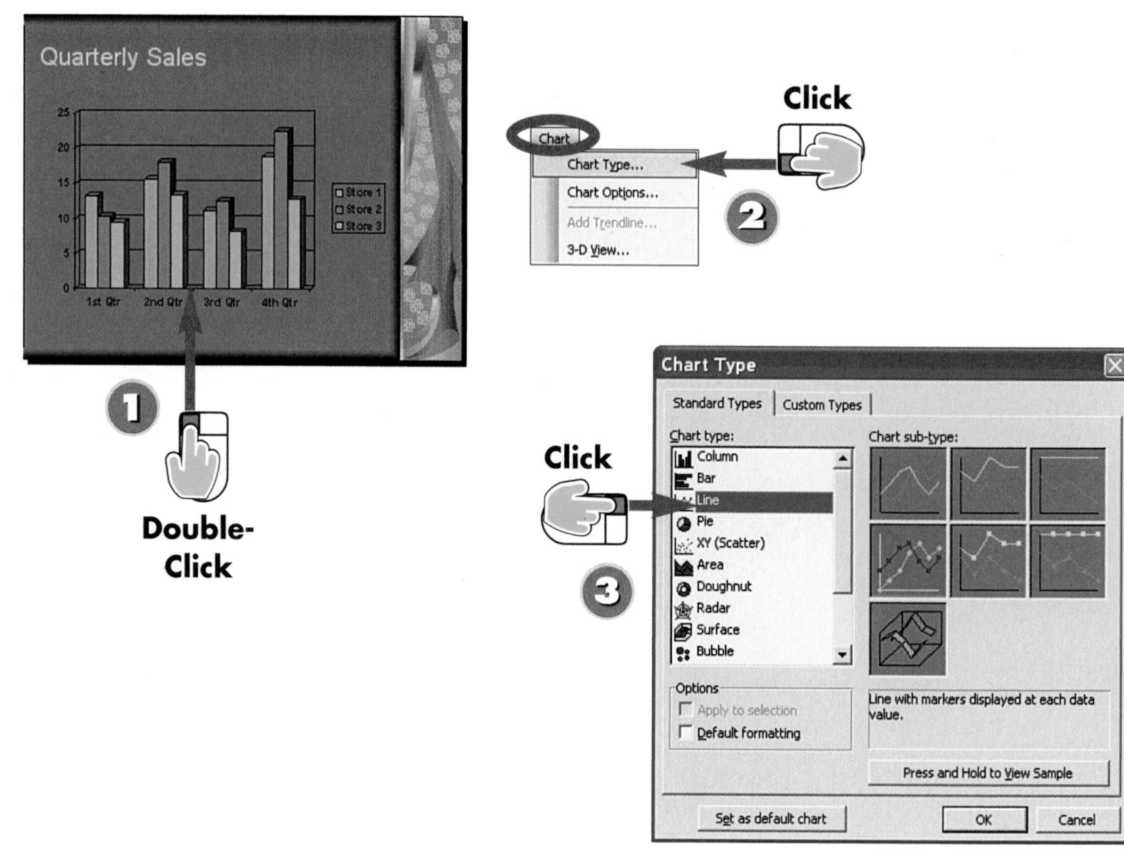

1. Double-click the chart.
2. Open the **Chart** menu and choose **Chart Type**.
3. The Chart Type dialog box opens. Click a chart type.

INTRODUCTION

By default, PowerPoint creates a column chart when you use the charting feature. You can, however, change the chart to another chart type, such as a pie chart or a line chart.

TIP

Which Chart Type Is Best?
The chart type you use depends on how you want to present the data. Use column, bar, and line charts to illustrate changes in values over time. Use pie charts to give percentage data a visual appearance.

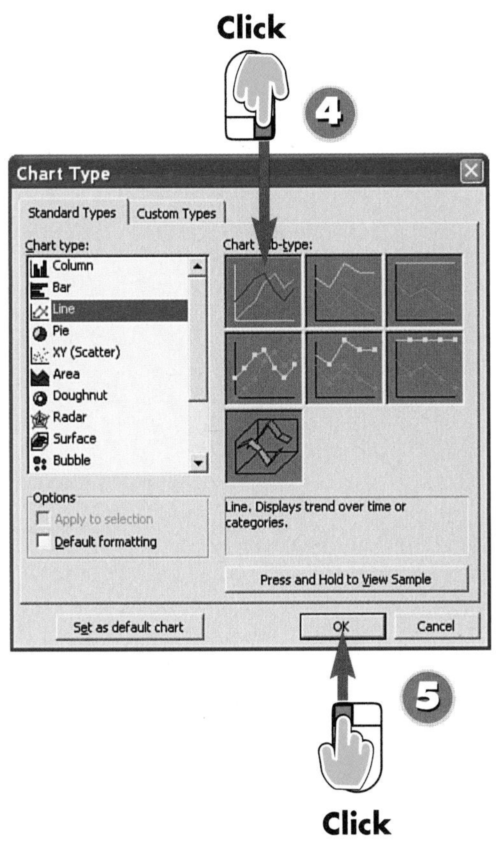

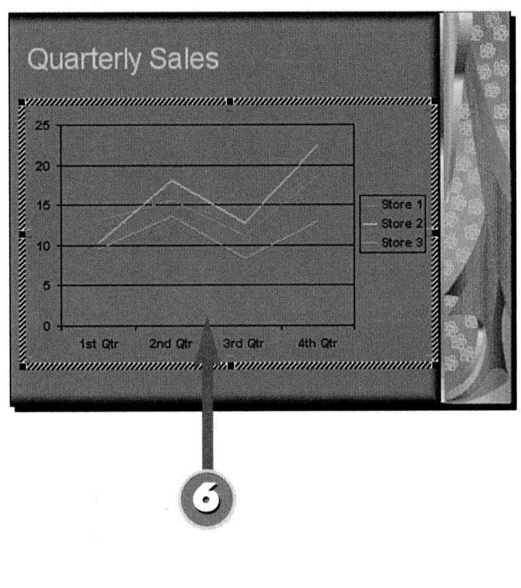

4. Click a chart sub-type.
5. Click **OK**.
6. PowerPoint changes the chart type on the slide.

TIP

Chart Shortcut
When you double-click a chart, several chart-related buttons are added to the Standard toolbar; click the **down arrow** next to the **Chart Type** button to display a list of chart types, and then click the one you want to apply.

TIP

Exiting Chart Edit Mode
When you double-click a chart, PowerPoint switches you to Chart Edit mode and displays the chart along with the datasheet. To return to your slide, click anywhere outside the chart or datasheet.

TIP

Hiding the Datasheet
In Chart Edit mode, click the **View Datasheet** button on the Standard toolbar to hide or display the datasheet.

Changing the Data Plot

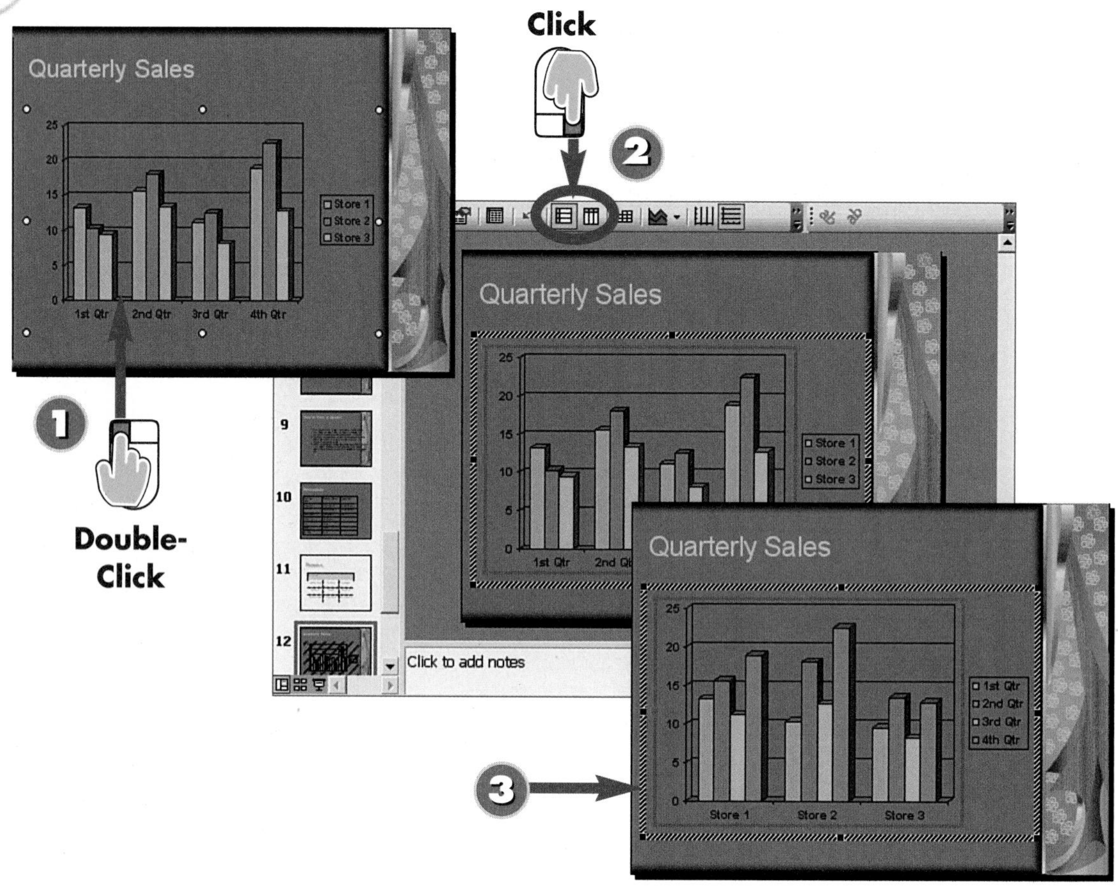

Click

Double-Click

Double-click the chart.

Click the **By Row** or **By Column** button in the Standard toolbar.

PowerPoint changes the data plot.

INTRODUCTION

You can change the way in which your data is presented in a chart by changing the data plot. Data is plotted based on how you enter it into the datasheet, by row or by column. However, you can switch it around to change the data plot.

TIP

Displaying the Datasheet
Click the **View Datasheet** button on the Standard toolbar to hide or display the datasheet. For example, you might hide the datasheet to better see the chart area.

Adding the Datasheet to the Chart

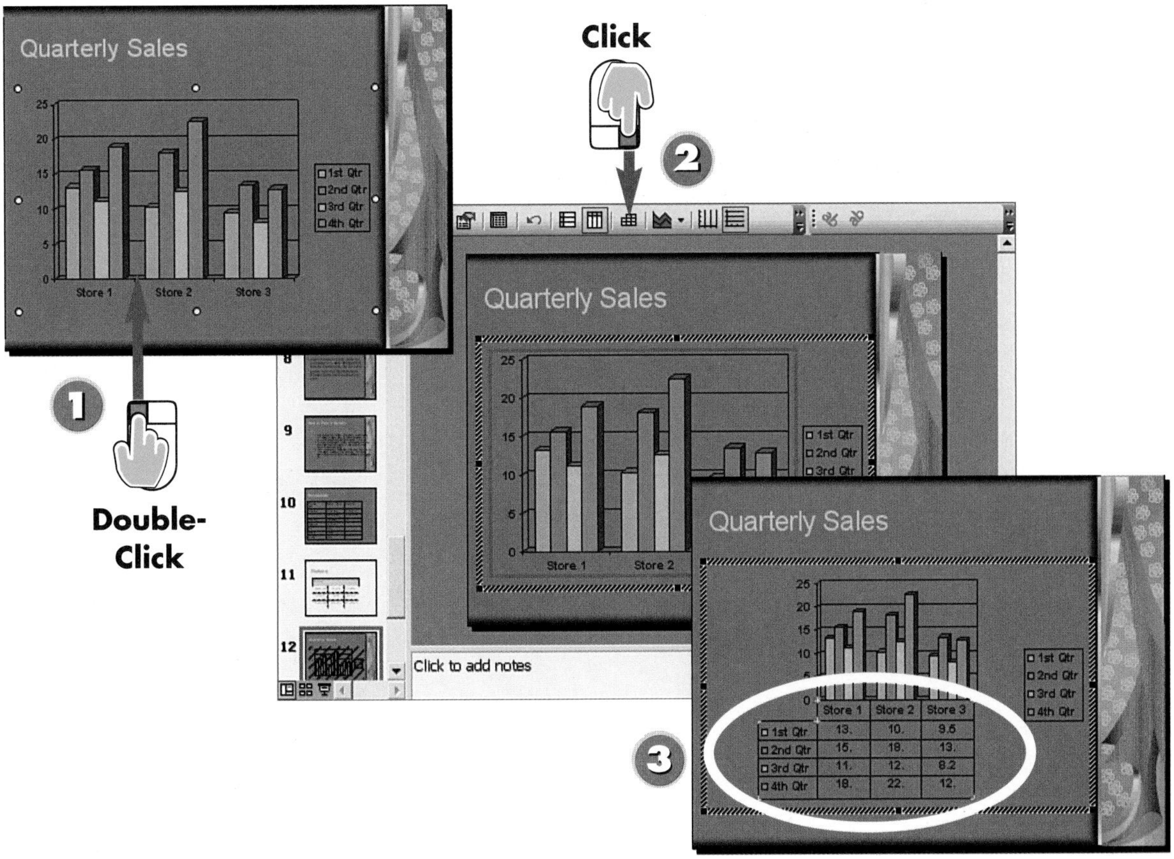

1. Double-click the chart.

2. Click the **Data Table** button on the Standard toolbar.

3. PowerPoint adds the datasheet to the chart.

End

INTRODUCTION

By default, when you finish creating a chart, it displays on your slide without the datasheet that you used to enter values. You can, however, choose to display the datasheet as part of the chart to show your audience how you created the chart, or to print out with the slide.

TIP

Removing the Datasheet
To remove the datasheet from the chart, double-click the chart, and then click the **Data Table** button again. The button toggles the datasheet on and off.

Adding Chart Titles

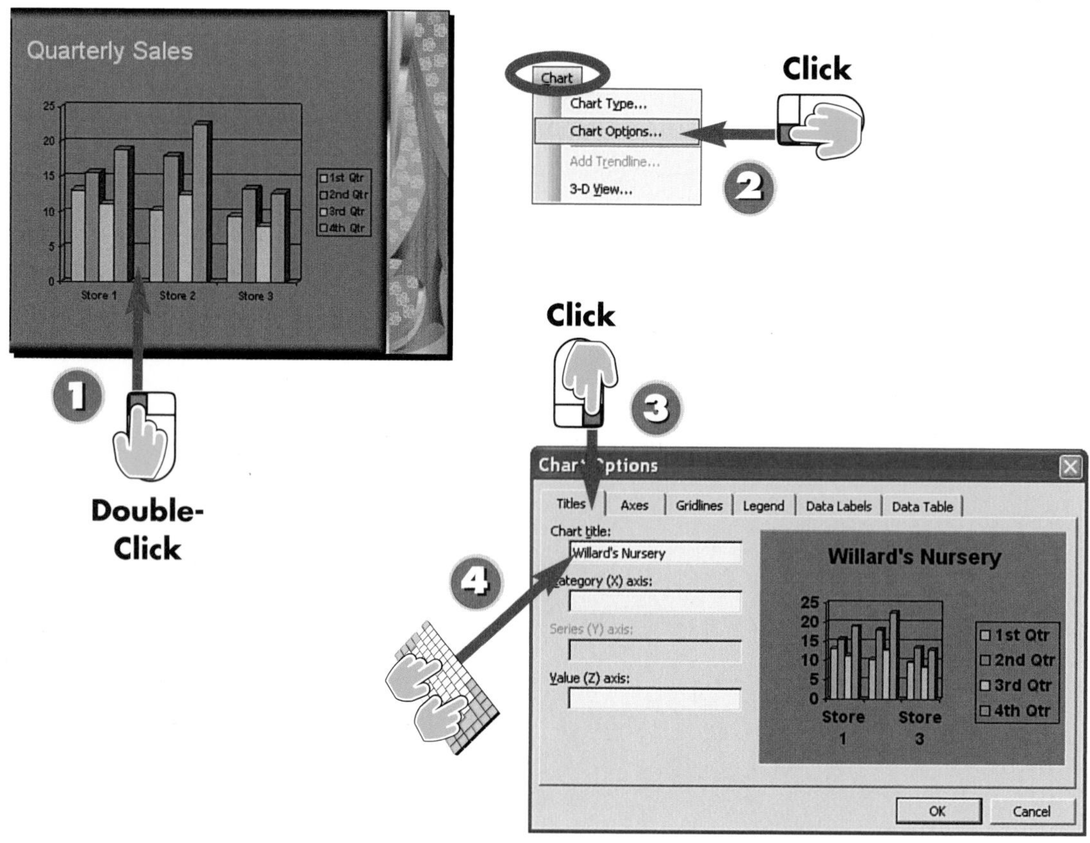

1. Double-click the chart.
2. Open the **Chart** menu and choose **Chart Options**.
3. The Chart Options dialog box opens. Click the **Titles** tab.
4. Click in the **Chart Title** field and type a chart title.

INTRODUCTION

By default, PowerPoint charts do not include chart titles, but you can add a title using the Chart Options dialog box. You can also add titles to the x and y axes.

TIP

Moving Chart Titles
Once you add a title to your chart, you can reposition it at any time. Click the title to select its text box, and then click and drag it to move it on the chart.

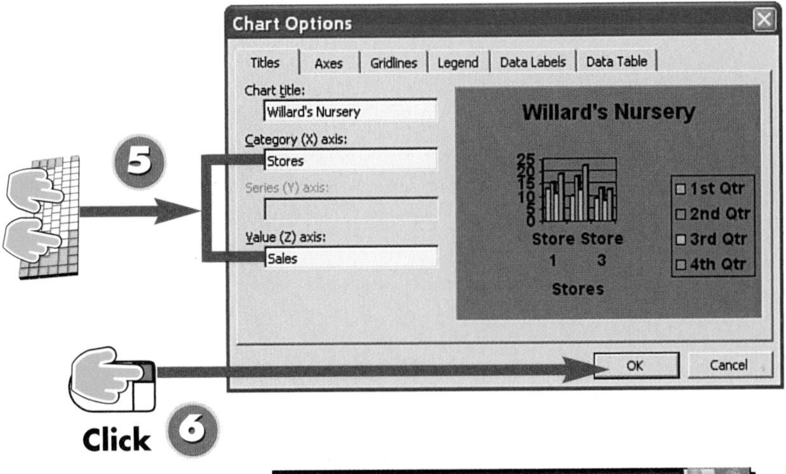

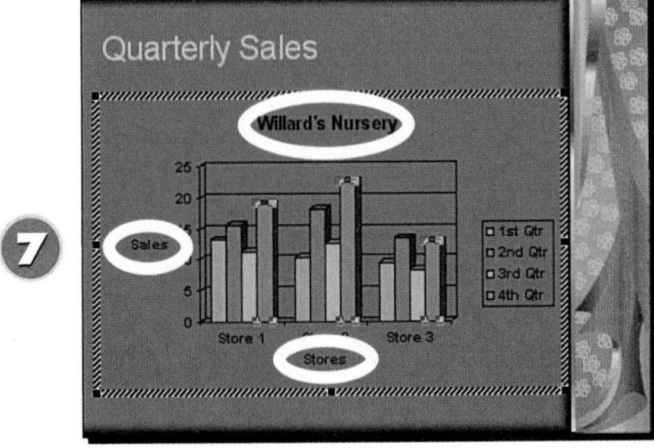

5. Optionally, click inside an axis box and type a title for the axis.

6. Click **OK**.

7. PowerPoint adds the titles to the chart.

TIP

Title Heading or Chart Title?
If your slide layout already includes a title text box, you might not need an additional chart title.

TIP

Removing a Chart Title
To remove a title after you have added it to your chart, simply click the title text box and press the **Delete** key on your keyboard. You can also reopen the Chart Options dialog box to the **Titles** tab and delete the title. To do so, double-click the chart, open the **Chart** menu, and choose **Chart Options**.

Changing Chart Options

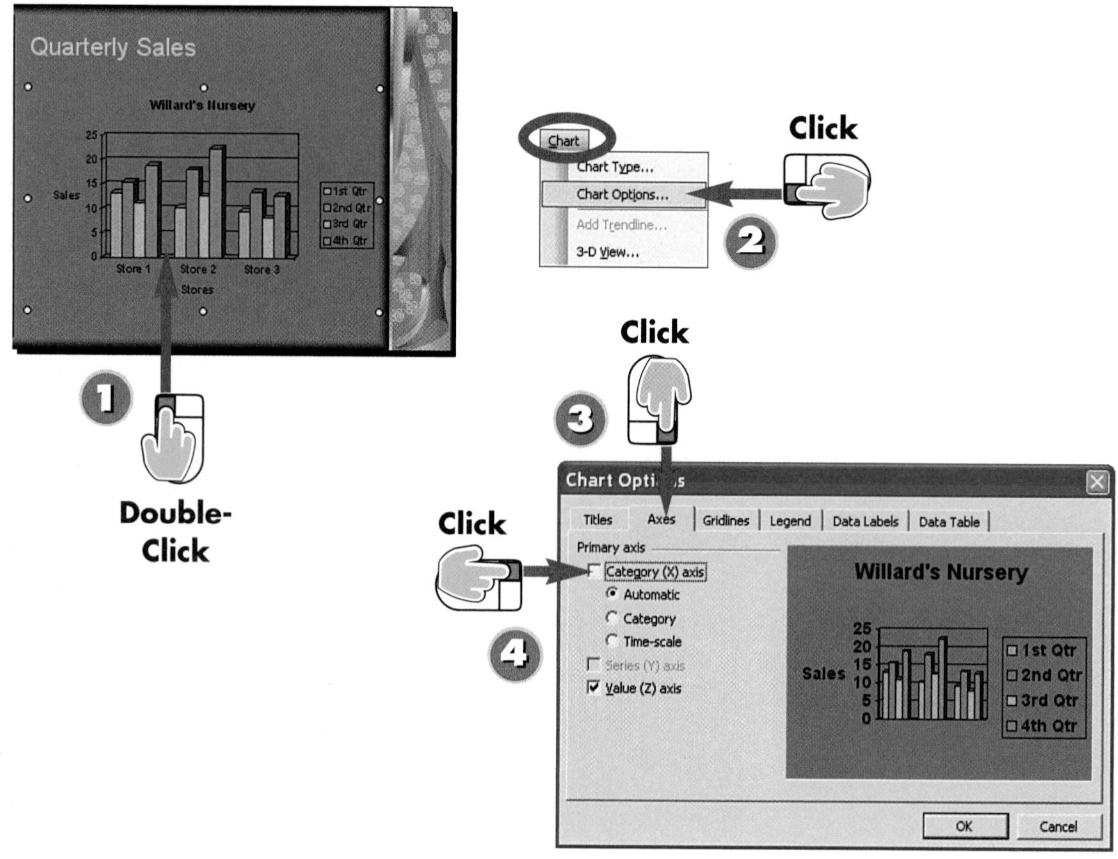

1. Double-click the chart.
2. Open the **Chart** menu and choose **Chart Options**.
3. The Chart Options dialog box opens. Click the **Axes** tab.
4. Click an axis check box to display or hide the axis label. A check mark indicates that the label is displayed, while no check mark indicates that the label is hidden.

INTRODUCTION

Using the Chart Options dialog box, you can display or hide axis labels, gridlines, and data labels; and control the placement of the legend. Each tab in the dialog box offers options for controlling what appears on your chart and lets you preview what the changes look like before applying them to the chart.

TIP

Which Axis Is Which?
The x axis is the horizontal axis on the chart. The y axis is the vertical axis on the chart.

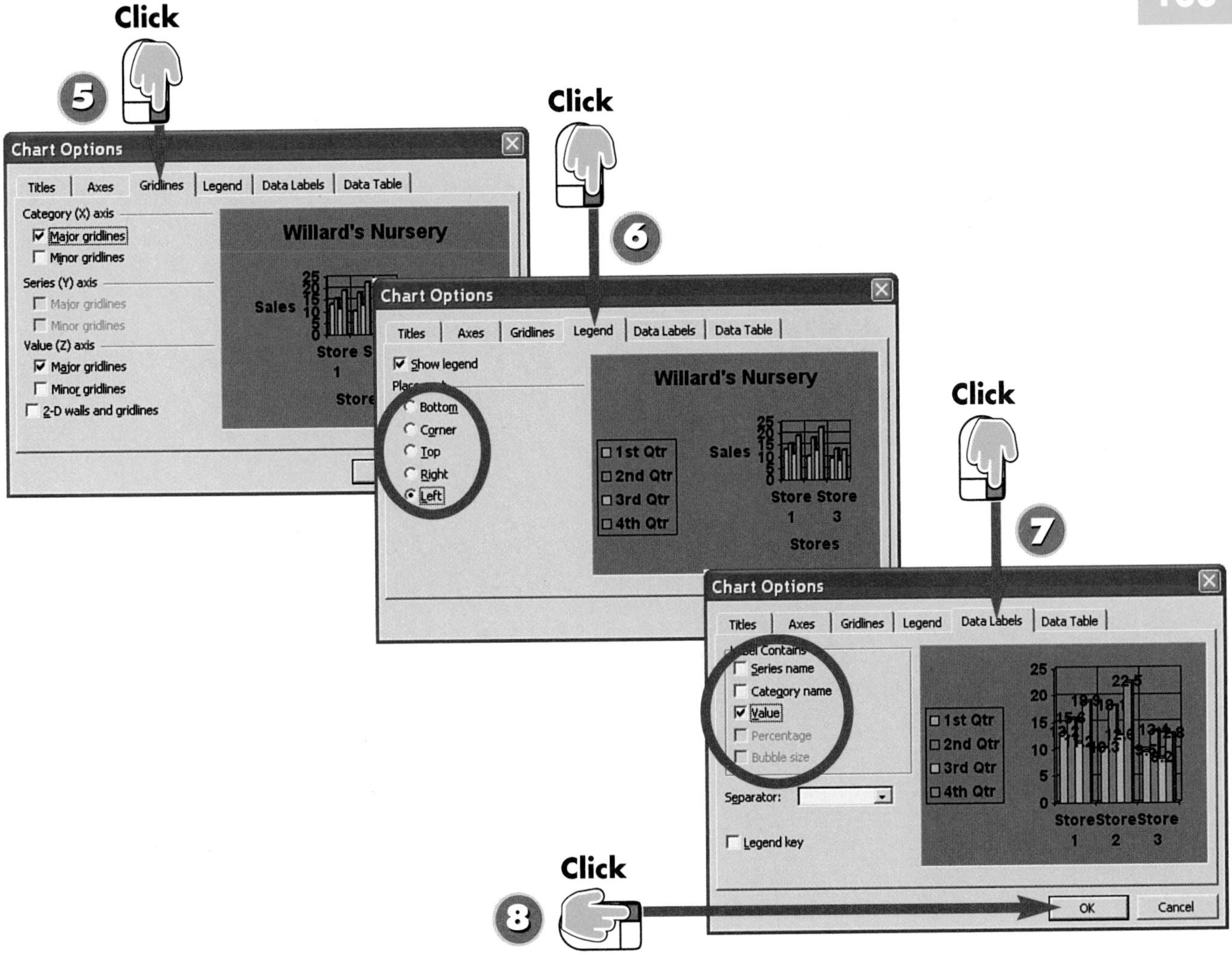

5. Click the **Gridlines** tab, and click the gridlines you want displayed or hidden.
6. Click the **Legend** tab, and click the placement option you want to apply.
7. Click the **Data Labels** tab, and click the labels you want displayed or hidden.
8. Click **OK** to close the dialog box and apply your changes.

TIP

Turning Off Your Legend
Legends explain the color scheme for the data in your chart, but you may decide to turn yours off to free up space or if the chart data is pretty self-explanatory. To do so, open the Chart Options dialog box to the **Legend** tab and deselect the **Show Legend** check box.

TIP

Data Label Clutter
By default, your chart's data labels are turned off because data labels tend to add clutter to charts. In addition, the more values you plot, the harder it is to read the labels. If your chart is simple, however, you can turn the labels on.

Rotating the Axis Labels

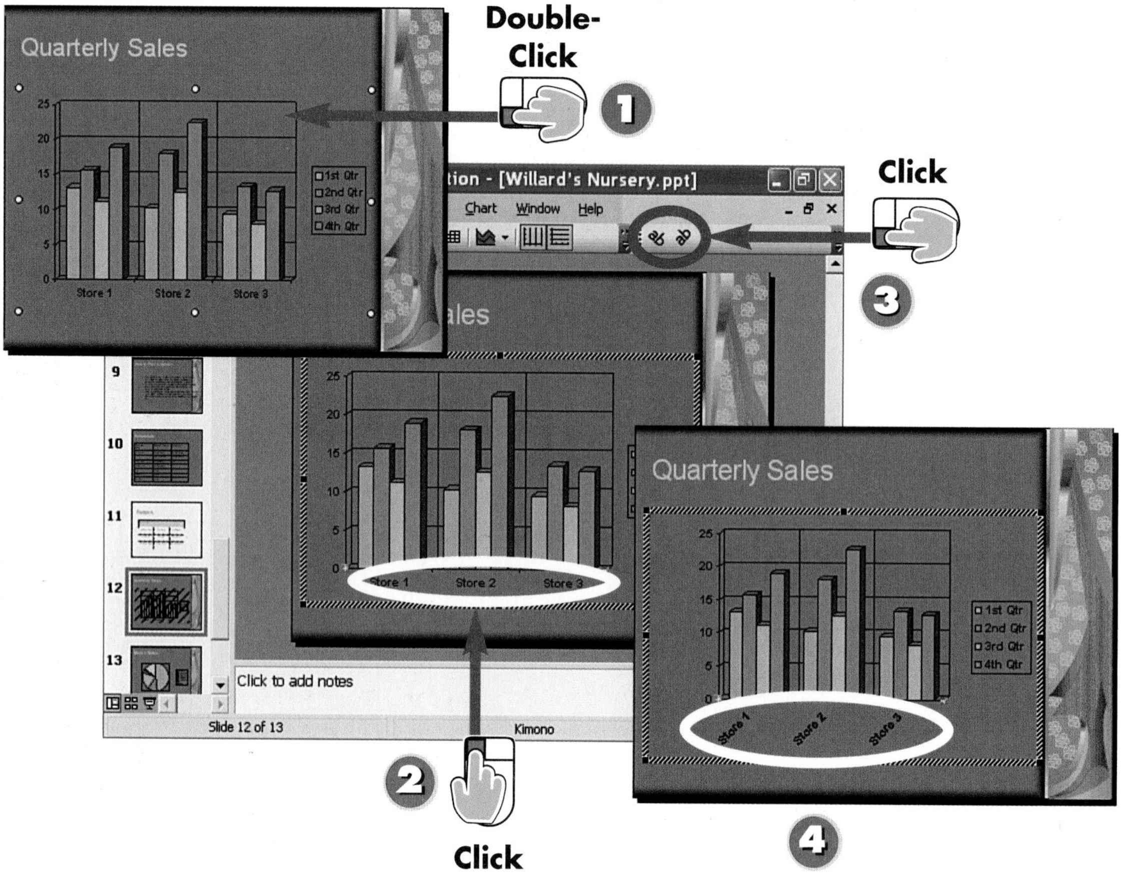

1. Double-click the chart.
2. Click the axis you want to edit.
3. Click the **Angle Clockwise** or **Angle Counterclockwise** button on the Formatting toolbar.
4. PowerPoint angles the labels.

INTRODUCTION

If your axis labels are long, you can rotate them slightly to make them easier to read. For example, if your x-axis labels bump up against each other because of your chart's size or the amount of data it contains, you can angle the labels to make them more legible.

TIP

Toggling On or Off
The **Angle Clockwise** and **Angle Counterclockwise** buttons toggle the angled labels on or off. To return to regular text, simply click the appropriate angle button again.

Formatting Chart Numbers

Double-Click

Click

Click & Drag

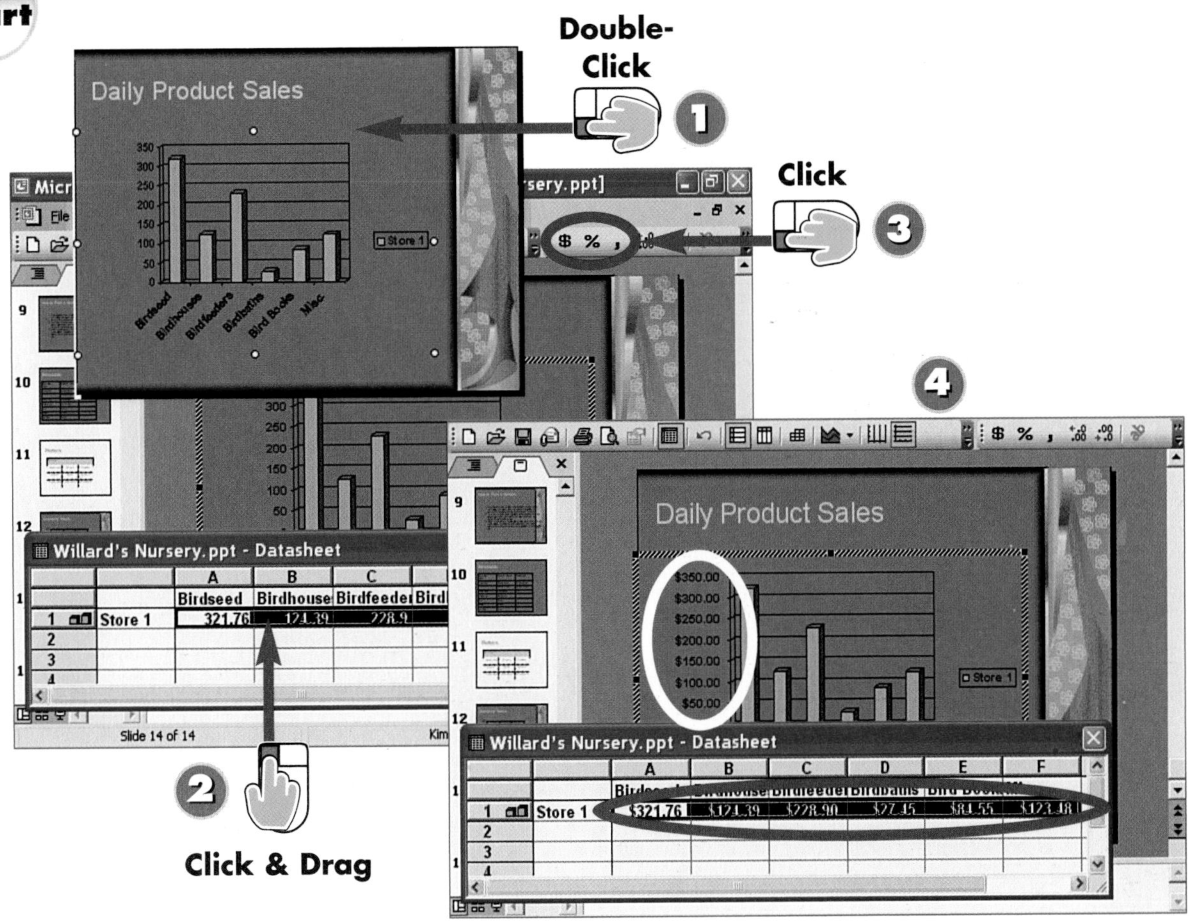

1. Double-click the chart.

2. In the datasheet, click and hold while dragging the mouse across the chart numbers you want to format.

3. Click the **Currency**, **Percent**, or **Comma** button on the Formatting toolbar.

4. PowerPoint applies the formatting to the numbers in the datasheet and on the chart.

INTRODUCTION

You can apply number formatting to your datasheet to make your chart data display currency, percent, or comma symbols.

TIP

My Datasheet Is Missing!
If your datasheet is hidden, click the **View Datasheet** button on the Standard toolbar in Chart Edit mode to display the datasheet again.

TIP

Controlling Decimals
To change the number of decimal places displayed in the data, click the **Increase Decimal** or **Decrease Decimal** buttons on the Formatting toolbar.

Formatting the Data Series

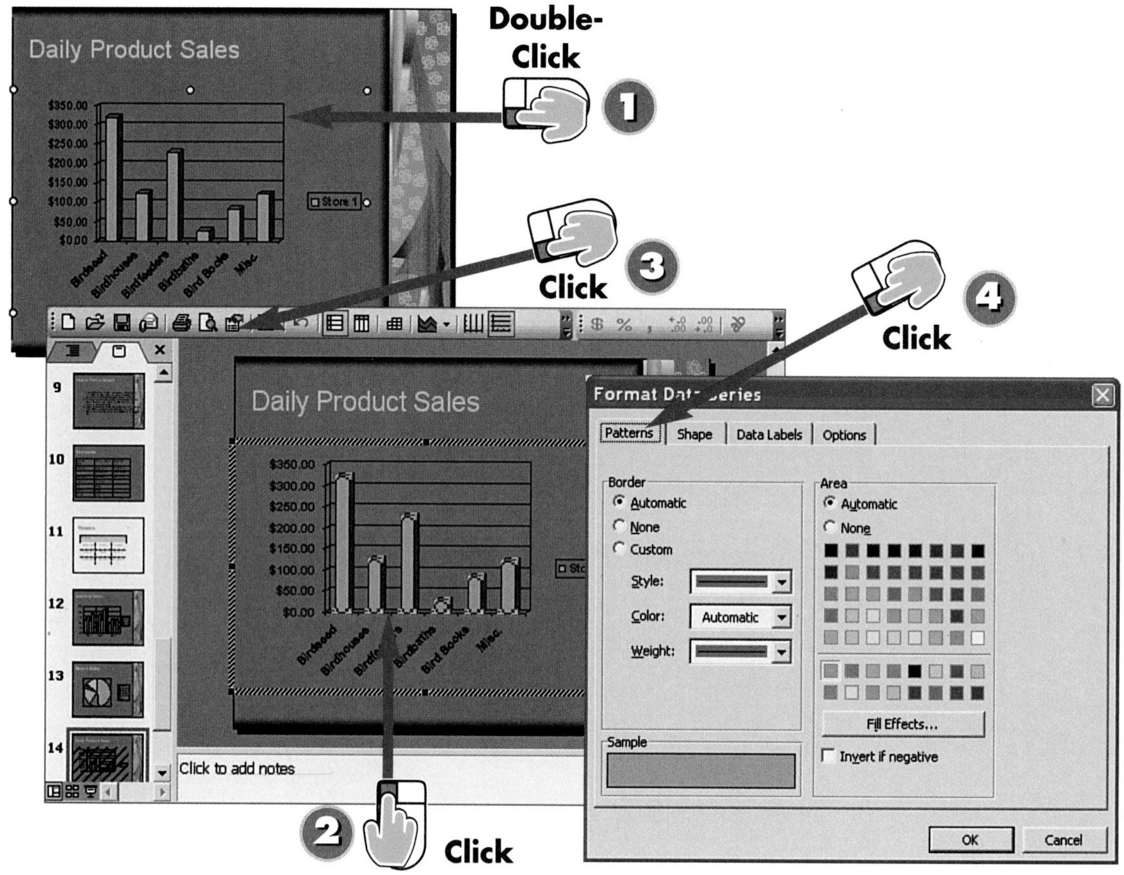

1. Double-click the chart.
2. Click the data series you want to change.
3. Click the **Format Data Series** button.
4. The Format Data Series dialog box opens. Click the **Patterns** tab.

INTRODUCTION

Another way in which you can customize your chart is to choose a different fill color for your chart data, also called the *data series.* For example, you might choose colors to go with your slide's color scheme or to make your data more legible to your audience.

TIP

Quick Color

You can also click the **Fill Color** button on the Formatting toolbar and select a color from the pop-up color palette to change the fill color of your data series.

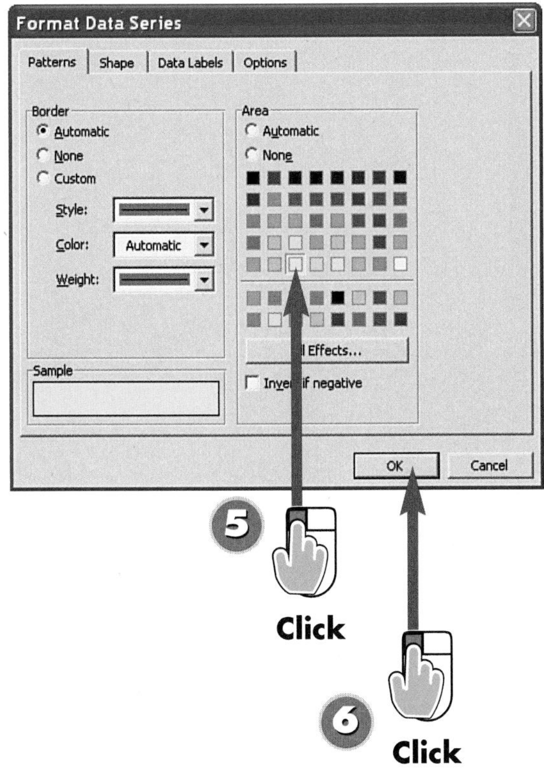

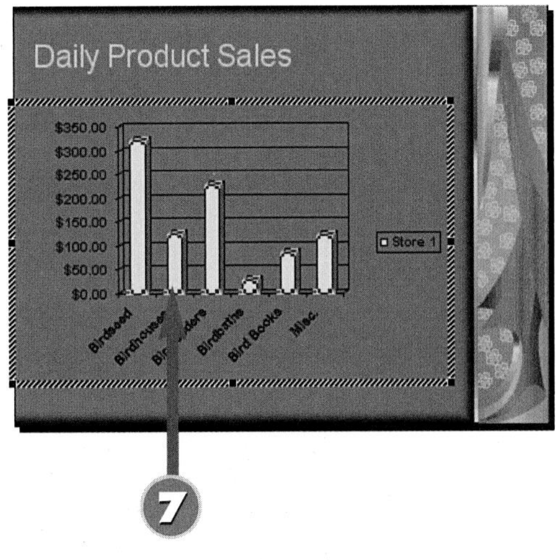

5. Click a fill color.

6. Click **OK**.

7. PowerPoint applies the new color to the data series.

TIP

Border Control
You can use the **Border** options in the Format Data Series dialog box's **Patterns** tab to change the outline that surrounds the data series. You'll find options for setting a line color as well as line thickness.

TIP

Formatting Legend Colors
You can format the colors used in your chart's legend using the Format Legend dialog box, which you open by double-clicking the legend. To apply a color to the legend's background, choose a color in the **Patterns** tab. To change the font, click the **Font** tab and select another.

Adding a Diagram

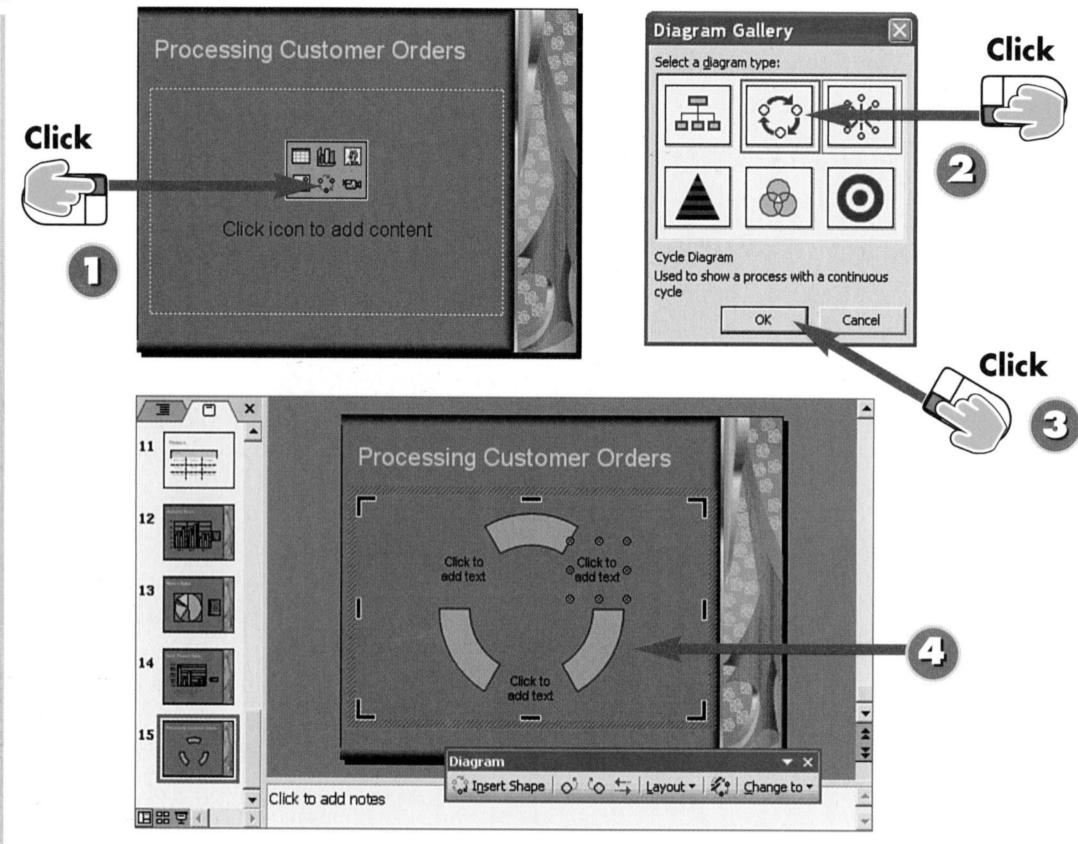

1. Click the **Insert Diagram** icon in the placeholder slide object.
2. The Diagram Gallery dialog box opens. Click the type of diagram you want to use.
3. Click **OK**.
4. PowerPoint creates the diagram and places it on the slide along with the Diagram toolbar.

INTRODUCTION

You can create diagrams to show cycles, hierarchy patterns, and more. PowerPoint's diagram feature includes organizational charts, cycle, radial, pyramid, Venn, and target diagram types. When you add a diagram, PowerPoint inserts it onto your slide as a slide object, along with placeholder text.

TIP

Adding Organization Charts
Although classified as a type of diagram, organization charts work a bit differently. See the task "Adding an Organization Chart" to learn how to add one to your slide.

TIP

Building a Diagram from Scratch
You need not use a layout that contains a diagram placeholder; you can add a new diagram to any slide. Simply click the **Insert Diagram** button on the Drawing toolbar and add a diagram as shown in these steps.

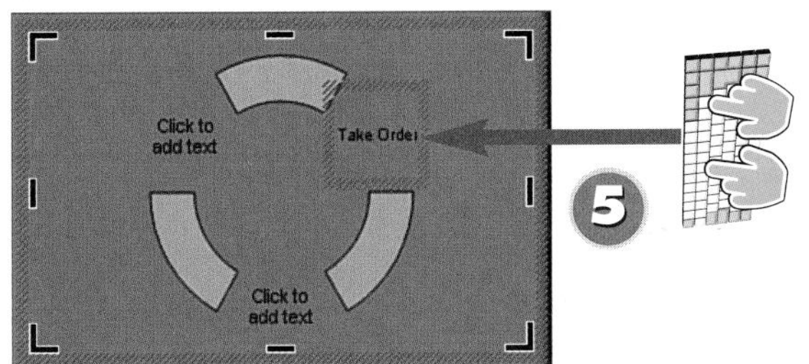

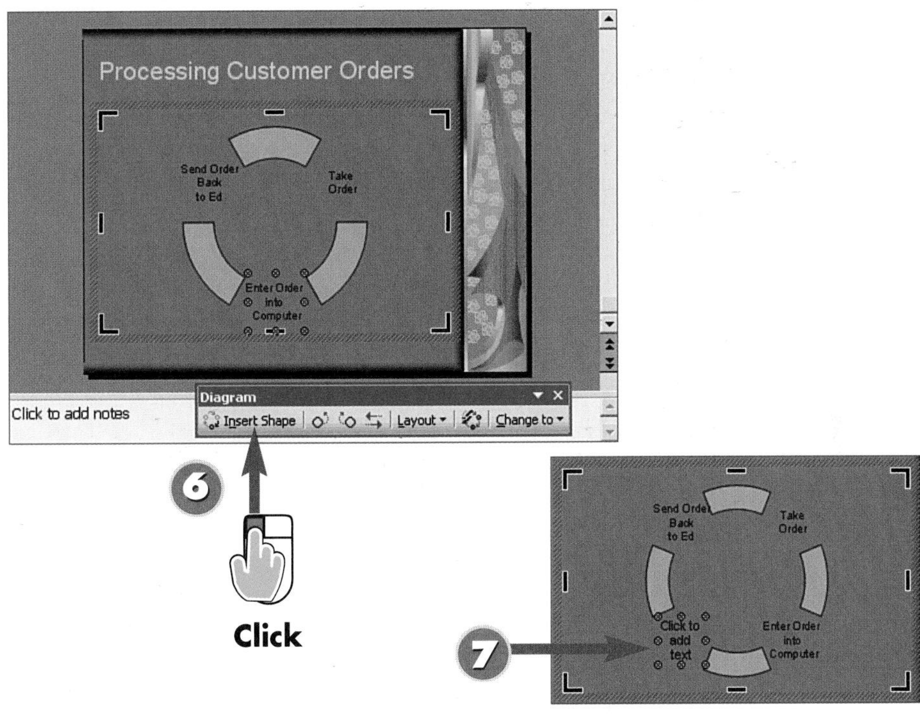

5. Click each placeholder text box and type your own diagram text.

6. Click **Insert Shape** to add another shape to your diagram.

7. PowerPoint inserts the new shape and another text box for your diagram text. The new shape appears and assumes the next position in the order of the diagram's hierarchy.

End

TIP

Reversing the Order
You can click the **Reverse Diagram** button on the Diagram toolbar to reverse the order of the shapes in your diagram.

TIP

Resizing Diagrams
Click the **Layout** button on the Diagram toolbar to reveal several commands for controlling the size of the diagram. Select the **Fit Diagram to Contents** command to resize the diagram around the current contents.

TIP

Changing Flow
You can click the **Move Shape Forward** or **Move Shape Backward** buttons in the Diagram toolbar to change the position of the current shape in the diagram.

Changing the Diagram Style

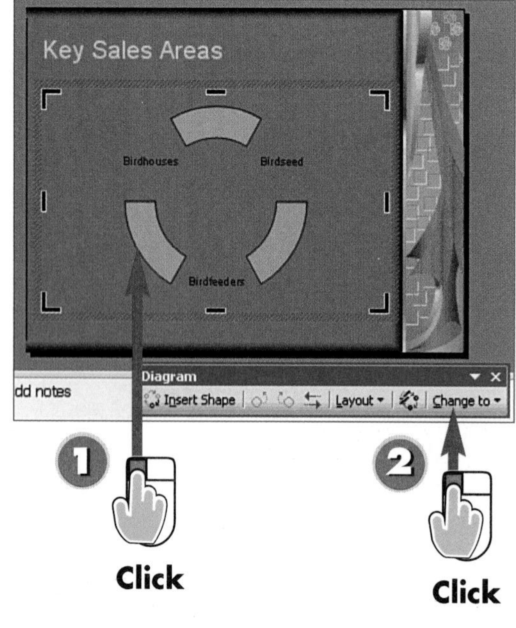

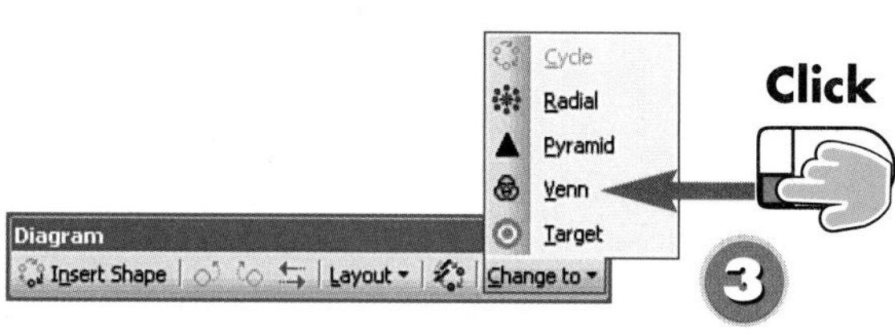

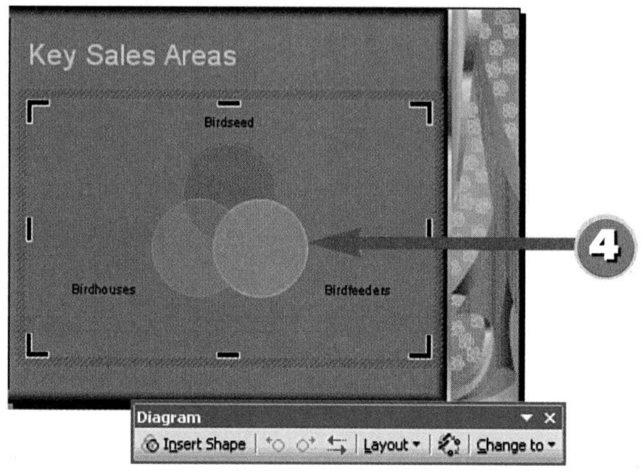

1. Click the diagram to select it.
2. Click the **Change To** button on the Diagram toolbar.
3. Click a new style.
4. PowerPoint applies the style.

INTRODUCTION

If you added a diagram to your slide, you can swap diagram styles at any time. Using the Diagram toolbar, you can assign another diagram style without affecting any data you have previously entered into the diagram.

TIP

Changing Text Formatting

To assign another font to your diagram text, simply select the text and click the **down arrow** next to the **Font** button on the Formatting toolbar to choose another font style.

TIP

Diagram Styles

The diagram style you should choose depends on the order in which you want to present the diagram flow. For example, a cycle diagram shows continuous flow in a circular pattern, while a radial diagram shows outward flow from one source.

Formatting a Diagram

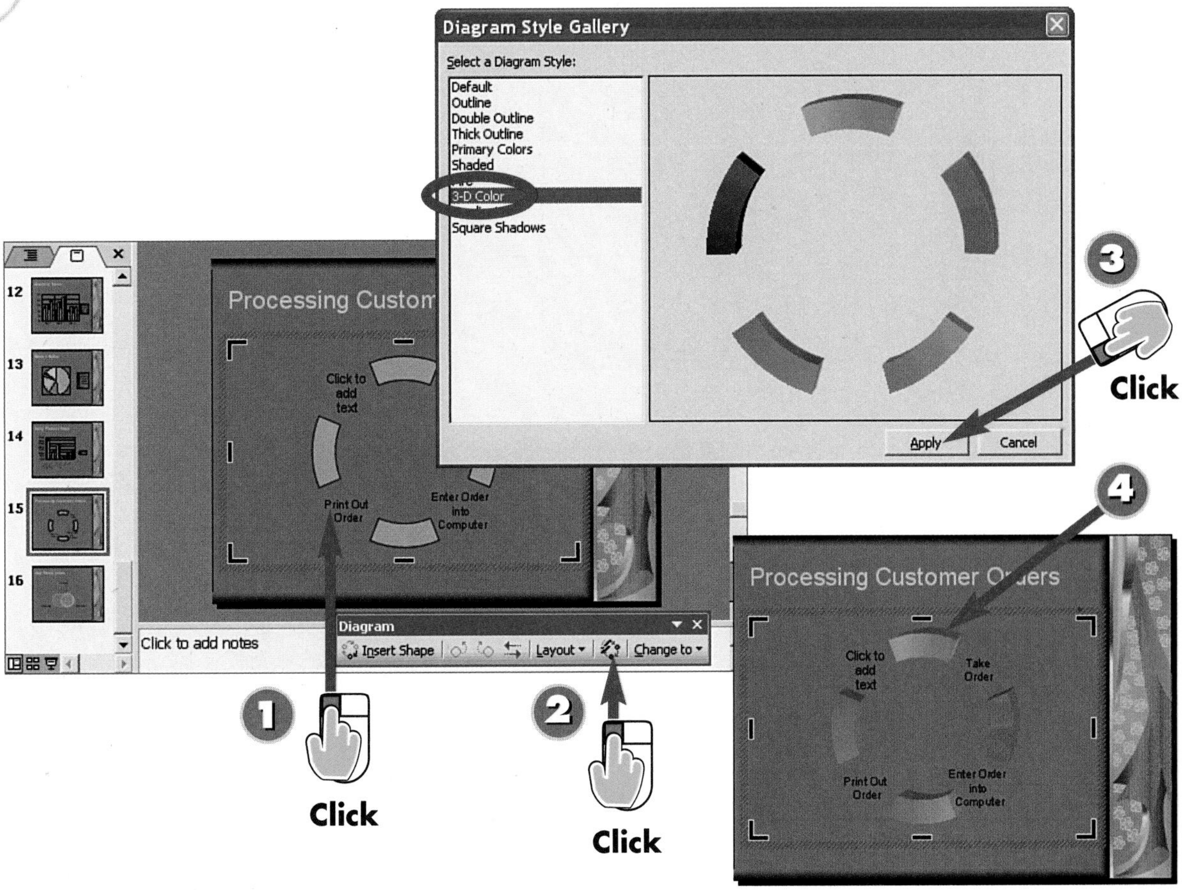

1. Click the diagram to select it.

2. Click the **AutoFormat** button on the Diagram toolbar.

3. The Diagram Style Gallery dialog box opens. Click a style and click **Apply**.

4. PowerPoint applies the style.

INTRODUCTION

When you add a diagram to a slide, PowerPoint applies default formatting to the diagram. With the AutoFormat feature, you can change the diagram's shape, colors, and style to something more compatible with your presentation design.

Adding an Organization Chart

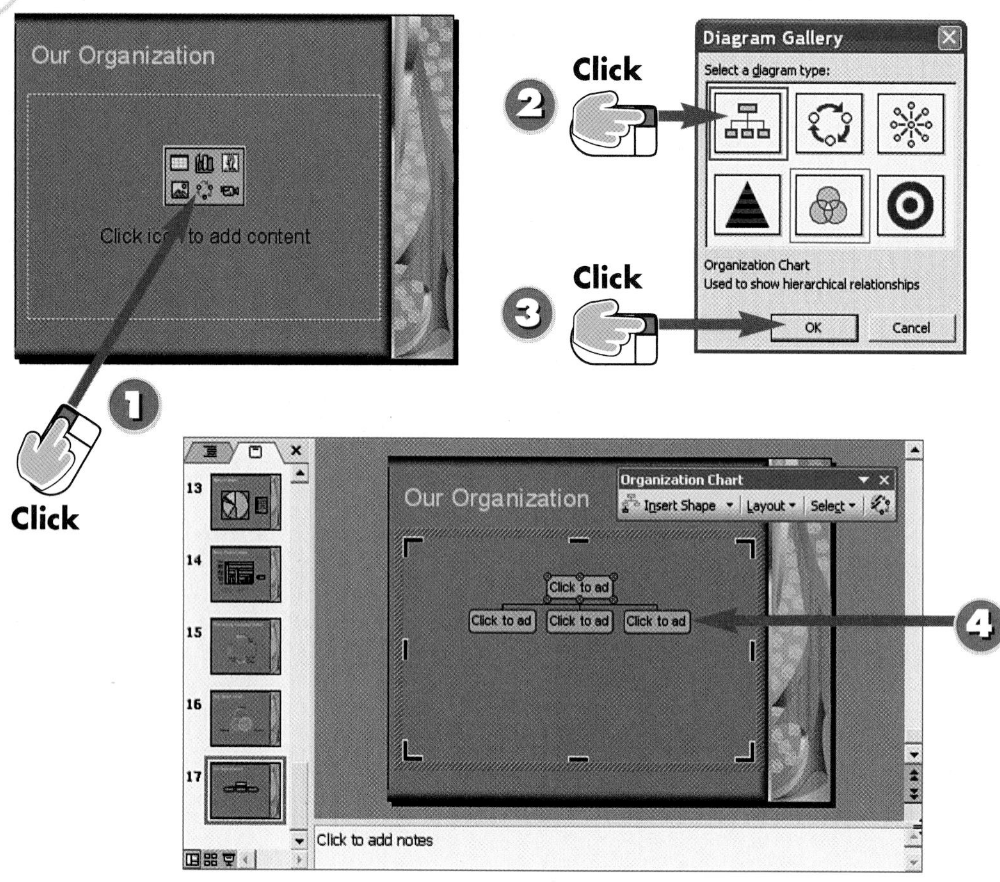

1. Click the **Insert Diagram** icon in the placeholder slide object.

2. The Diagram Gallery dialog box opens. Click the **Organization Chart** option.

3. Click **OK**.

4. PowerPoint creates the chart and places it on the slide along with the Organization Chart toolbar.

INTRODUCTION

Add an organization chart to a slide to show a structure, such as a corporate structure or a chain of command. You can then add shapes to the chart to extend the structure. Organization chart shapes are classified as subordinate, coworker, or assistant, and are connected by lines called *connecting lines*. Subordinate shapes are added directly below the current shape. Coworker shapes are added to the right of the current shape. Assistant shapes are added off to the side, yet below the current shape.

TIP

Using Another Layout
By default, PowerPoint builds your organization chart using a standard layout that starts with one shape at the top, like a pyramid. You can choose from several other layouts if you click the **Layout** button on the Organization Chart toolbar.

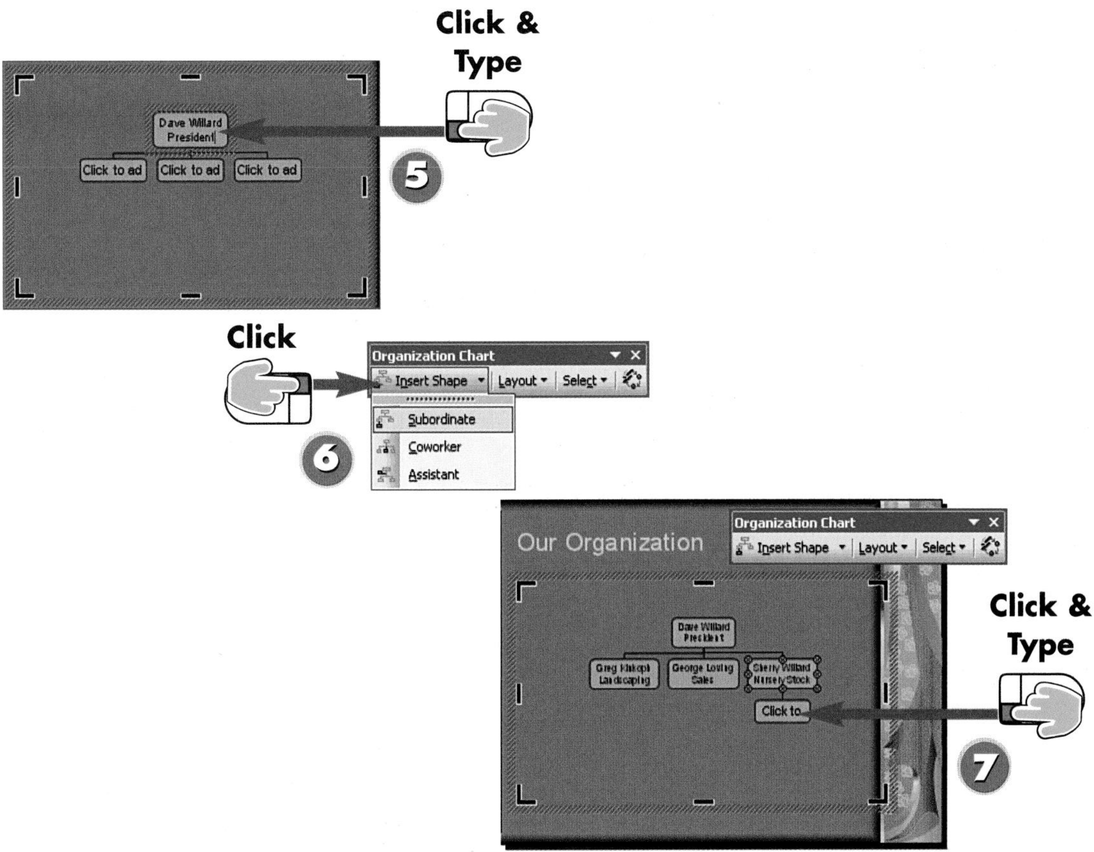

5 Click a shape and type your own chart text; repeat for each shape in the organization chart.

6 To add another block to the chart, click the shape you want to add a new shape to, click the **Insert Shape** button on the Organization Chart toolbar, and click a shape type.

7 PowerPoint adds the shape and connects it to the current shape. Click the new shape and type the desired text.

TIP

Changing the Formatting

You can use the AutoFormat feature to change the organization chart style. Click the **AutoFormat** button on the Organization Chart toolbar to open the Organization Chart Style Gallery dialog box, where you can choose from a variety of different shapes and styles for your chart. Click a style, and click **Apply**.

TIP

Adding a New Organization Chart

You need not use a layout that already contains a diagram placeholder; you can add a new organization chart to any slide. Click the **Insert Diagram** button on the Drawing toolbar.

Adding a Microsoft Excel Chart

Click

Click

Click

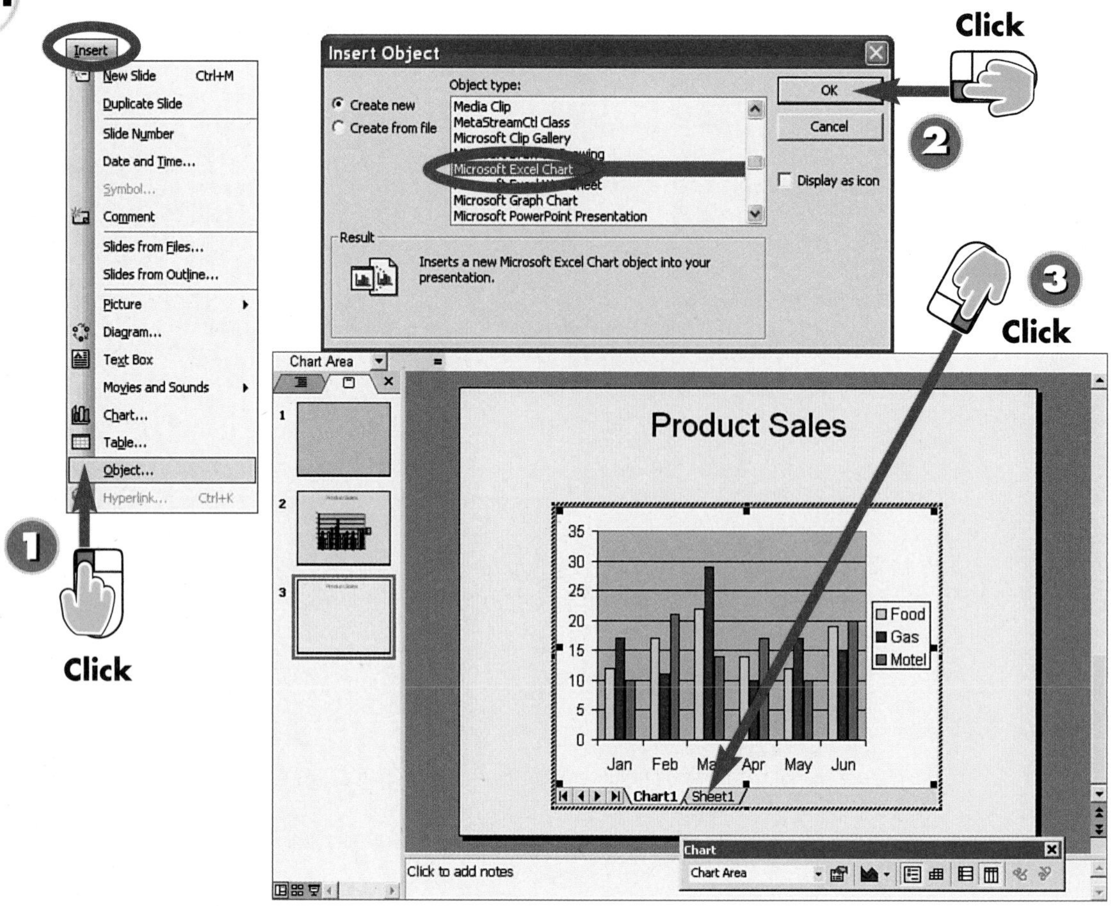

1. Open the **Insert** menu and choose **Object**.

2. The Insert Object dialog box opens. Click **Excel Chart** and click **OK**.

3. PowerPoint displays a worksheet, a chart and the Chart toolbar. Click the **Sheet1** tab.

INTRODUCTION

If you are an experienced Microsoft Excel user, you can add a new Excel chart and worksheet to your slide and enter your own chart data. When you activate this feature, a single worksheet and a chart sheet display on your slide. The toolbars also include Excel tools, such as the AutoSum and Paste Function tools, which you can use to create formulas and format the worksheet cells.

TIP

Zooming

You might need to zoom your view of the chart to better see the data you want to enter. See Part 1 to learn more about zooming in or out to see slides.

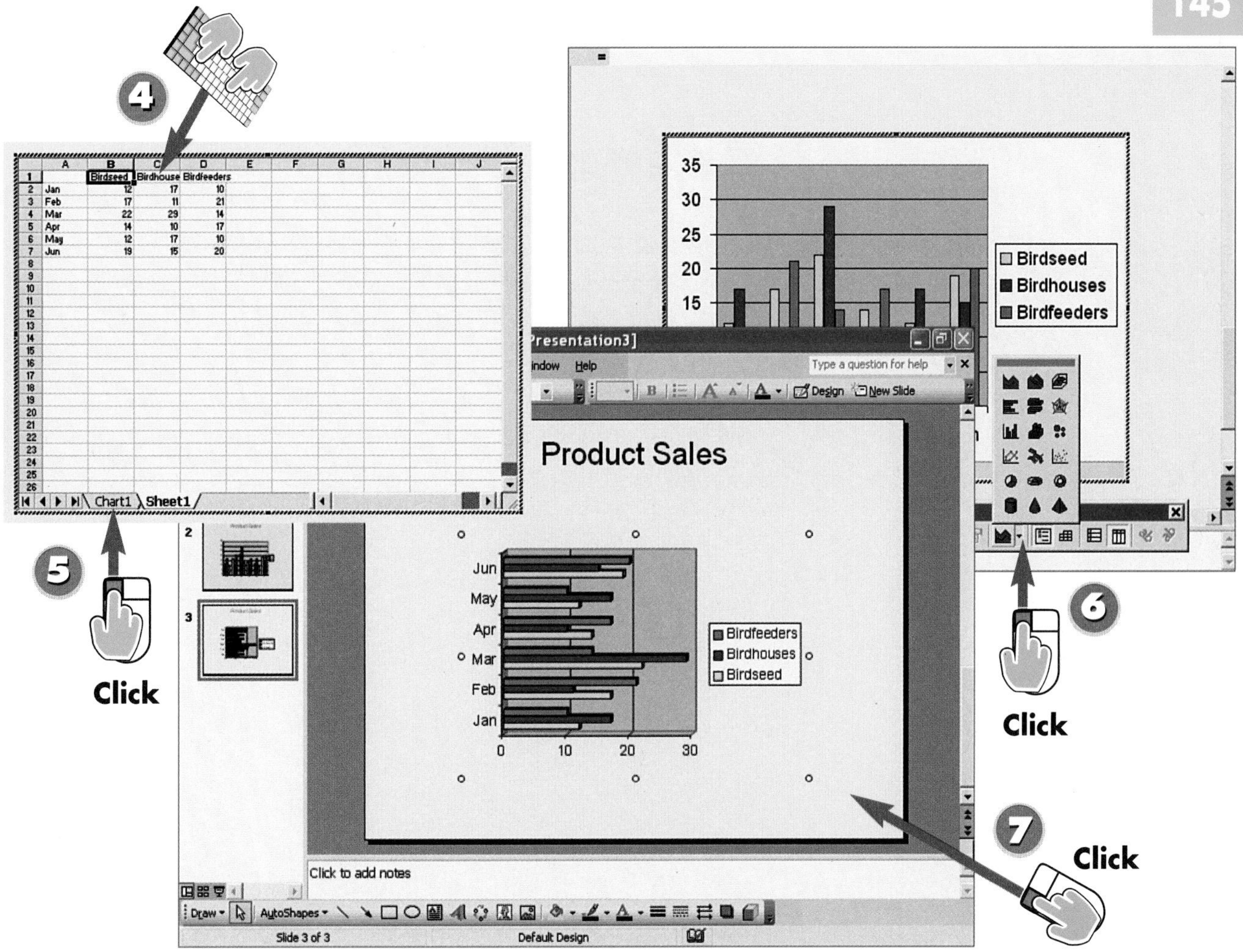

4 Enter your chart data.

5 Click the **Chart1** tab to view the data as a chart.

6 To change the chart type, click the **Chart Type** button in the Chart toolbar and select a type from the options that appear.

7 The new chart type is applied. Click anywhere outside the chart to deselect the chart.

TIP

Editing a Chart
To return to the worksheet you used to create the chart, double-click on the chart.

TIP

Adding a Worksheet
To add a plain worksheet—but no Excel chart—to your slide, open the **Insert** menu and choose **Object** to open the Insert Object dialog box. Select **Microsoft Excel Worksheet** and click **OK**. A single worksheet is added.

TIP

Adding an Existing Chart
Use the Copy and Paste commands to add an existing Excel chart to a slide. Open Excel, select the chart, and click the **Copy** button. Return to PowerPoint, click where you want the chart to go, and click the **Paste** button.

PART 8

Adding Tables

One of the best ways to organize and present data to your audience is through the use of tables. You can add and edit tables to present lists such as schedules, products and prices, or any other multi-columned data.

You can enhance plain tables in PowerPoint by formatting table cells, adding borders and shadows, and more. You can also make edits to the table structure, such as expanding column widths and row heights.

Slide with Table

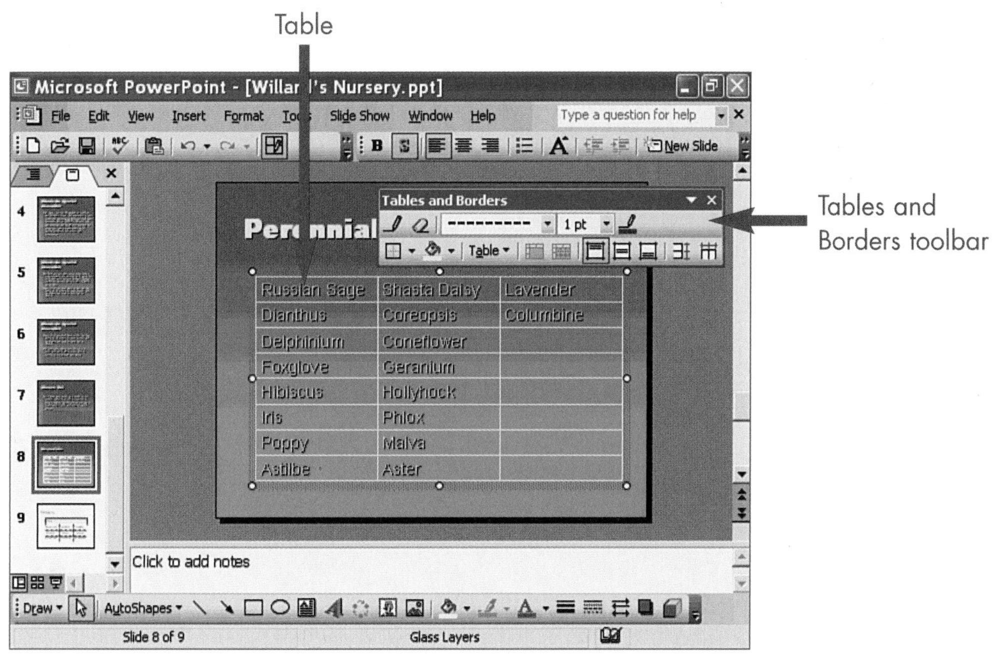

Adding a Table

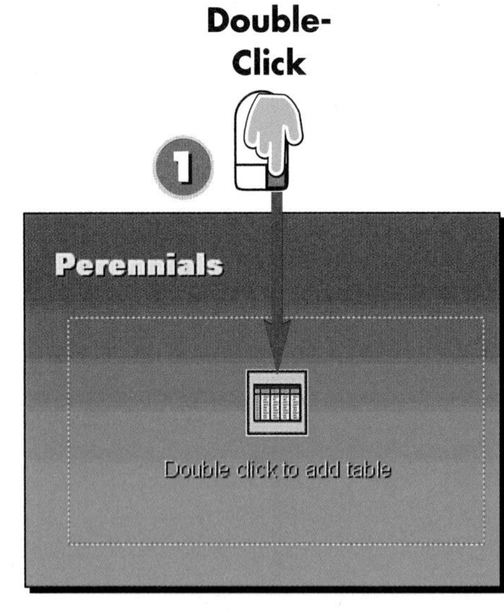

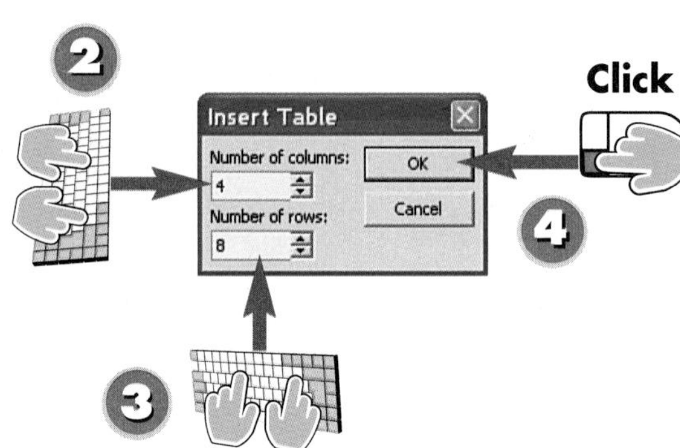

1. Double-click the table object on the slide.
2. PowerPoint displays the Insert Table dialog box. Type the number of columns you want in the table.
3. Type the number of rows you want in the table.
4. Click **OK**.

INTRODUCTION

A table is a great way to organize data, especially data suited for multiple columns and rows. PowerPoint tables are composed of intersecting columns and rows that form *cells*. Cells commonly hold text, but can also hold pictures or clip-art images. The easiest way to add a table is to choose a slide layout that includes a table object.

TIP

Finding a Table Layout

Under the category **Other Layouts** in the Slide Layout pane, you can find a layout that includes a title and a table. Many of the other layouts include the versatile object menu that allows you to add different slide objects.

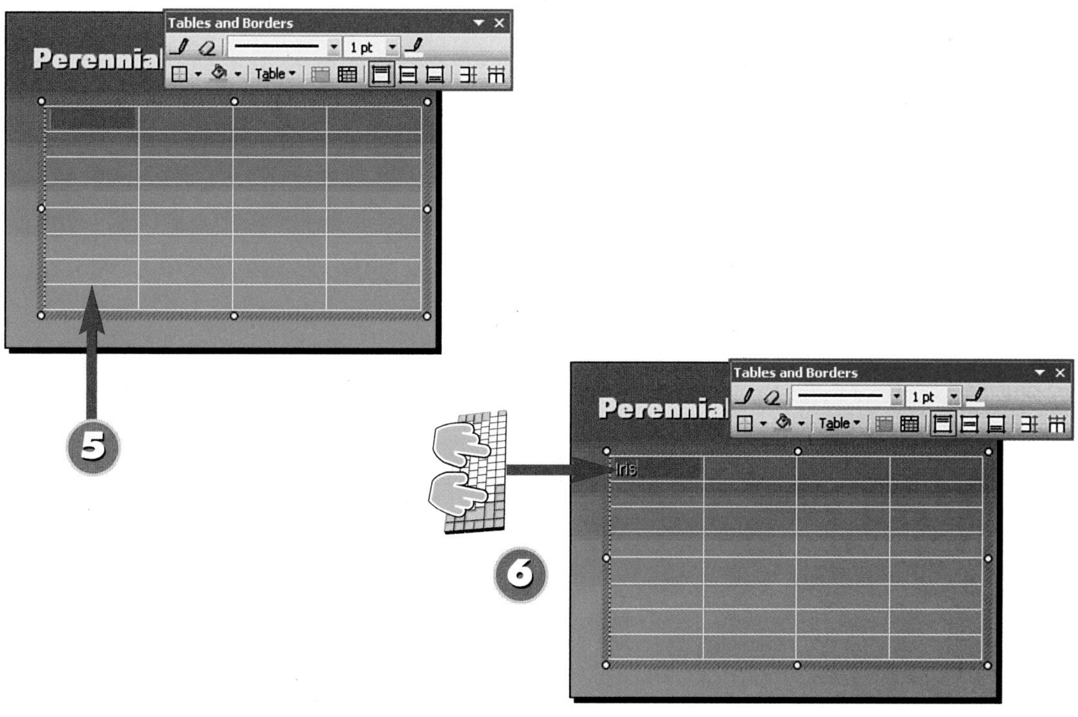

5 PowerPoint creates the table and displays the Tables and Borders toolbar.

6 Click inside a table cell and start typing to add text to the table. You can press the Tab key to move from cell to cell.

TIP

Drawing Your Own Table

To create custom tables, click the **Tables and Borders** button on the Standard toolbar; this opens the Tables and Border toolbar with the Draw Table button selected. Then, click and drag to create the table border, and click and drag within the table border to create columns and rows. Alternatively, open the **Insert** menu and choose **Table**, and specify the number of columns and rows.

TIP

Deleting a Table

To remove a table you no longer need, click the table border to select the entire table, and press the **Delete** key on your keyboard. This removes the table and any text contained within the table cells.

Changing Row Height or Column Width

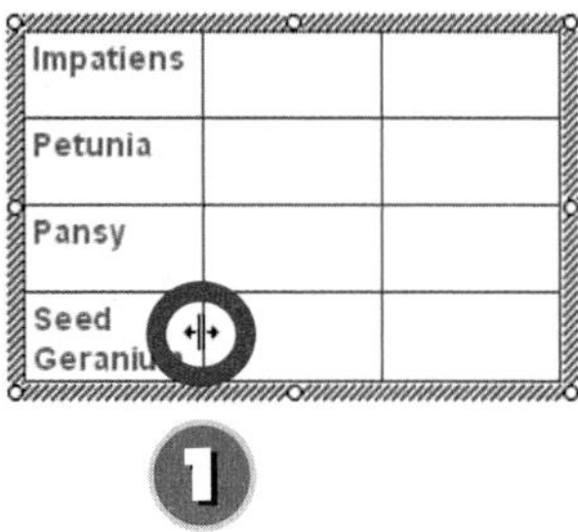

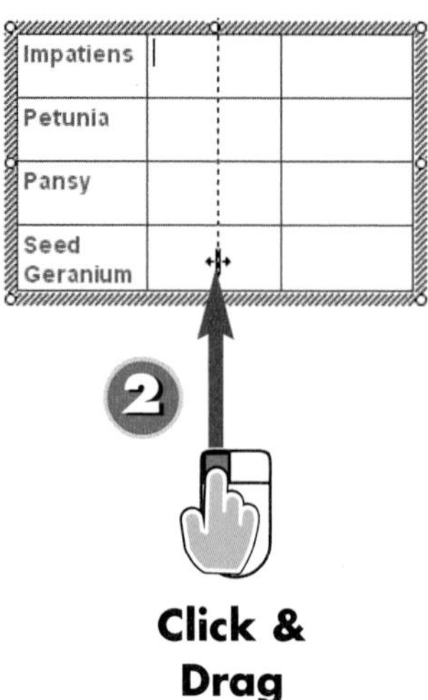

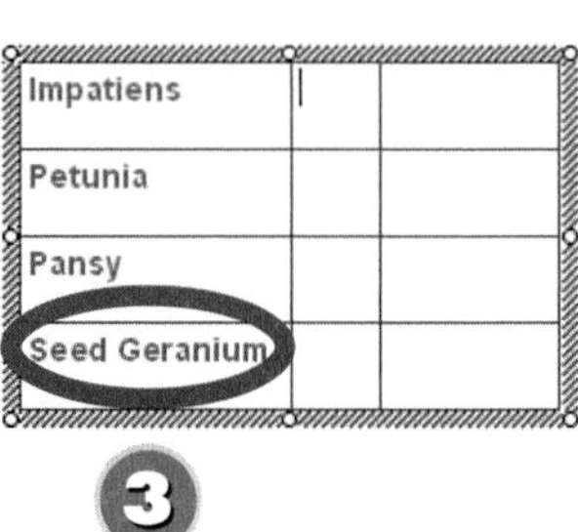

1. Move the mouse pointer over the edge of the row or column you want to adjust. The pointer becomes a double-sided arrow.
2. Click and drag the row edge up or down to increase or decrease the row height, or drag the column edge left or right to increase or decrease the column width.
3. Release the mouse button; the row height or column width is adjusted.

INTRODUCTION

You can easily adjust the height of a table row or the width of a table column to accommodate text or an image in the table cells.

TIP

Automatic Resizing
When you click inside a table cell and start typing, PowerPoint automatically adjusts the row height to include all the text.

Adding a Row or Column

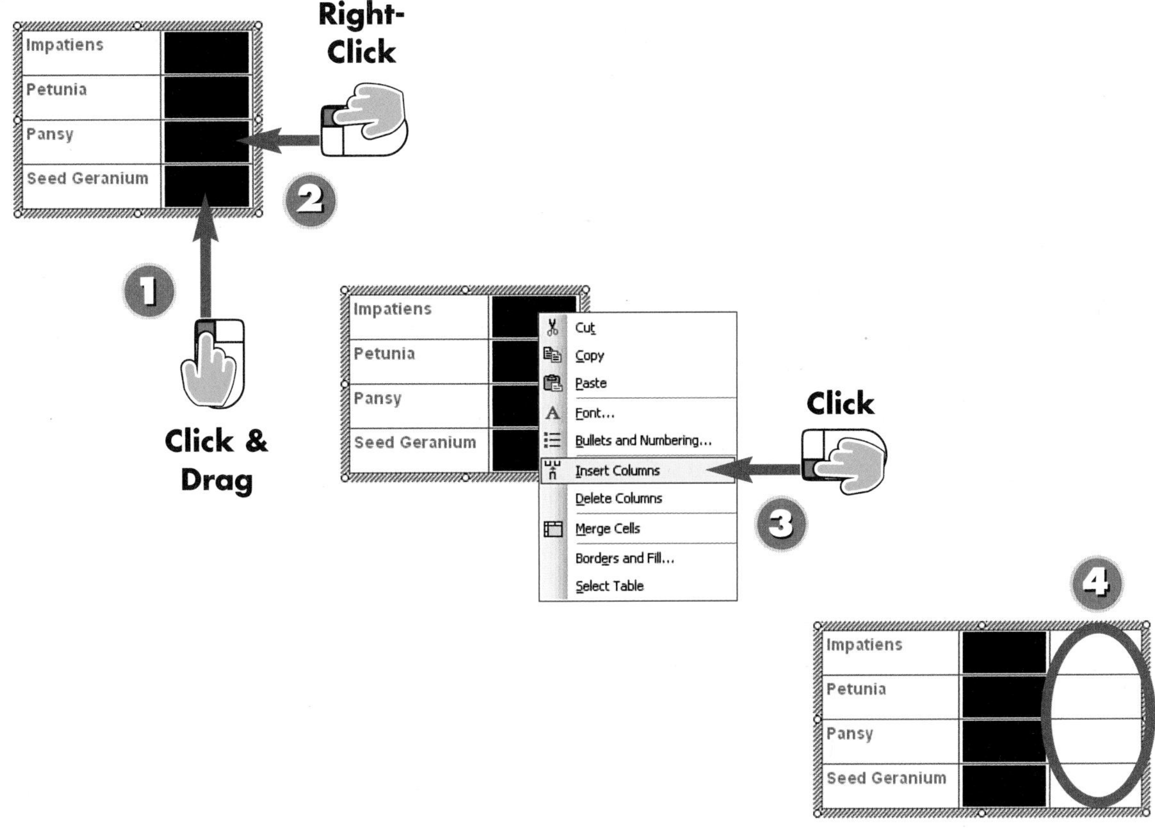

1. Click and drag over all the cells in a row to select the row, or click and drag over all the cells in a column to select the column.
2. Right-click the selected row or column.
3. Select **Insert Rows** or **Insert Columns** from the shortcut menu that appears.
4. PowerPoint adds a new row or column to the table.

INTRODUCTION

You can add more rows or columns to accommodate additional text in your slide table. When inserting rows, PowerPoint inserts the new row directly above the current row. When inserting columns, PowerPoint inserts the new column directly to the left of the current column.

TIP

Using the Toolbar
If the Tables and Borders toolbar is displayed, you can click the **Table** drop-down arrow, and then select whether to add a new column or row and specify where it should be placed. To display the toolbar, click the **Tables and Borders** button.

TIP

Resizing Your Table
If your table grows beyond the borders of your slide, you can resize the table to make it fit. Click the table border to select the entire table, and then drag a corner of the table to resize the table.

Deleting a Row or Column

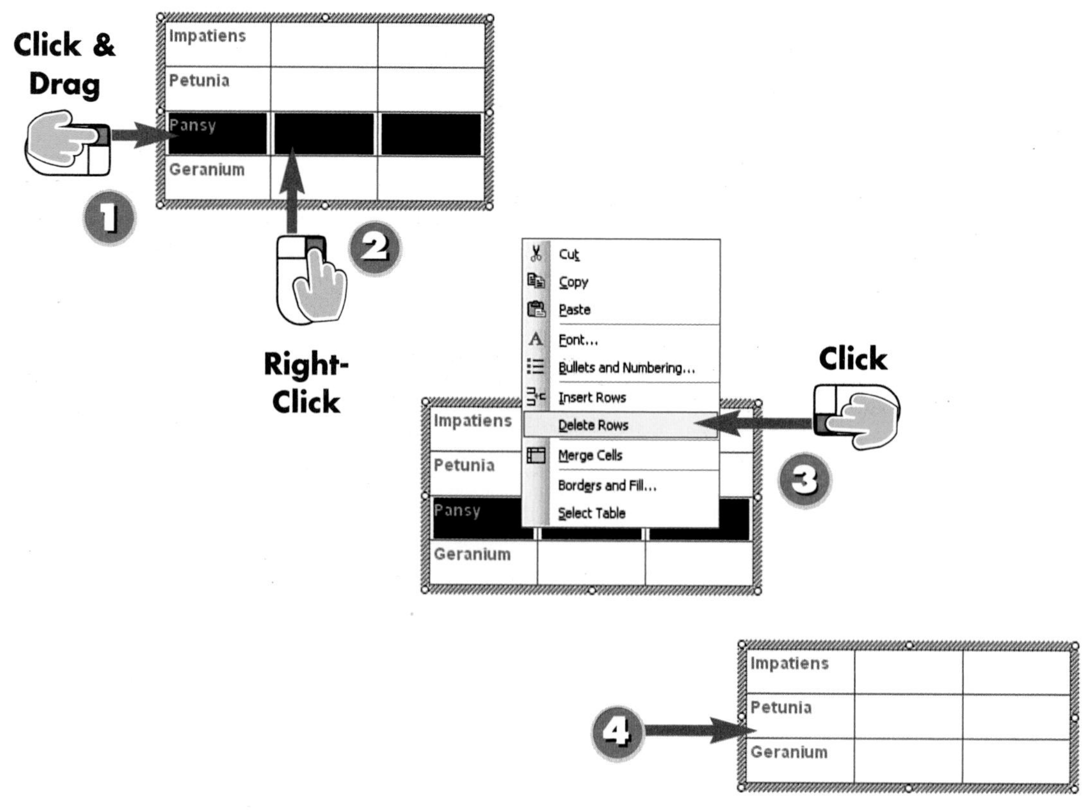

1. Click and drag over all the cells in a row to select the row, or click and drag over all the cells in a column to select the column.
2. Right-click over the selected row or column.
3. Select **Delete Rows** or **Delete Columns** from the shortcut menu that appears.
4. PowerPoint removes the selected row or column and shifts the remaining rows or columns to replace the deletion.

INTRODUCTION

You can quickly remove a row or column that you no longer need in your table. Removing a row or column also removes any text or images in the table cells.

TIP

Deleting Table Text
To remove table data rather than the row or column, drag over the cells and press the **Delete** key on your keyboard.

Combining Table Cells

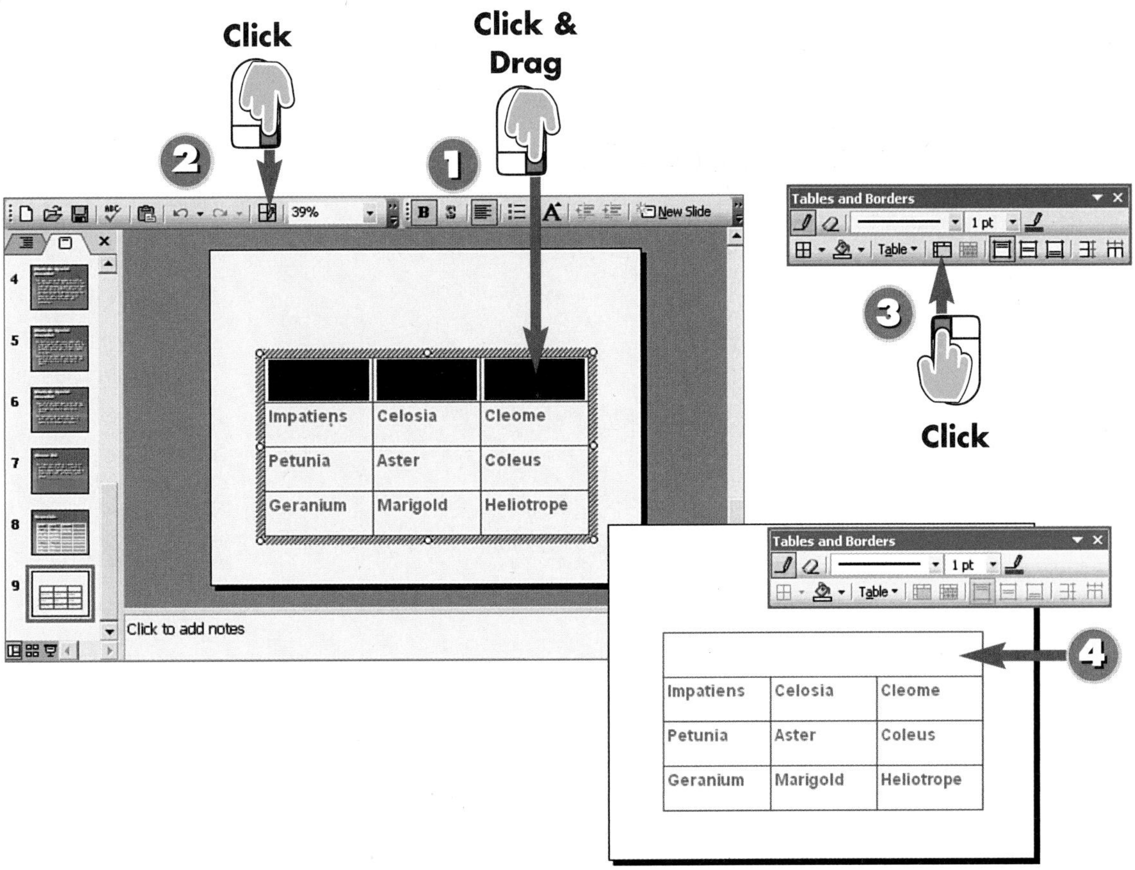

1. Click and drag over all the cells that you want to combine.
2. Click the **Tables and Borders** button on the Standard toolbar to open the Tables and Borders toolbar.
3. Click the **Merge Cells** button on the Tables and Borders toolbar.
4. PowerPoint merges the cells.

INTRODUCTION

You can merge two or more cells in a PowerPoint table to create one cell. This technique is commonly used to create a title cell that appears at the top of the table. You can also merge cells to combine a list of data or create a larger table cell to insert a picture, for example.

TIP

What Happens to Existing Text?
If you apply the Merge Cells command to table cells that already contain text, PowerPoint merges the cells and lists the data from each on a separate line within the new cell.

Splitting Table Cells

Start

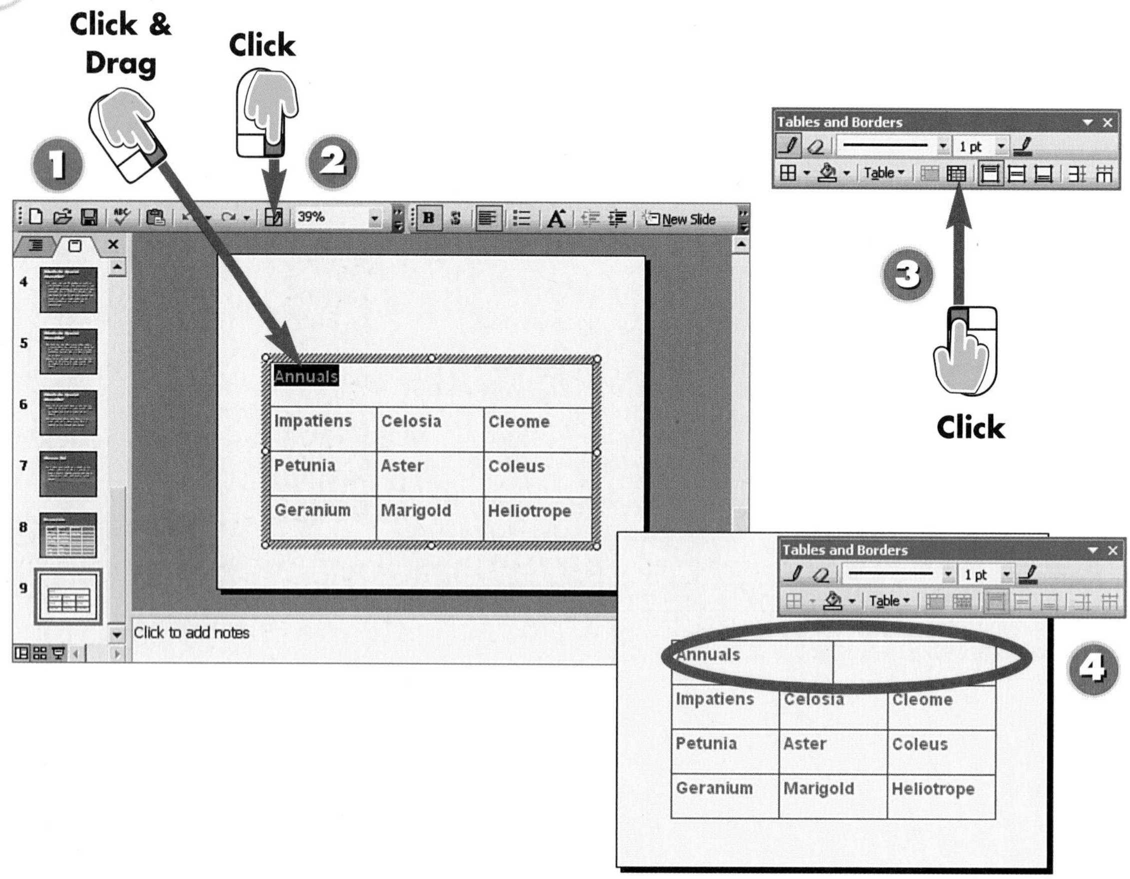

1. Click and drag over the cell that you want to split.
2. Click the **Tables and Borders** button on the Standard toolbar to open the Tables and Borders toolbar.
3. Click the **Split Cell** button on the Tables and Borders toolbar.
4. PowerPoint splits the cell into two cells.

INTRODUCTION

You can split a table cell into two separate cells. Splitting cells allows you to create customized cells within your table to suit your data needs.

TIP

Using the Other Toolbar Buttons

You can use the various tools in the Tables and Borders toolbar to customize your table structure. For example, you can click the **Draw Table** button and drag the tool over cells to add new lines to your table, splitting existing cells into separate cells. In addition, you can click the **Eraser** button and drag over table lines to erase cell borders and merge cells.

Changing Cell Background Color

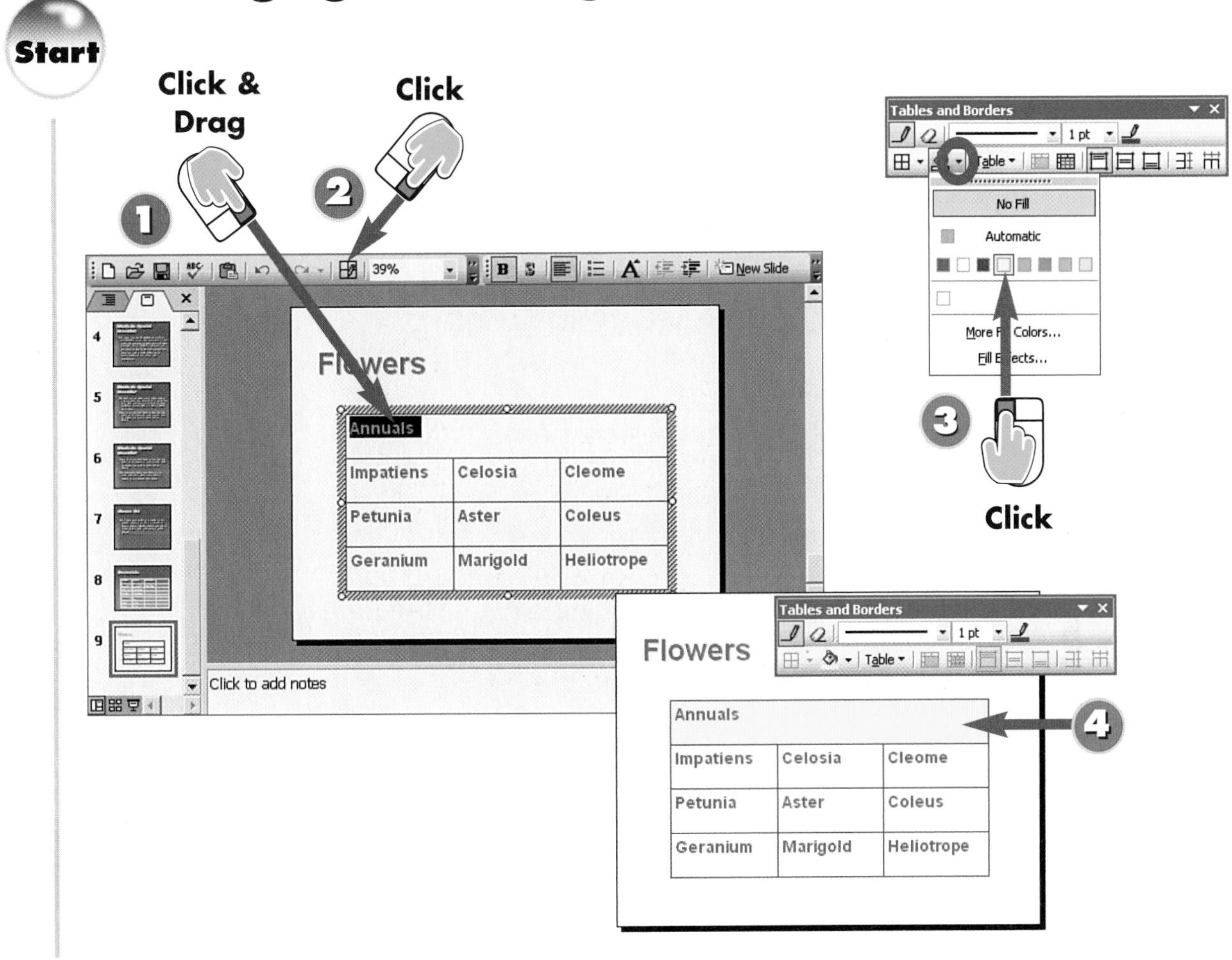

Click & Drag

Click

Click

1. Click and drag over the cell or cells to which you want to add a background color.

2. Click the **Tables and Borders** button on the Standard toolbar to open the Tables and Borders toolbar.

3. Click the **down arrow** next to the **Fill Color** button on the Tables and Borders toolbar, and click a color in the menu that appears.

4. PowerPoint applies the color to the selected cells.

INTRODUCTION

You can use color to emphasize different cells in your PowerPoint tables. By assigning different background colors behind table cells, you can customize the appearance of your table. Be sure to use a color that complements the table text; a color that conflicts with the text color will make the text illegible.

TIP

Accessing More Colors

You can use the **More Fill Colors** and **Fill Effects** options on the Fill Color menu to assign additional colors, textures, or patterns to your table cells. See Part 6, "Changing the Appearance of Slides," to learn more about how these features work when applied to slide backgrounds. You can use the same techniques to customize table cell backgrounds.

Aligning Cell Text

Click

Click & Drag

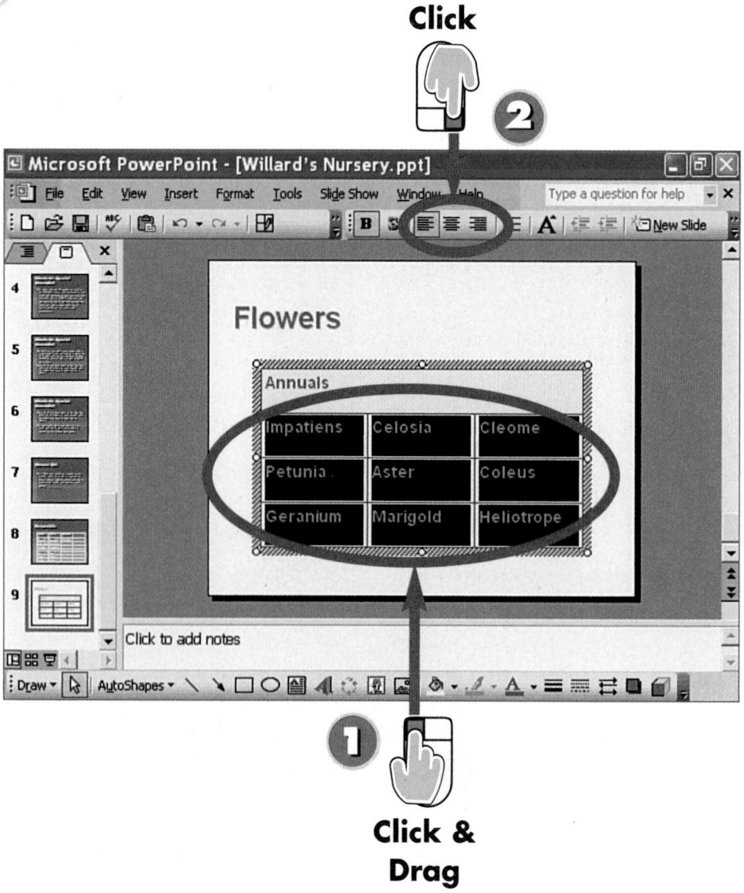

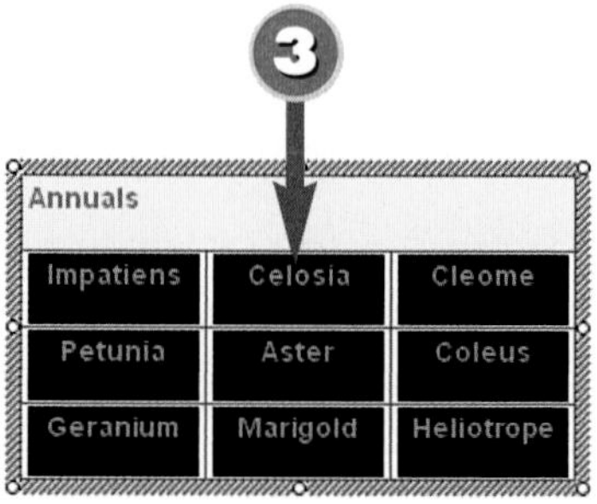

1. Click and drag over the cell or cells to which you want to change alignment.
2. Click the **Align Left** button to align text to the left, the **Center** button to center text, or the **Align Right** button to align text to the right.
3. PowerPoint applies the new alignment. In this example, the cell text is centered horizontally in the cell.

INTRODUCTION

By default, when you type table text, the text is aligned to the left in each cell. You can quickly change the alignment using the alignment buttons on the Formatting toolbar. You can also adjust the vertical alignment of your table text. By default, PowerPoint vertically aligns cell text to appear at the top of the cell, but you can set the alignment to the center or bottom of the table cell.

TIP

Selecting the Entire Table

To quickly select all the cells in your table for editing, simply click the table border. You can also click the **Table** button on the Tables and Borders toolbar and then click **Select Table**.

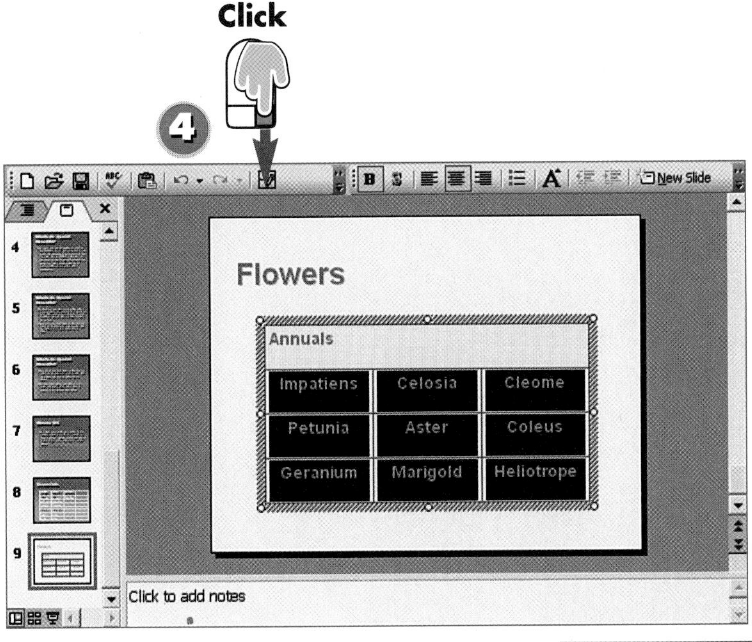

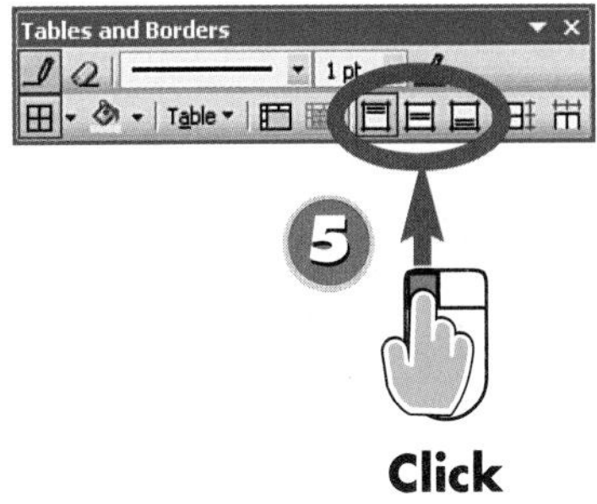

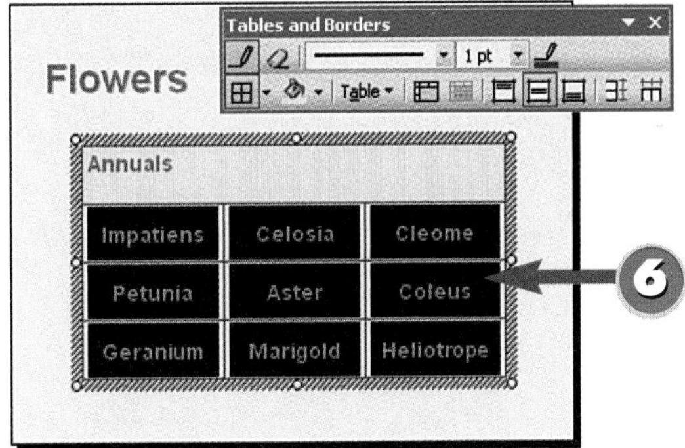

4. To change the vertical alignment of the text in selected cells, click the **Tables and Borders** button on the Standard toolbar.
5. Click **Align Top** to align text to the top of the cell, **Center Vertically** to center the text vertically in the cell, or **Align Bottom** to align the text to the bottom of the cell.
6. PowerPoint applies the new alignment. In this example, the cell text is centered vertically in the cell.

TIP

Closing the Toolbar
When you finish editing your table, you can close the Tables and Borders toolbar by clicking the **Tables and Borders** button on the Standard toolbar, which toggles the toolbar on or off. You can also close it by clicking the toolbar's **Close** button.

Changing Table Borders

Start

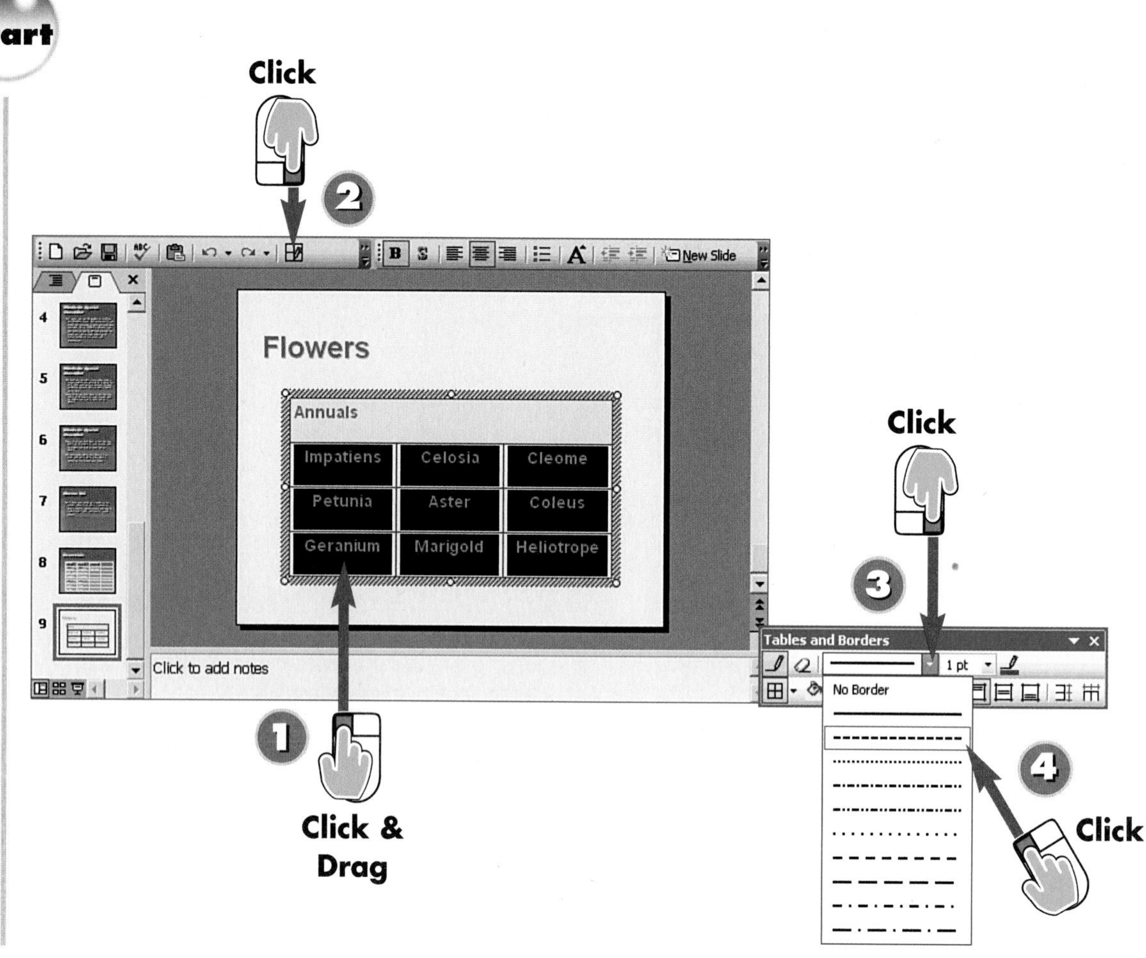

1. Click and drag over the cells you want to edit.
2. Click the **Tables and Borders** button on the Standard toolbar to open the Tables and Borders toolbar.
3. To change the border style, click the **Border Style** drop-down arrow.
4. Select a style from the list.

INTRODUCTION

Another way to customize your slide tables is to format the borders surrounding the table cells. For example, you might add a thick border around cells containing important data. This helps to draw attention to the data.

TIP

Controlling Border Thickness

To make a border appear thicker or thinner, click the down arrow next to the **Border Width** button in the Tables and Borders toolbar and choose a line width for the border.

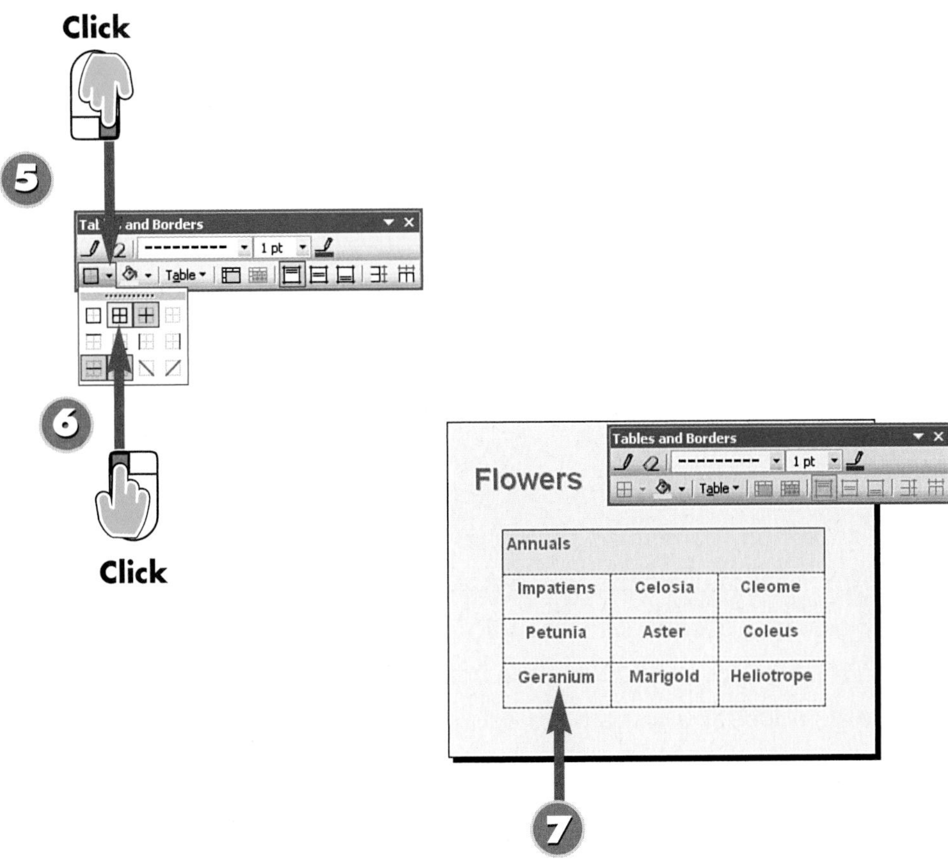

5 Click the **down arrow** next to the **Borders** button on the Tables and Borders toolbar.

6 Select the type of border you want. For example, click the **All Borders** option to apply the customized border to all sides of the selected table cells.

7 PowerPoint applies the settings to the selected cells.

TIP

Adding Color
Add color to your cell borders to really make them stand out. To do so, click the **Border Color** button in the Tables and Borders toolbar and choose a color for the border.

TIP

Adding Color Behind the Cells
You can add background color behind any cell in your table. See the task "Changing Cell Background Color" earlier in this part to learn more.

PART 9

Adding Multimedia Elements

You can punch up your presentation by adding multimedia elements—such as sound effects, movies, background music, recorded narration, and more—to your slides. Each multimedia element, or clip, you add to a slide becomes a slide object that you can then manipulate. You can add a single multimedia object, or include several on the same slide.

You can choose from a variety of prerecorded sound clips from PowerPoint's clip-art collection, as well as animated GIF files. You can also add your own video clips, such as footage you record with a digital camcorder. You can even record your own sounds and narration to go along with your presentation, or you can instruct PowerPoint to play background music from a music CD-ROM. A few well-placed multimedia objects can really make your slide show come to life.

Sound Clips

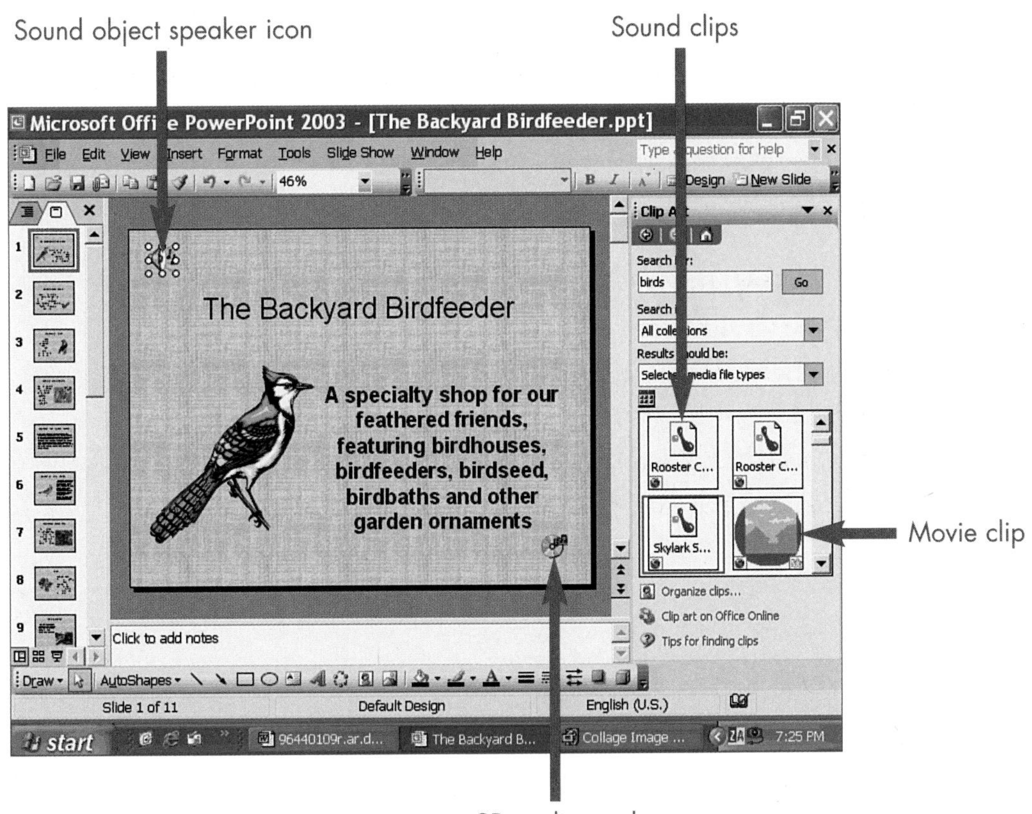
Sound object speaker icon
Sound clips
Movie clip
CD audio track
Microsoft Office PowerPoint 2003 - [The Backyard Birdfeeder.ppt]
The Backyard Birdfeeder
A specialty shop for our feathered friends, featuring birdhouses, birdfeeders, birdseed, birdbaths and other garden ornaments
Click to add notes
Slide 1 of 11
Default Design
English (U.S.)
Organize clips...
Clip art on Office Online
Tips for finding clips

Adding a Sound Clip with the Clip Organizer

Start

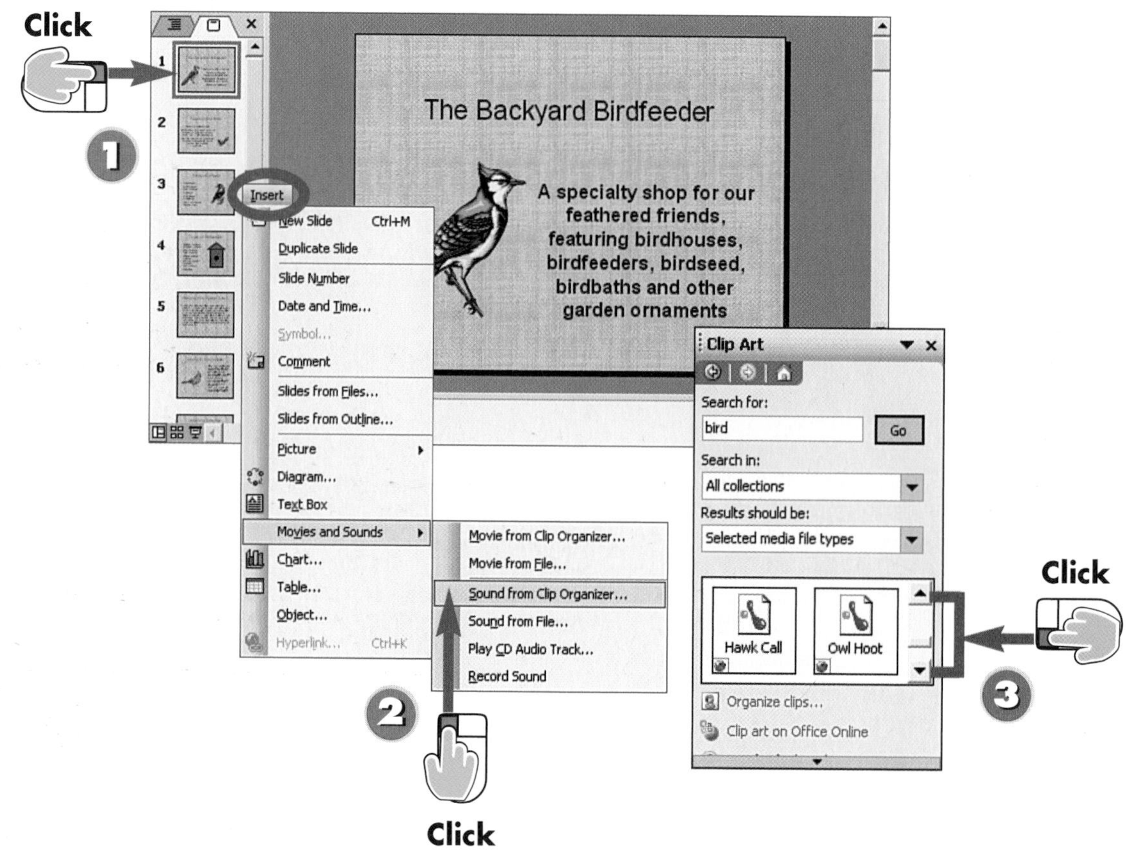

1. Click the slide to which you want to add a sound.
2. Open the **Insert** menu, choose **Movies and Sounds**, and select **Sound from Clip Organizer**.
3. The Clip Art Task pane opens, listing available sound clips. Click the scroll arrows to search through the list for sounds.

INTRODUCTION

The Clip Art gallery includes multimedia clips in addition to clip art. You can choose from a variety of prerecorded sound clips to enhance your slides, and can preview the available sound clips before applying them to your slides.

TIP

Using a Multimedia Placeholder
If your slide layout contains a Media Clip icon, you can click it to open the Media Clip dialog box and sift through the various sound and movie clips. Click the one you want, and click **OK** to add it to your slide.

TIP

Finding More Sounds
To locate more sound clips, click the **Clip Art on Microsoft.com** link at the bottom of the Clip Art Task pane and log on to the Microsoft Web site to browse for more clips.

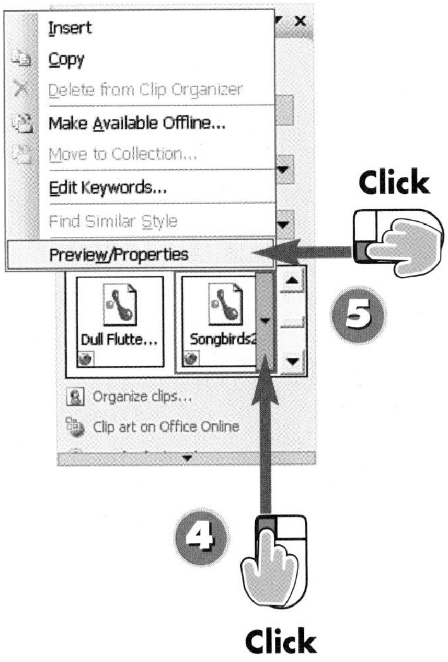

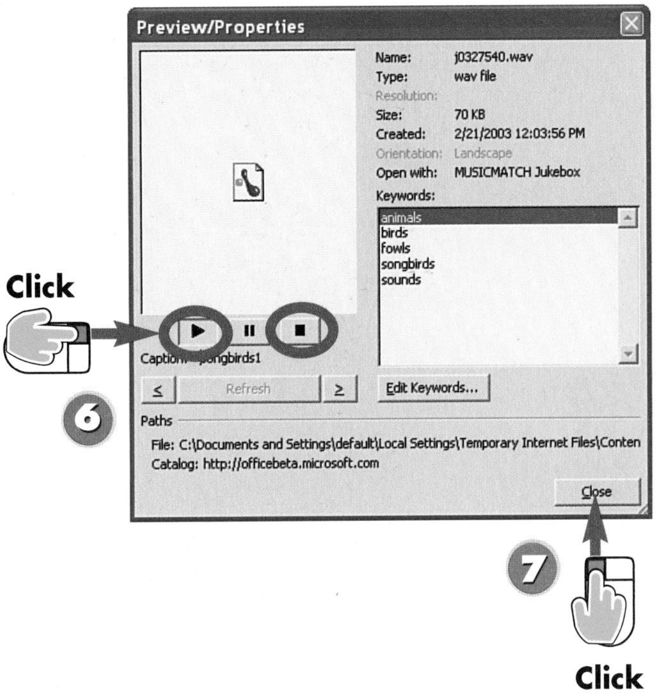

4. To preview a sound, move the mouse pointer over the sound clip icon and click the drop-down arrow.

5. Click **Preview/Properties** in the menu that appears.

6. The Preview/Properties dialog box opens and plays the sound clip. Click the **Stop** button to stop the sound from playing, or click the **Play** button to play the sound again.

7. Click **Close**.

TIP

Sound Clip File Format

The sound clips available in the Clip Art Task pane are WAV files, a popular sound file on the Web.

HINT

Checking the Playing Time

After you add the clip to the slide, you can check its playing time by right-clicking the speaker icon and selecting **Edit Sound Object** from the menu that appears. The Sound Options dialog box opens, displaying the playing time as well as options for controlling the sound.

Adding a Sound Clip with the Clip Organizer (Continued)

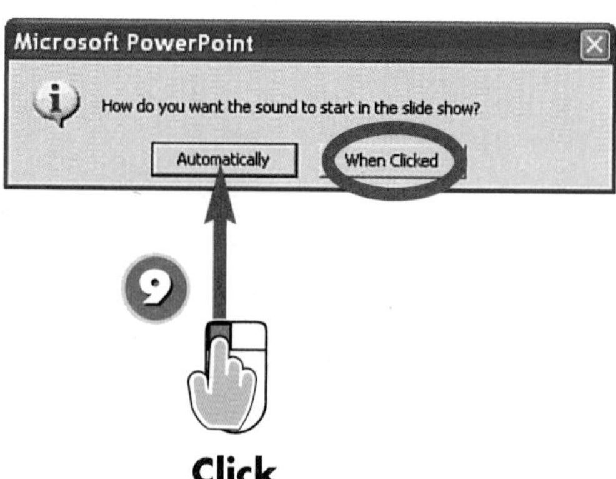

8. When you locate a sound clip you want to use, click the clip to add it to your slide.

9. Click **Automatically** to have the sound play automatically when the slide is displayed in your presentation, or **When Clicked** if you want to activate the sound clip manually.

TIP

Sound Clips as Slide Objects

Sound clips appear as speaker icons on the slide, and as a slide object, they can be moved around the slide and resized.

HINT

Playing the Clip During the Show

If you opted to play the clip when clicked, you can click the speaker icon at any time the slide is onscreen to play the sound.

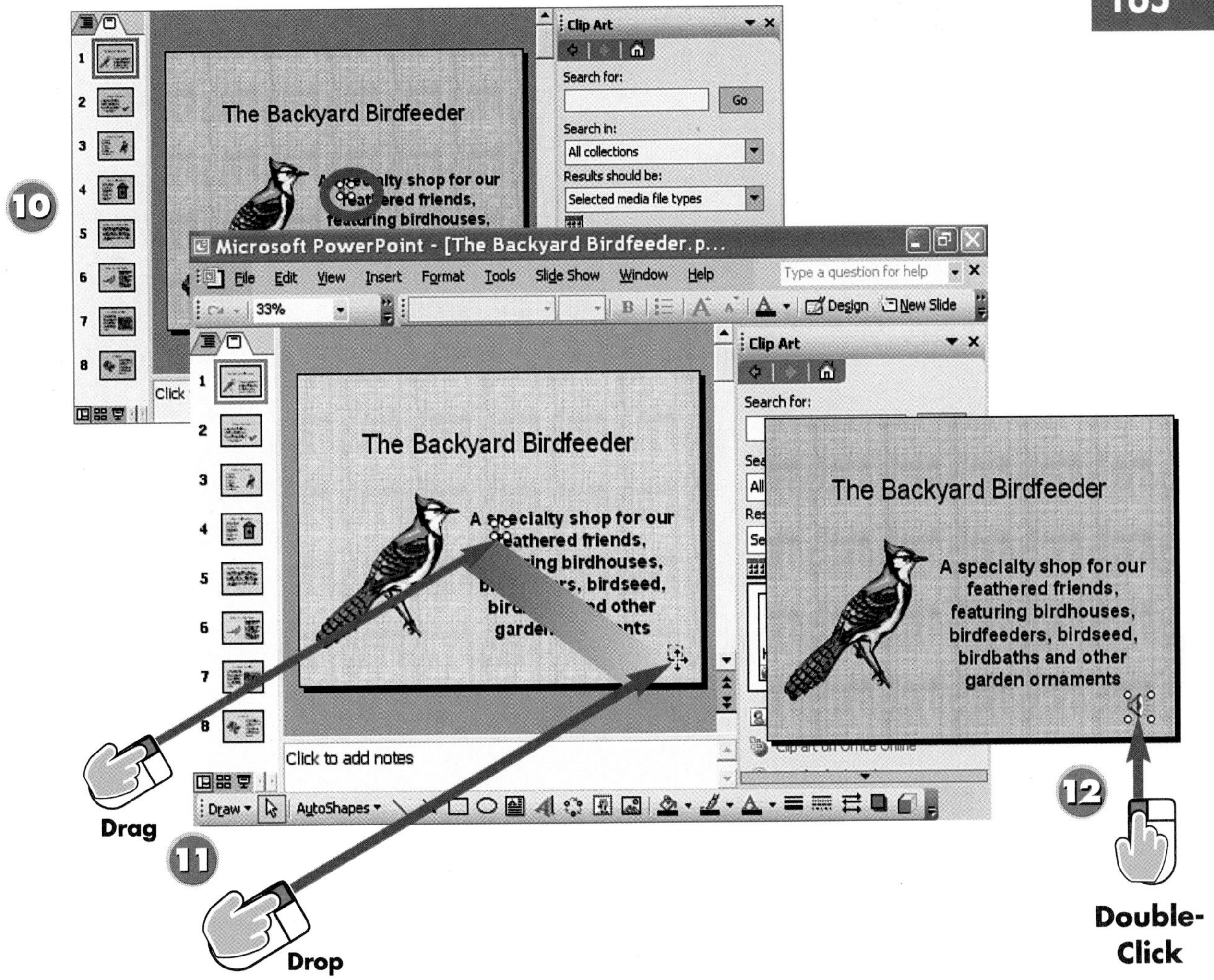

10 PowerPoint adds a speaker icon to your slide to represent the clip and leaves the Clip Art Task pane open.

11 Click and drag the speaker icon to the corner of your slide.

12 Double-click the icon to play the sound.

Hiding the Clip

TIP

If you chose to play the clip automatically, you can drag the speaker icon off of the slide so it remains a part of the slide, but not visible to your audience.

Removing a Clip

TIP

To remove a clip from your slide, click the speaker icon and press the **Delete** key on your keyboard.

Viewing the Show

TIP

To learn more about viewing your presentation as a slide show, see Parts 10 and 12.

Adding a Sound File

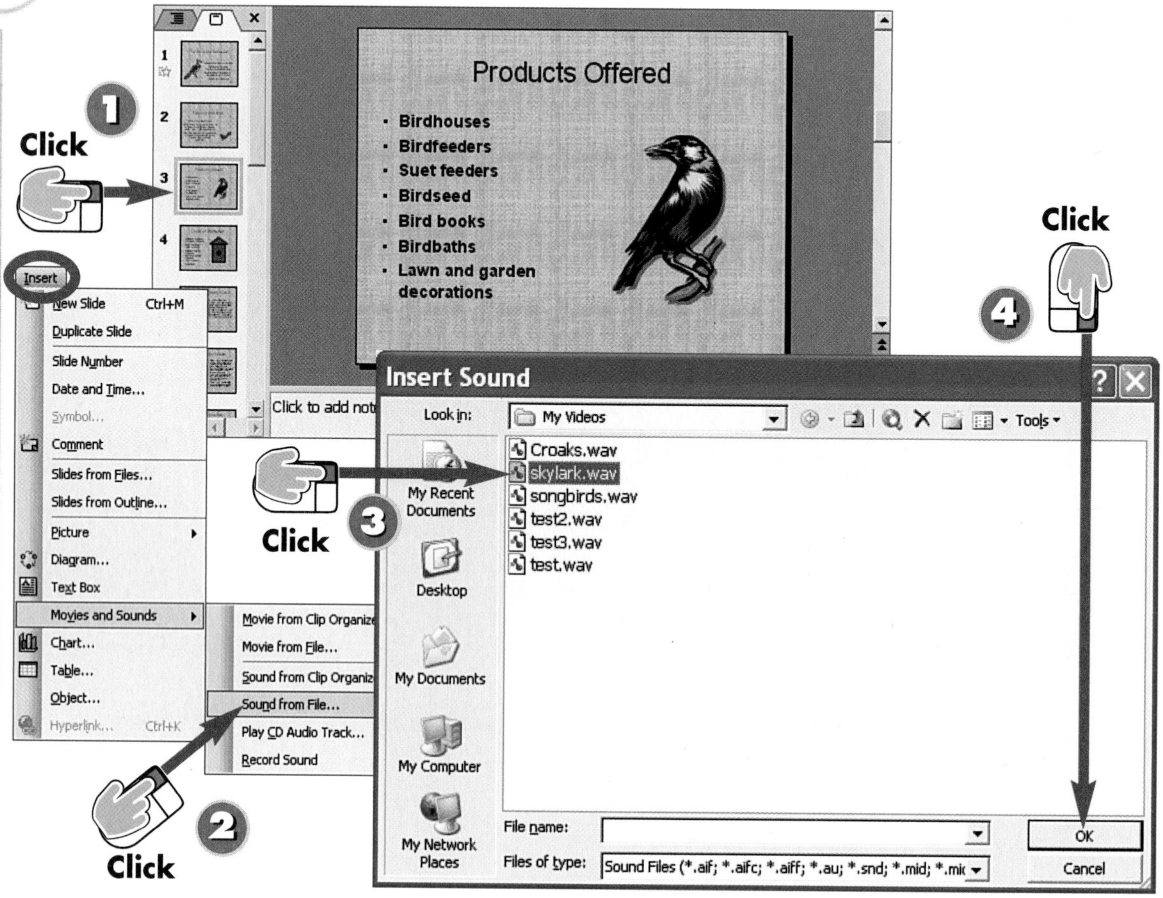

1. Click the slide to which you want to add a sound.
2. Open the **Insert** menu, choose **Movies and Sounds**, and select **Sound from File**.
3. The Insert Sound dialog box opens. Locate and select the sound file you want to add.
4. Click **OK**.

INTRODUCTION

You aren't limited to using sound files found in the Clip Art Gallery in your presentations. If you like, you can add sound files that you obtain from other sources. All sound clips appear as speaker icons on the slide. When adding a sound file, you can choose to have the sound file play automatically or only when its icon is clicked.

TIP

Supported Sound Formats

You can add AIFF, AU, MIDI, MP3, Windows Media, and other popular sound file formats to your PowerPoint slides.

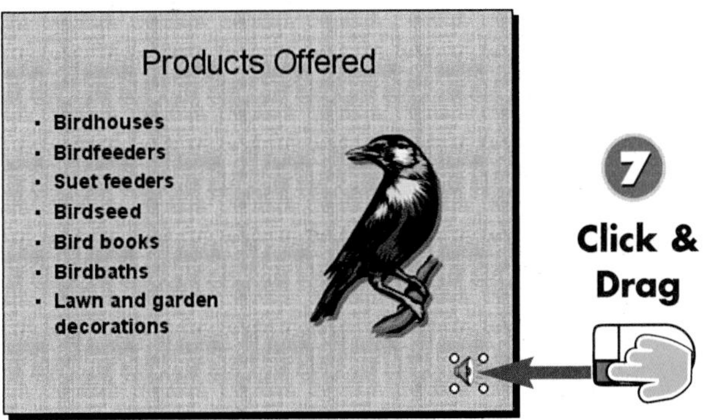

5 Click **Automatically** to have the sound play automatically when the slide is displayed in your presentation, or **When Clicked** if you want to activate the sound clip manually.

6 PowerPoint adds a speaker icon to your slide representing the clip.

7 Click and drag the speaker icon to the corner of your slide. You can double-click the icon to play the sound.

TIP

Moving the Icon

For best visual results, it's a good idea to move the speaker icon for your sound file to a less noticeable location on your slide. Click and drag the icon to a corner or an empty area of your slide.

TIP

Removing a Clip

To remove a clip from your slide, click the speaker icon and press the **Delete** key on your keyboard.

CAUTION

Linking or Embedding

If your sound file is more than 100KB in size, PowerPoint adds a link to the file rather than embedding it on the slide. If you share your presentation with someone else you'll need to include the sound file along with the PowerPoint file.

Recording Sounds

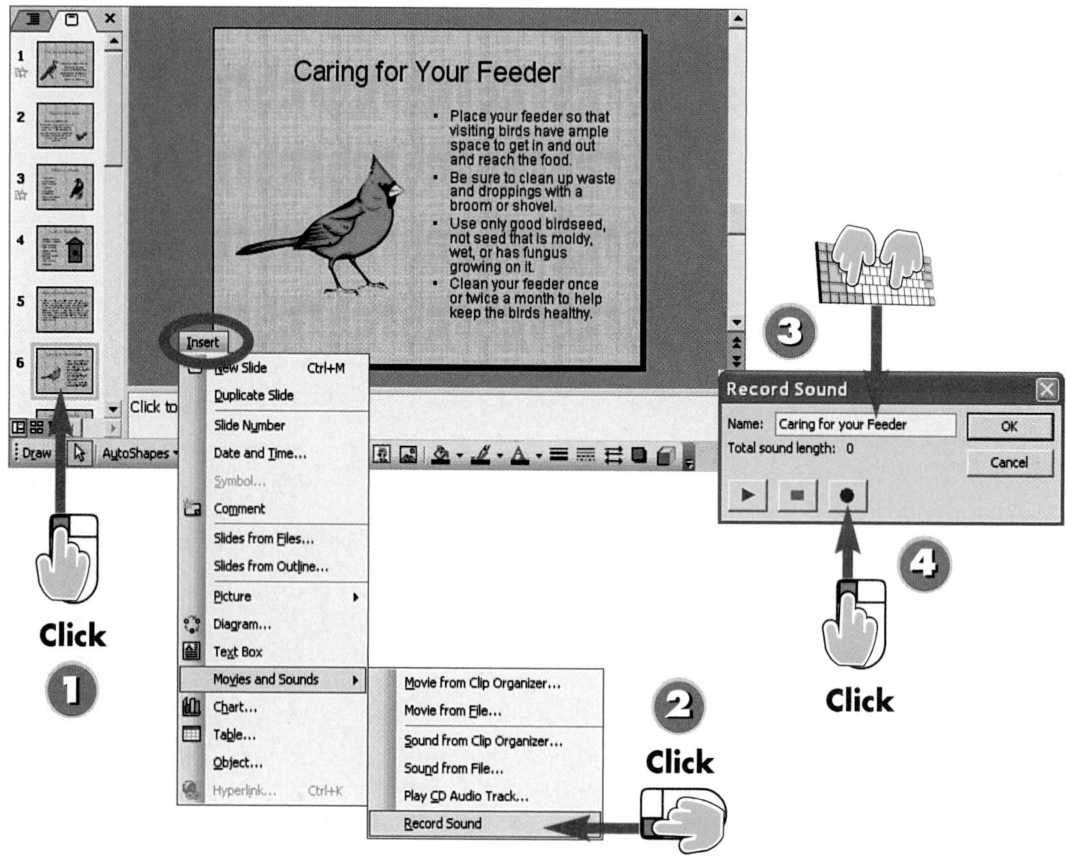

1. Click the slide to which you want to add a recorded sound.
2. Open the **Insert** menu, choose **Movies and Sounds**, and select **Record Sound**.
3. The Record Sound dialog box opens. Type a name for the sound in the **Name** field.
4. Click the **Record** button to begin recording, and speak into your computer's microphone or recording device.

INTRODUCTION

In addition to including prerecorded sounds on your slides, you can record new sounds to use in a presentation. In order to do this, your computer needs to have a microphone installed on it.

TIP

Recording Sound Effects
You can use your computer microphone to record more than your voice. With a little creativity, you can create your own sound effects.

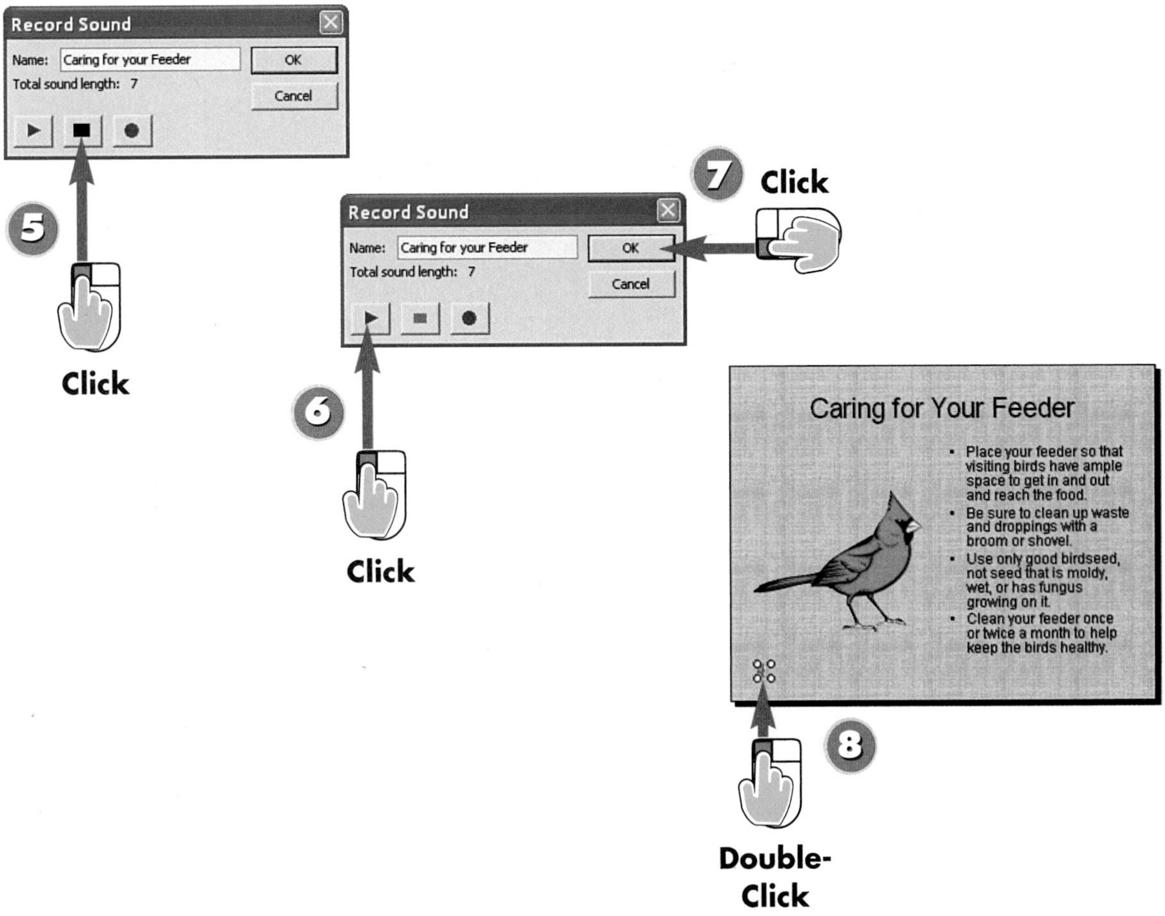
Record Sound
Name: Caring for your Feeder
Total sound length: 7
OK
Cancel
5
Click
Record Sound
Name: Caring for your Feeder
Total sound length: 7
OK
Cancel
6
Click
7 Click
Caring for Your Feeder
Place your feeder so that visiting birds have ample space to get in and out and reach the food.
Be sure to clean up waste and droppings with a broom or shovel.
Use only good birdseed, not seed that is moldy, wet, or has fungus growing on it.
Clean your feeder once or twice a month to help keep the birds healthy.
8
Double-Click

5. When you finish recording the sound, click the **Stop** button.

6. To play back the sound, click **Play**.

7. Click **OK**.

8. PowerPoint adds the sound to your slide as a speaker icon. Double-click the speaker icon to play the recorded sound.

End

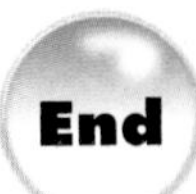

TIP

Moving the Icon
You MIGHT need to move the speaker icon for the recorded sound so it does not interfere with other slide objects. Click and drag the icon to reposition it on the slide.

TIP

Playing the Sound During the Show
When you run your slide show and reach the slide containing the recorded sound, you must click the speaker icon on the slide to play the recording. See Parts 10 and 12 to learn more about running a slide show.

Adding Narration

Start

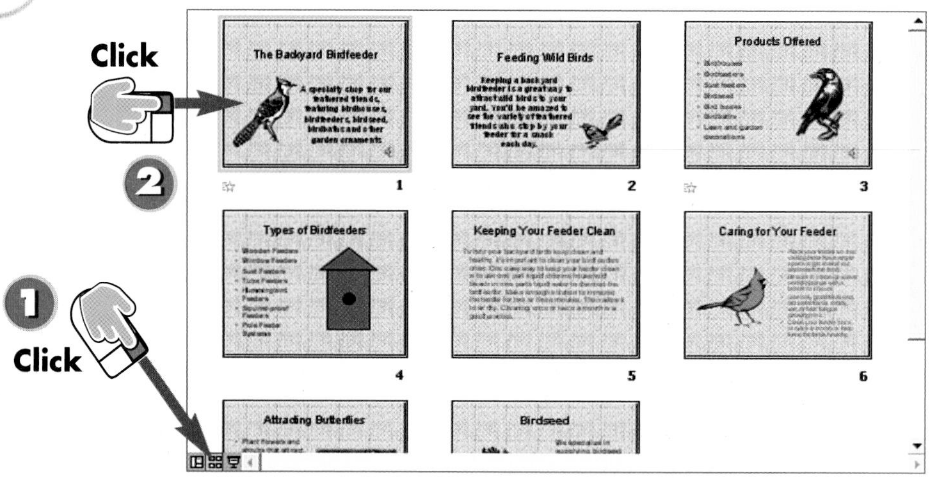

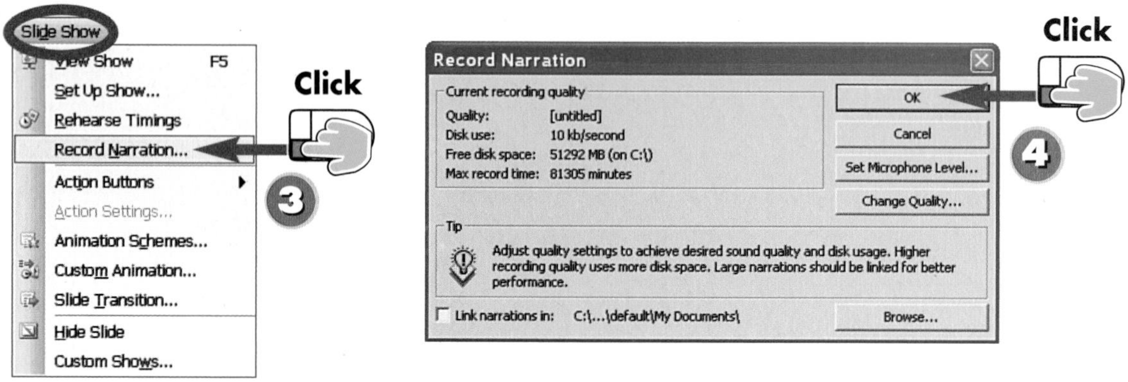

1. Click the **Slide Sorter View** button to switch to Slide Sorter view.
2. Click the first slide in the presentation.
3. Open the **Slide Show** menu and choose **Record Narration**.
4. The Record Narration dialog box opens. Click **OK** to begin.

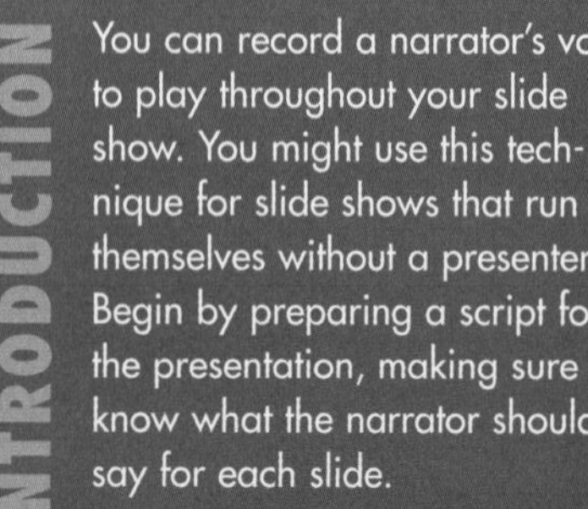

INTRODUCTION

You can record a narrator's voice to play throughout your slide show. You might use this technique for slide shows that run by themselves without a presenter. Begin by preparing a script for the presentation, making sure you know what the narrator should say for each slide.

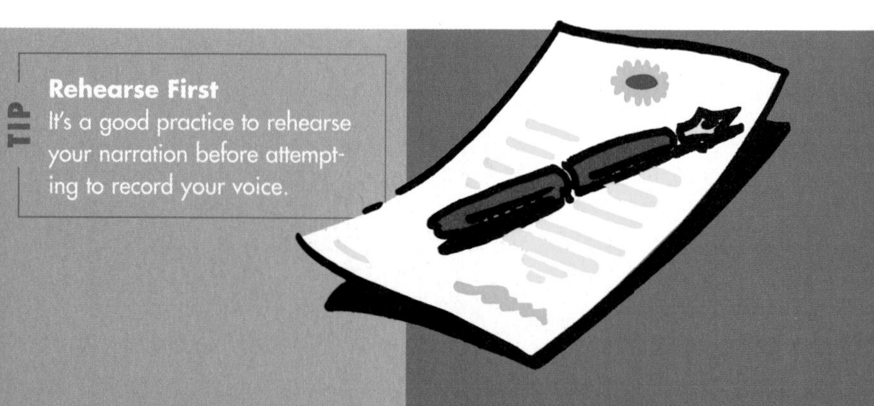

TIP

Rehearse First

It's a good practice to rehearse your narration before attempting to record your voice.

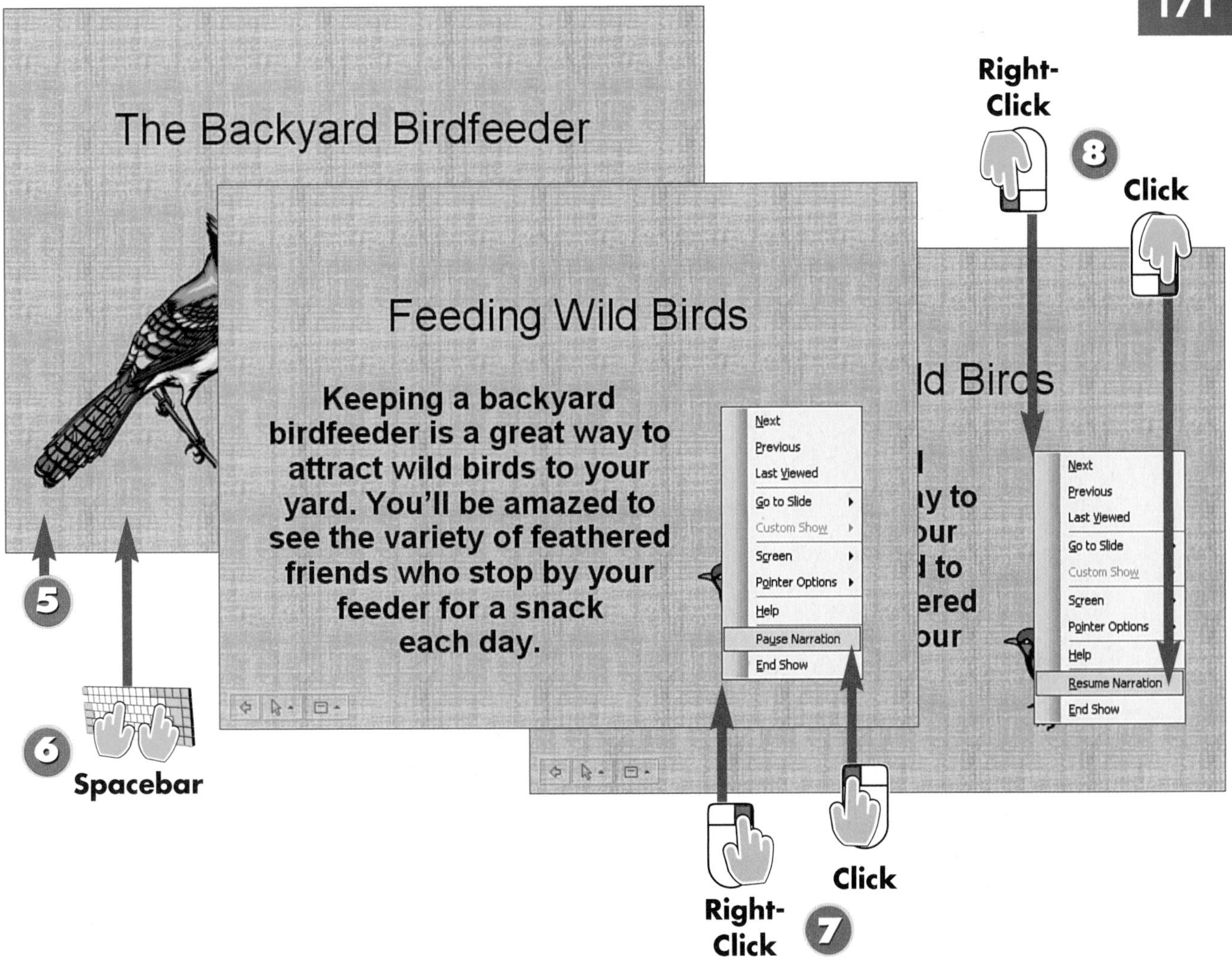

The Backyard Birdfeeder

Feeding Wild Birds

Keeping a backyard birdfeeder is a great way to attract wild birds to your yard. You'll be amazed to see the variety of feathered friends who stop by your feeder for a snack each day.

Next
Previous
Last Viewed
Go to Slide
Custom Show
Screen
Pointer Options
Help
Pause Narration
End Show

Next
Previous
Last Viewed
Go to Slide
Custom Show
Screen
Pointer Options
Help
Resume Narration
End Show

5

6 Spacebar

7 Right-Click Click

8 Right-Click Click

5. PowerPoint displays the first slide. Speak into your microphone to record the narration for the slide.

6. Press the **Spacebar** to continue to the next slide.

7. To pause your recording at anytime, right-click the slide and click **Pause Narration** in the shortcut menu that appears.

8. To resume your recording, right-click the slide and click **Resume Narration** in the shortcut menu that appears.

TIP

Checking Your Microphone

Click the **Set Microphone Level** button in the Record Narration dialog box to test your microphone before recording. Then, speak into the microphone and watch the monitor scale for changes in display. If you see fluctuations in the scale, you know the microphone is working. You can move the slider to adjust the volume level. Click **OK** when finished testing your equipment.

Adding Narration (Continued)

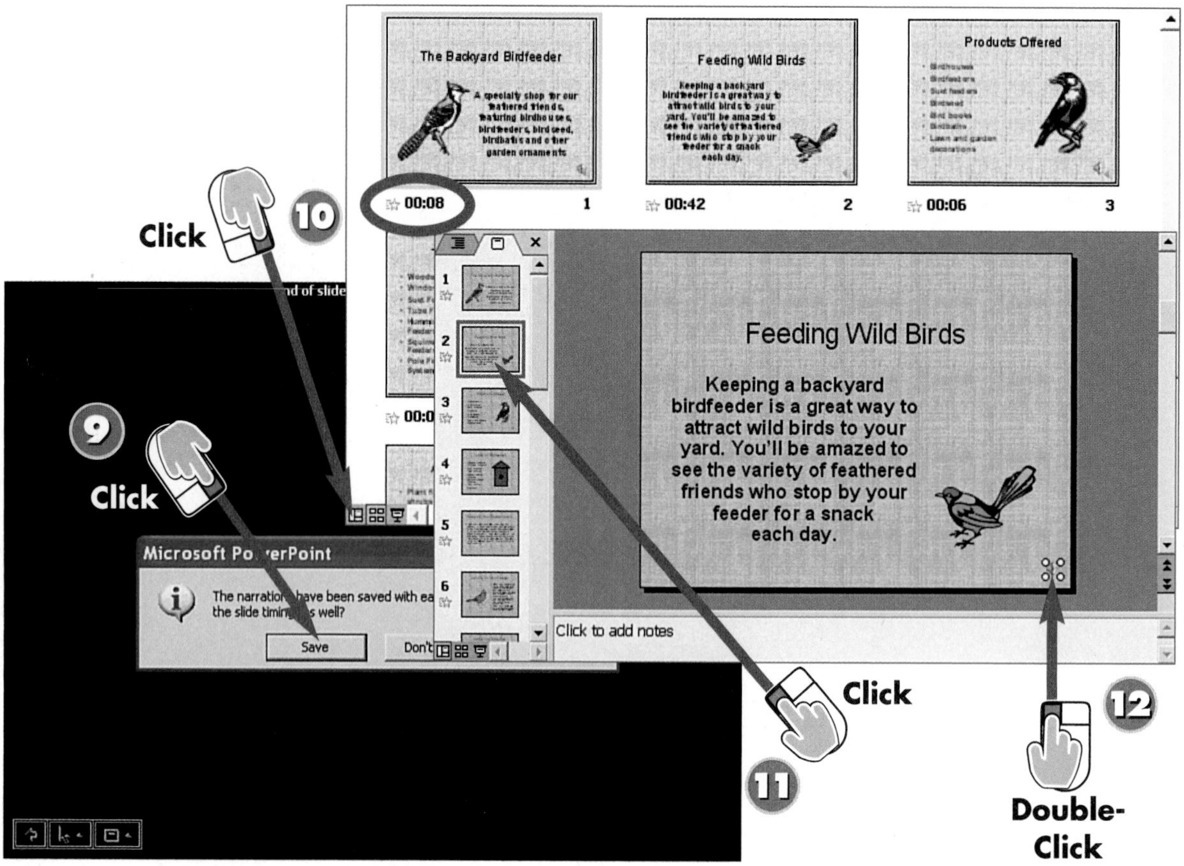

9. At the end of the slide show, a dialog box appears. Click **Save** to save the slide timings along with the narration.

10. PowerPoint returns you to Slide Sorter view and displays the narration times beneath each slide. Click the **Normal View** button to return to Normal view.

11. Click a slide containing narration.

12. Double-click the speaker icon to hear the recording for that slide.

> **TIP**
>
> **Removing Narration from a Slide**
>
> To remove the narration for a particular slide, display the slide in Normal view, click the speaker icon, and press the **Delete** key on your keyboard.

> **TIP**
>
> **Temporarily Turning Off the Narration**
>
> To turn off the narration but keep the recording as part of your presentation, open the **Slide Show** menu and choose **Set Up Show** to open the Set Up Show dialog box. Then, deselect the **Show Without Narration** check box and click **OK**.

Playing a Music CD with a Presentation

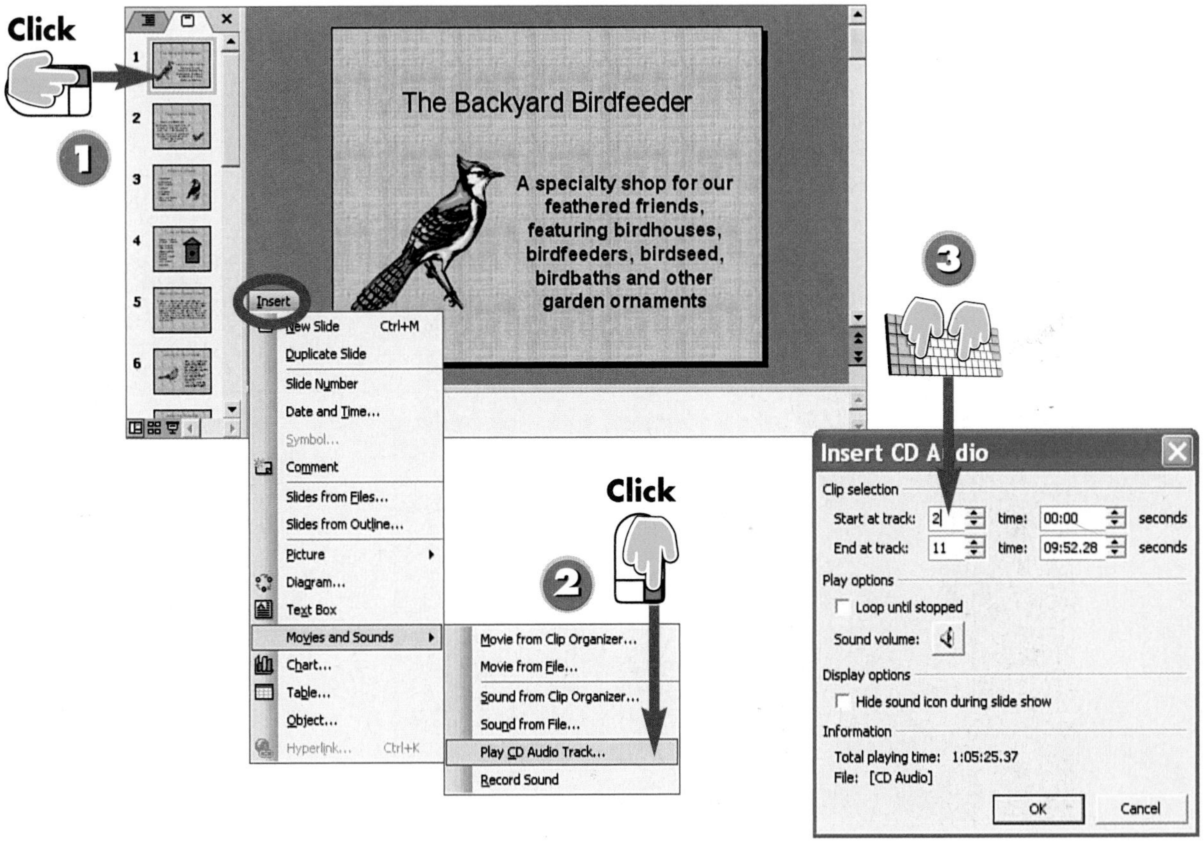

1. After you insert the CD into your computer's CD-ROM drive, click the first slide in your presentation.
2. Open the **Insert** menu, choose **Movies and Sounds**, and select **Play CD Audio Track**.
3. The Insert CD Audio dialog box opens. Click the **Start at Track** field and type the track number of the first track you want to play.

See next page

INTRODUCTION

Another way to add sound to your presentation is to play a music CD along with the show. Music CDs provide great background music, and you can set the music up to play along with as many slides as you need.

CAUTION

Using Another Computer
If you plan to show your presentation on another computer, be sure that computer has a CD-ROM drive to accommodate your slide-show music.

Playing a Music CD with a Presentation (Continued)

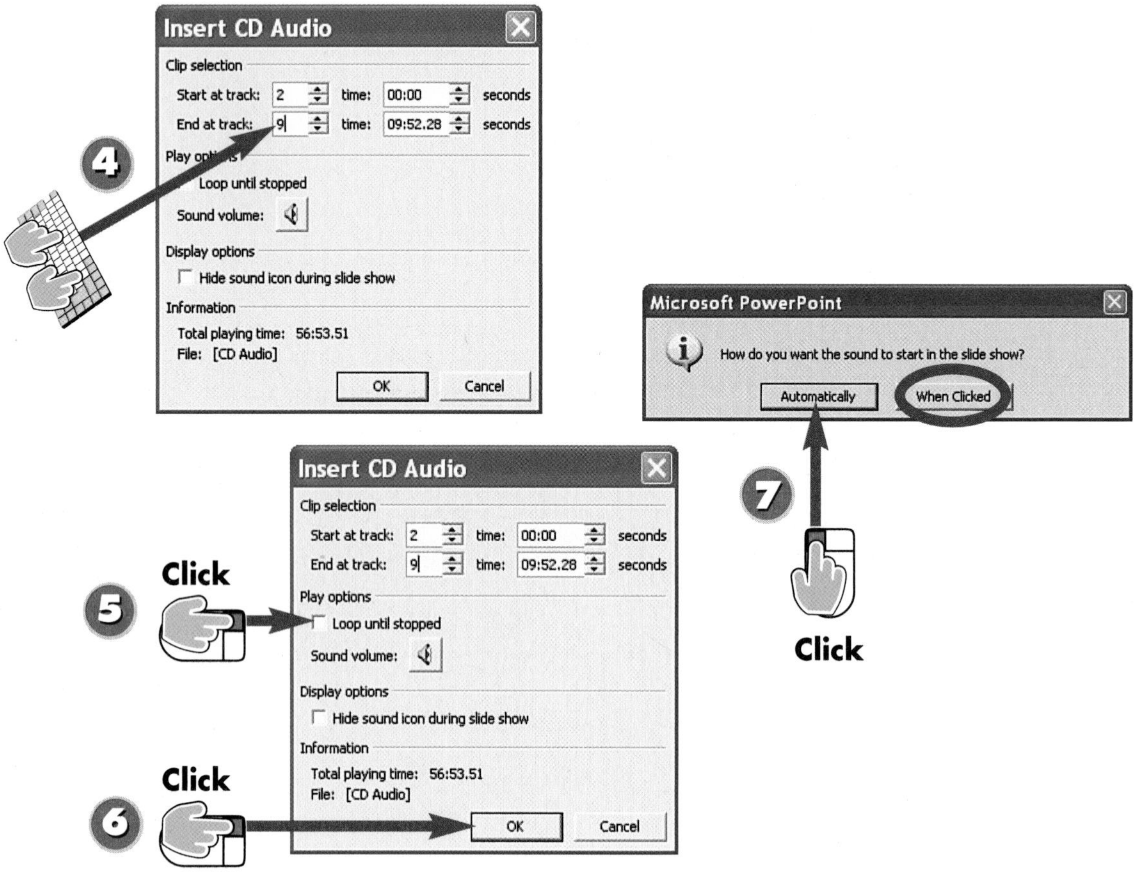

4. Click the **End at Track** field and type the track number of the last track you want to play.
5. Click the **Loop Until Stopped** check box to make the music play continually.
6. Click **OK**.
7. Click **Automatically** to have the CD play as soon as the slide is displayed in your presentation, or **When Clicked** if you want to activate the CD manually.

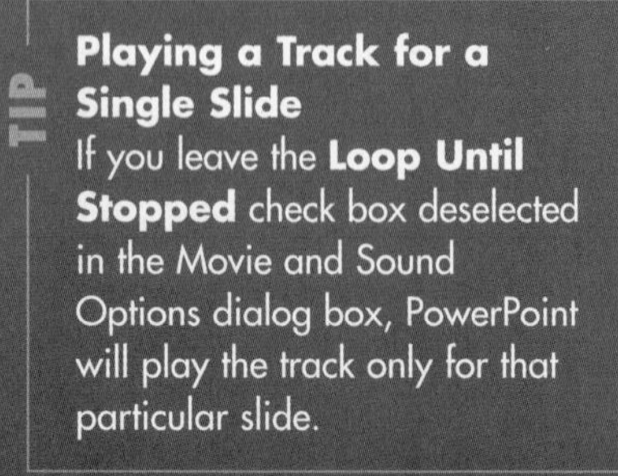

Playing a Track for a Single Slide

If you leave the **Loop Until Stopped** check box deselected in the Movie and Sound Options dialog box, PowerPoint will play the track only for that particular slide.

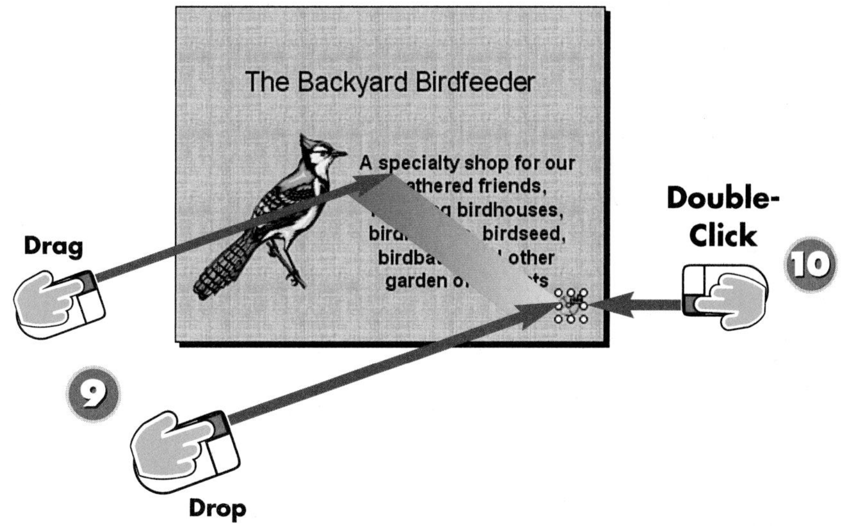

8 PowerPoint adds a CD icon to the current slide.

9 Click and drag the CD icon to the corner of your slide.

10 Double-click the CD icon to play the CD.

CAUTION

A Reminder
Don't forget to put your music CD in before you start your slide show during an actual presentation.

TIP

Changing the Object Order
If your slide includes sound and movie clips as well as instructions for playing a CD, you may need to arrange the order in which each object is played. To do so, open the **Slide Show** menu and choose **Custom Animation** to open the Custom Animation pane. Click the object you want to change in the list order and click a reorder button to move the item up or own in the list.

Adding a Movie Clip with the Clip Organizer

Start

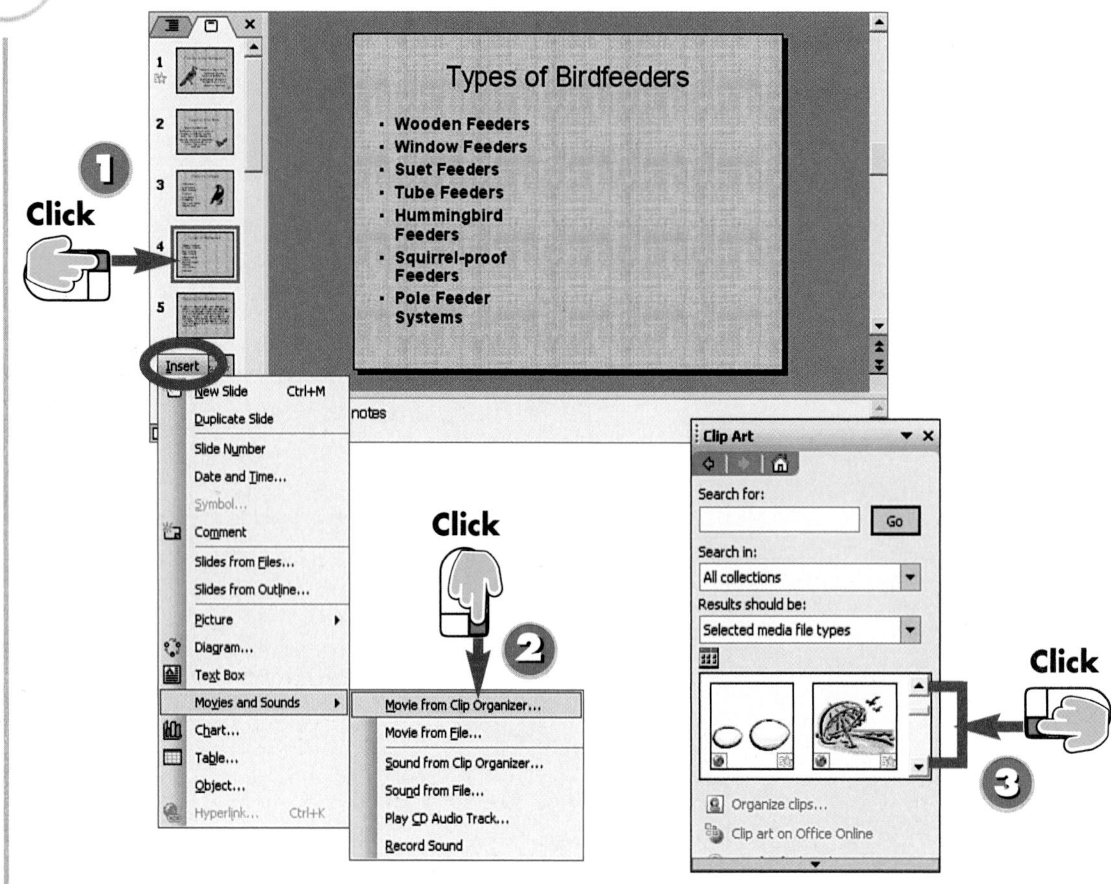

1. Click the slide to which you want to add a movie clip.
2. Open the **Insert** menu, choose **Movies and Sounds**, and select **Movie from Clip Organizer**.
3. The Clip Art Task pane opens, listing the available movie clips. Click the scroll arrows to search through the list.

INTRODUCTION

Another way you can enhance your presentation's message is through the use of movie or video clips. The Clip Art gallery includes a variety of short animated art clips in addition to regular clip art. You can preview any movie clip before applying it to your slide.

TIP

Using a Multimedia Placeholder
If your slide layout contains a Media Clip icon, you can click it to open the Media Clip dialog box and sift through the various sound and movie clips. Click the one you want, and click **OK** to add it to your slide.

TIP

Finding More Movies
To locate more movie clips, click the **Clip Art on Microsoft.com** link at the bottom of the Clip Art Task pane and log on to the Microsoft Web site to browse for more clips.

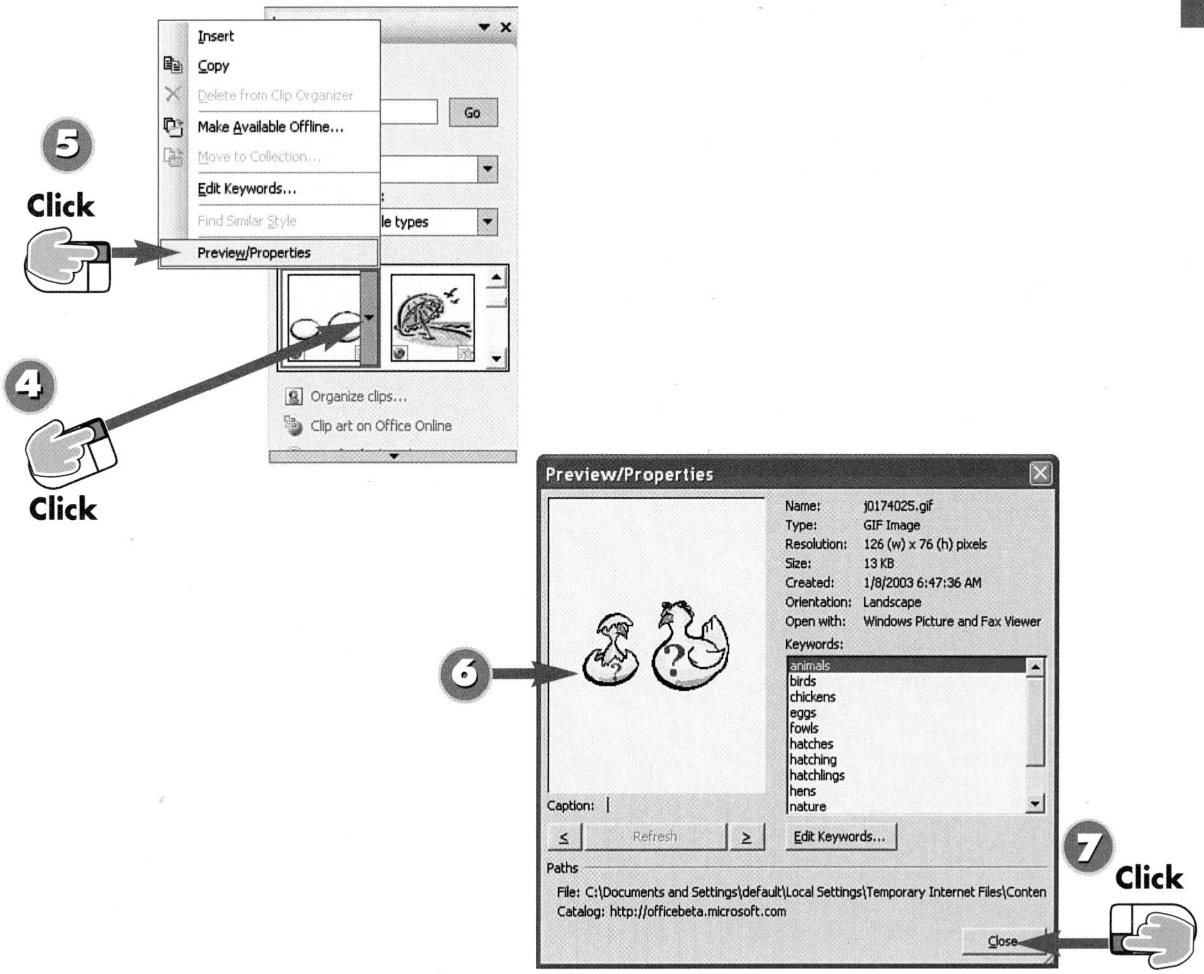

4. To preview a movie clip, move the mouse pointer over the movie clip icon and click the drop-down arrow.

5. Click **Preview/Properties** in the menu that appears.

6. The Preview/Properties dialog box opens and plays the movie clip.

7. Click **Close**.

See next page

TIP

Movie Clip File Format

The movie clips available in the Clip Art Task pane are animated GIF files, a popular movie file format on the Web.

Adding a Movie Clip with the Clip Organizer (Continued)

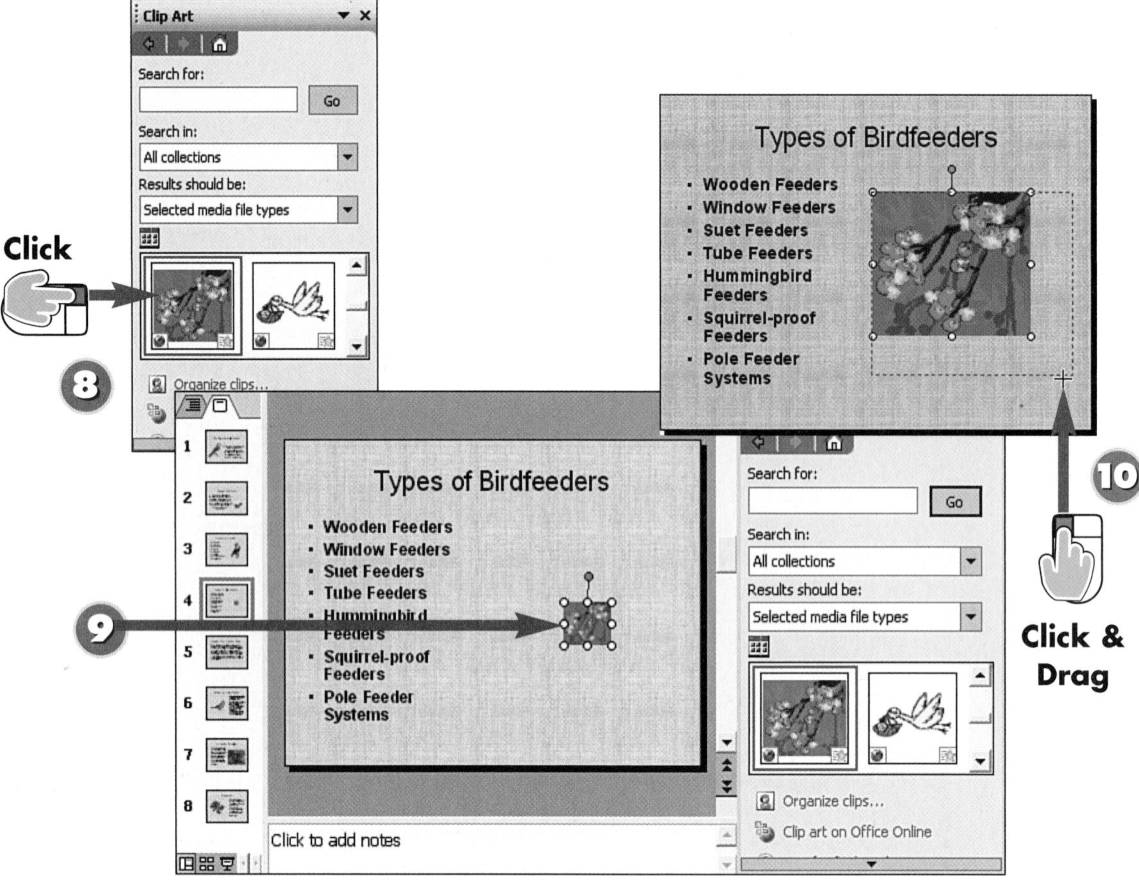

8 When you locate a movie clip you want to use, click the clip to add it to your slide.

9 PowerPoint adds the clip to the slide and leaves the Clip Art Task pane open.

10 You can click and drag the clip to change its position on the slide, and you can drag a handle surrounding the clip to resize the clip.

TIP
Movie Clips as Slide Objects
Movie clips appear as slide objects when you add them to a slide, which means you can move and resize the objects.

TIP
Finding a Clip
You can use PowerPoint's Search feature to look for a particular kind of movie clip. In the Clip Art Task pane, click inside the **Search For** box and type a keyword describing the type of clip you want, and then click **Go**.

TIP
Closing the Task Pane
To close the Clip Art Task pane to free up workspace, click the pane's **Close** button.

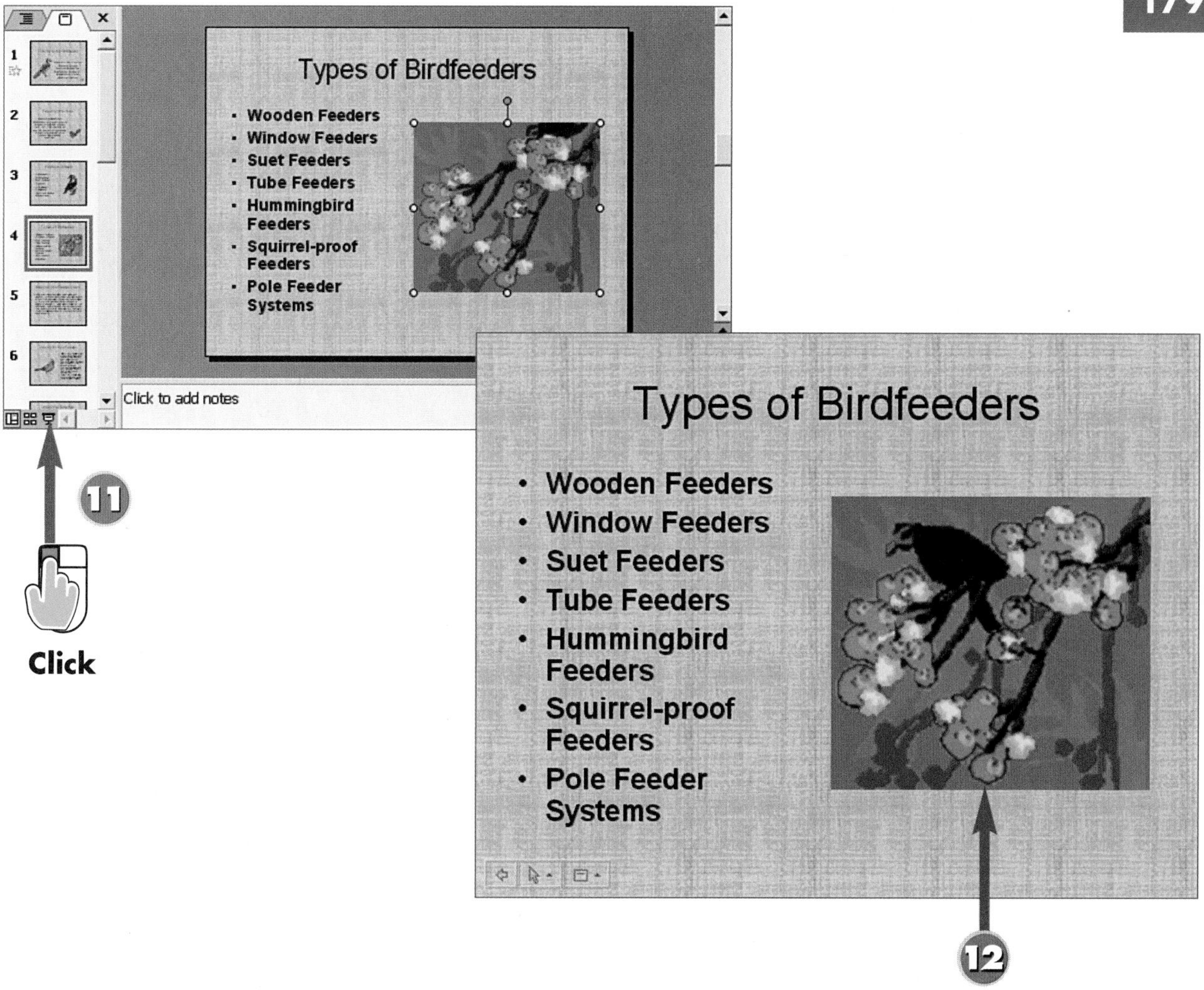

Click

11 To play the clip, first click the **Slide Show View** button.

12 PowerPoint displays the slide in full-screen mode, and the movie clip plays automatically. Press the **Esc** key to exit the slide show and return to Normal view.

Adding Non-GIF Clips
If you add a movie that is not an animated GIF clip, an additional prompt box appears asking you how you want to play the clip. You can choose to play it automatically or when clicked.

Removing a Clip
To remove a clip from your slide, click the clip and press the **Delete** key on your keyboard.

Viewing the Show
To learn more about viewing your presentation as a slide show, see Parts 10 and 12.

Adding a Movie File

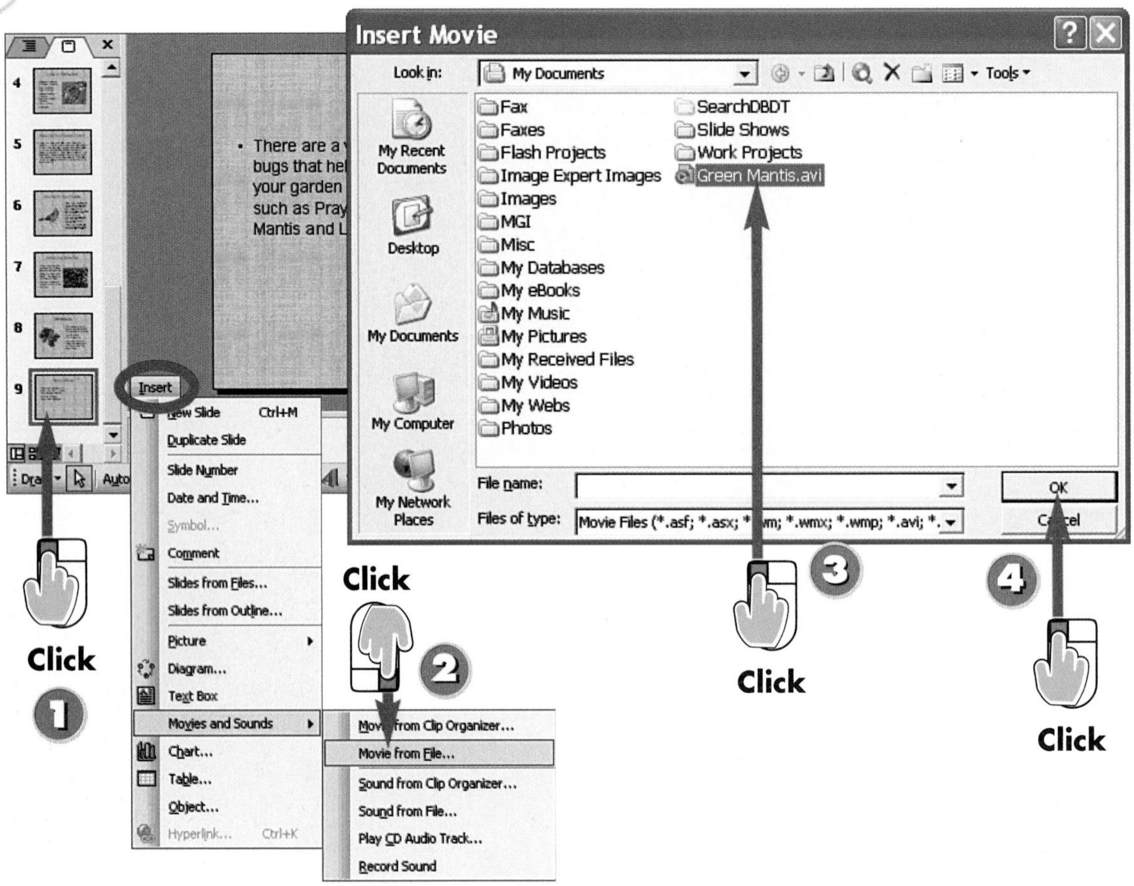

1. Click the slide to which you want to add a movie clip.
2. Open the **Insert** menu, choose **Movies and Sounds**, and select **Movie from File**.
3. The Insert Movie dialog box opens. Locate and select the movie file you want to use.
4. Click **OK**.

INTRODUCTION

You can add other types of movie files to your slides besides animated clip-art GIFs. For example, you can add video files stored on your computer, such as digital camcorder footage. Once you add a movie clip to your slide, you can move and resize the clip object just as you do other slide objects.

TIP

Supported Movie Files
PowerPoint supports popular video file formats, such as AVI and MPEG.

TIP

Moving Clips
You can reposition your clip by dragging it to a new location. See Part 5 to learn more about working with slide objects on the slide.

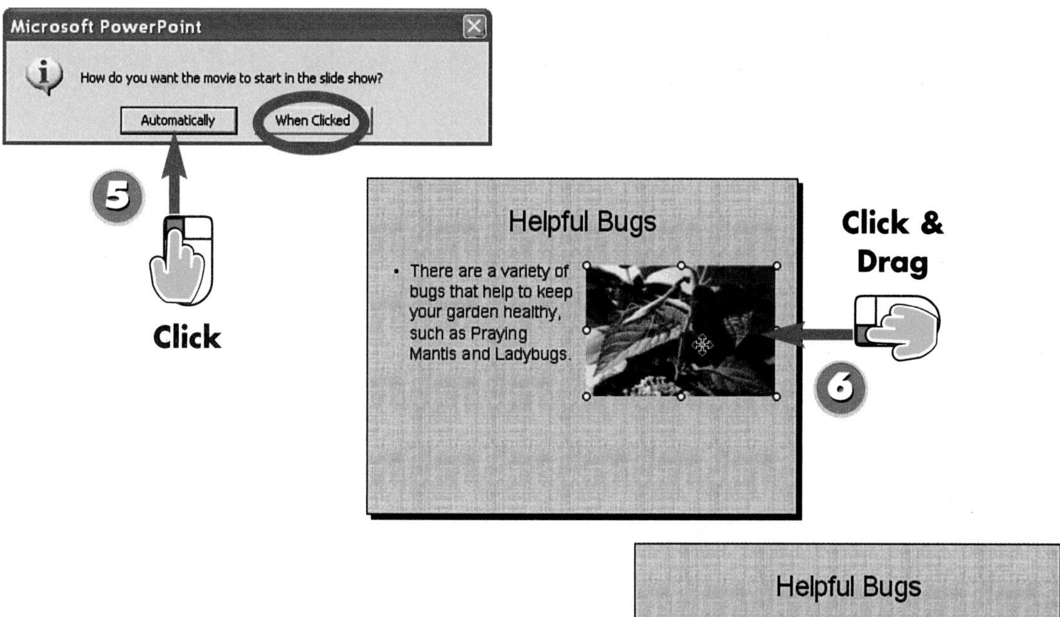

5. Click **Automatically** to have the clip play automatically when the slide is displayed in your presentation, or **When Clicked** if you want to activate the clip manually.
6. Click and drag the clip to reposition it on the slide, or click and drag a handle to resize the clip.
7. Double-click the clip to play the movie.

TIP

My Clip Won't Play!
If you insert an animated GIF clip, it does not play when double-clicked. Use Slide Show view to view the clip.

TIP

Removing a Clip
To remove a clip from your slide, click the clip and press the **Delete** key on your keyboard.

CAUTION

Resizing Movie Clips
Use caution when resizing movie clips. Most video files play best at their original size. Enlarging the slide object can make the clip appear grainy during playback.

PART 10

Fine-Tuning a Presentation

After you have created the bulk of your presentation, you can add finishing touches that affect how your presentation plays for the audience. You can use PowerPoint's Slide Sorter view to see and work with all the slides in your presentation at once.

As you preview your slide show, you might find it needs some special elements to make the presentation more interesting. For example, you can add transitions to control how one slide segues into the next. You can also choose from a variety of animation effects that control how slide objects appear on a slide. You can make your slide title text seem to crawl across the screen, or you can make a bulleted list appear one bullet at a time.

PowerPoint also includes features for creating speaker notes and audience handouts. This portion of the book tells you how to prepare your slide show for final presentation.

The Custom Animation Task Pane

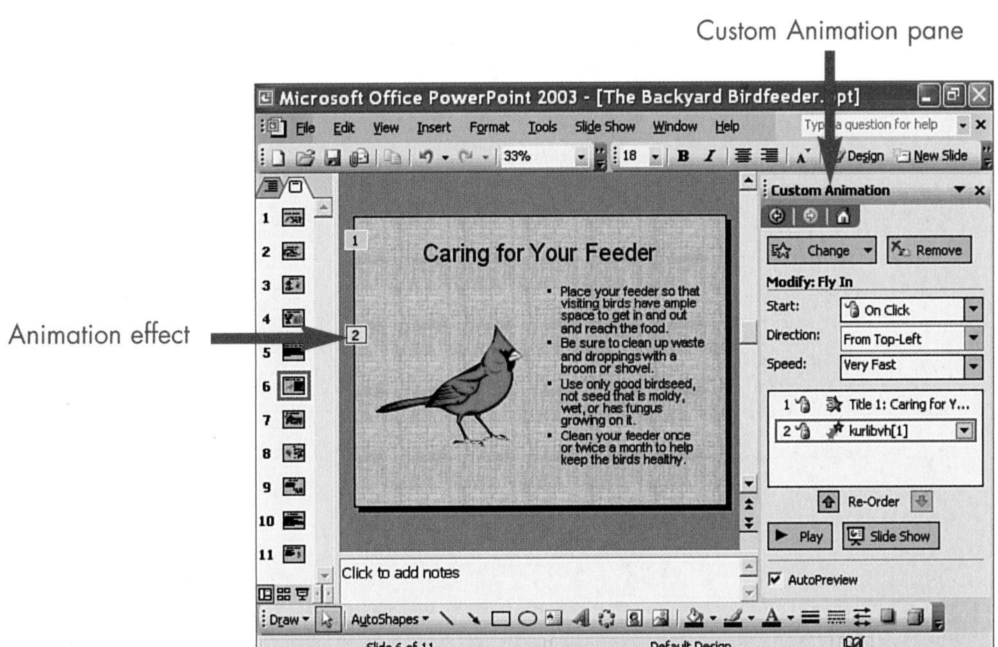

Rearranging Slides in Slide Sorter View

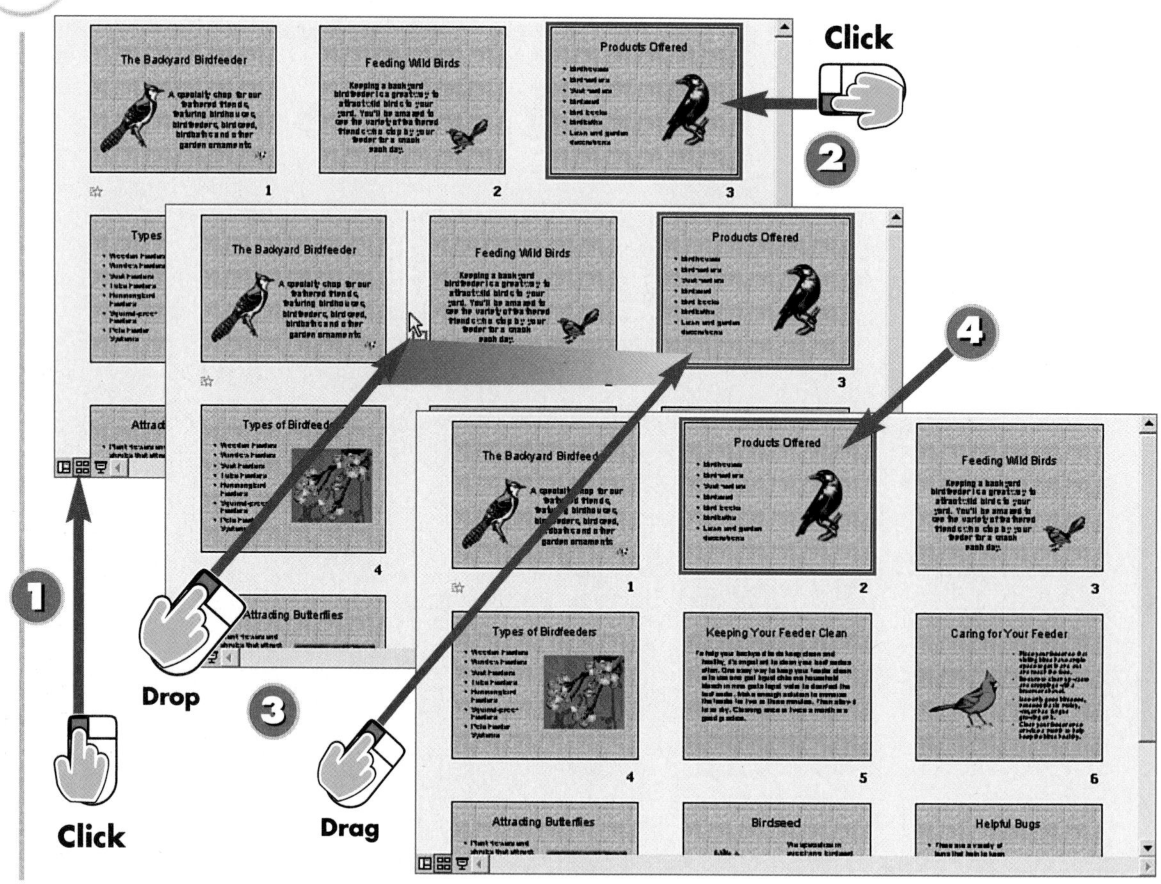

1. Click the **Slide Sorter View** button.
2. Click the slide you want to rearrange.
3. Drag the slide to a new location in the show.
4. Release the mouse button, and the slide is moved.

INTRODUCTION

You can use Slide Sorter view to see all the slides in your presentation and make changes to the order of the slides. Simply drag the slides around in Slide Sorter view to change their position in the slide show.

TIP

Moving Multiples
To move more than one slide at a time, press and hold the **Ctrl** key while clicking on the slides you want to move.

TIP

Hiding a Slide
You can hide a slide in Slide Sorter view so that it doesn't appear in the show itself, yet remains part of the presentation file. Click the slide, open the **Slide Show** menu, and choose **Hide Slide**.

Deleting a Slide in Slide Sorter View

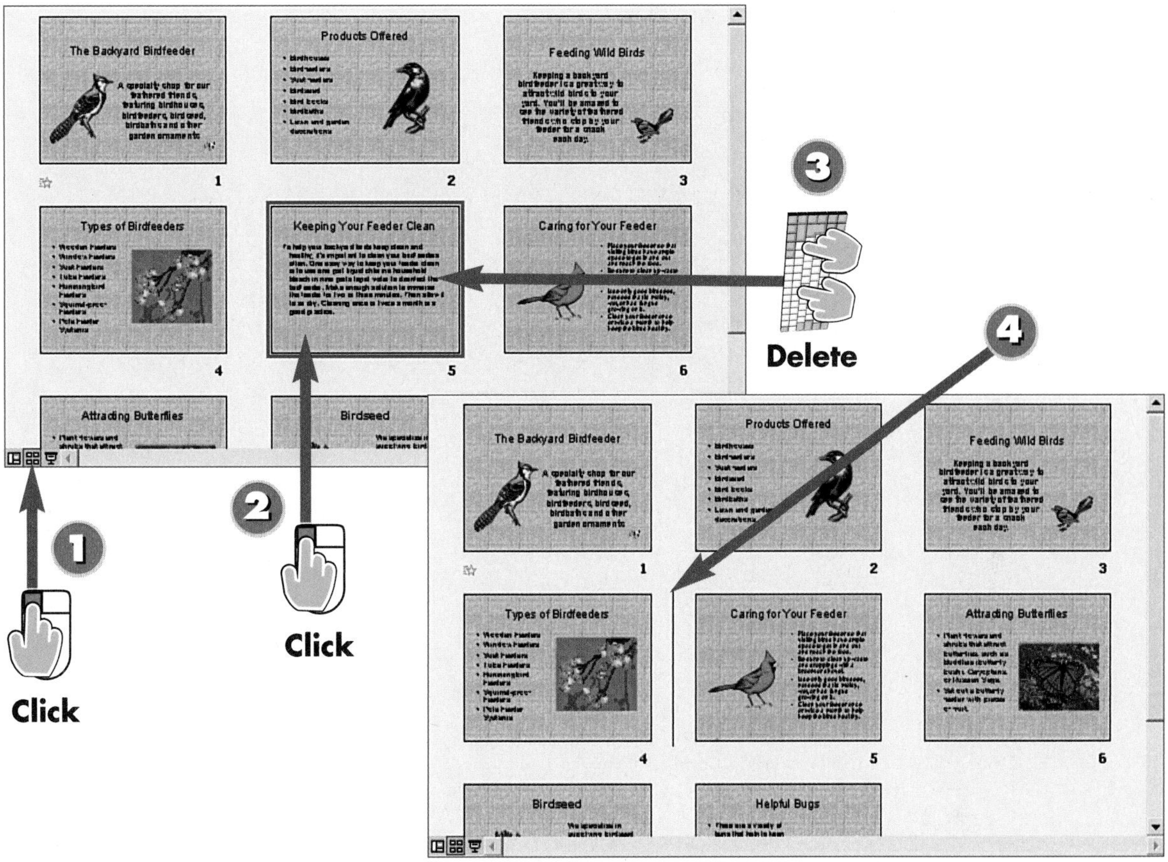

1. Click the **Slide Sorter View** button.
2. Click the slide you want to delete.
3. Press the **Delete** key on your keyboard.
4. PowerPoint removes the slide and renumbers the other slides automatically.

INTRODUCTION

After reviewing your slides in Slide Sorter view, you might need to remove a slide you no longer need. Just remember, removing the slide removes any information included on the slide.

TIP

Oops!
If you accidentally removed the wrong slide, click the **Undo** button on the toolbar to bring it back again.

Adding Slides from Another Presentation

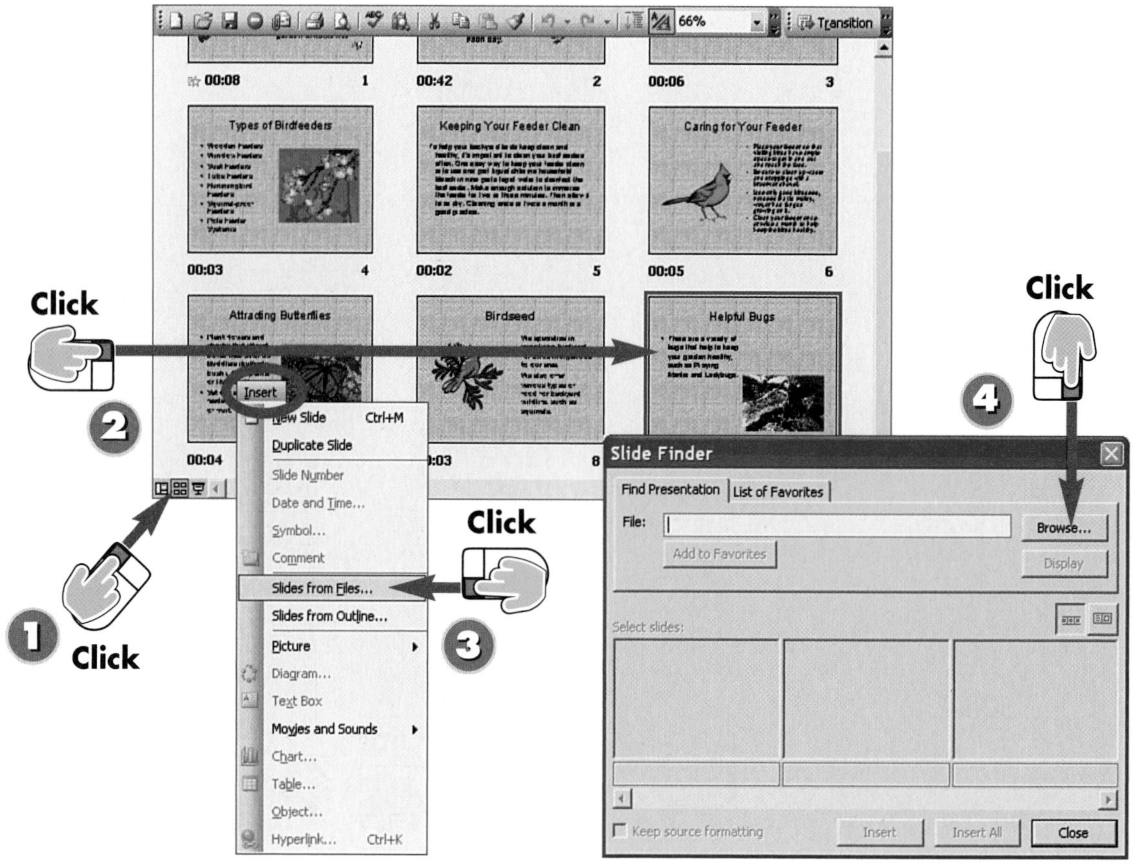

1. Click the **Slide Sorter View** button.
2. Click the slide you want to appear immediately before the new slides.
3. Open the **Insert** menu and choose **Slides from Files**.
4. The Slide Finder dialog box opens. Click the **Browse** button.

INTRODUCTION

You can reuse slides you created for other presentations and insert them into your current slide show. PowerPoint copies the slides from one presentation to the other and matches the newly inserted slides to the current slide design.

TIP

Linking to a Presentation

You can turn slide text into a hyperlink to another presentation or to a single slide in another presentation. (The slide or slides you are linking to, however, must be on the same computer or network server.) To do so, select the text and click the **Insert Hyperlink** button. In the Insert Hyperlink dialog box, click **Existing File or Web Page**, and then select the file in the Link to File dialog box. Click **OK** twice to close both dialog boxes.

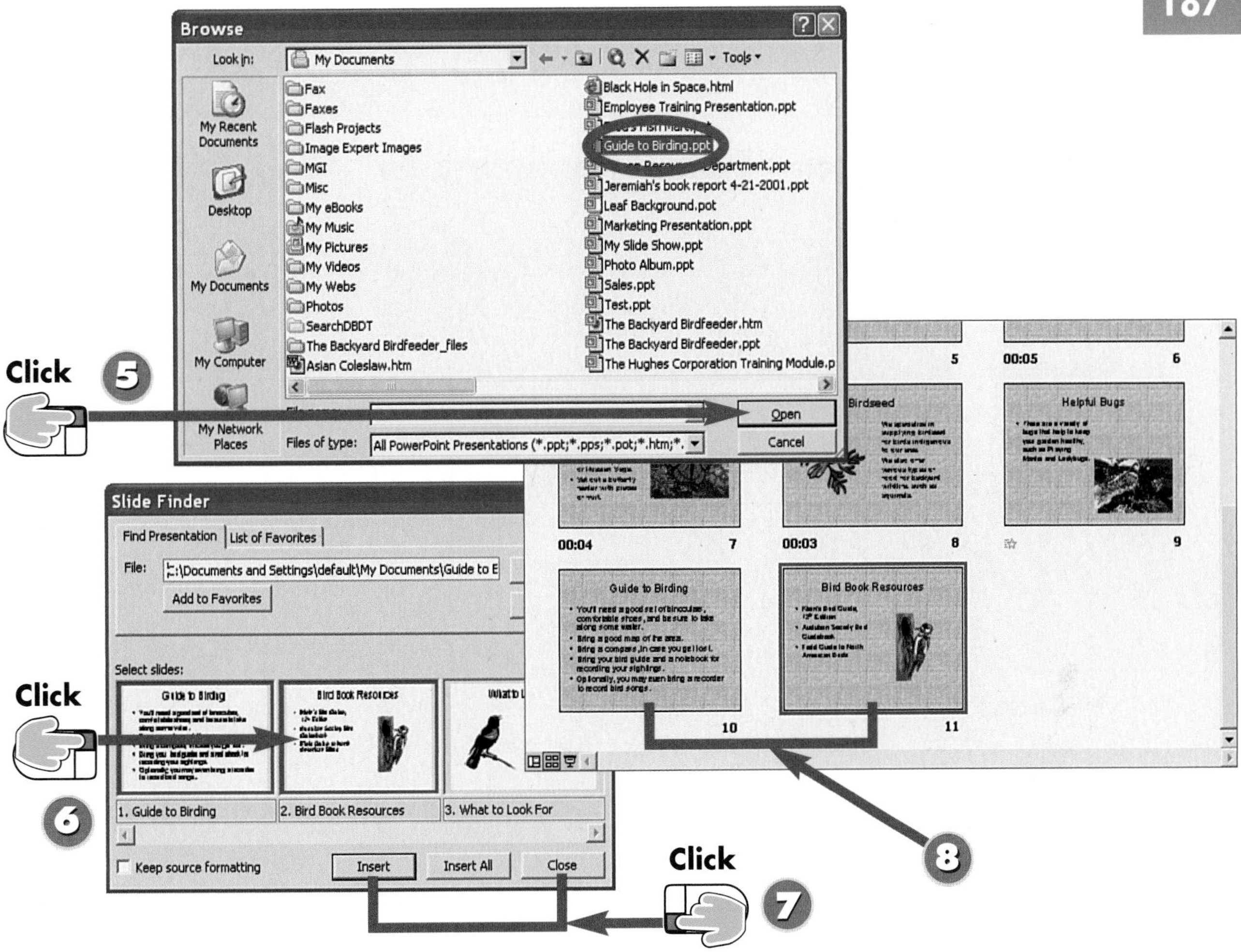

5. The Browse dialog box opens. Locate and select the presentation containing the slides you want to copy and click the **Open** button.

6. In the Slide Finder dialog box, click each slide you want to add to the current presentation.

7. Click the **Insert** button, and then click **Close**.

8. PowerPoint adds the slides.

TIP

Keeping the Original Slide Design?
If you want the new slides to retain their original slide design, click the **Keep Source Formatting** check box in the Slide Finder dialog box.

TIP

Scroll Away
You can use the scroll buttons in the Slide Finder dialog box to scroll through the available slides.

TIP

Inserting Them All
If you are sure you want to insert copies of all the slides in the presentation, click the **Insert All** button in the Slide Finder dialog box.

Creating a Summary Slide in Slide Sorter View

Start

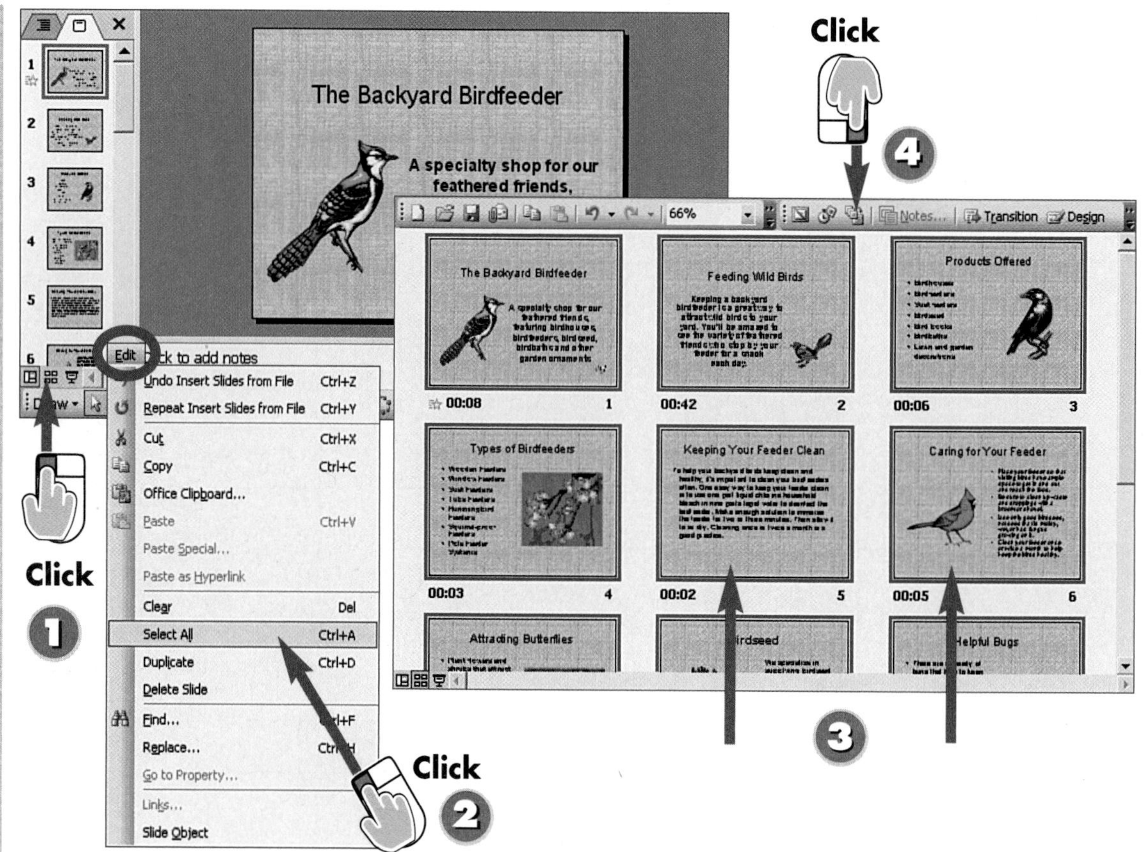

1. Click **Slide Sorter View** button.
2. Open the **Edit** menu and choose **Select All**.
3. PowerPoint selects all the slides in your presentation.
4. Click the **Summary Slide** button in the Formatting toolbar.

INTRODUCTION

PowerPoint's summary slides act as a table of contents for your presentation. A summary slide displays all the titles of your slides as a bulleted list. You can use summary slides when you want to introduce your topics at the start of the slide show.

TIP

Outline View

You can also create summary slides using PowerPoint's Outline view. See Part 3 to learn more about building presentations based on outlines.

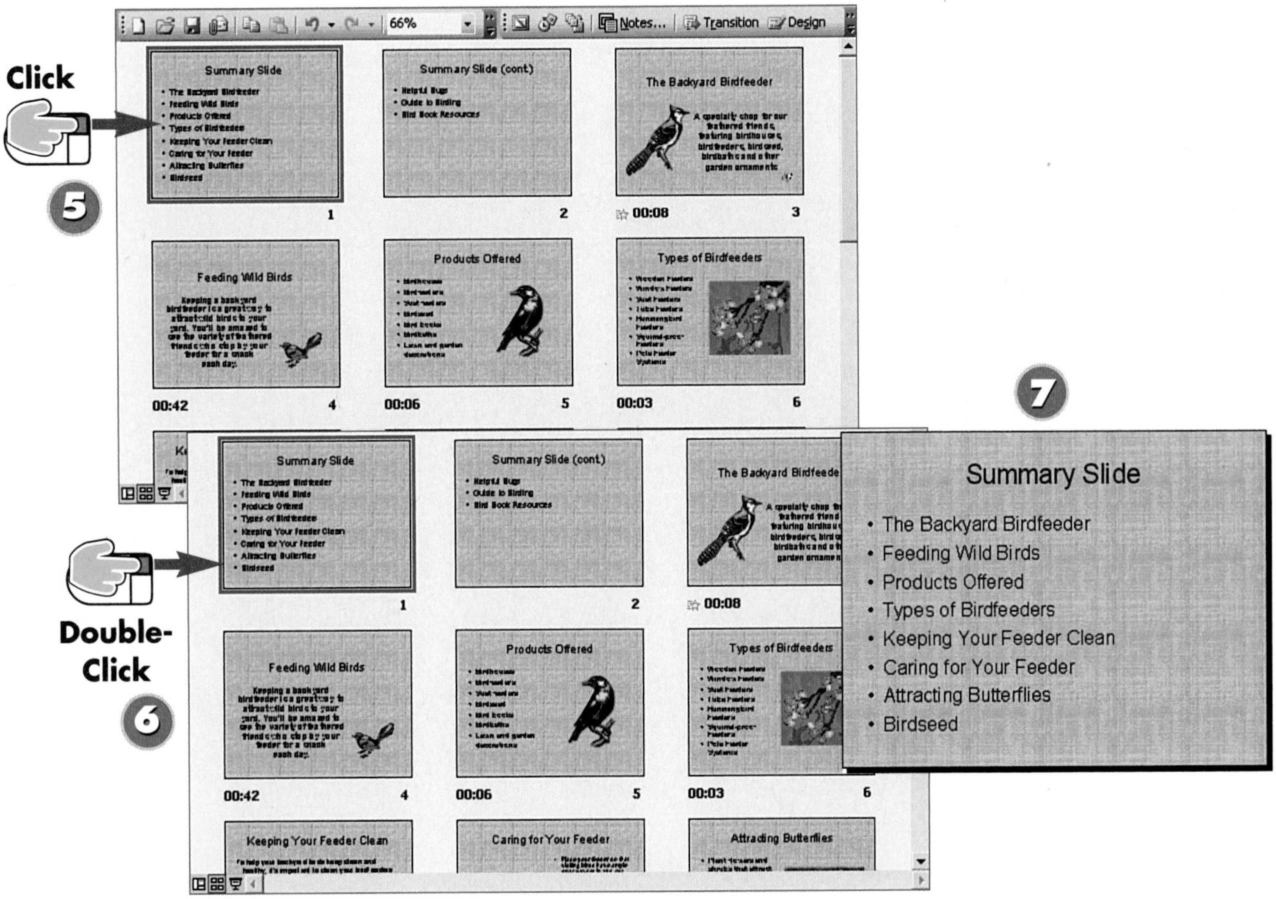
Click
5
Double-Click
6
7
Summary Slide
• The Backyard Birdfeeder
• Feeding Wild Birds
• Products Offered
• Types of Birdfeeders
• Keeping Your Feeder Clean
• Caring for Your Feeder
• Attracting Butterflies
• Birdseed
Summary Slide (cont)
The Backyard Birdfeeder
Feeding Wild Birds
Products Offered
Types of Birdfeeders
Keeping Your Feeder Clean
Caring for Your Feeder
Attracting Butterflies
00:08
00:42
00:06
00:03
66%
Notes...
Transition
Design

5. PowerPoint inserts a summary slide at the beginning of your presentation.

6. To view the summary slide, double-click the slide.

7. You can edit the slide text as needed.

End

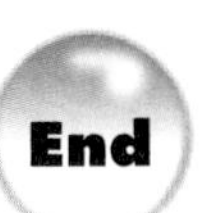

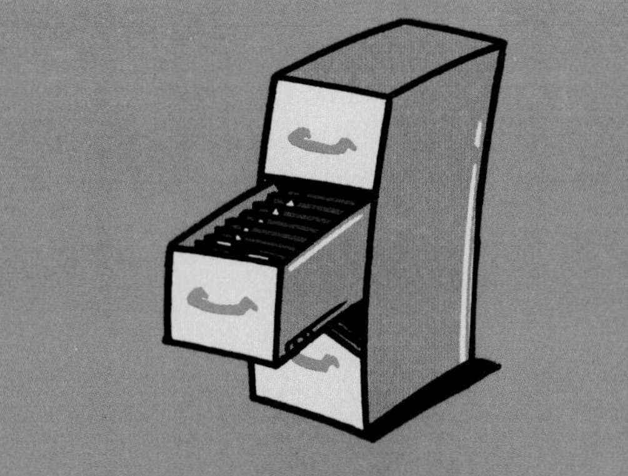

TIP

Working with Text
See Part 4 to learn more about working with slide text, including formatting and editing the text.

TIP

Two Summary Slides
If your presentation is long, PowerPoint might insert two summary slides in order to list all the slide titles.

Adding Slide Transitions

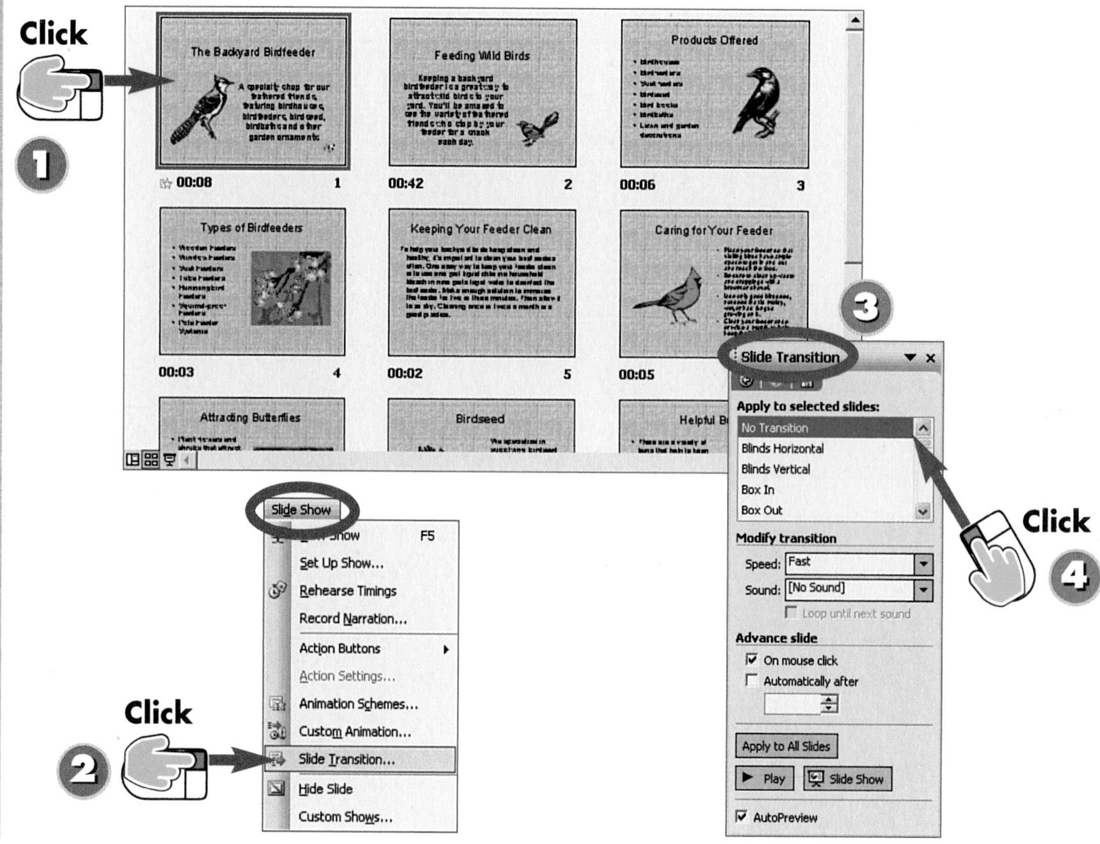

1. In Slide Sorter view, click the slide to which you want to add a transition.
2. Open the **Slide Show** menu and choose **Slide Transition**.
3. The Slide Transition Task pane opens and lists the available transitions.
4. Click the transition you want to apply.

INTRODUCTION

You can use slide transitions to control the way in which one slide moves to the next slide in the show. PowerPoint offers a wide variety of transition effects, including dissolves, fades, and more. You can also control the speed of the transition to make it play slower or faster in the show.

TIP

Opening the Slide Transition Task Pane

You can also open the Slide Transition Task pane by clicking the **Transition** button on the Formatting toolbar.

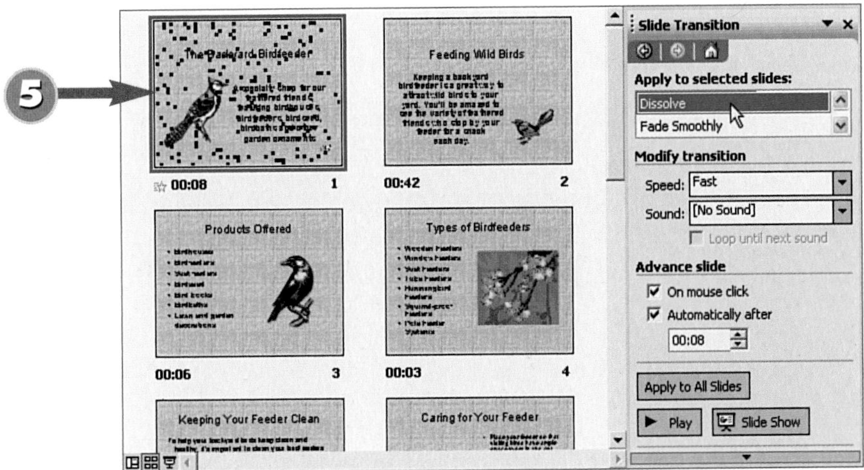

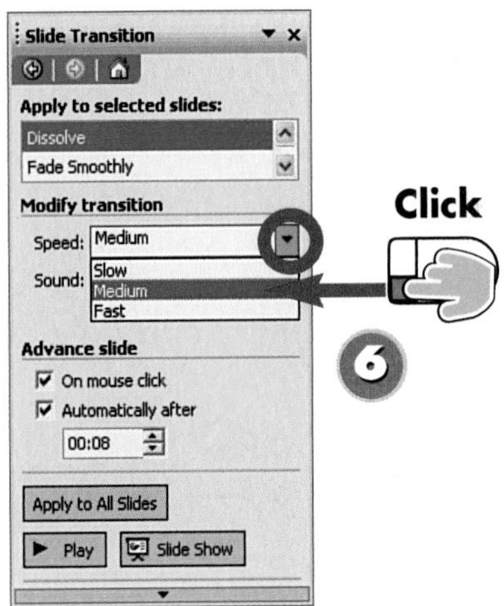

5 PowerPoint applies the transition and shows you a preview of the effect.

6 To change the transition speed, click the **down arrow** next to the **Speed** field in the Task pane and select **Slow**, **Medium**, or **Fast**.

TIP

Applying to All
To use the same transition for every slide in your presentation, click the **Apply to All Slides** button at the bottom of the Slide Transition Task pane.

TIP

Removing a Transition
To rid your slide of a transition you no longer want, select the slide and click the **Transition** button to open the Slide Transition Task pane. Scroll to the top of the transition list and click **No Transition**. PowerPoint removes the effect.

TIP

Viewing the Show
To see your transitions in action, click the **Slide Show View** button to start the slide show. Press **Esc** at any time to exit the show and return to the PowerPoint window.

Assigning an Animation Scheme

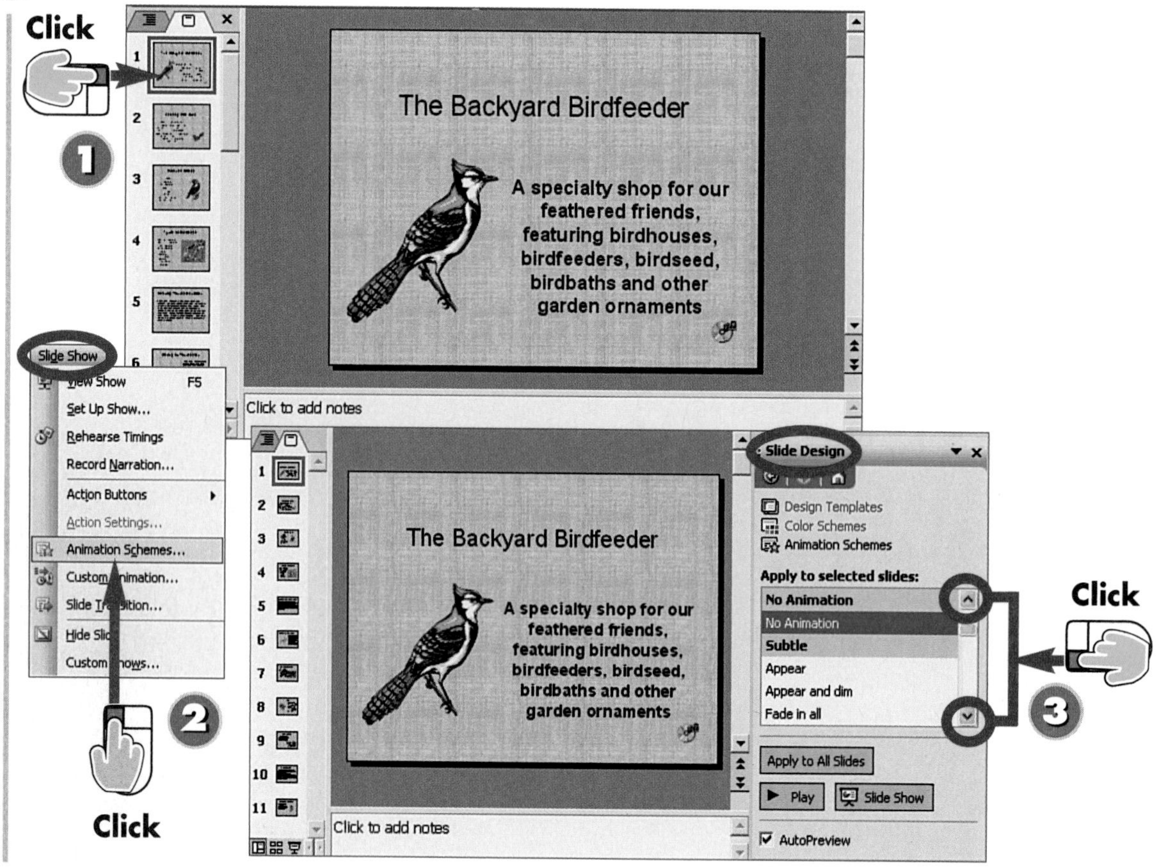

1. In Normal view, click the slide to which you want to assign an animation scheme.

2. Open the **Slide Show** menu and choose **Animation Schemes**.

3. PowerPoint opens the Slide Design Task pane and lists the available animation schemes. Use the scroll arrows to scroll through the list.

INTRODUCTION

PowerPoint offers a variety of animated effects, called *animation schemes*, that you can add to your slides. You can use animation schemes to add movement to the slide elements. For example, you can assign an animation scheme that makes the slide's text boxes appear to fade into the slide or swoop in from a different direction. When you assign an animation scheme, it animates all the elements on a slide.

TIP

Animating a Single Slide Object

You can assign an animation effect to a single slide element rather than to the entire slide. See the next task, "Animating a Single Slide Object," to learn more.

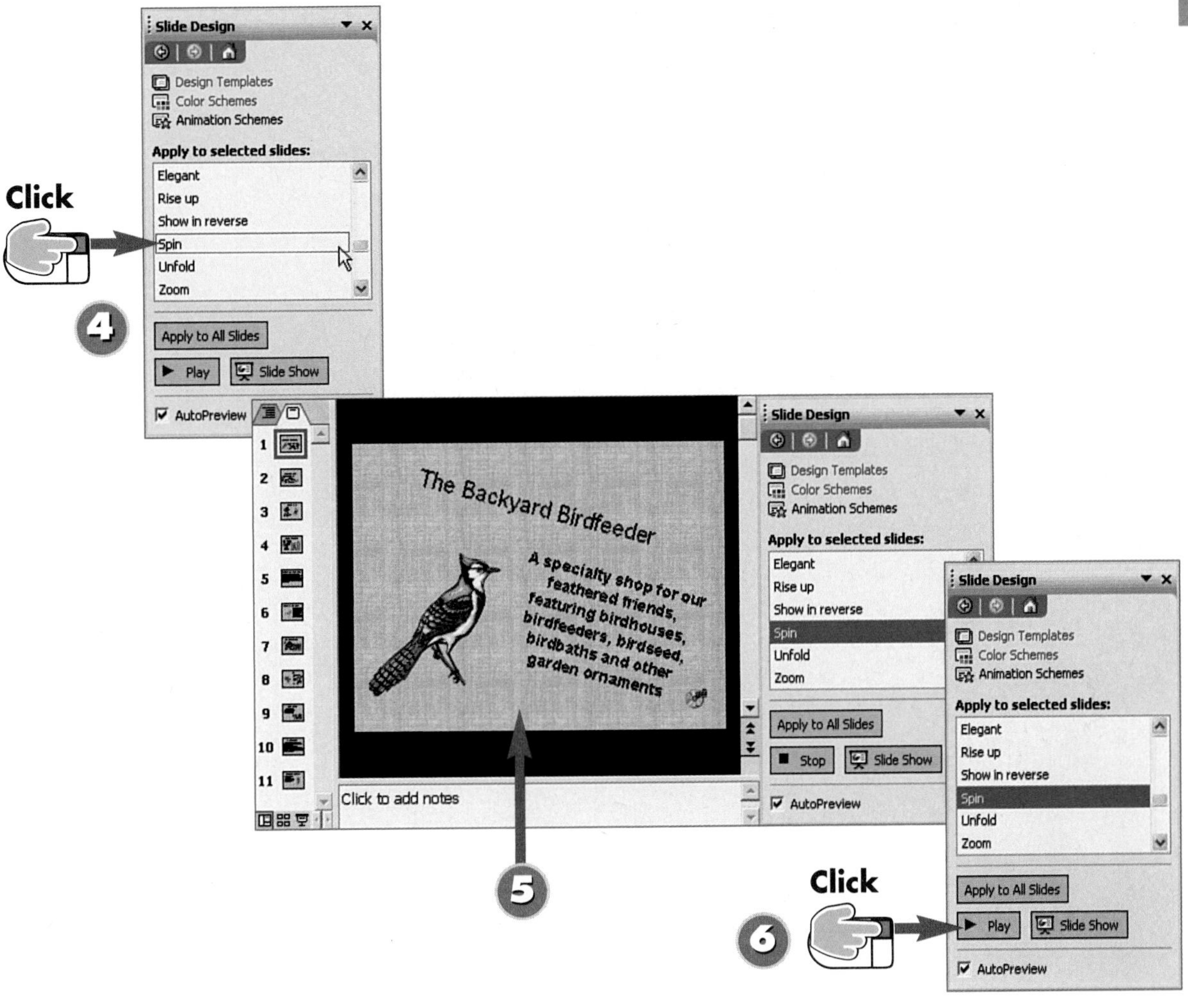

4. Click a scheme.

5. PowerPoint assigns the scheme and previews the animation effect.

6. Click the **Play** button to view the effect again.

Removing a Scheme

To remove an animation scheme from a slide, first select the slide, then select **No Animation** from the list of available animation effects in the Slide Design Task pane.

Assigning to All Slides

To assign the same animation scheme to all the slides in your presentation, click the **Apply to All Slides** button in the Slide Design Task pane.

CAUTION

Animation Overload

Don't get too carried away assigning animation schemes to your presentation. Too many special effects will detract from your presentation message.

Animating a Single Slide Object

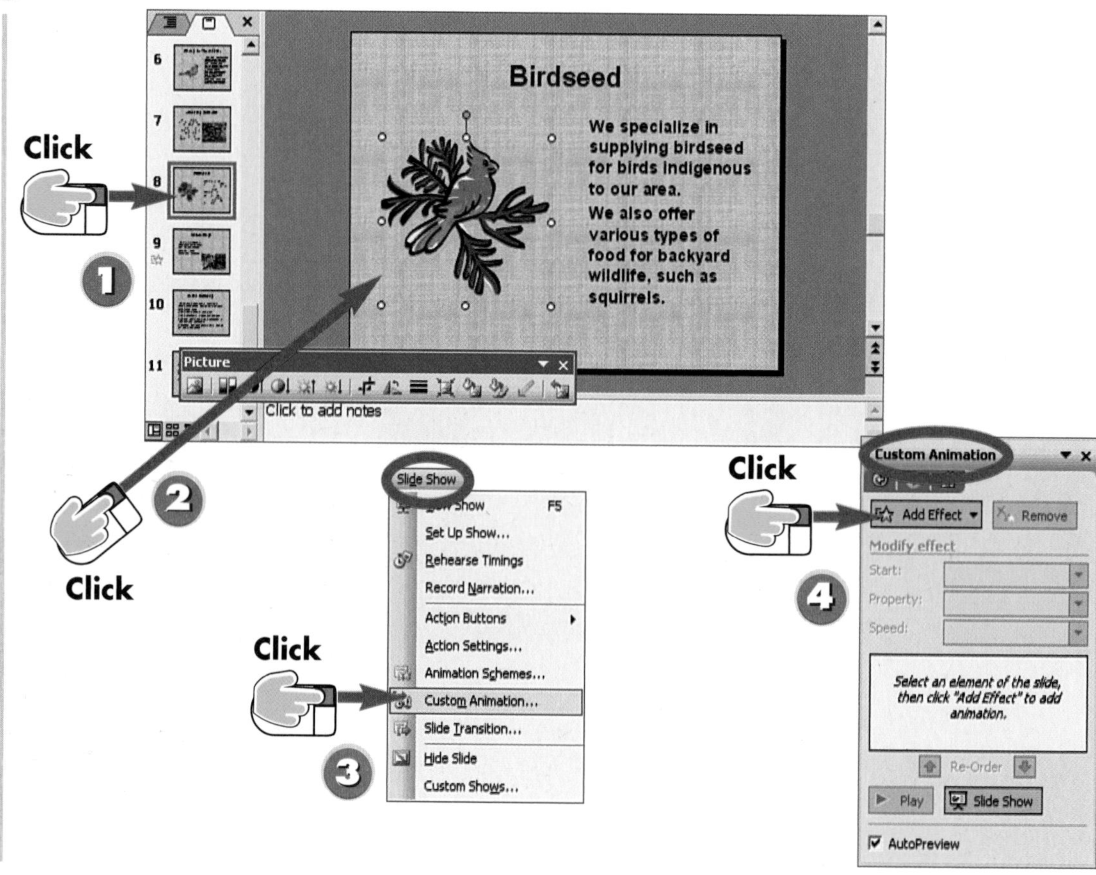

1. In Normal view, click the slide to which you want to assign custom animation.
2. Click the slide object you want to animate.
3. Open the **Slide Show** menu and choose **Custom Animation**.
4. PowerPoint opens the Custom Animation Task pane. Click the **Add Effect** button.

INTRODUCTION

In addition to animation schemes that you can apply to animate an entire slide, you can also customize PowerPoint animation effects and apply them to a single slide element. For example, you might want a clip-art object to spin onto the slide, or animate a single text box for emphasis. You can use multiple custom animations in a slide. You can assign animations effects to text boxes, clip art, pictures, bulleted lists, charts, and graphs.

TIP

Animating the Entire Slide

You can assign an animation effect to an entire slide rather than to a single slide element. See the previous task, "Assigning an Animation Scheme," to learn more.

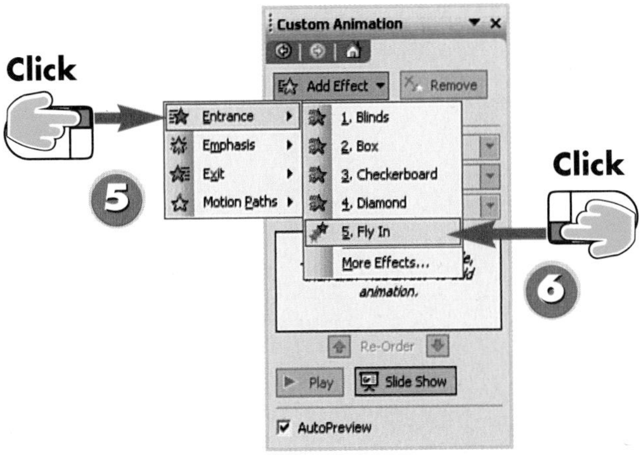

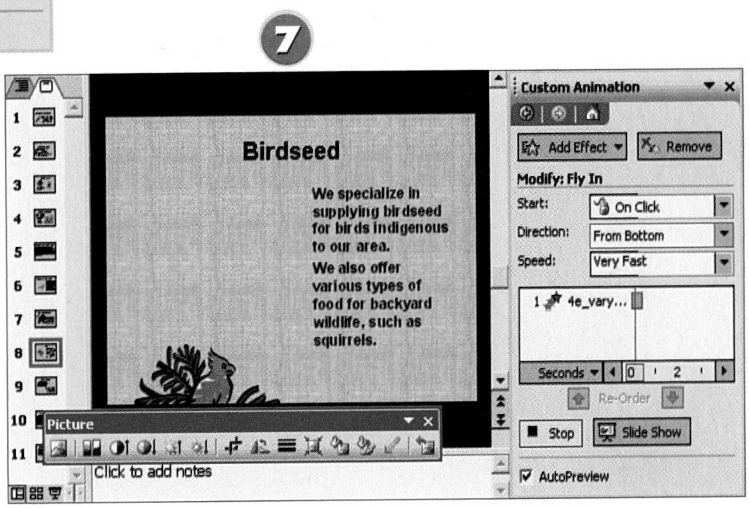

Click

5

Click

6

7

5 Click an effect category (here, **Entrance**).

6 Click an animation (in this case, **Fly In**) .

7 PowerPoint assigns the animation to the selected slide object and previews the animation effect.

TIP

Understanding Effect Categories

Use Entrance effects to animate objects onto the slide. Use Emphasis effects to draw attention to an object already appearing on the slide. Use Exit effects to make objects disappear off the slide. Use Motion Path effects to make slide objects animate across the slide following a path.

TIP

Changing the Animation Order

If you are assigning more than one animation effect to a slide, you can control the order of the effects. See the next task, "Changing the Animation Order," to learn more.

Changing the Animation Order

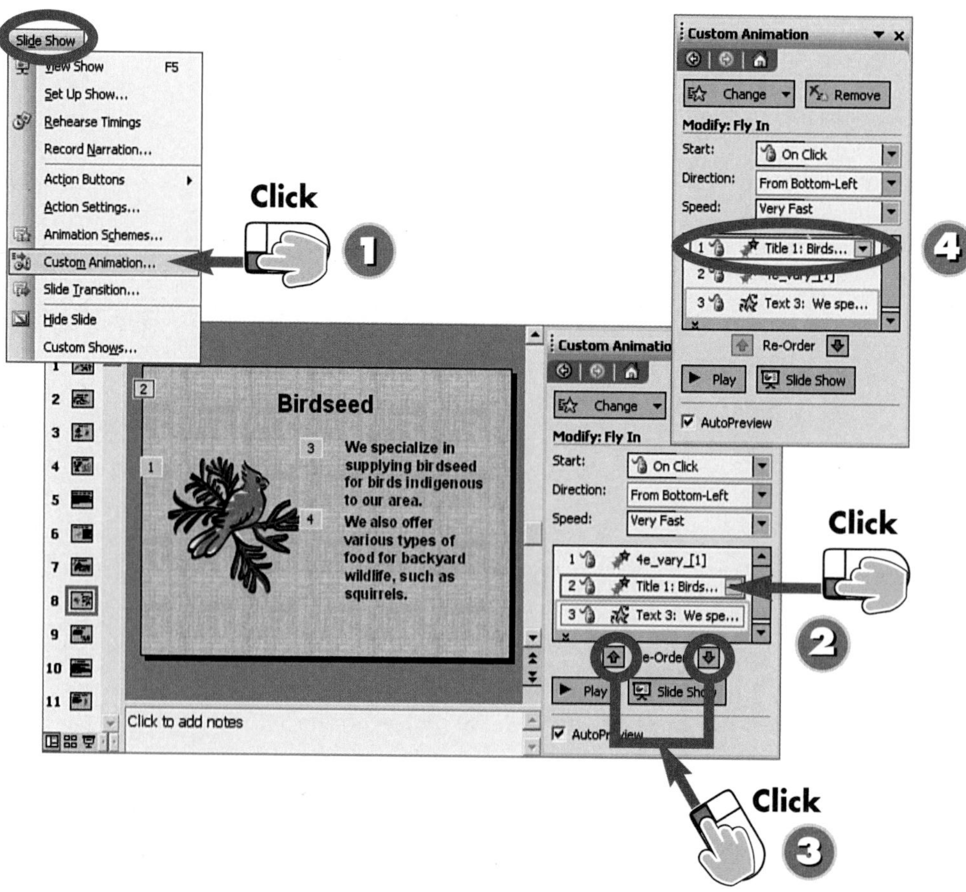

1. Open the **Slide Show** menu and choose **Custom Animation**.
2. PowerPoint opens the Custom Animation Task pane. Click the effect you want to reorder.
3. Click the **Up** or **Down Re-Order** button to change the effect's order in the list.
4. PowerPoint moves the effect in the list.

INTRODUCTION

If you assign more than one custom animation effect to a slide, you can control the order in which each effect appears on the slide. Each animation effect is numbered in PowerPoint. The numbers do not appear on the actual slides during the presentation, but you can reorder the effect numbers in the Custom Animation pane to control the order of appearance.

TIP

Adding Effects

See the previous task, "Animating a Single Slide Object," to learn more about assigning animation effects to various slide elements.

Adding Sounds to Animations

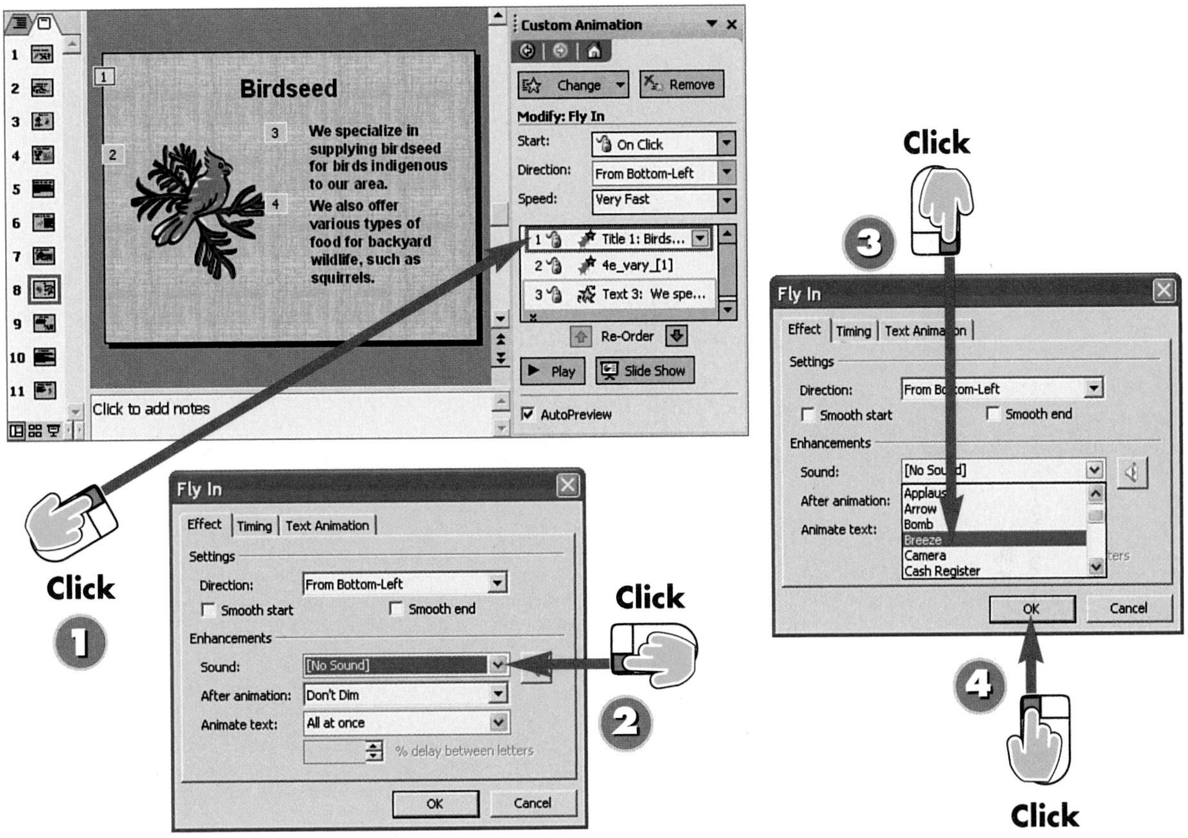

1. In the Custom Animation Task pane, double-click the animation to which you want to add a sound. (See step 1 of the preceding task if you need help opening this Task pane.)
2. PowerPoint opens the effect's associated dialog box. Click the **down arrow** next to the **Sound** field.
3. Click a sound.
4. Click **OK** to apply it to the effect.

INTRODUCTION

To make your animation effects appear even livelier, you can add sound effects. For example, you can add a cash-register sound to an animated chart, or applause to a title. PowerPoint includes a variety of prerecorded sounds you can add to animations.

TIP

Adding Effects

See the task "Animating a Single Slide Object" to learn more about assigning custom animation effects to various slide elements.

TIP

Removing Sounds

To remove a sound associated with an animation, repeat the steps shown here and click **No Sound** from the drop-down list in the effect's dialog box.

Customizing Animation Effects

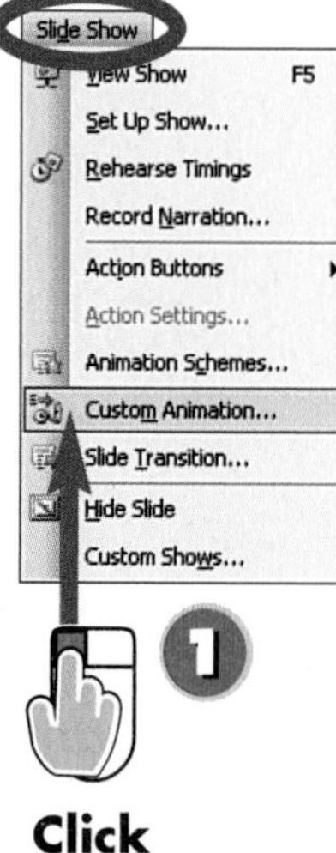

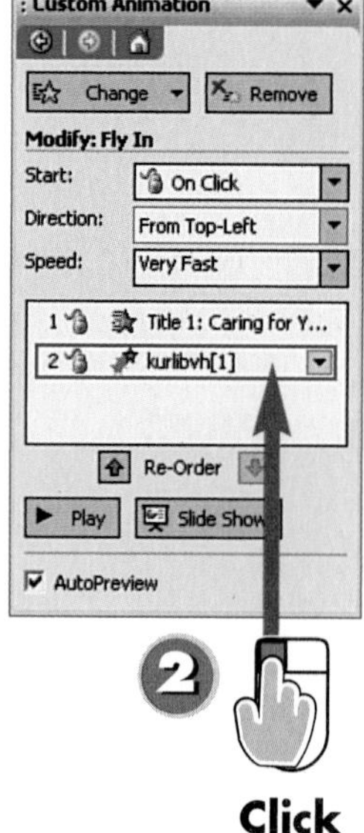

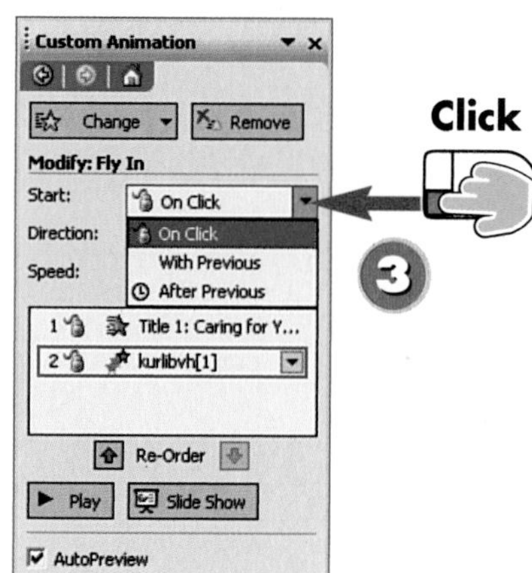

1. Open the **Slide Show** menu and choose **Custom Animation**.
2. The Custom Animation Task pane opens. Click the effect you want to customize.
3. Click the **down arrow** next to the **Start** field and select how you want the effect to be activated on the slide.

INTRODUCTION

You can use the Custom Animation pane to customize how an animation effect starts, the speed at which it plays, and the direction in which it enters or exits the slide.

TIP

Start Options

The Custom Animation pane offers three ways to activate a custom effect. Choose the **On Click** start option to make the animation effect play only when you click the slide. Choose the **With Previous** option if you want the effect to play simultaneously with the previous animation effect. Choose the **After Previous** option to start the effect after the previous effect ends.

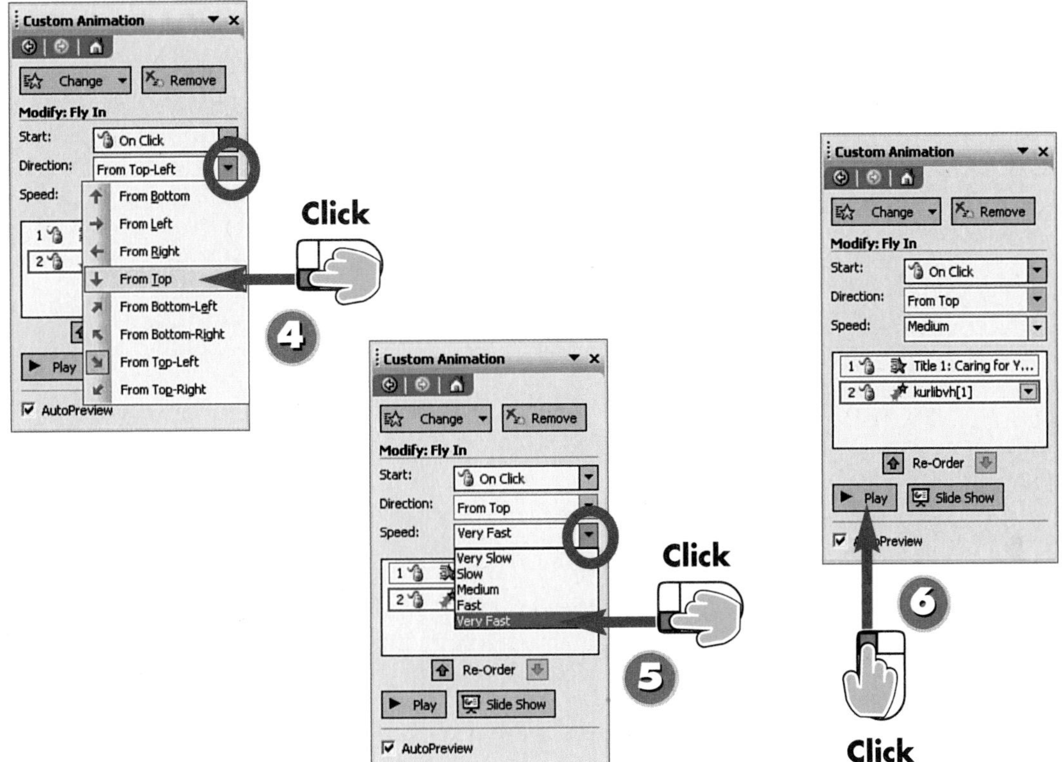

4. Click the **down arrow** next to the **Direction** field and select a direction for the effect.

5. Click the **down arrow** next to the **Speed** field and select a speed for the effect.

6. To view the custom settings, click the **Play** button in the Custom Animation Task pane.

TIP

Assigning Multiple Effects

You can assign multiple animation effects to a single slide object and control the order of appearance. See the task "Changing the Animation Order" to learn more about reordering your effects.

TIP

Removing Animations

To remove an animation effect you no longer want, click the effect in the Custom Animation Task pane list box and click the **Remove** button.

Adding Action Buttons

In Normal view, click the slide to which you want to assign an action button.

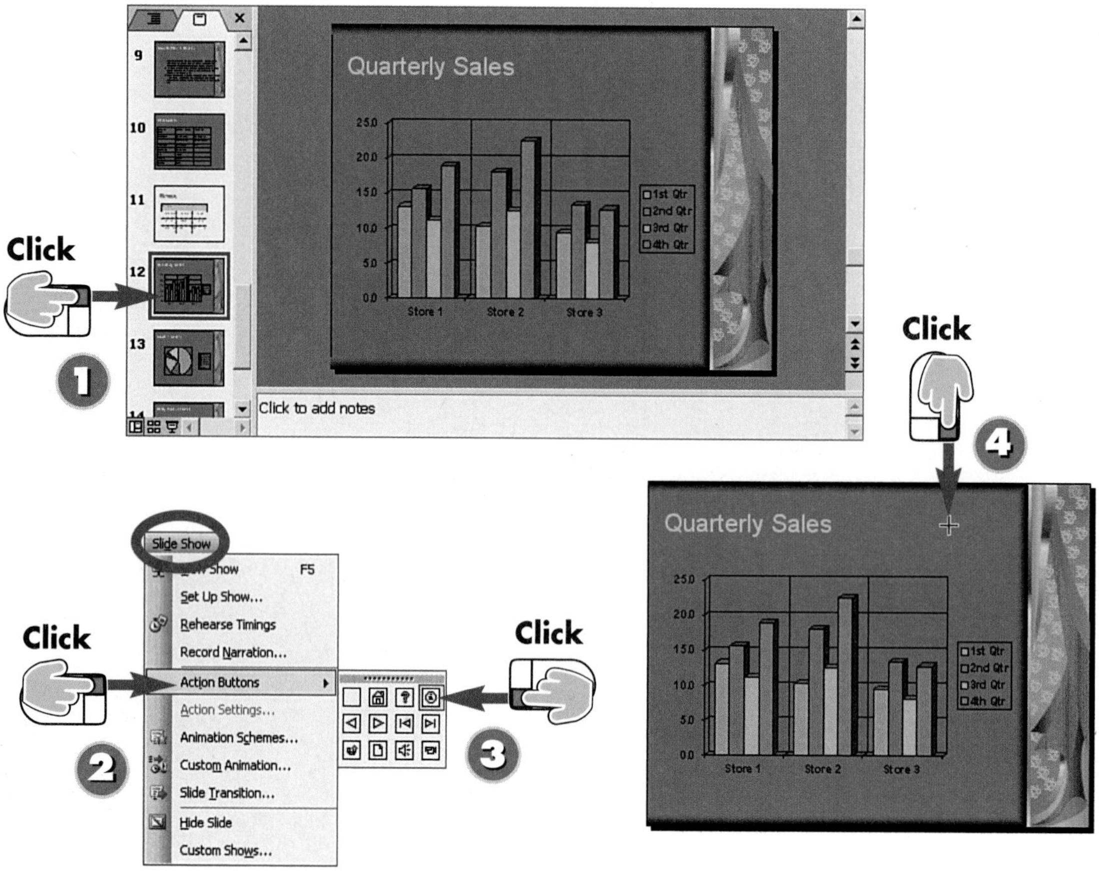

Open the **Slide Show** menu and choose **Action Buttons**.

Click an action button in the submenu that appears.

Click on the slide where you want to insert the action button.

INTRODUCTION

You can add action buttons to your slides that allow you to move back and forth to other slides during the presentation. For example, if you want to refer back to an important chart on the first slide in the presentation, you can add action buttons to other slides that allow you to jump back to the first slide whenever you need to.

TIP

Action Button Ideas

You can use action buttons in a variety of ways. For example, if your presentation is self-viewing, you can insert **Next Slide** and **Previous Slide** buttons that take the user back or forward a slide as the user reads at his or her own pace.

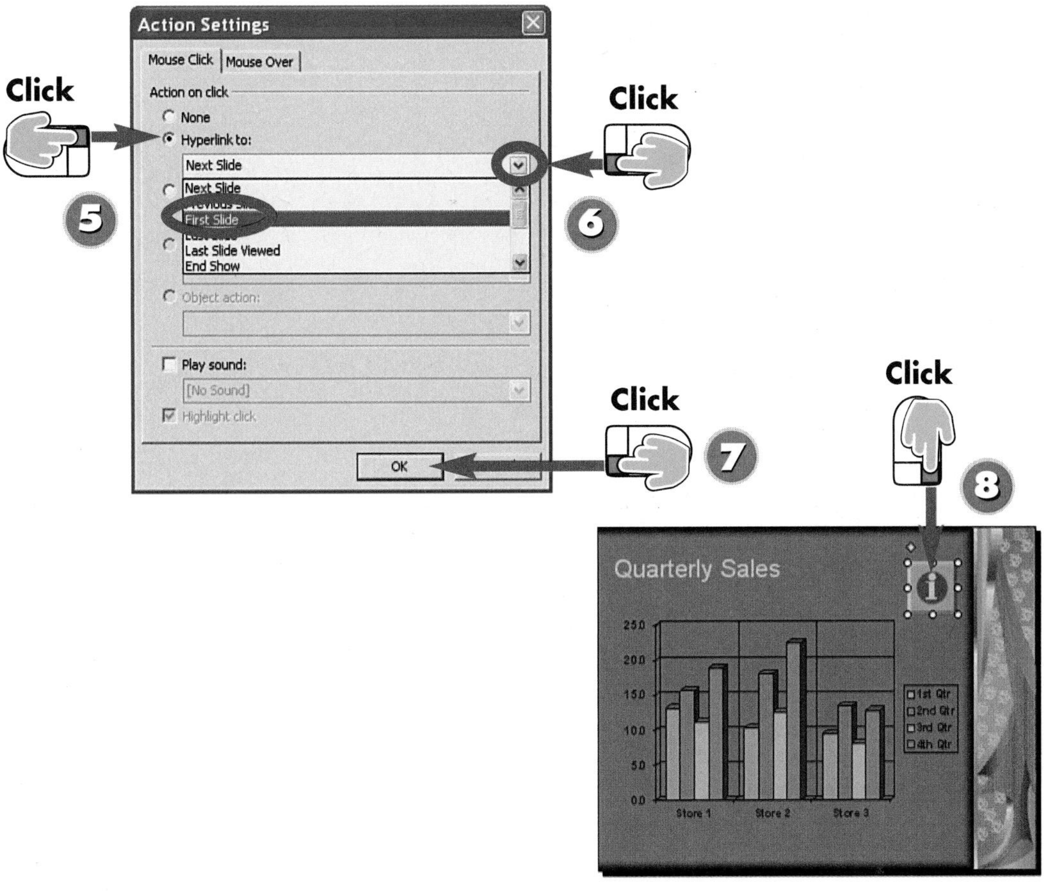

5 The Action Settings dialog box opens. Click the **Hyperlink to** option button.

6 Click the drop-down arrow and select the slide you want to jump to.

7 Click **OK**.

8 PowerPoint adds the action button to the slide. When you view the show, you can click the button to activate the link.

TIP

Moving and Resizing Action Buttons
You can move and resize action buttons just as you do other slide objects. See Part 5 to learn more about working with slide objects.

TIP

Activating a Program
You can use the **Run Program** option in the Action Settings dialog box to associate a program with the action button. When clicked, the button activates the program. You'll need to enter the path location of the program you want to execute, and the program must reside on the same drive or network as the slide show file.

Creating Speaker Notes

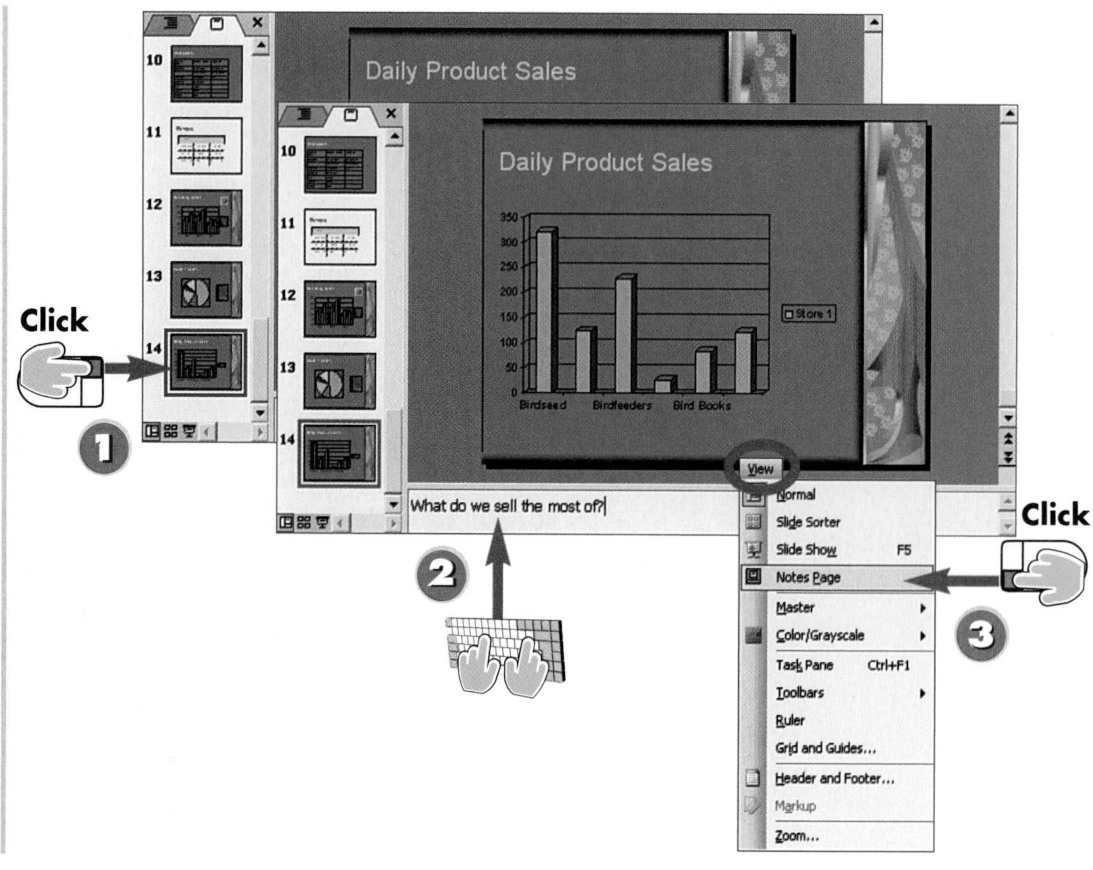

1. In Normal view, click the slide to which you want to add notes.
2. Click in the Notes pane and type the note information.
3. Open the **View** menu and choose **Notes Page**.

INTRODUCTION

You can use the Notes pane in Normal view mode to add notes about each slide. Speaker notes can help you present important information associated with each slide. Switch to Notes Page view to see and edit your notes.

TIP

Increasing the Pane Size
If the Notes pane appears too small in Normal view, you can increase the pane size. Move the mouse pointer over the top edge of the Notes pane, then click and drag to resize the pane.

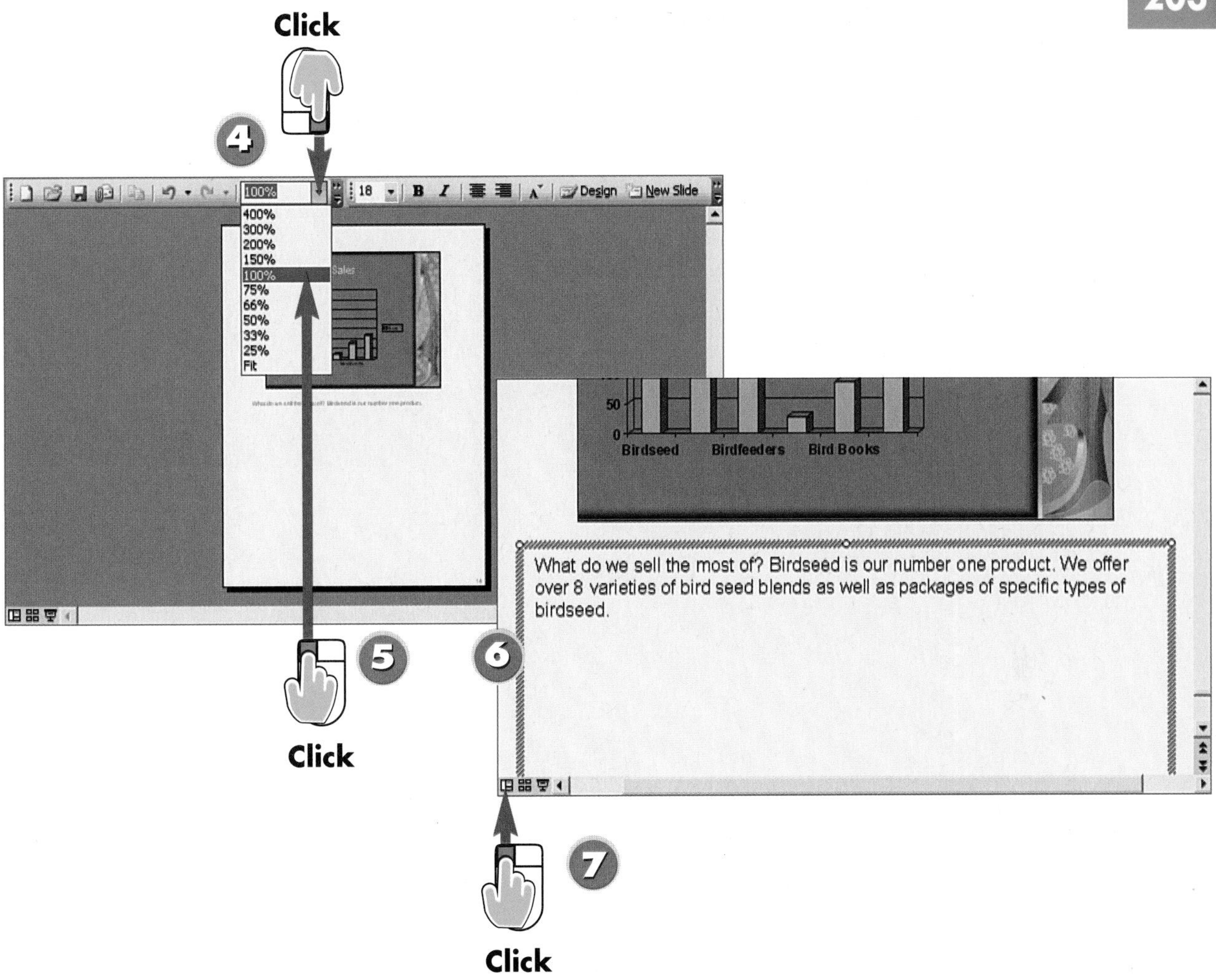

4. The Notes page appears. Click the down arrow next to the **Zoom** field.

5. Select a magnification percentage.

6. PowerPoint zooms your view of the Notes page. You can edit and format the Notes page using the same formatting controls for editing slide text.

7. Click the **Normal View** button to exit Notes Page view.

TIP

Scrolling Along Notes Pages
While in Notes Page view, you can use the scroll arrows on the right side of the screen to scroll through each slide in your presentation and view the associated notes.

TIP

Printing Notes
You can use PowerPoint's printing options to print out your notes and use them during the presentation. See the task "Printing a Presentation" to learn more.

Printing a Presentation

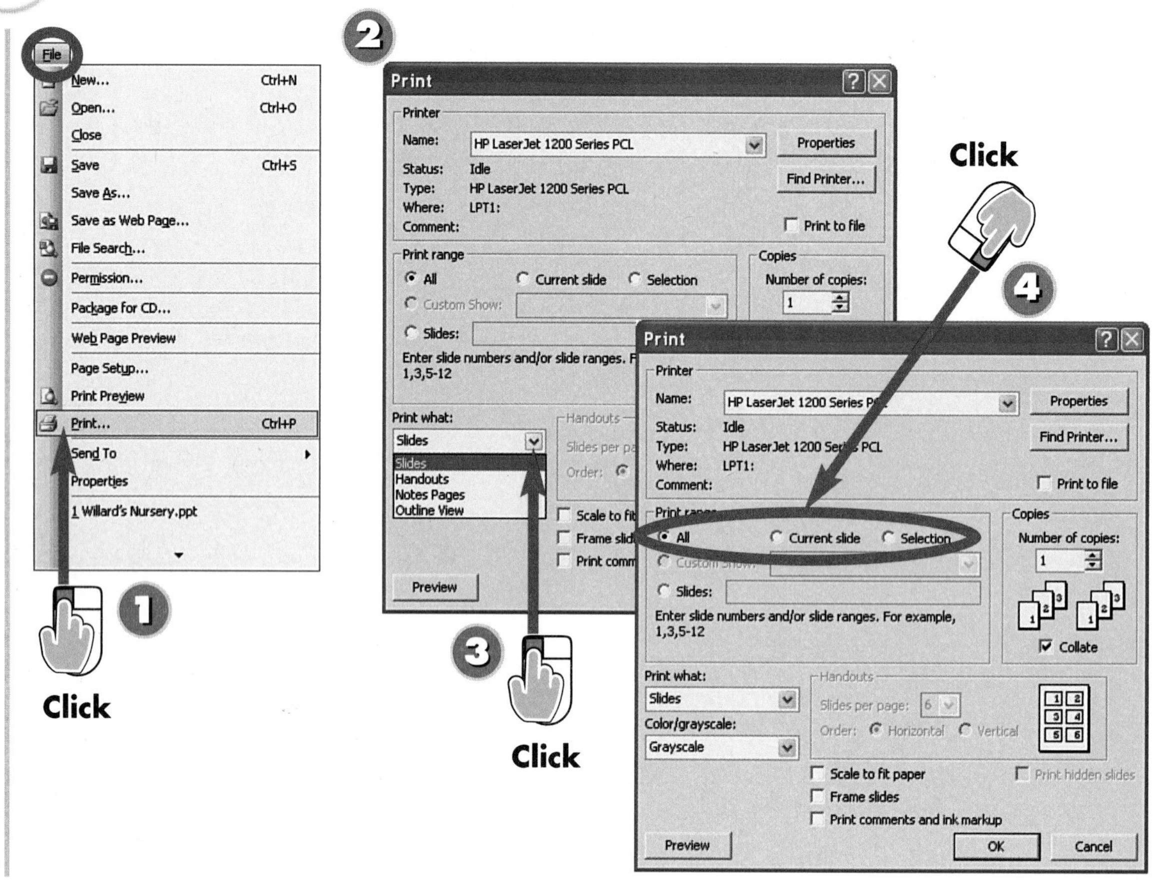

1. Open the **File** menu and choose **Print**.

2. PowerPoint opens the Print dialog box.

3. Click the **down arrow** next to the **Print What** field and select the presentation item you want to print. In this example, **Slides** is selected.

4. Click a print range. You can choose to print just the current slide, all the slides in the presentation, or selected slides.

INTRODUCTION

PowerPoint's printing options include a variety of settings to control how your slides are printed out. You can choose to print out individual slides or to group several slides on one page to create audience handouts. You can also choose to print out your speaker notes along with the slides.

TIP

Printing Audience Handouts

If you want to turn your slides into handouts that you can give to your audience, select the **Handouts** option in the Print dialog box and set the number of slides to print per page.

TIP

Printing Notes

To print slide notes, click the **Print What** drop-down arrow in the Print dialog box and select **Notes Pages**.

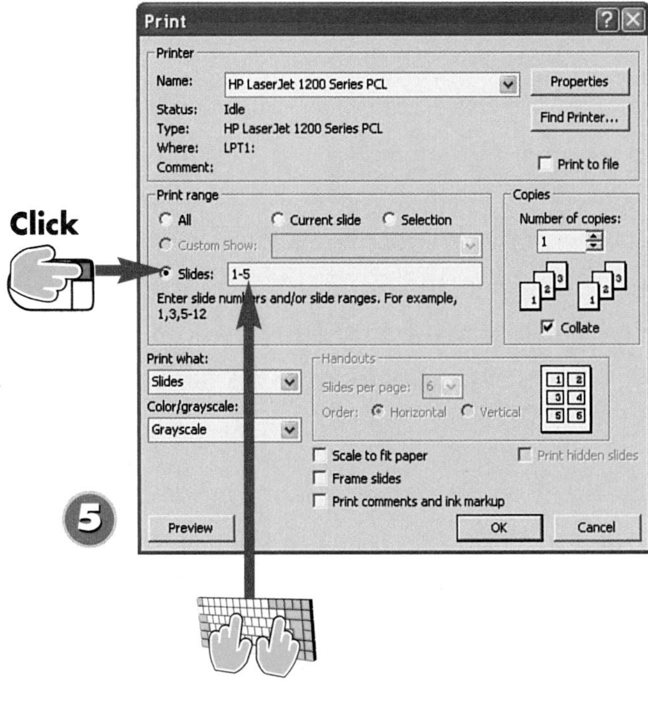

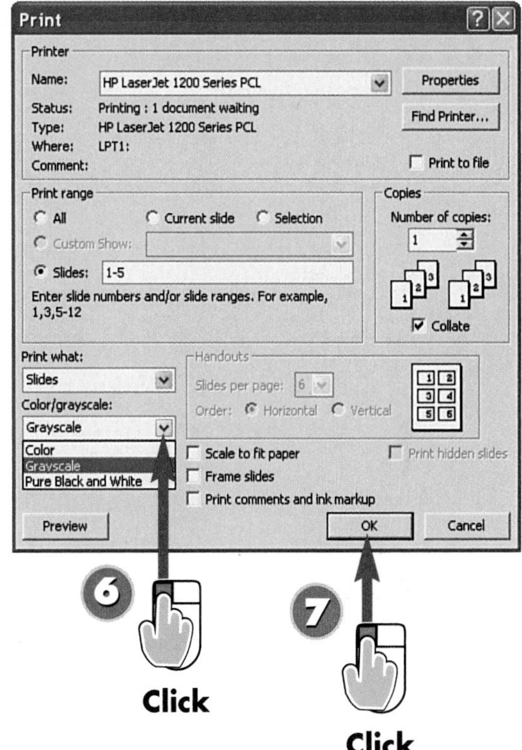

5 To print specific slides, click the **Slides** option and type the slide numbers.

6 Click the **down arrow** next to the **Color/grayscale** field and select whether you want to print color, grayscale, or black and white printouts of your slides.

7 Click **OK** to start printing the slides.

TIP

More Printing Options
If you need to control whether your slides print out in landscape or portrait style, click the **Properties** button in the Print dialog box. This opens your printer's Properties dialog box. Click the **Layout** tab and choose a printing direction: **Landscape** or **Portrait**.

TIP

Printing an Outline
You can also choose to print just the text outline of your presentation without all the slide and visuals. In the Print dialog box, click the **Outline View** option in the **Print What** drop-down list.

PART 11

Collaborating with Others

If you collaborate with others to create presentations, PowerPoint offers several useful features to help you and your colleagues edit presentation materials. Your presentation can be viewed by multiple reviewers, and PowerPoint tracks feedback offered by each person. You can then combine all the review documents into a finished slide show.

You can also use comments to add notes about slide elements and text. Comments are helpful when you want to insert reminders to yourself about checking a fact or adding an explanation about a slide element. Users who review your presentation can also use the Comment feature to add comments to your slides.

You can share your presentation with others via email or as a Web page. For example, if the person you want to view a presentation does not have PowerPoint installed, you can save your slide show on a Web page and allow them to view it in a Web browser.

The Revisions Task Pane

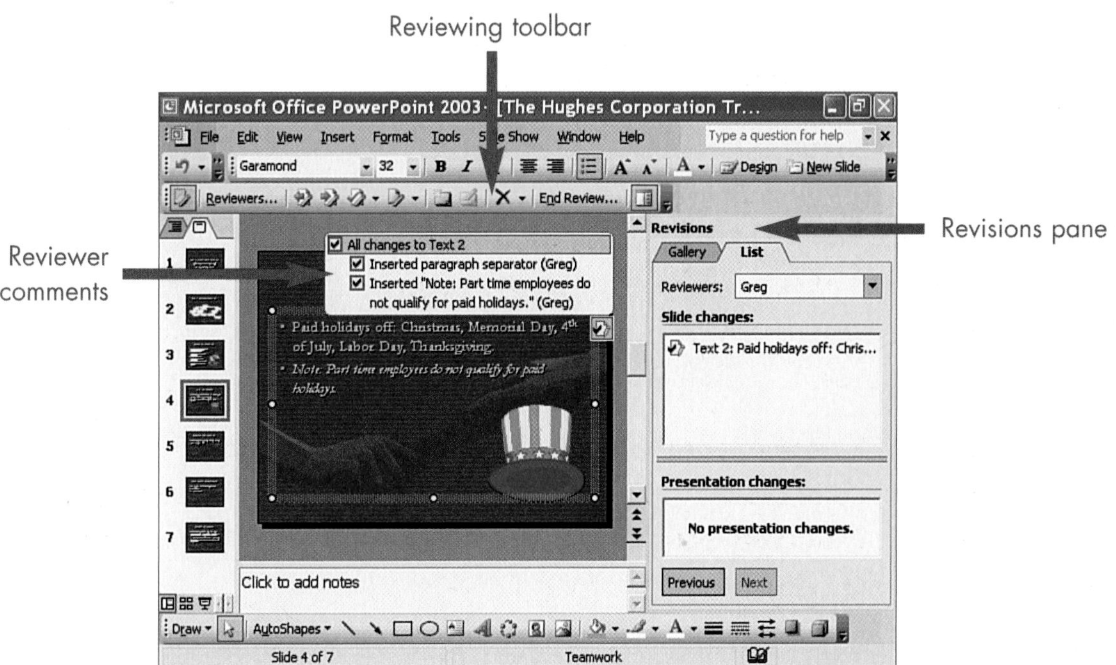

Adding a Comment

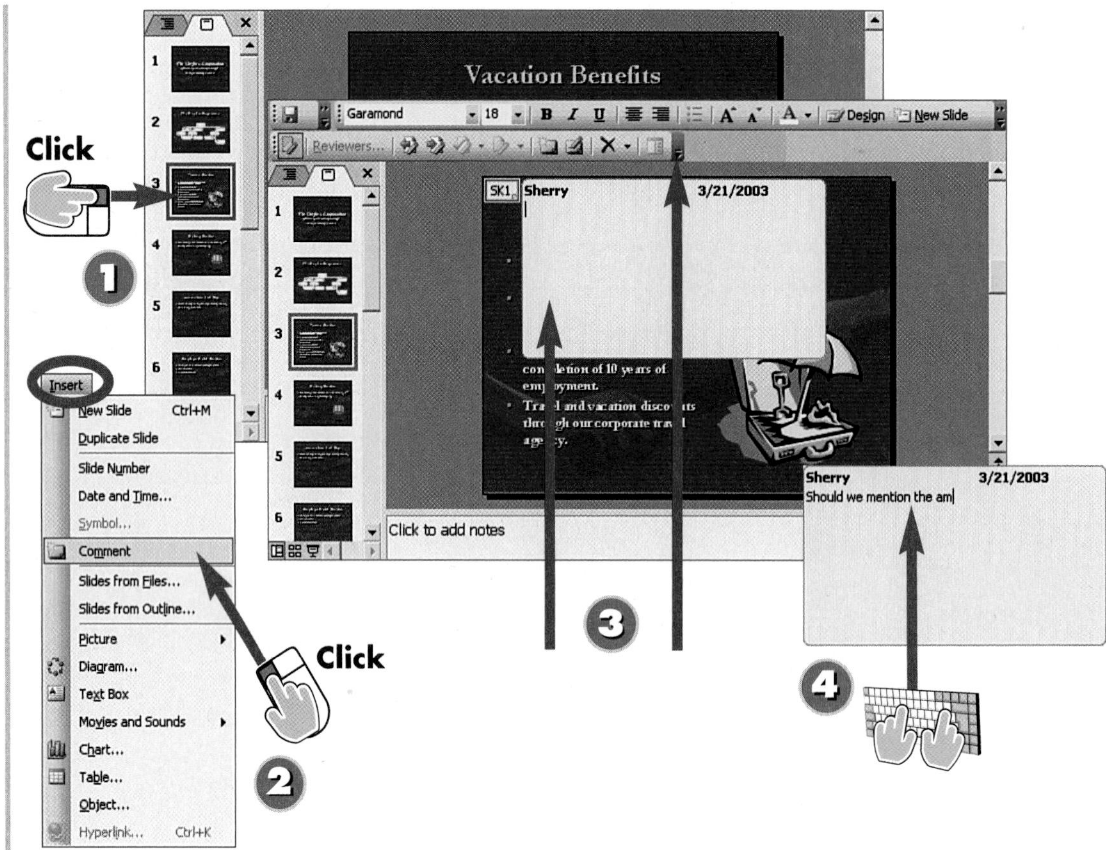

1. In Normal view, click the slide to which you want to add a comment.
2. Open the **Insert** menu and choose **Comment**.
3. PowerPoint displays a yellow comment box with your name and the current date filled in, along with the Reviewing toolbar.
4. Type the comment text you want to add to the slide.

INTRODUCTION

If you are working with others to create a presentation, you can use comments to add feedback about a slide. You can also use comments to add notes to yourself, such as a reminder about updating data, or an explanation about your choice of clip art. Comments do not appear when you view the actual slide show.

TIP

Printing Comments
The Print dialog box has a **Print Comments and Ink Markup** check box you can select if you want to print any comments associated with the slides you want to print. Refer to Part 10 to learn how to print a presentation.

TIP

Reviewer Comments
If you use PowerPoint's reviewing features to collaborate with others on a slide show, your reviewers can also use the Comment feature to add comments to your slides.

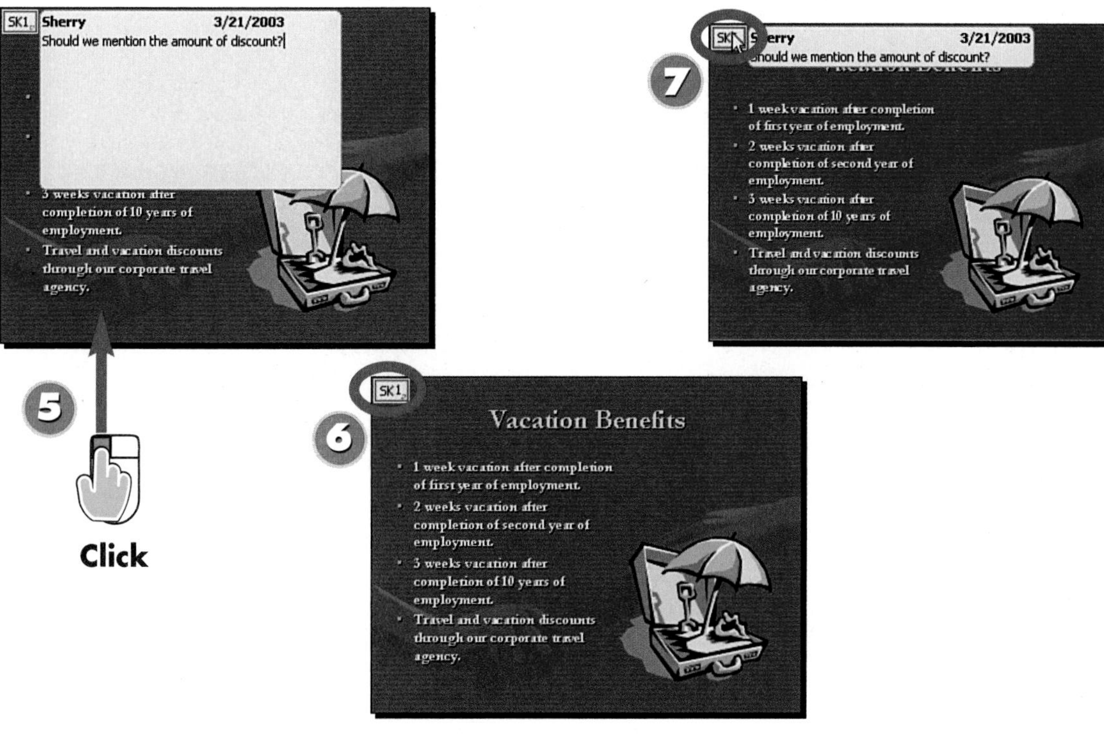

5. Click outside the comment box.

6. The comment box closes and a comment marker containing your initials appears on the slide.

7. To view the comment again, move the mouse pointer over the comment marker.

TIP

Removing a Comment
Right-click a comment marker and select **Delete Comment** to remove the comment from the slide.

TIP

Editing Comments
To open a comment box and add or edit the text, simply double-click the comment marker, and type in the comment box.

Saving a Presentation for Multiple Reviewers

Start

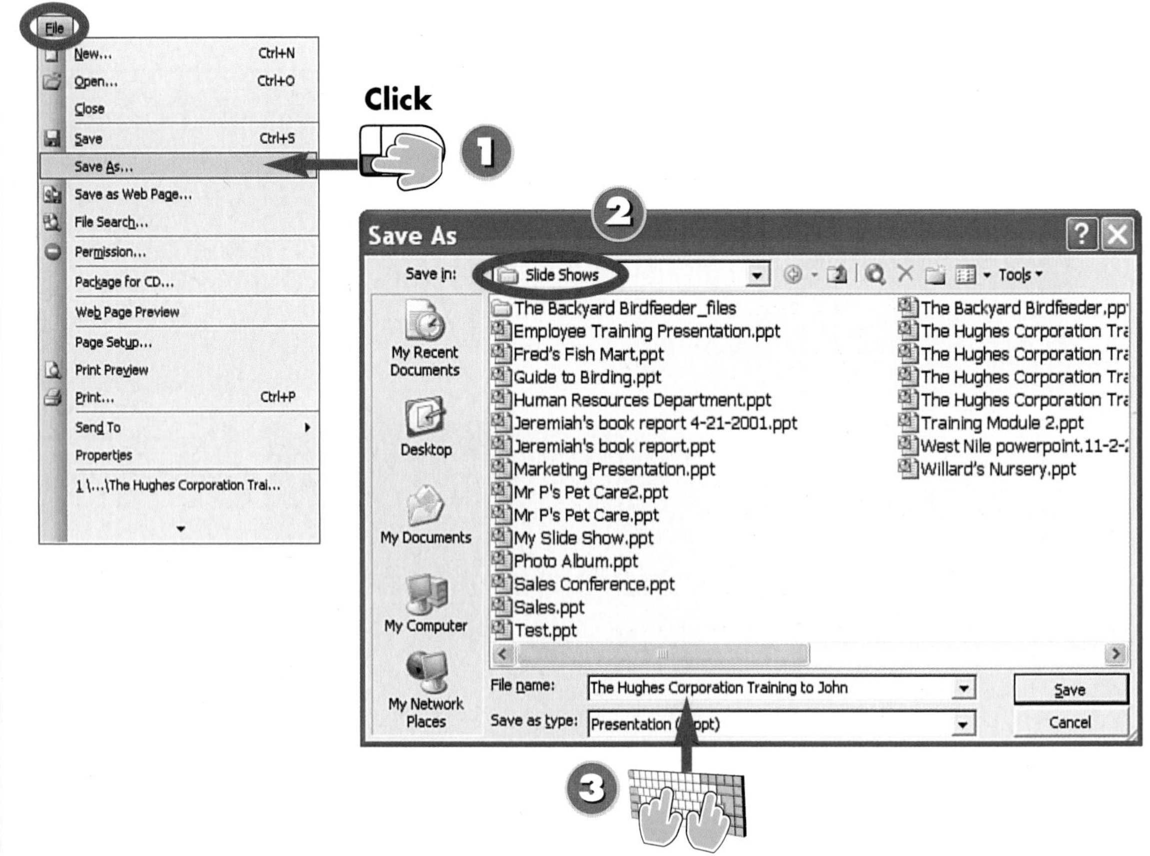

1. With the presentation you want to distribute to others displayed onscreen, open the **File** menu and choose **Save As**.
2. The Save As dialog box opens. Select a folder or drive to save the file to, or use the default folder.
3. Type a name for the review file in the **File Name** field.

INTRODUCTION

PowerPoint offers a unique feature for users who collaborate to build a presentation. You can save a presentation as a review file and distribute it to others for their feedback. After each person has reviewed the file, you can combine the review files into one presentation.

CAUTION

Warning!
If you distribute your review files to be viewed on another computer, the user might not be able to access the multimedia files associated with your slide show. If you want the reviewer to be able to work with the multimedia files as well, be sure to distribute the clips along with the review file.

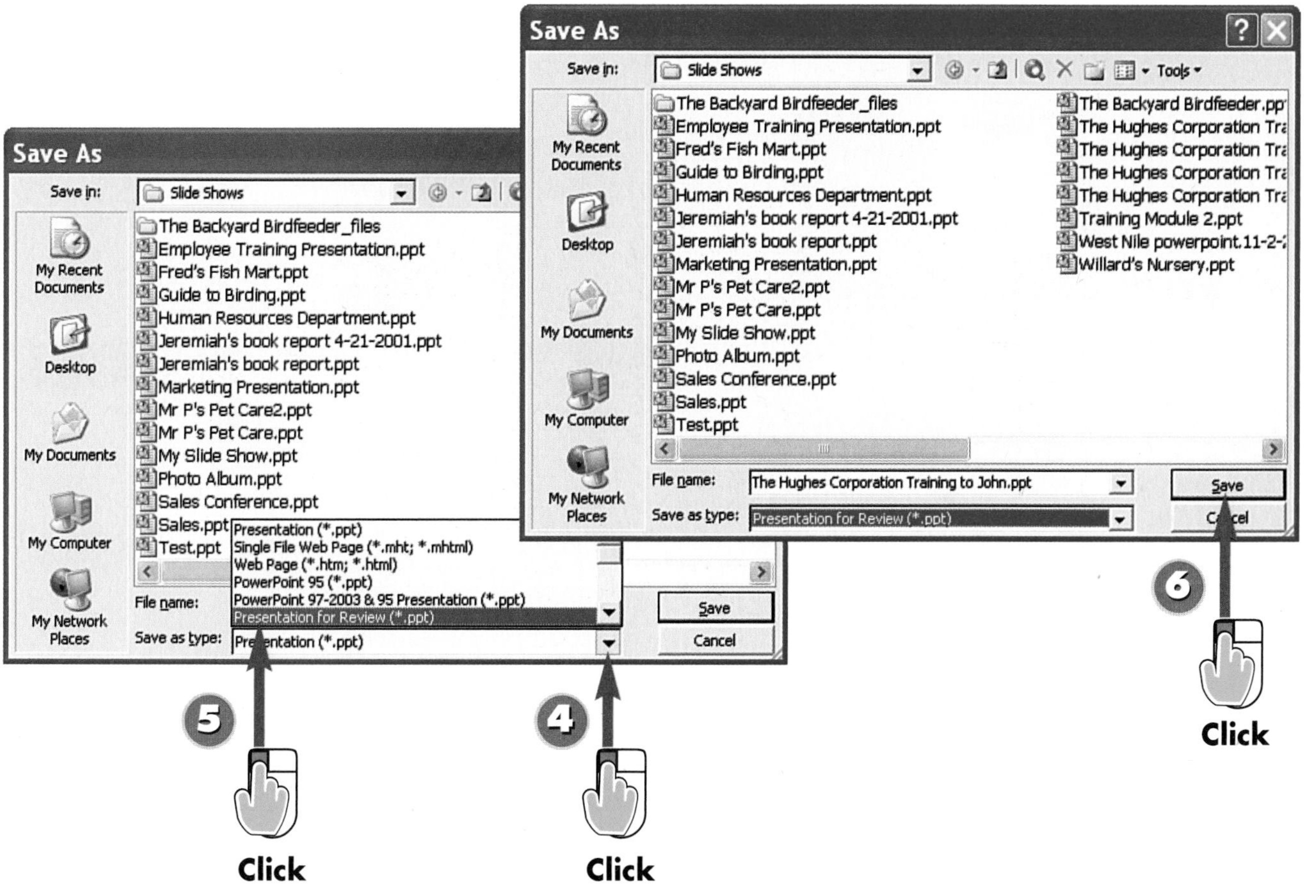

4. Click the **down arrow** next to the **Save as Type** field.

5. Click **Presentation for Review**.

6. Click **Save**. Repeat steps 1–6 to save more copies of the same file to distribute to different reviewers.

TIP

Naming Ideas

To help keep your review files separate and easy to distinguish, consider naming each one after the person to whom you want to distribute a copy.

TIP

Information Rights Management

To prevent unauthorized users from accessing your file, you can download and install PowerPoint's new Information Rights Management Client feature and set up restricted permissions. Open the **File** menu and choose **Permission**, and link to the Microsoft Web site to learn more about this feature.

Merging Review Files

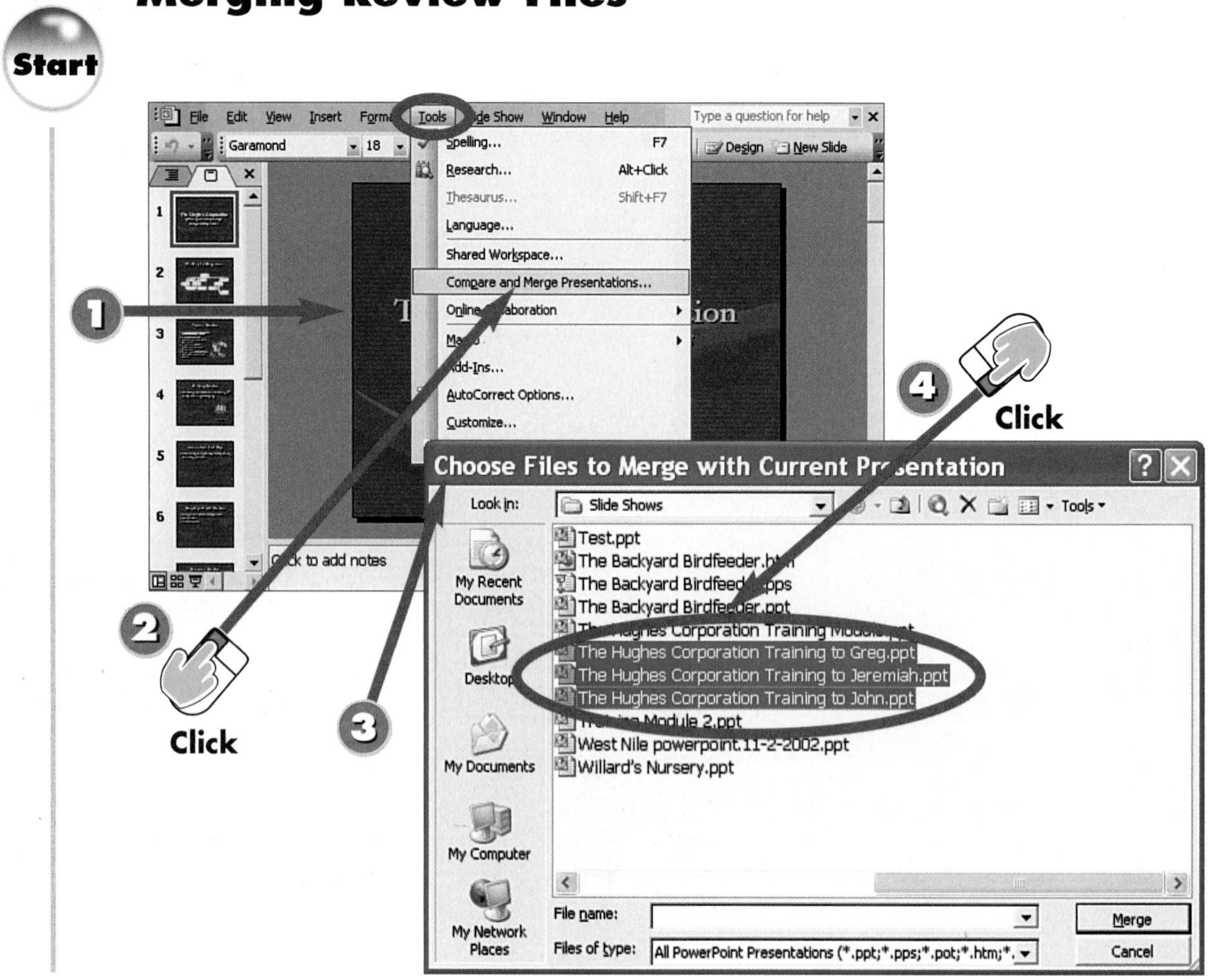

1. Upon receiving the reviewed files back from the reviewers, open the original presentation file in PowerPoint.
2. Open the **Tools** menu and choose **Compare and Merge Presentations**.
3. The Choose Files to Merge with Current Presentation dialog box opens.
4. Locate and select the review files you want to combine. To select multiple files, press and hold the **Ctrl** key while clicking the filenames.

INTRODUCTION

When you distribute a review file to others, they can open the file in PowerPoint and make any changes to the slide show. After they review the presentation, they can save their changes and return the file to you. You can then merge the review files with the original slide show and view all the changes.

TIP

Selecting Files
When selecting multiple files that are listed right next to each other, you can click the first filename, press and hold the **Shift** key, then click the last file. If the files are scattered, press and hold the **Ctrl** key while clicking files.

TIP

Creating Review Files
See the previous task, "Saving a Presentation for Multiple Reviewers," to learn how to create review files.

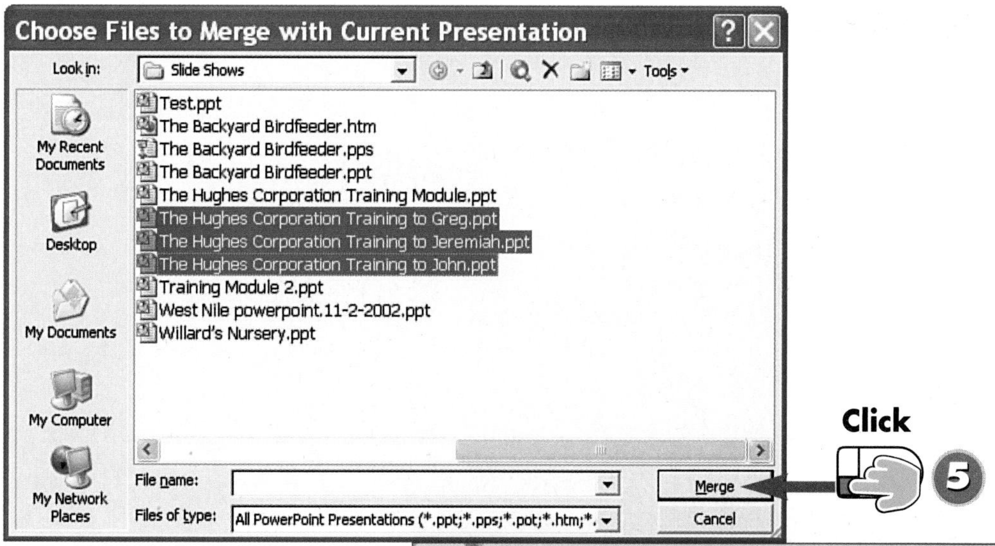

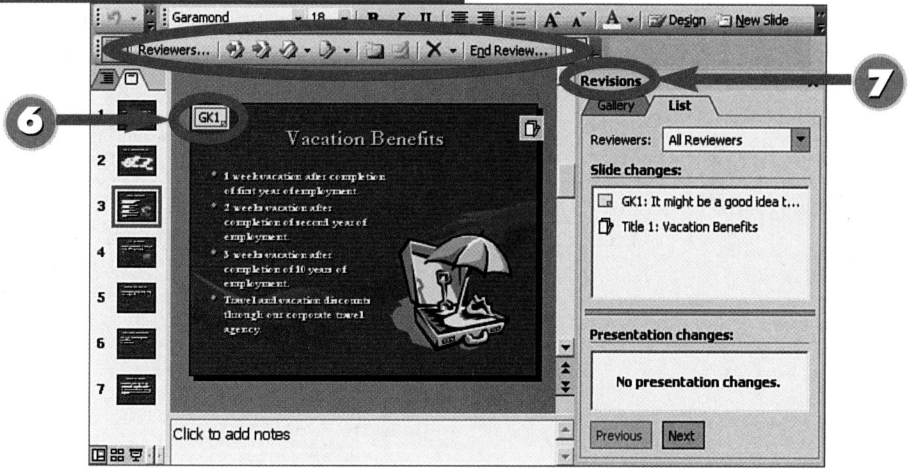

5 Click **Merge**.

6 PowerPoint combines all the files with the original file and displays markers in each location where a change occurs.

7 PowerPoint also displays the Reviewing toolbar and the Revisions Task pane.

TIP

Reviewing the Changes
See the next task, "Reviewing Changes in a Review File," to learn more about checking the changes in the merged review file.

TIP

Toggle the Toolbar
You can turn the Reviewing toolbar on or off as needed. Select **View**, **Toolbars**, **Reviewing**.

Reviewing Changes in a Review File

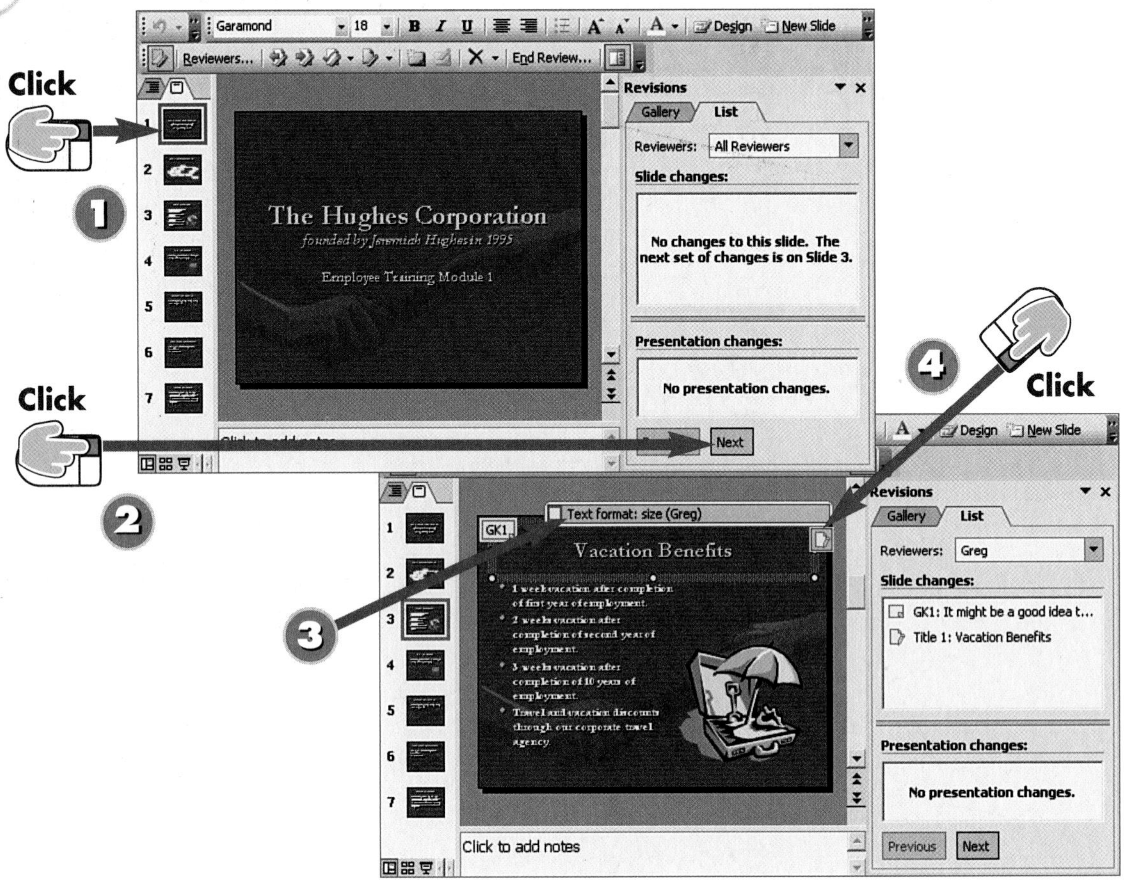

1. In Normal view, click the first slide in the presentation.
2. Click the **Next Item** button on the Reviewing toolbar or click the **Next** button in the Revisions pane.
3. PowerPoint jumps to the first change in the presentation.
4. Click the review box to display details about the requested change.

INTRODUCTION

After merging review files from your collaborators, you can review the suggested changes and decide which ones to keep and which ones to ignore. If two or more people reviewed the presentation, each reviewer's changes are color-coded on the slides.

TIP

Merging Files First

See the previous task, "Merging Review Files," to learn how to combine review files before checking for changes.

TIP

Previewing Changes

Click the **Gallery** tab in the Revisions Task pane to see a preview of how each slide might look in the presentation if the suggested changes are implemented.

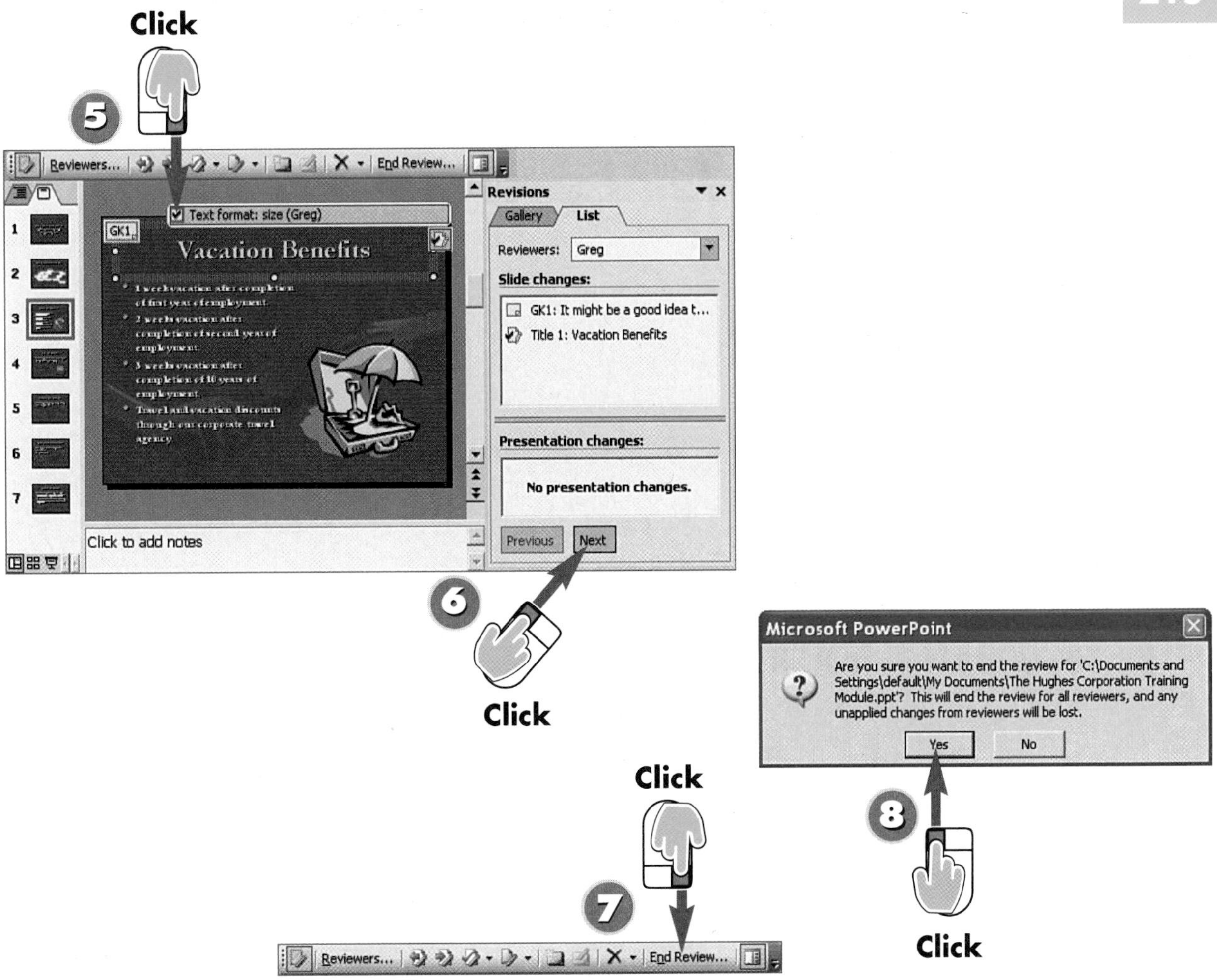

Click

Click

Click

Click

5 Click the check box to apply the change, or leave the check box empty to ignore the change.

6 Repeat steps 2–5 to continue reviewing all the changes in the presentation.

7 When finished reviewing the presentation, click the **End Review** button on the Reviewing toolbar.

8 PowerPoint displays a prompt box. Click **Yes** to end the review and remove all the markers in the file.

TIP

Hiding Markers
You can click the **Markup** button on the Reviewing toolbar to toggle between hiding and displaying the change markers on your slides.

TIP

Conflicting Changes
If two or more reviewers suggest different changes to the same item, a red change marker appears on the slide. You can choose which person's change to implement, or ignore them all.

TIP

Toolbar Shortcuts
You can use the **Apply** and **Unapply** buttons on the Reviewing toolbar to apply or ignore reviewer changes in your slides. Use the **Next Item** and **Previous Item** buttons to move back and forth between changes.

Emailing a Presentation

Start

Click

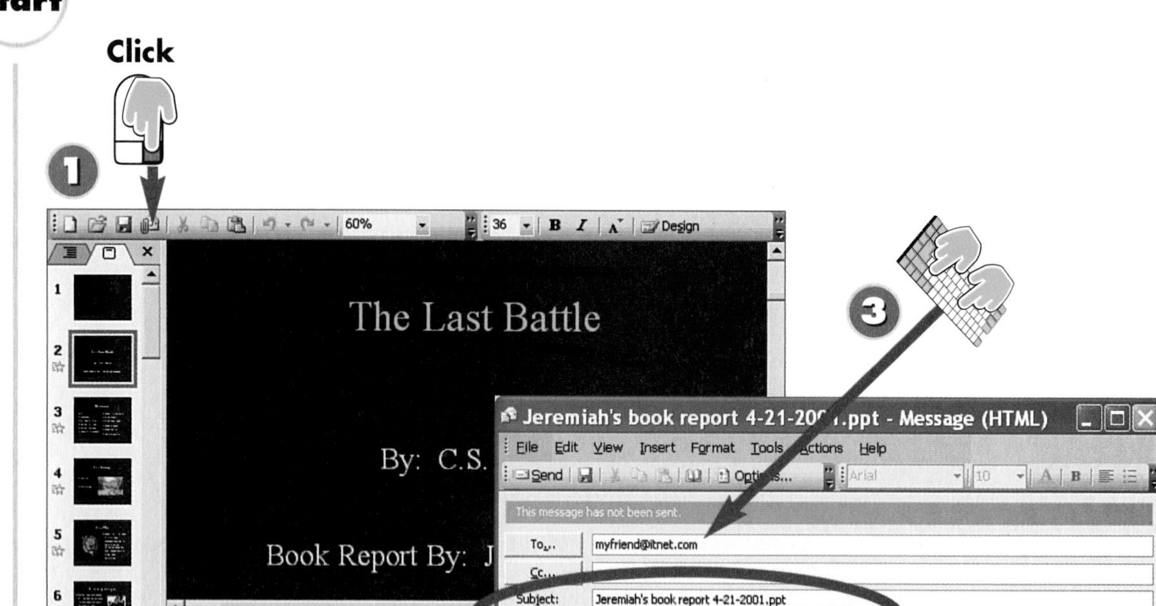

1. With the PowerPoint file you want to email displayed onscreen, click the **E-mail (As Attachment)** button on the Standard toolbar.
2. An email message window appears with the presentation file already attached to the message and the subject header filled in.
3. Type the email address of the person to whom you want to send the file.

INTRODUCTION

Another way to collaborate with others is to email your presentation file. You can email your current file without leaving the PowerPoint program window.

CAUTION

Warning!
To view the presentation, the person to which you email the file must have PowerPoint installed on their computer.

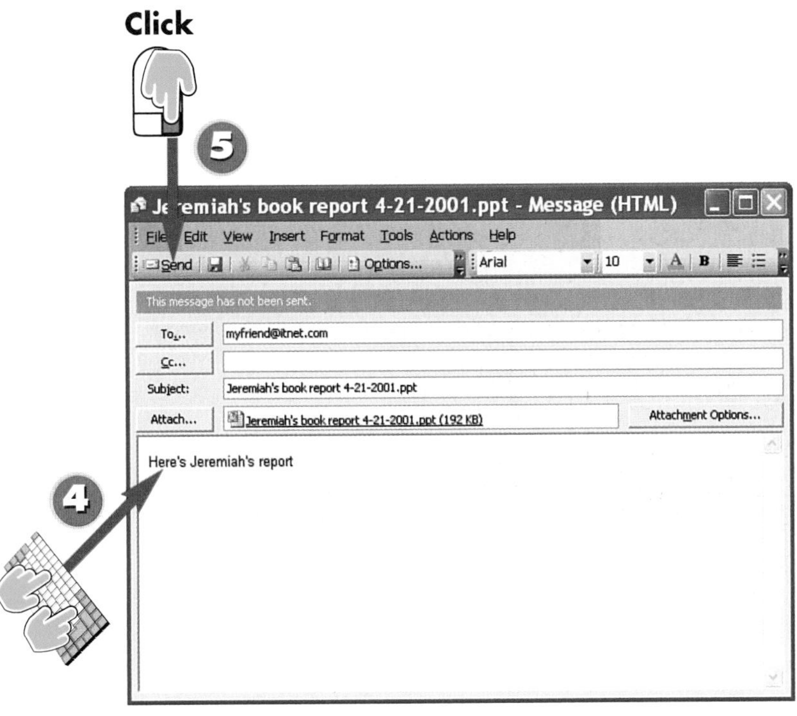

4. Click the message area and type any text you want to accompany the presentation.

5. Click **Send** to email the file.

CAUTION

Connecting to the Web
If you are not connected to the Internet, you might need to log on first in order to send the file.

Saving a Presentation as a Web Page

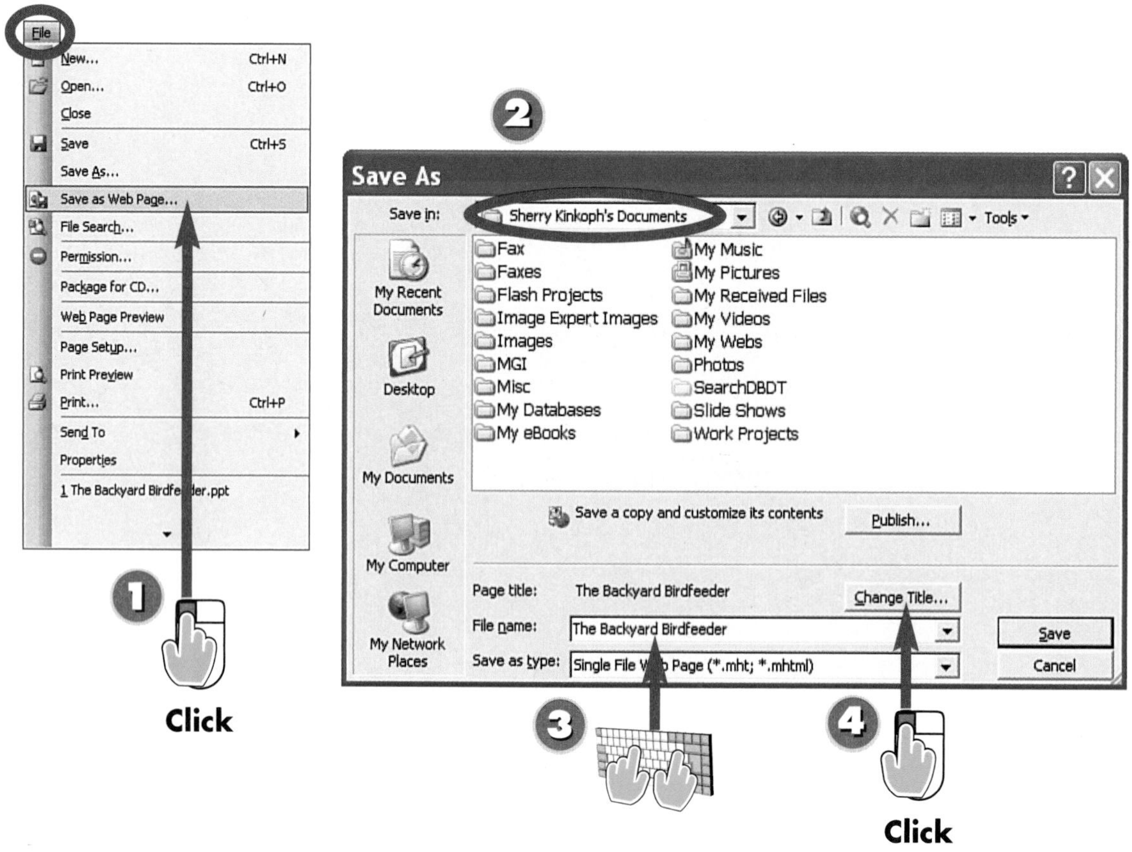

1. With the PowerPoint file you want to share displayed onscreen, open the **File** menu and choose **Save as Web Page**.
2. The Save As dialog box opens. Select a folder or drive to save the file to, or use the default folder.
3. Type a name for the Web page file in the **File Name** field.
4. To create a title for the browser window that displays the presentation, click the **Change Title** button.

INTRODUCTION

Yet another way to collaborate with others is to share your presentation as a Web page. For example, if you want a colleague or friend to view a slide show, yet you know the person doesn't have PowerPoint, you can save your presentation as an HTML file, which the intended recipient can view using a Web browser. (Web page browsers are quite common and the HTML format is an easy way to share files.) You can also save your presentation as a Web page to post on a server and allow Internet users to view the show.

TIP

What Is HTML?
HTML stands for *hypertext markup language*, a special file format used to create Web pages.

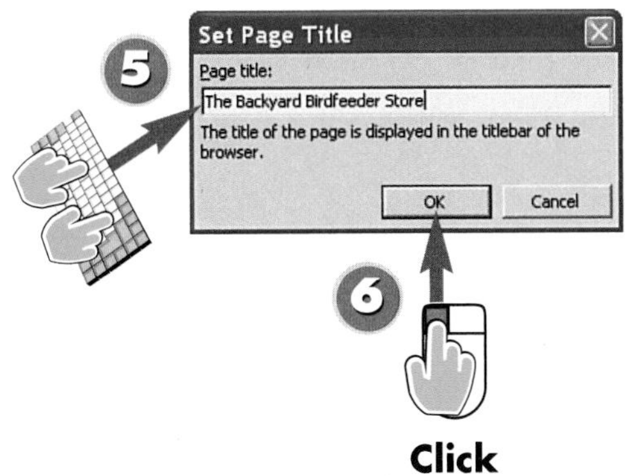

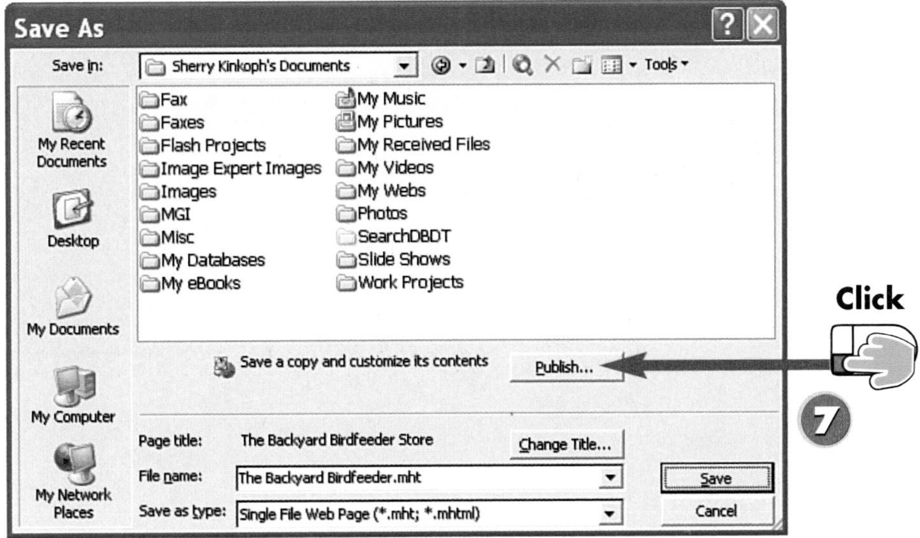

5 The Set Page Title dialog box opens. Type a title for the page in the **Page Title** field.

6 Click **OK**.

7 Click the **Publish** button.

TIP

Using the Preview Feature

You can preview how your slide show looks as a Web page before saving it as an HTML file. Open the **File** menu and choose **Web Page Preview** to open your default Web browser and view the presentation.

Saving a Presentation as a Web Page (Continued)

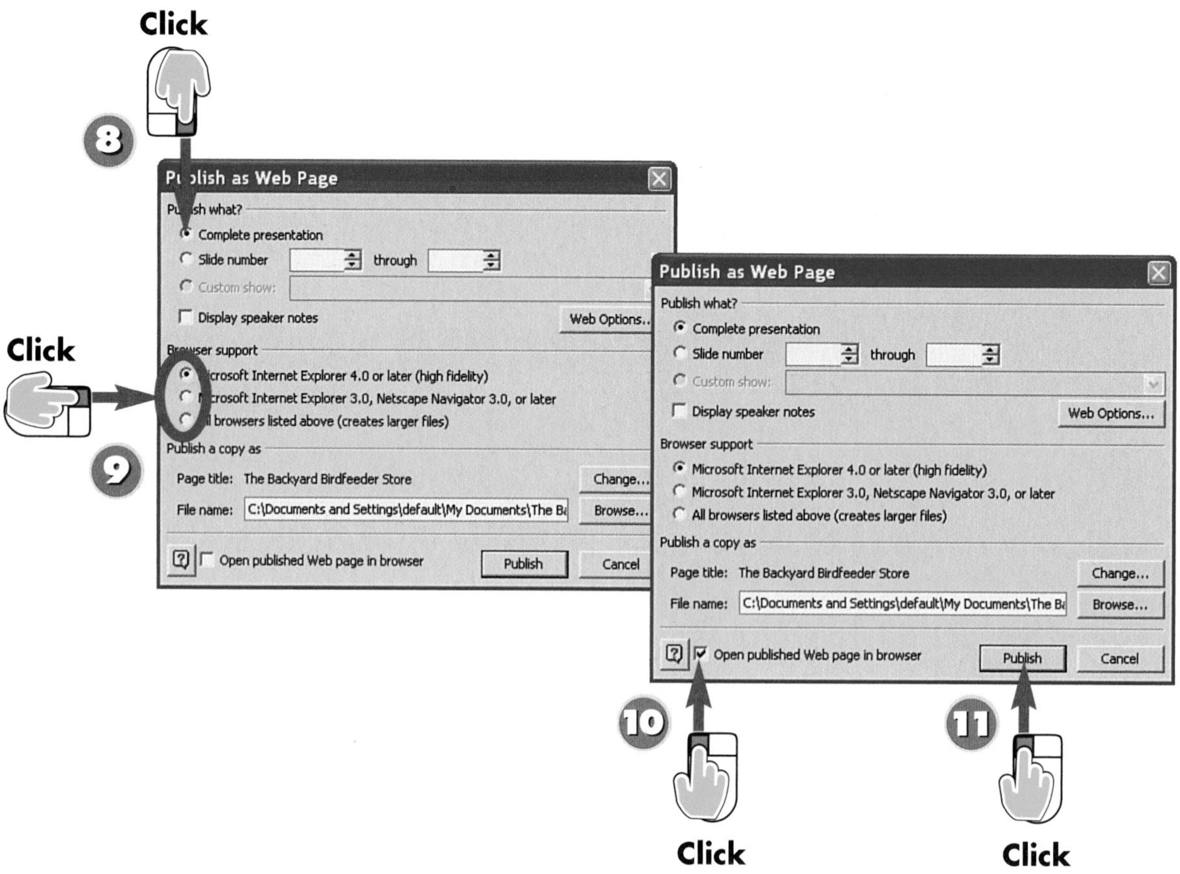

8. The Publish as Web Page dialog box opens. Click the **Complete Presentation** option button.
9. Click the type of browser support you want to apply.
10. Click the **Open Published Web Page in Browser** check box to select it.
11. Click the **Publish** button.

Publishing to a Server

TIP

If you want to save your presentation as an HTML file for other Internet users to view, you must publish the file to a Web server—a computer that stores Web pages. Contact your network administrator or Internet service provider to learn more.

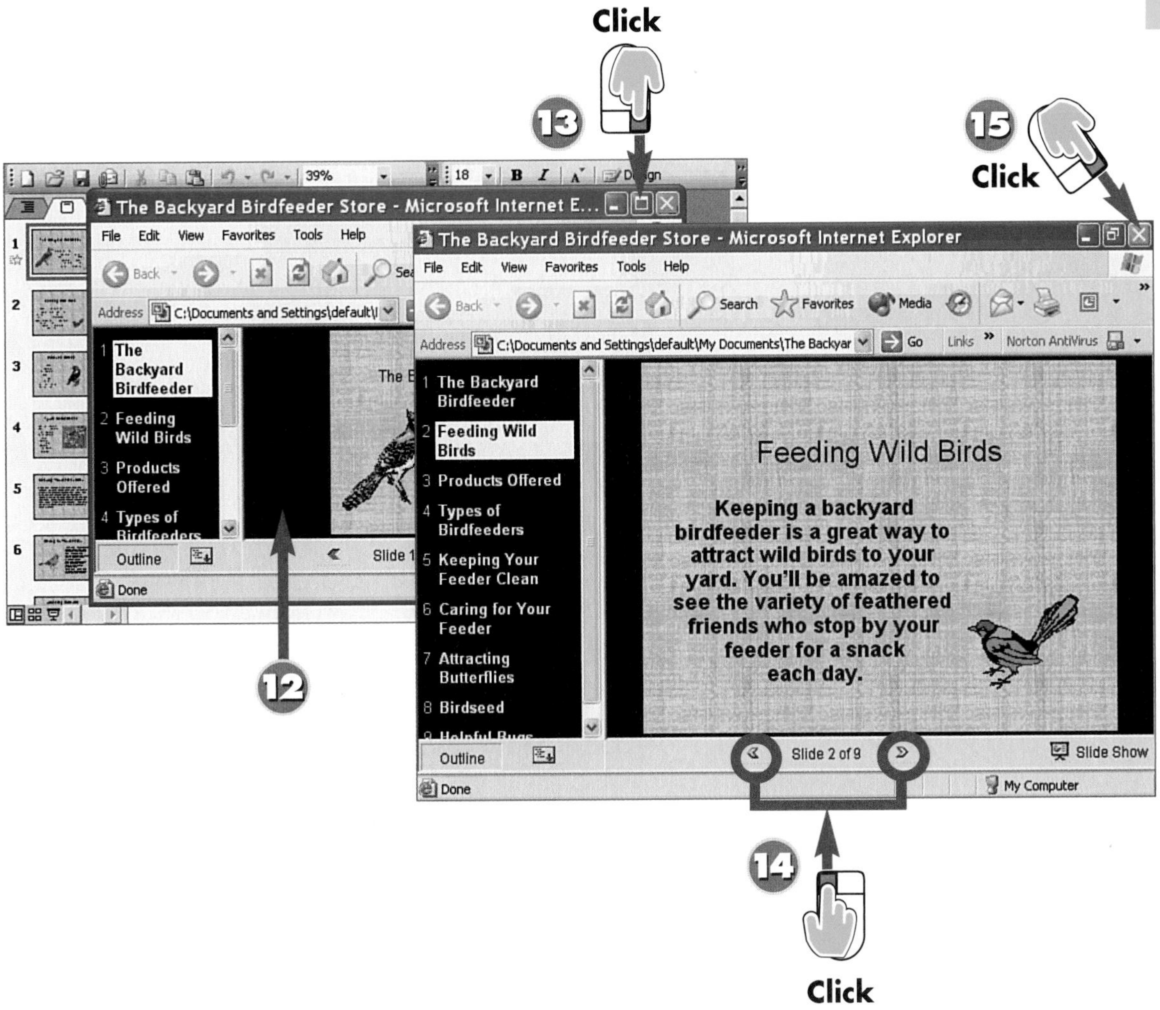

12 PowerPoint saves your presentation and opens your Web browser to enable you to view the slide show.

13 Click the browser's **Maximize** button to enlarge the viewing area.

14 Click the arrow buttons to move back and forth between each slide.

15 When you finish previewing the show, click the browser's **Close** button to return to the PowerPoint window.

TIP

Viewing the Full Show
Users can see your full-screen slide show on the Web page by clicking the **Slide Show** button at the bottom of the browser window.

CAUTION

Hiding Speaker Notes
If you are publishing your presentation on the Internet, you might not want your speaker notes visible to others. Be sure to deselect the **Display Speaker Notes** check box in the Publish as Web Page dialog box before clicking the **Publish** button and creating the HTML file.

PART 12

Running a Presentation

You can tell PowerPoint exactly how you want your slide show to run. You can choose to present the show yourself, or set up a slide show to run on its own. You can also set the show up as a self-guided presentation, allowing the user to view and interact with the show at his or her own pace.

If you plan on giving the presentation yourself, PowerPoint includes a variety of tools you can use to assist you with the show, including a tool for rehearsing the presentation.

If you want to take your show on the road, so to speak, PowerPoint includes a feature for transferring your presentation package to a CD-ROM. The Package for CD feature creates a compact file along with all the necessary multimedia clips, narration, and other slide items needed to run the show.

A Running Slide Show

The Rehearse Timings command

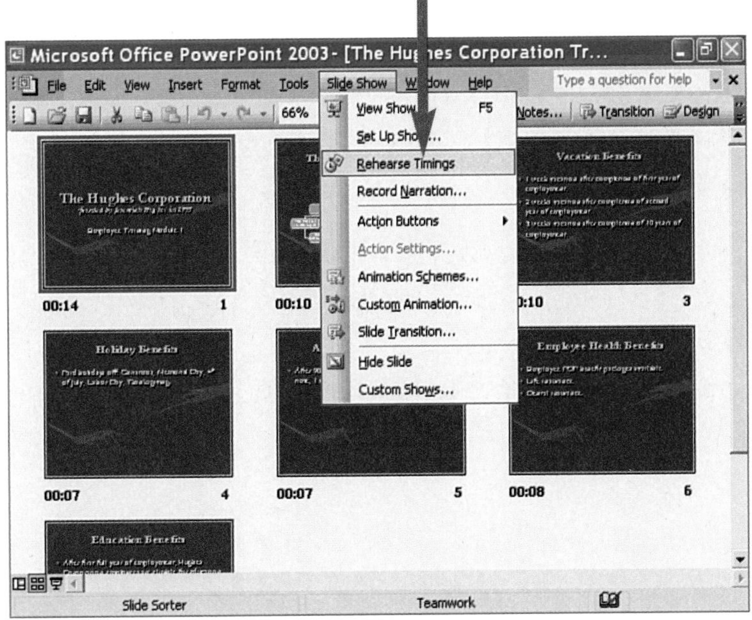

Setting Up a Slide Show

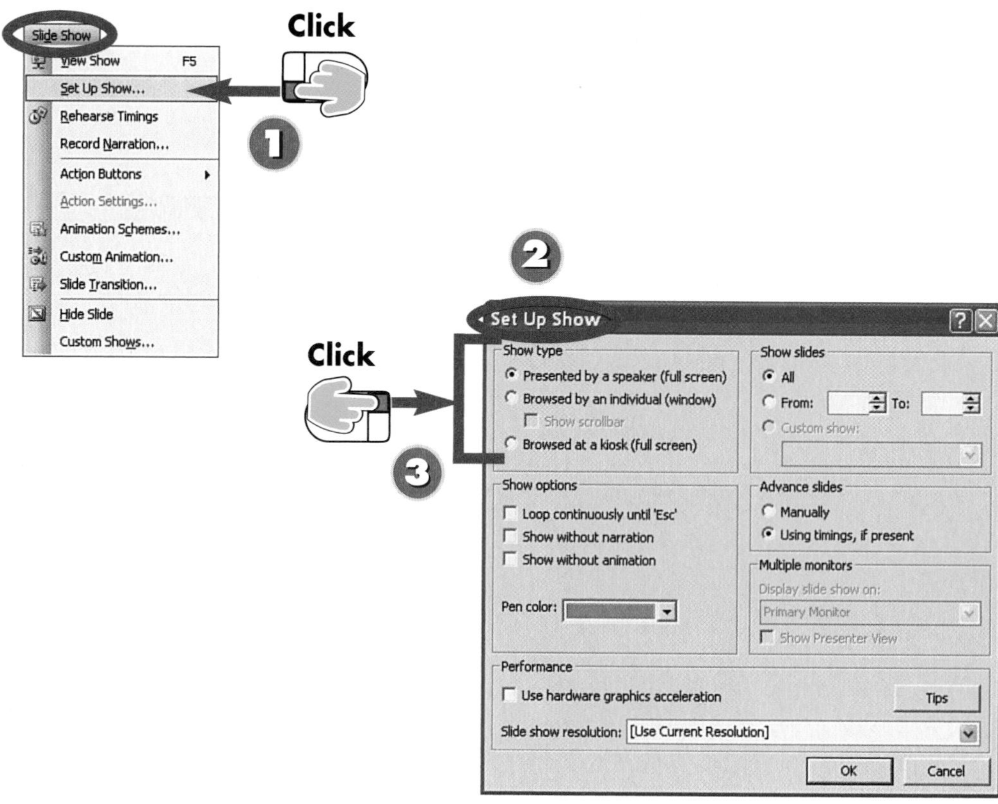

1. With the slide show you want to set up displayed onscreen, open the **Slide Show** menu and choose **Set Up Show**.
2. The Set Up Show dialog box opens.
3. Click the type of show you want to present. You can choose to present the show yourself, to allow a user to browse at his or her own pace, or to make the show play by itself.

INTRODUCTION

You can tell PowerPoint exactly how you want to present your slide show. You can choose to present the show yourself, or allow users to view it on their own. You can even set the slide show up to run by itself, such as at a trade show kiosk.

TIP

Browsed at a Kiosk
To present a self-running slide show, select the **Browsed at a Kiosk** option in the Set Up Show dialog box. By default, PowerPoint sets up this type of show to run in a continuous loop.

TIP

Show Options
If your slide show includes narration or animation effects, you can choose to turn them on or off using the **Show Options** check boxes in the Set Up Show dialog box.

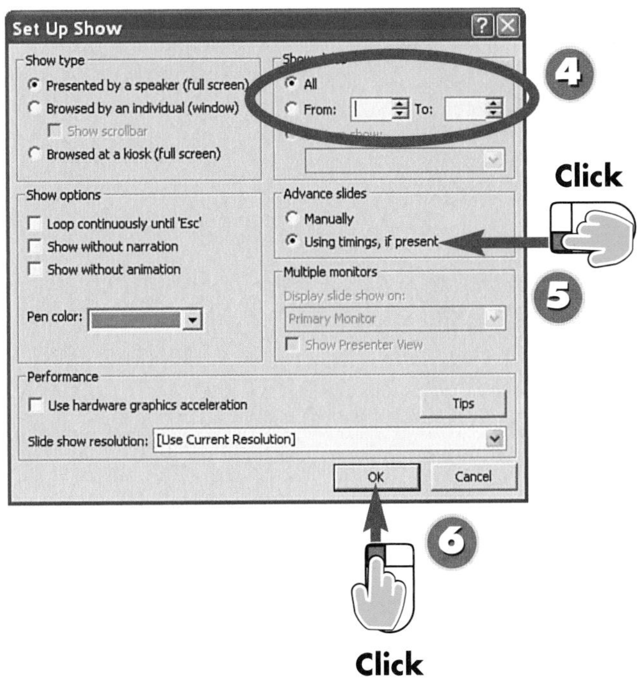

4. By default, PowerPoint includes all the slides when presenting the slide show. If you like, however, you can specify a range of slides to play.

5. Select how you want the slides to advance in the show—either manually by the presenter, or using rehearsed timings.

6. Click **OK** to apply the new settings.

TIP

Manual Versus Rehearsed Timings

When presenting a show manually, you control when each slide advances with a click on the screen. When you use rehearsed timings, the show moves at the pace you specify. See the task "Rehearsing a Presentation" to learn more about setting rehearsed timings for a show.

Rehearsing a Presentation

Start

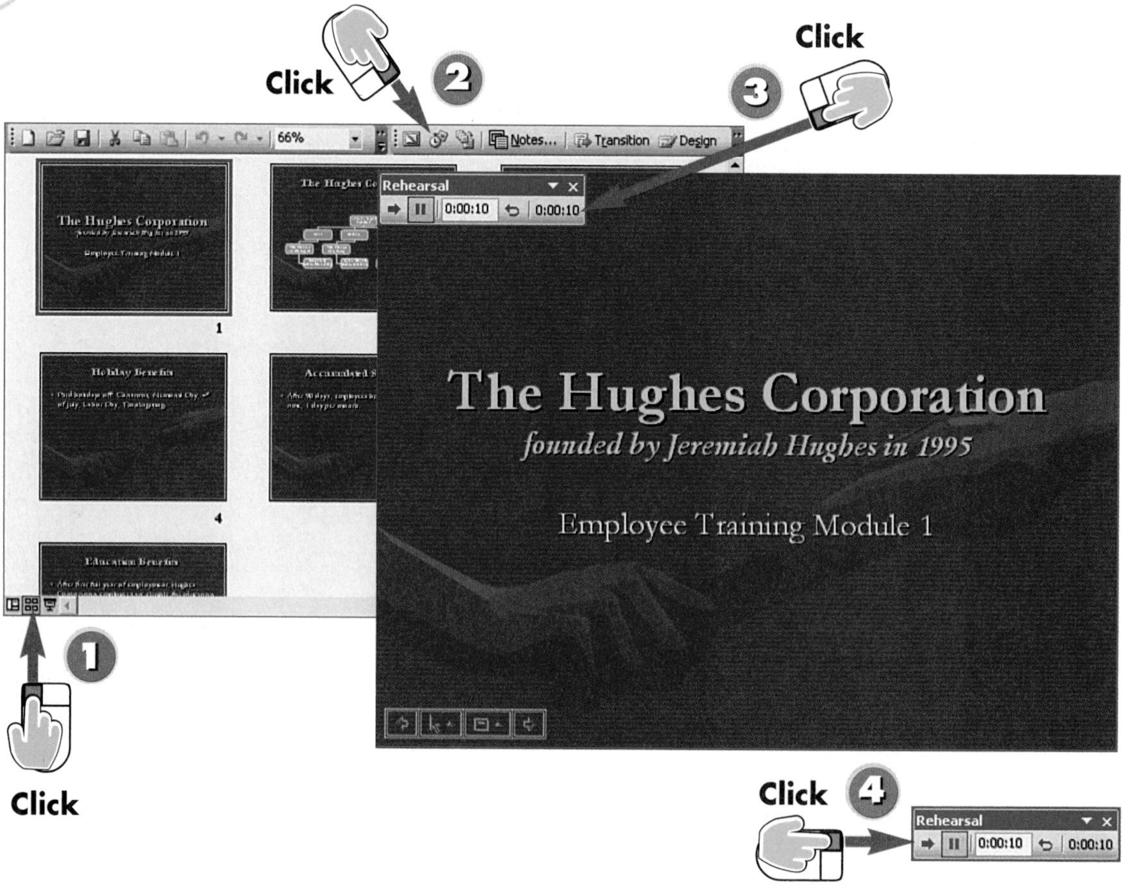

1. Click the **Slide Sorter View** button.

2. Click the **Rehearse Timings** button on the Formatting toolbar.

3. PowerPoint switches to Slide Show mode, displaying the first slide and the Rehearsal toolbar, and starts a timer.

4. Rehearse what you want to say while this slide is displayed. When you are ready to advance to the next slide, click the **Next** button on the Rehearsal toolbar.

INTRODUCTION

You can use PowerPoint's Rehearsal feature to time exactly how long each slide is displayed during the course of the show. The Rehearsal feature records the timings and displays them along with the slides in Slide Sorter view mode.

TIP

Slide Timing

When setting up timings for each slide, be sure to allow enough time for the audience to read everything on the slide, as well as view any animation or multimedia clips.

TIP

Pausing the Rehearsal

If you need to pause your slide show during rehearsal, click the **Pause** button on the Rehearsal toolbar.

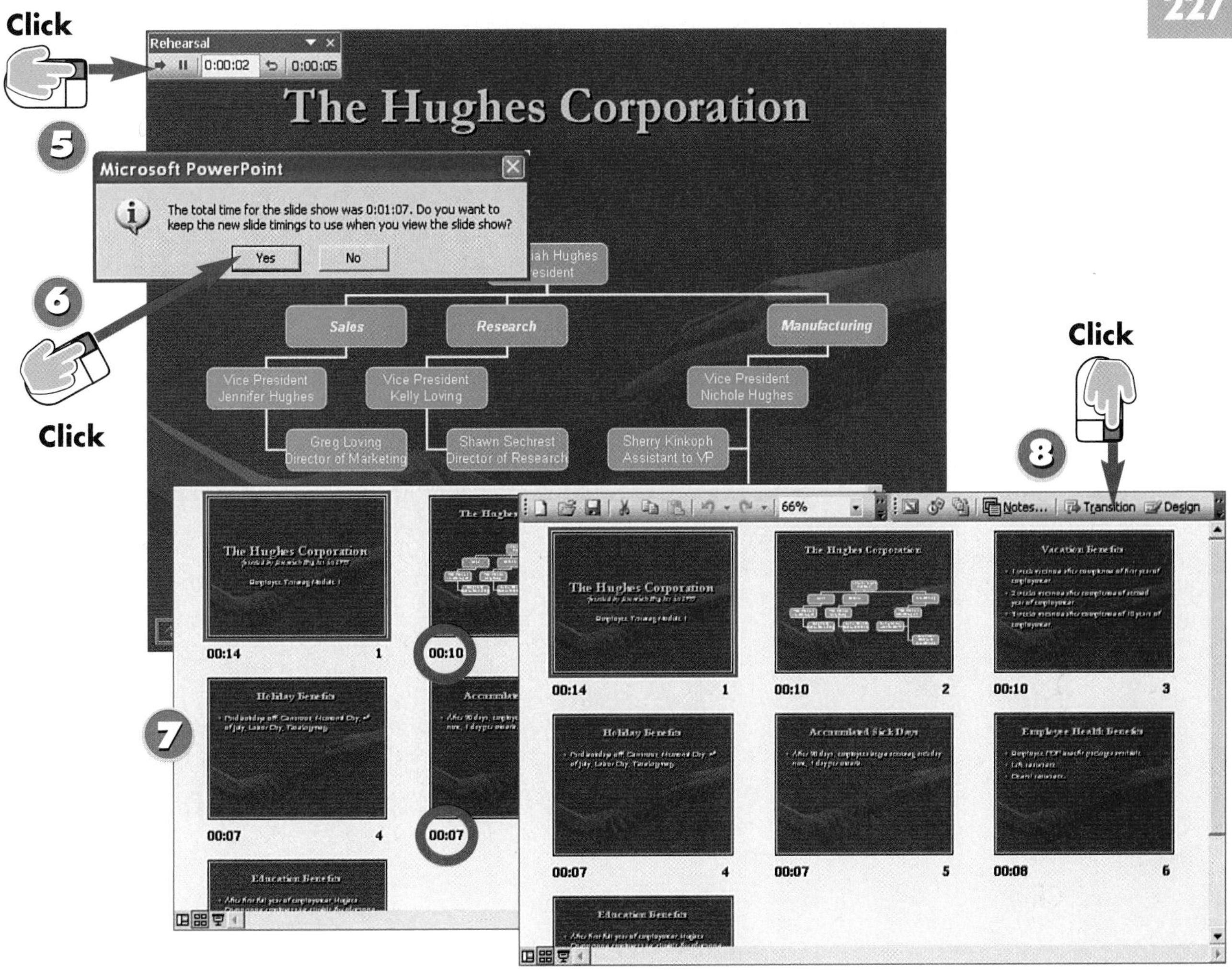

5. Repeat step 4 for each slide in the presentation.

6. When the slide show is finished, click **Yes** to record the timings.

7. PowerPoint displays the timings beneath each slide.

8. To view or change the timings, click the **Transition** button to open the Slide Transition Task pane and view the Advance Slide settings.

TIP

Redoing the Timing
If you make a mistake in the recorded time for a slide during the rehearsal, click the **Repeat** button on the Rehearsal toolbar to reset the timer and start again.

TIP

Changing Timings
You can adjust the slide's timings in the Slide Transition Task pane. Click the slide whose timing you want to alter in Slide Sorter view, then click the **Up** or **Down** arrows beneath the **Automatically After** check box.

TIP

Same Timings
To make all the slides use the same timings, click the **Apply to All** Slides button in the Transition Task pane.

Viewing a Presentation

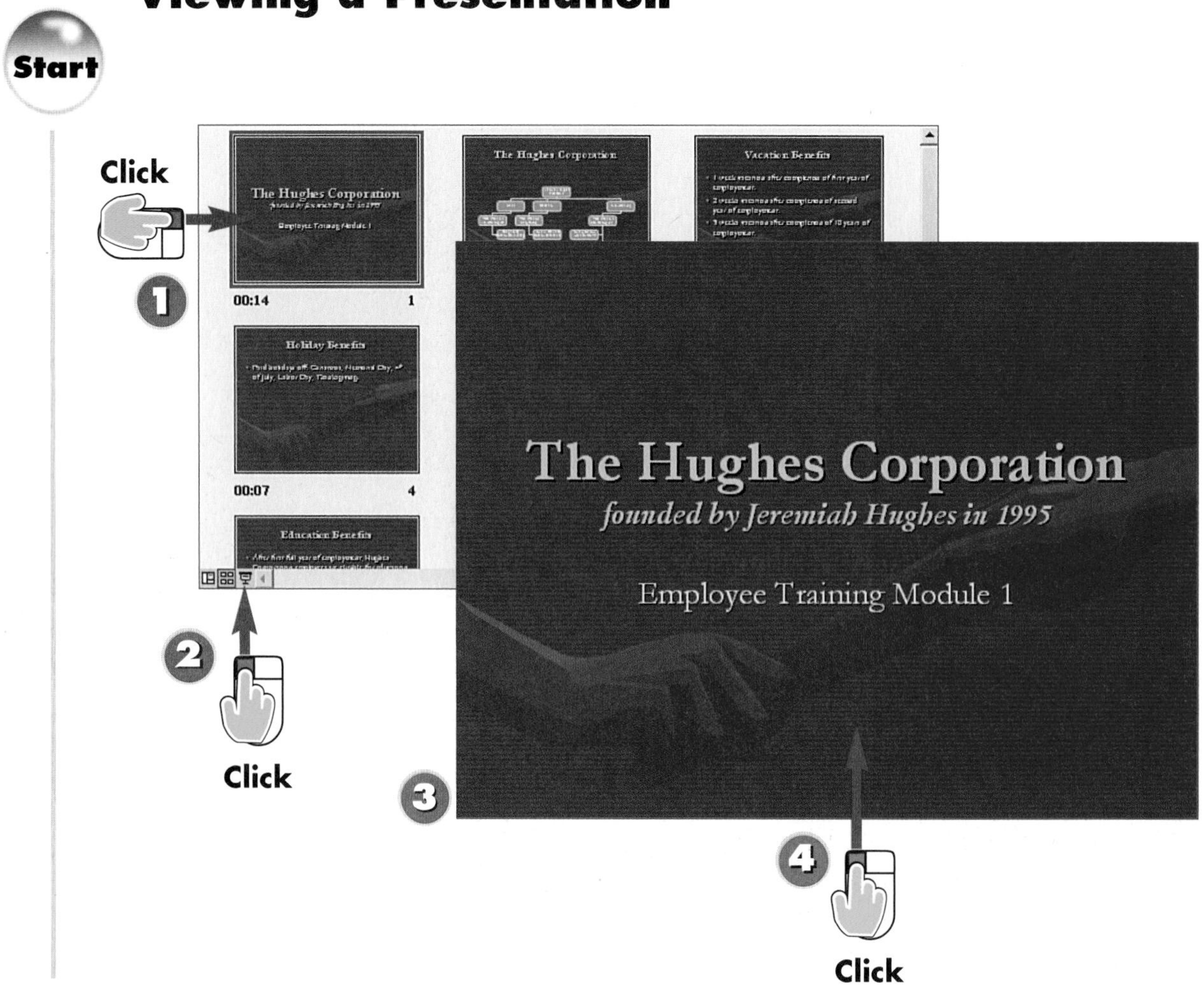

1. Click the first slide in the presentation.
2. Click the **Slide Show View** button.
3. PowerPoint displays the first slide in full-screen mode.
4. Click on the slide to advance to the next slide.

INTRODUCTION

You can use Slide Show view to view a presentation. As your slide show plays, you can manually tell PowerPoint when to advance to the next slide, return to the previous slide, or exit the show before it ends.

TIP

Navigation Shortcuts
You can press the **Spacebar** on the keyboard to advance to the next slide, or you can press the **Backspace** key to return to the previous slide. To display a specific slide, type the slide number and press **Enter**.

TIP

Navigation Bar
You can use the Navigation bar that appears in the corner of your slide show to control the show. Click the arrow buttons to move back and forth between slides, or click the middle buttons to reveal slide show control menus.

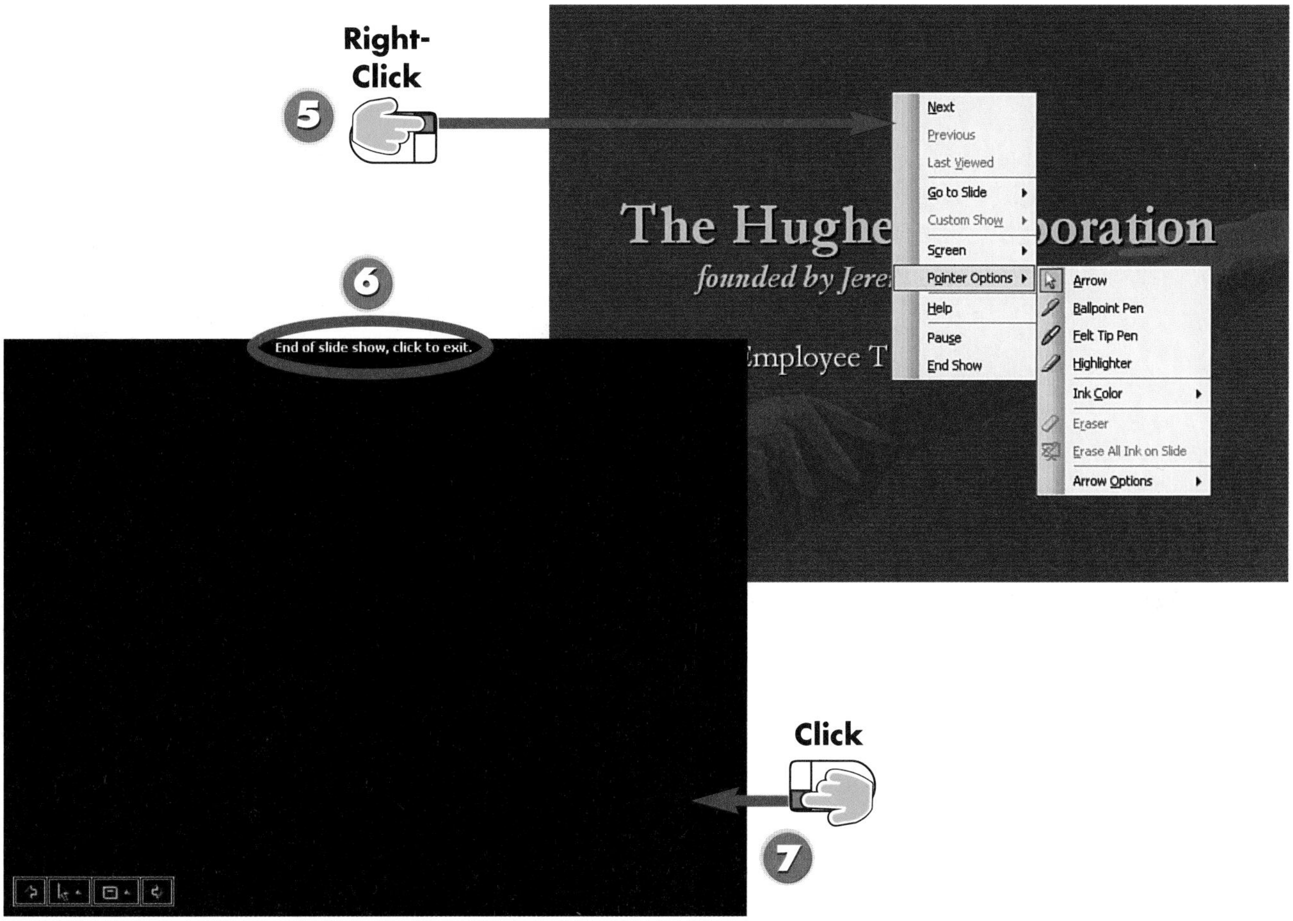

Right-Click

Click

5 To display commands for controlling the slide show, right-click over a slide; select a command from the shortcut menu that appears.

6 Repeat step 4 until you reach the black screen indicating the end of the show.

7 Click the screen to end the show and return to the PowerPoint window.

TIP

Pausing the Show
To pause the show at any time, press the **B** key to make the screen go black, or press the **W** key to make the screen go white. To continue, press the **B** or **W** key again.

TIP

Drawing on Your Slides
PowerPoint includes several pen tools you can use to mark on the slides as you present them in Slide Show mode. Right-click on the slide, select **Pointer Options**, and choose **Ballpoint Pen** or **Felt Tip Pen**. If you prefer a highlighter pen, select **Highlighter**. You can now click and drag the mouse pointer on the screen to draw on the screen. To change pen color, right-click the slide, select **Pointer Options**, choose **Ink Color**, and select a color. To erase any markings on the slide, press the **E** key on the keyboard.

Creating a Custom Slide Show

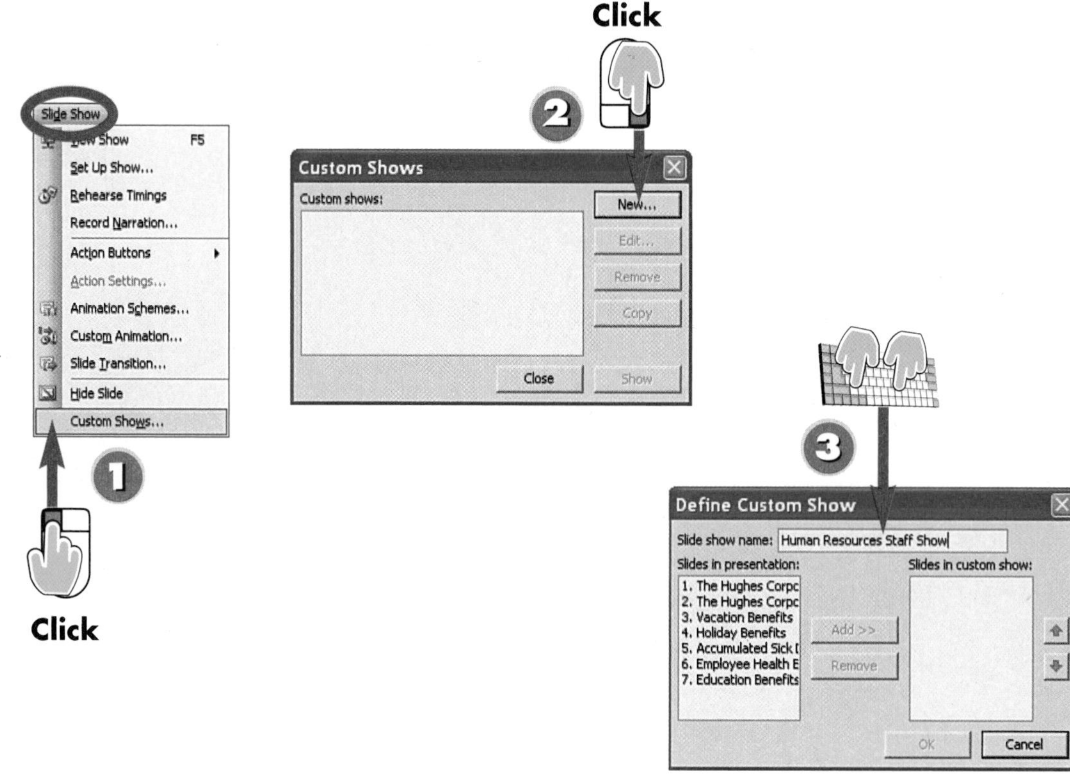

1. With the presentation you want to customize displayed onscreen, open the **Slide Show** menu and choose **Custom Shows**.

2. The Custom Shows dialog box opens. Click the **New** button.

3. The Define Custom Show dialog box opens. Type a name for the custom show in the **Slide Show Name** field.

INTRODUCTION

You can pull together several slides from within your presentation to create a custom show. For example, you may need to show all your slides to a management team, but leave out a few confidential slides to show the rest of the department. You can create numerous custom shows within your main slide show.

CAUTION

Warning!
If you make changes to the slides in the original presentation, the changes also appear in the slides of the custom show.

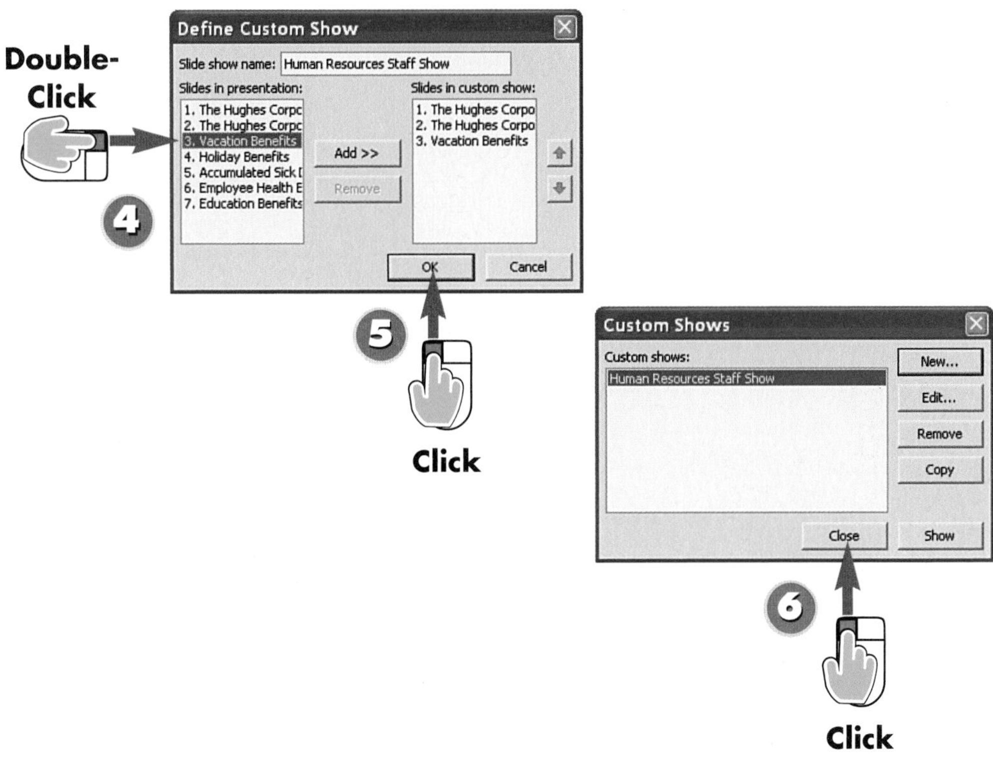

4. Double-click each slide you want to include in the custom show.

5. Click **OK**.

6. PowerPoint lists the name of the custom show in the **Custom Shows** list. Click the **Close** button to exit the dialog box.

TIP

Rearranging the Slide Order
To change the order of the slides listed in the Define Custom Show dialog box, select a slide, then click the **up arrow** or **down arrow** button to change the slide's position in the list.

TIP

Removing a Slide
To remove a slide from a custom show, click the show you want to edit, and then click the **Edit** button. Double-click the slide you want to remove from the list on the right side of the dialog box. The slide is removed.

TIP

Summoning a Custom Show
To view a custom show, open the **Slide Show** menu and choose **Custom Shows** to open the Custom Shows dialog box. Select the show and click the **Show** button to start the presentation.

Packing Your Presentation onto a CD

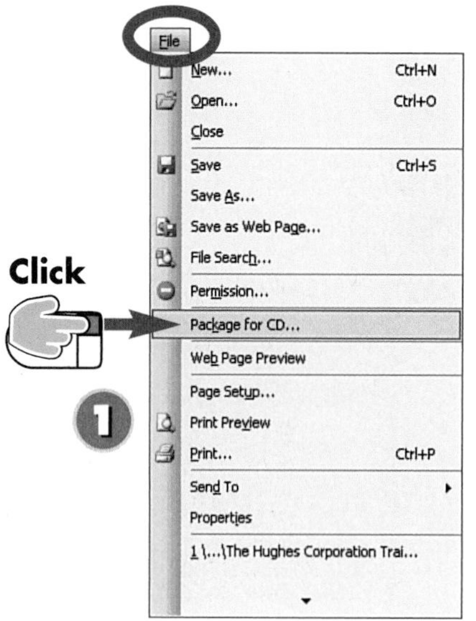

1. After you insert a writable CD into your CD-ROM drive, open the **File** menu and choose **Package for CD**.
2. The Package for CD dialog box opens. Type a name for the CD in the **Name the CD** field.
3. Click the **Copy to CD** button.

INTRODUCTION

If you need to take your presentation on the road, you can use PowerPoint's Package for CD feature. The Package for CD feature helps you bundle the presentation along with the necessary multimedia clips and other elements onto a CD-ROM.

CAUTION

Windows XP

The Package for CD feature works only with Windows XP or later. If you're using an earlier operating system, you can use the feature only to package the presentation to a folder, network drive, or floppy disk, and only if you do not include the PowerPoint viewer with the package.

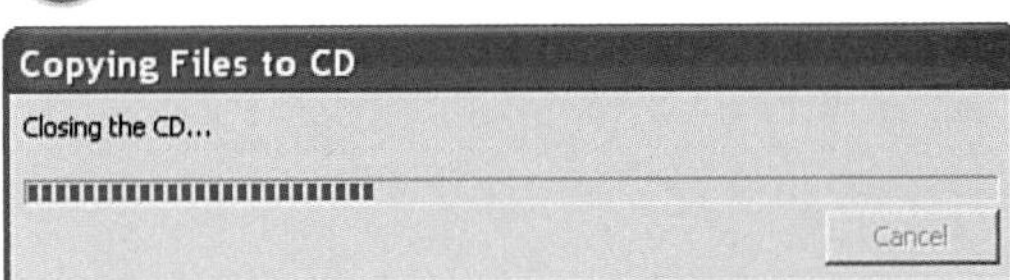

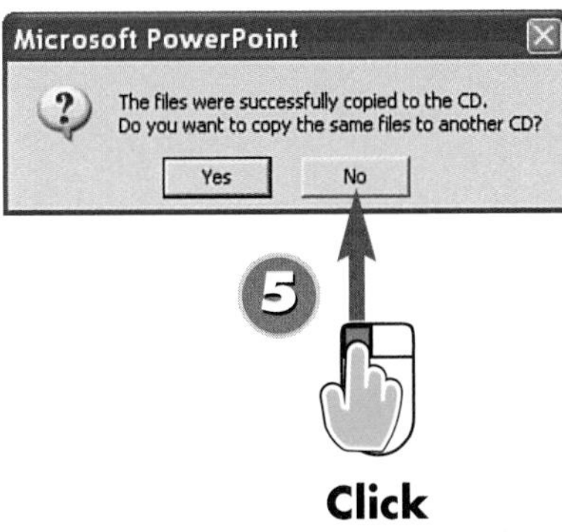

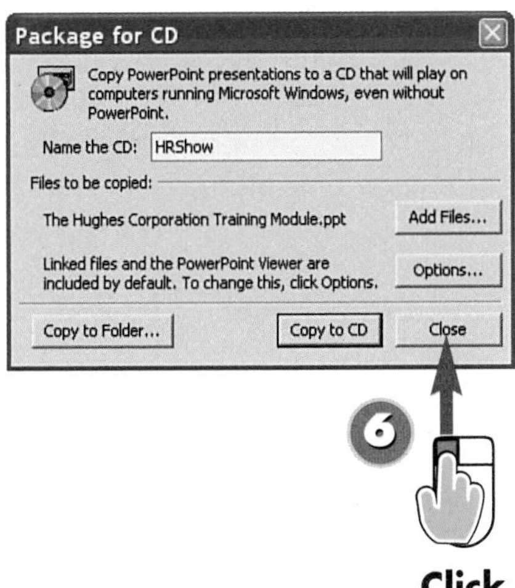

4. PowerPoint copies the related presentation files, including any multimedia clips.

5. PowerPoint informs you when the copying is complete, and asks if you want to copy the files to another CD. Click **No**.

6. Click **Close** to exit the Package for CD dialog box.

TIP

No PowerPoint?
The Package for CD feature automatically includes a PowerPoint Viewer in case the computer you are using to show the presentation does not currently have PowerPoint installed. The PowerPoint Viewer is simply a scaled-down version of PowerPoint for viewing presentations.

TIP

The PowerPoint Viewer Won't Open My Presentation!
The PowerPoint Viewer can only open PowerPoint files from PowerPoint 97 or later. It does not allow you to view presentations created in earlier versions of PowerPoint.

Glossary

A

active cell The selected cell in a table. You can enter or edit text in the active cell.

active document The slide document that is currently selected in your software window.

active window In a multiple-window environment, the window that you are currently using, or that is currently selected. Only one window can be active at a time, and keystrokes and commands affect the active window.

alignment The way text lines up against the margins of a slide text object or text box, or within the width of a table column.

Animation effects Special animating effects you can assign to slide objects, such as text or clip art, that present one slide item at a time. (Also called *build effects*.)

AutoContent wizard A PowerPoint feature that walks you through the process of creating a slide-show presentation.

AutoShapes Predrawn shapes you can add to slides. AutoShapes are found on the Drawing toolbar.

B

background The area behind the slide elements, or directly behind any individual slide object. Backgrounds can be changed to other colors, patterns, or textures.

body text The text containing the main points of your slide message. Body text can consist of a series of bullet points or other paragraphs that appear under the slide title.

browser A program for surfing the Internet (such as Netscape or Internet Explorer).

build effect A special effect in a PowerPoint slide show that presents one slide item at a time.

C

cell The intersection of a column and a row in table.

chart A graphical representation of worksheet data. Charts are linked to the data from which they were created and are automatically updated when the source data changes.

chart area The entire region surrounding the chart, just outside the plot area. When the chart area is selected, uniform font characteristics can be applied to all text in the chart.

chart type The way chart data is displayed; column, bar, and pie are common chart types.

Chart wizard A wizard that guides you through the steps required to create a new chart or to modify settings for an existing chart.

clip art A predrawn illustration or graphics object you can insert into an Office file. Microsoft Office comes with a collection of clip-art files you can use to illustrate your documents.

Clipboard *See **Windows Clipboard**.*

Close box A small box with an X in it that's located in the upper-right corner of every Windows window; click it to close the program or file or item in the window.

color scheme A coordinated, built-in color palette you can apply to your slides.

command An instruction that tells the computer to carry out a task or perform an action.

cursor The flashing vertical line that shows where text is entered. Also referred to as the *insertion point.*

D

datasheet A worksheet that supplies the underlying data for a chart.

document A file you create with a program such as PowerPoint. A document can be saved with a unique filename by which it can be retrieved.

download To transfer a file from the Internet to your computer through telephone lines and a modem.

drag and drop A technique for moving or copying data from one location to another. Select the item to be moved or copied, hold down the left mouse button, drag the item to a new location, and release the mouse button to drop it in place.

E

export The process of converting and saving a file to be used in another program. *See also **import**.*

F

fill color A color that fills a selected shape or background.

floating palette A palette that can be dragged away from its toolbar.

floating toolbar A toolbar that is not docked at the edges of the application window. A floating toolbar stays on top of other windows within the application window.

font A typeface, such as Arial or Tahoma.

font formatting Characteristics you can apply to text to change the way it looks; these include bold, italic, color, and font size.

footer Text that appears at the bottom of every slide. *See also **header**.*

formatting Commands you apply to data to change the way it looks or appears in a file. Formatting controls range from text formatting to formatting for objects such as graphics.

G

gradient effect A blending effect that combines two colors to create a fill color for shapes or backgrounds.

graphics object A line or shape (button, text box, ellipse, rectangle, arc, picture) you draw using the tools on the toolbar, or a picture you paste into a file.

group To combine one or more objects to act as a single object, which you can then move or resize.

H

handles Small black squares located around the perimeter of selected graphics objects, chart items, or chart text. By dragging the handles, you can move, copy, or size the selected object, chart item, or chart text.

handouts A PowerPoint feature that lets you create paper handouts to go along with the slide presentation.

header Text that appears at the top of every printed page. *See also* ***footer***.

HTML Stands for Hypertext Markup Language, a special file format for Web pages.

hyperlink Colored, underlined text that you can click to open another file or go to a Web address.

I

import The process of converting and opening a file that was stored or created in another program. *See also* **export**.

insertion point A flashing vertical line that shows the text entry point. Also referred to as the *cursor*.

Internet The worldwide network of networks, by which everyone is connected to everyone else.

Internet Explorer A popular Web browser program included with Microsoft Office.

Internet service provider (ISP) A private enterprise that provides a server through which you can connect to the Internet, usually for a small fee (also called *local service provider* and *mail service*).

intranet A miniature Internet that operates within a company or organization.

J–L

landscape The horizontal orientation of a page; opposite of *portrait*, or vertical, orientation.

layout A preset arrangement of slide objects that you can apply to a slide. Slide layouts control the positioning of text boxes, clip art, tables, and more.

legend A chart element you can add to Excel charts that tells what each data series on the chart represents.

link To copy an object, such as a graphic or text, from one file or program to another so that a dependent relationship exists between the object and its source file. The dependent object is updated whenever the data changes in the source object.

local service provider *See* ***Internet service provider***.

M

masters The underlying templates that control the formatting and placement of slide objects. PowerPoint includes masters for slides, handouts, and notes.

maximize To enlarge the program window to its maximum screen size.

Meeting Minder A feature that allows you to take onscreen notes during a presentation.

minimize To reduce the program window to a button on the taskbar.

N–O

Normal view A view in PowerPoint that allows you to see the current slide.

notes pages Text pages containing notes about your slides that you can print out to accompany your slide show.

Notes pane The area below the Slide pane that allows you to add text notes about the slide.

object A table, chart, graphic, text box, or other form of information you create and edit. An object can be inserted, pasted, or copied into any slide.

Office Assistant Animated Office help system that provides interactive help, tips, and other online assistance.

Outline view A view that enables you to see your presentation in the form of an outline.

P

Pack and Go wizard A special program within PowerPoint for copying a presentation and any supporting files along with a PowerPoint viewer for viewing the presentation.

palette A box containing choices for color and other special effects. A palette appears when you click a toolbar button, such as Border or Fill Color. *See also* ***floating palette***.

Photo Album A feature that allows you to turn a group of pictures into individual slides to make a presentation.

plot area The area of a chart in which data is plotted. In 2D charts, it is bounded by the axes and encompasses the data markers and gridlines. In 3D charts, the plot area includes the chart's walls, axes, and tick-mark labels.

portrait The vertical orientation of a page; opposite of *landscape*, or horizontal, orientation.

PowerPoint A presentation program designed to create and view slide-show programs and other types of visual presentations.

PowerPoint Viewer A program for viewing PowerPoint presentations, particularly useful for people who do not have access to the PowerPoint program.

presentation A group of slides that present information or a message to an audience.

Preview A view that displays your document as it will appear when you print it. Items such as text and graphics appear in their actual positions.

Q–S

ScreenTips Helpful notes that appear on your screen to explain a function or feature of PowerPoint.

server A computer used on the Internet or a network environment that stores email messages, Web pages, and other data.

shadow A formatting effect you can apply to slide objects to create the appearance of shadows behind the object.

shortcut keys Keyboard keys you can press to perform commonly used commands instead of using the mouse.

slide A single document or page in a PowerPoint presentation.

Slide design A preset design you can assign to your slide that includes formatting and background colors or artwork.

Slide Master The underlying template that controls the formatting and placement of slide objects.

slide object Slide objects act as containers for specific slide elements, such as text, clip art, or a chart.

Slide pane The area in the middle of the PowerPoint window that displays the current slide. You can view the Slide pane in Normal and Outline view modes.

slide show A visual presentation you can create with PowerPoint which uses text, graphics, and other effects. Use slide shows for business presentations, training presentations, and other tasks that require visual presentations.

Slide Sorter view A view in PowerPoint that allows you to see all the slides in a presentation and arrange their order in the slide show.

Speaker notes Text pages containing notes about your slides that you can print out to accompany your slide show and assist you with your presentation.

T

table Data that is stored in rows and columns.

taskbar The horizontal bar across the bottom of the Windows desktop; it includes the Start button and buttons for any programs, documents, or items that are open.

Task pane The vertical pane that appears on the right side of the PowerPoint window; it includes shortcuts and options for various PowerPoint features and tasks.

template Templates provide predesigned patterns on which PowerPoint presentations can be based.

text box A slide object used for presenting text in a slide. Also called a text object.

title A text box that appears at the top of a slide to display the main heading.

toolbar A collection of frequently used commands that appear as icon buttons you can click to activate.

transition Determines how the slide show moves from one slide to another in a presentation, such as a fade or dissolve.

U–Z

URL (uniform resource locator) A Web site address.

Web *See **World Wide Web**.*

Windows Clipboard A temporary holding area in computer memory that stores the last set of information that was cut or copied (such as text or graphics). You transfer data from the Clipboard by using the Paste command. The Windows Clipboard can hold up to 12 cut or copied items.

wizards A set of dialog boxes that ask you questions to walk you through processes such as creating a file or an object based on your answers.

WordArt A program within PowerPoint for creating text effects, such as curved text.

World Wide Web (WWW) The part of the Internet where Web sites are posted and available to Web browsers.

x-axis On most charts, categories are plotted along the x-axis. On a typical column chart, the x-axis is the horizontal axis.

y-axis On most charts, data values are plotted along the y-axis. On a typical column chart, the y-axis is the vertical axis. When a secondary axis is added, it is a secondary y-axis.

Index

NUMBERS

D

G – H

I

N

T